Sabine Hake
The Nazi Worker

Interdisciplinary German Cultural Studies

Edited by
Irene Kacandes

Volume 35

Sabine Hake

The Nazi Worker

The Culture of Work and the End of Class

DE GRUYTER

ISBN 978-3-11-221488-6
e-ISBN (PDF) 978-3-11-100432-7
e-ISBN (EPUB) 978-3-11-100475-4
ISSN 1861-8030

Library of Congress Control Number: 2023935923

Bibliographic information published by the Deutsche Nationalbibliothek
The Deutsche Nationalbibliothek lists this publication in the Deutsche Nationalbibliografie;
detailed bibliographic data are available on the internet at http://dnb.dnb.de.

© 2025 Walter de Gruyter GmbH, Berlin/Boston
This volume is text- and page-identical with the hardback published in 2023.
Cover image: akg-images / Fotoarchiv für Zeitgeschichte
Printing and binding: CPI books GmbH, Leck

www.degruyter.com

For Fred, from Freiburg with Love

Preface

The Nazi Worker: The Culture of Work and the End of Class is the second in a three-volume project on German working-class culture. *The Proletarian Dream* (2017) follows the emergence of the proletariat as a social imaginary from the pre-Wilhelmine years to the end of the Weimar Republic. *The Nazi Worker* (2023) draws on the discourse of *Arbeitertum* (workerdom), including its socialist, nationalist, and populist elements, to reconstruct the shift from class to race in the new culture of work established during the Nazi dictatorship. The third volume examines the very different working-class cultures in East and West Germany and connects both to the legacies of fascism and communism and the changing face of class and work during the 1950s and 1960s.

Covering about one hundred years, from the 1863 founding of Social Democracy to the protest movements of 1968, the larger project is based on extensive archival research and takes a historically based interdisciplinary approach. The forgotten archives of working-class culture are rediscovered with three main goals in mind: to show the relevance of working-class culture to modern German history, culture, and society; to recognize the worker as the main protagonist in very different social imaginaries and political ideologies; and to make sense of historical dis/continuities and processes of adaptation and appropriation. As indicated by the original subtitle – *Socialism, Culture, and Emotion* – these connections are especially important as regards the power of symbolic politics and social imaginaries, the appeal of populism and ethnonationalism, and the ongoing debates on the end of class and the future of work.

Contents

Preface —— VII

Glossary and Abbreviations —— XI

List of Illustrations —— XIII

Acknowledgments —— XV

Introduction —— 1

Chapter 1
From Proletariat to Workerdom, in the Name of the People —— 21

Chapter 2 Conversion Stories: Turning Communists into Nazis —— 49

Chapter 3
The Revisionist Project of Workers' Poetry —— 74

Chapter 4
The *Thingspiel* and the Performance of Class —— 97

Chapter 5
Pride in Work: On Workers' Sculpture and Industrial Painting —— 124

Chapter 6
Joy in Work: On Industrial Photography and Film —— 154

Chapter 7
The German Worker and the Beauty of Labor —— 190

Afterword —— 221

Select Bibliography —— 225

Index of Names —— 229

Glossary and Abbreviations

Amt Rosenberg (Rosenberg Office)
Amt "Schönheit der Arbeit" (Beauty of Labor Office)
Arbeiterdichtung (workers' poetry)
Arbeiterschaft (workers, working class)
Arbeitertum (literally: workerdom)
Arbeitsfreude (joy in work)
Arbeitsstolz (pride in work)
Betriebsgemeinschaft (factory community)
Bewegungsfilm (Nazi movement film)
Bewegungsroman (Nazi movement novel)
BPRS Bund proletarisch-revolutionärer Schriftsteller (League of Proletarian-Revolutionary Writers)
CDU Christlich Demokratische Union Deutschlands (Christian Democratic Union of Germany)
DAF Deutsche Arbeitsfront (German Labor Front)
DAP Deutsche Arbeiterpartei (German Workers' Party)
GDK Große Deutsche Kunstaustellung (Great German Art Exhibition)
Gleichschaltung (forced coordination of German culture and society in the Nazi dictatorship)
Kampfbund für deutsche Kultur (Fighting League for German Culture)
Kampfzeit (Nazi term for the party's early years during the Weimar Republic)
KdF Kraft durch Freude (Strength through Joy)
KPD Kommunistische Partei Deutschlands (Communist Party of Germany)
Leistungsschau (achievement exhibition)
NS-Musterbetrieb (National Socialist model factory)
NSBO Nationalsozialistische Betriebszellenorganisation (National Socialist Factory Cell Organization)
NSDAP Nationalsozialistische Deutsche Arbeiterpartei (National Socialist German Workers' Party)
RAD Reichsarbeitsdienst (Reich Labor Service)
RSK Reichsschrifttumskammer (Reich Chamber of Literature)
Neue Sachlichkeit (New Objectivity)
SED Sozialistische Einheitspartei Deutschlands (Socialist Unity Part of Germany)
SPD Sozialdemokratische Partei Deutschlands (Social Democratic Party of Germany)
Systemzeit (derogatory Nazi term for the Weimar Republic)
Thingspiel (choric theater or choral drama/play)
USPD Unabhängige Sozialdemokratische Partei Deutschlands (Independent Social Democratic Party of Germany)
Volk (folk, people, race)
Volksdichtung (folk poetry)
Volksgemeinschaft (folk community, people's community, national community)
Volkstum (folkdom, folklore)
Volkstümlichkeit (folksiness, popularity)
Werkgemeinschaft (work community)
Werkmann (working man)

List of Illustrations

In Germany, access to the visual archives of National Socialism remains a problem. Complete journal runs are missing from libraries or not available for digitalization. Meanwhile, heirs of artists from the period and museums with such holdings are sometimes suspicious of critical research. These are the main reasons for the heavy reliance on low-quality reproductions of Nazi-era publications and the dearth of illustrations where some should have been included.

Cover Image: II. WK – Rüstung 1942 / WW II – armament 1942. akg-images / Fotoarchiv für Zeitgeschichte.

1.1 Mjölnir (Hans Schweitzer), "Unsere letzte Hoffnung Hitler" (1932), Bildarchiv Foto Marburg, www.fotomarburg.de.
1.2 Mjölnir (Hans Schweitzer), "Schluß jetzt: Wählt Hitler!" (1932), bpk/Deutsches Historisches Museum/Arne Psille.
4.1 Richard Euringer, *Deutsche Passion 1933*, Theater des Volkes Berlin, 1935, set design by Traugott Müller, photograph by René Fosshag. Institut für Theaterwissenschaft der FU Berlin, Theaterhistorische Sammlungen Nachlass Traugott Müller.
4.2 Thingstätte auf dem Brandberge, Halle (Saale), Sammlung Katharina Bosse, reprinted in *Thingstätten: Von der Bedeutung der Vergangenheit für die Gegenwart* (Bielefeld: Kerber, 2020), 92. With permission of the author.
4.3 *Triumph des Willens* (1935) Reichsarbeitsdienst sequence (c. 38'), screen captures.
4.4 *Triumph des Willens* (1935) Reichsarbeitsdienst sequence (c. 38'), screen captures.
4.5 Kurt Heynicke, *Der Weg in Reich*, Reichsfestspiele 1935, Thingstätte auf dem Heiligen Berg Heidelberg, set design by Traugott Müller, photograph by René Fosshag. Institut für Theaterwissenschaft der FU Berlin, Theaterhistorische Sammlungen Nachlass Traugott Müller.
5.1 Fritz Koelle, *Der Blockwalzer* (1929, 190 cm), Melusinenplatz (today: Karl-Preis-Platz), Munich. Public domain, Wikimedia Commons.
5.2 Fritz Koelle, *Der Hammermeister* (1932, 200 cm), in Ernst Kammerer, *Fritz Koelle* (Berlin: Rembrandt, 1939), 36.
5.3 Fritz Koelle, *Hochofenarbeiter* (1935, 200 cm), in Kammerer, *Ernst Koelle*, 44.
5.4 Fritz Koelle, *Hochofenarbeiter* (1938, 420 cm), in Kammerer, *Ernst Koelle*, 60.
5.5 Erich Mercker, *Aus Deutschlands Schmiede* (1940), VG Bild-Kunst, Bonn 2022.
5.6 Erich Mercker, *Abend am Hochofen* (1920). Courtesy of Collection of the Grohmann Museum at Milwaukee School of Engineering, Milwaukee, Wisconsin.
5.7 Erich Mercker, *Im Reiche der Hochöfen* (1942). Courtesy of Collection of the Grohmann Museum at Milwaukee School of Engineering, Milwaukee, Wisconsin.
6.1 Paul Wolff, *Arbeit! 200 Tiefdruckbildseiten*. Text by Paul Georg Ehrhardt (Berlin: Volk und Reich, 1937), 168. Courtesy of Dr. Paul Wolff & Tritschler, Historisches Bildarchiv, D-77654 Offenburg.
6.2 "Wer schaffen will, muß fröhlich sein!" Courtesy bpk/Deutsches Historisches Museum, Raumbild-Verlag Otto Schönstein/Walter Tröller.
6.3 Eugen Diesel, ed., *Das Werk: Technische Lichtbildstudien* (Königstein im Taunus: Karl Robert Langewiesche, 1931), frontispiece.
6.4 *Arbeitertum* 6.10 (1937), cover.
6.5 *Arbeitertum* 9.13 (1939), cover.
6.6 *Arbeitertum* 10.34 (1941), cover.

6.7   Wolff, *Arbeit!*, 50.
6.8   Wolff, *Arbeit!*, 77.
6.9   Erna Lendvai-Dircksen, *Arbeit formt das Gesicht*. Aus dem Archiv der Henschelwerke, words by Emil Maier-Dorn (Magdeburg: Wohlfeld, 1938), n.p.
6.10 Lendvai-Dircksen, *Arbeit formt das Gesicht*, n.p.
6.11 Lendvai-Dircksen, *Arbeit formt das Gesicht*, n.p.
6.12 *Acciaio/Arbeit macht glücklich* (Walter Ruttmann, 1933), Deutsches Filminstitut & Filmmuseum, Frankfurt am Main/Plakatarchiv/Nachlass Erich Meerwald.
6.13 *Hände am Werk* (Walter Frentz, 1935), Bundesarchiv PLAK 105/14321.
6.14 Woman worker with aerial bomb, Maschinenfabrik Meer, Mönchengladbach, February 1941, Ruth Hallersleben/Fotoarchiv Ruhrmuseum.
7.1   Edmund Schultz, ed., *Die veränderte Welt: Eine Bilderfibel unserer Zeit*, with texts by Ernst Jünger (Breslau: Wilhelm Gottlieb Korn, 1933), 49.
7.2   Anatol von Hübbenet, ed., *Das Taschenbuch Schönheit der Arbeit* (Berlin: Verlag der DAF, 1938), 79.
7.3   *Das Taschenbuch "Schönheit der Arbeit,"* 124.
7.4   "So und nicht so" and "Schönheit der Arbeit. Wir helfen mit," posters reprinted in *Die Form* 10.7 (1935): 190.
7.5   "Arbeitsfreude" posters, reprinted in *Die Form* 10.7 (1935): 191.

Acknowledgments

Archival research for this book was supported by a 2016 Wolfsonian-FIU Fellowship at the Wolfsonian Museum in Miami Beach, which holds a truly unique collection. The FRIAS Alumni Program at the Albert-Ludwigs-Universität Freiburg allowed me to take full advantage of the German interlibrary loan system during the summer of 2017; my heartfelt thanks to the entire FRIAS staff, and to Roland Muntschick in particular. The 2020 Ailsa Bruce Mellon Visiting Senior Fellowship at the Center for Advanced Visual Studies (CASVA) at the National Gallery of Art in Washington, DC, provided an ideal setting for thinking about art historical questions in dialogue with a remarkable group of scholars. The completion of a first draft was made possible by a fall 2021 Faculty Research Assignment (FRA) from the University of Texas at Austin. Throughout the years, the generosity of the donor of the Texas Chair, Walter Wetzels, who passed away in 2020, has allowed me to indulge my passion for archival research and take on a multivolume book project.

Early versions of chapters were presented at conferences and colloquia in the United States and Europe: at the Kunstwissenschaftliche Institut München, the FRIAS HUMSS Colloquium, the Duke-UNC Germanic Studies Program, the Max Kade German-American Research and Resource Center at Indiana University-Purdue University, the Max-Planck-Institut für Bildungsforschung in Berlin, and the Humanities Institute at the University of Pittsburgh. Conferences at the University of Leuven, University of Manchester, Central University Vienna, as well as the annual conferences of the German Studies Association and the American Comparative Literature Association proved essential for testing new arguments. Closer to home, the Modern Studies Group organized by Linda Henderson and the Germanic Studies works-in-progress series offered collegial settings for constructive feedback. Judy Coffin, Tracie Matysik, Joan Neuberger, Yoav di Capua, and Ben Brower, the members of my writing group, read several chapters and gave valuable advice on everything from theoretical questions to stylistic matters. I have greatly benefitted from their critical acumen and generosity of spirit over the years. Special thanks to Patrick Jung who shared his work about Mercker and to Ofer Ashkenazi who helped out with Frentz. At De Gruyter Irene Kacandes, the editor of the Interdisciplinary German Cultural Studies, and humanities editor Stella Dietrich have enthusiastically supported the larger project from the very beginning. Monica Birth and Michael Thomas Taylor provided excellent copyediting, and Myrto Aspioti made sure that the publication process went smoothly. I am indebted to all of them.

Earlier versions of chapters have been published in the following journals and anthologies:

Chapter 1: "From Proletariat to Workerdom, in the Name of the People," *New German Critique* 142 (2021): 125–152. Copyright 2021, *New German Critique*, Inc. All rights reserved. Republished by permission of the publisher www.duke.press.edu.

Chapter 2: "Communists into Nazis: The Conversion of the German Worker," in *The Wider Arc of Revolution*, ed. Choi Chatterjee, Steven G. Marks, Mary Neuburger, and Steven Sabol (Bloomington: Slavica Press of Indiana University, 2019), 167–193.

Chapter 3: "Add, Delete, Replace: The Revisionist Project of Workers' Poetry," *Germanic Review* 96.1 (2021): 67–86.

Chapter 4: "Workers, Work, and the Thingspiel," special issue on "Produktionswelten der Massenkultur," ed. Antje Dietze and Maren Möhring, *Geschichte und Gesellschaft: Zeitschrift für historische Sozialwissenschaft* 46.1 (2020): 155–178.

Introduction

From the social imaginaries of the industrial age, the working class emerged as a driving force behind the calls for revolution and reform and the struggles for equality, freedom, and democracy. Promising alternatives to class society, the figure of the worker, or proletarian, came to occupy the center of a rich and diverse working-class culture that raised class consciousness, offered models of community, and functioned as an alternative or oppositional public sphere during the Wilhelmine Empire and the Weimar Republic. Yet the dreams of a classless society did not remain the prerogative of socialists and communists. In fact, the German worker also played a key role in the historical convergence of nationalist, antisemitic, and *völkisch* thought that gave rise to National Socialism. As the voice of grievances and resentments, this "other" worker became a powerful catalyst in the shift from class to race announced by the Nazi Party during the 1920s and implemented after 1933 through the making of the racial state.

With its distinctly German genealogy, the discourse of *Arbeitertum* (literally: workerdom) proves especially suited for examining these continuities on the level of representations and imaginations. The term's strangeness, its difference from "working man" or "working class" and its distance from actual working conditions and real workers, is acknowledged in the choice of an English neologism, with the suffix "-tum" or "-dom" designating a condition, state, or way of being. Confirming the function of discourse as social practice, workerdom after 1933 served three distinct but interrelated purposes: to disempower the working class, to reorganize the relationship between work and life, and to maintain support for the regime through a combination of coercion and consent. Aware of the growing significance of symbolic politics, the discourse of workerdom relied on specific techniques of aestheticization and emotionalization in establishing the new culture of work based on the legacies of the workers' movement and the discourses of folk, class, and community. More specifically, workerdom utilized specific techniques of adaptation and appropriation in mobilizing socialist, nationalist, and populist elements for an exclusionary communitarianism and, in the process, establishing a new culture of work in line with Nazi biopolitics.[1]

---

[1] The theoretical and methodological premises of this book are laid out in greater detail in the introduction to *The Proletarian Dream: Socialist, Culture, and Emotion in Germany, 1863–1933* (Berlin: De Gruyter, 2017). My use of social imaginary is informed by Cornelius Castoriadis, *The Imaginary Institution of Society*, trans. Kathleen Blamey (Cambridge: Polity, 1987) and Charles Taylor, *Modern Social Imaginaries* (Durham, NC: Duke University Press, 2004).

The book's seven chapters reconstruct the Nazis' selective appropriation and instrumentalization of socialist iconographies and terminologies through a strange cast of characters: well-known worker poets rewriting earlier poems in the idioms of *völkisch* thought, SA men penning semiautobiographical novels about their conversion to National Socialism, ordinary citizens submitting *Thingspiel* manuscripts to the Propaganda Ministry, self-taught artists making a good living painting industrial landscapes, commercial photographers taking pictures of workers in the factories, documentary filmmakers promoting big corporations and war-essential industries, and architects and designers planning every detail of the National Socialist model factory. Analyzing workerdom as a social fantasy requires that these images and stories be seen as both formative and transformative and read as an integral part of the admixtures of socialism, nationalism, and populism that have haunted German conceptions of class and community since the nineteenth century. Taking the promises of workerdom seriously also means paying close attention to the growing significance of psychological and aesthetic factors in the culture of work and the heightened role of symbolic politics – the pursuit of political goals through nonpolitical means – in all areas of public life.

The texts to be examined belong to the "minor" registers in which working-class culture assumed new functions after 1933: on the margins of official Nazi art and literature, at the intersection of propaganda, marketing, and research, through combinations of Nazi Sachlichkeit, the post-1933 version of New Objectivity, and updated versions of proletarian kitsch, and as part of the institutional culture of joy and pride promoted by the Deutsche Arbeitsfront (DAF, German Labor Front). Often dismissed by scholars as devoid of aesthetic quality and artistic value or classified as mere products of Nazi ideology, these texts do not belong to any recognized canons, archives, or histories. They have become invisible und unreadable even where they are on full view. In part, these difficulties reflect the contested status of workerdom within Nazi ideology itself – namely as a potentially dangerous legacy of the workers' movement and an overly ambitious project of Nazi ideologues and functionaries. In part, the continued indifference in German studies scholarship to this surprisingly vast and rich culture of work has to do with the close association of workerdom with the "failure" of the Weimar Left and the Nazi "corruption" of socialist ideas, on the one hand, and the "negligible" role of working-class culture and "diminished" relevance of questions of labor and class for contemporary debates on culture and identity, on the other. Yet like the *völkisch* writers chosen by George Mosse almost sixty years ago to research the ideological origins of the Third Reich, the proponents of workerdom can today become helpful guides into a strange world that existed only in the imagination but had powerful consequences for social and political reality.²

The Nazi Worker examines the strategies and processes through which the Nazis took elements of the workers' movement and translated its class-based politics into the racialized communitarianism of *Volksgemeinschaft* (folk community). These processes of adaptation and appropriation became both possible and necessary because of the growing significance of symbolic politics and the heightened role of culture as a site of collective identifications. Through the figure of the worker, the dream of community could be injected into the founding narratives about work that operated across the class divide in sustaining the dream of industrial modernity since the nineteenth century: the cult of the machine, faith in progress, and a belief in work as a means of self-emancipation. Under such conditions, the discourse of workerdom brought together three very different spheres of influence: the culture of the working class, which aligned class identifications with oppositional or alternative practices; the culture of industrial modernity, which combined the perspectives of organizational management, work psychology, and corporatist ideology; and the culture of ethnonationalism, which provided narratives of belonging through corresponding mechanisms of exclusion and othering. Two features proved especially crucial to the emotional appeal of workerdom: the masculinization of work, which is evident in the gendered nature of images and imaginaries and their contribution to the remasculinization of society, and the racialization of class, which can be traced in the connection to older discourses of folk community and German nationhood.³ Mutually constitutive, these structural conditions in turn allowed critics, writers, artists, photographers, and filmmakers to celebrate the German worker as a personification of workerdom and pro-

---

2 George Mosse, *The Crisis of German Ideology: Intellectual Origins of the Third Reich*, intr. Stephen A. Aschheim (Madison: University of Wisconsin Press, 2021). Methodologically speaking, something similar can be said about the connection between fascism and sexuality explored by Klaus Theweleit through his analysis of the novels written by Freikorps men in *Male Fantasies*, vol. 1, *Women Floods Bodies History;* vol. 2, *Male Bodies: Psychoanalyzing the White Terror*, trans. Erica Carter and Chris Turner (Minneapolis: University of Minnesota Press, 1987).
3 All images and stories discussed in this book involve male workers. With few exceptions, the discourse of workerdom had no place for women workers or questions of gender. As a way of foregrounding this aspect, the pronoun "he" will be used when referring to individual workers; a neutral pronoun would only obscure this discrepancy. The contribution of women workers to the history of industrialization and the workers' movement has been well documented. Here, the photographic history of factory work offered in Wolfgang Ruppert, *Die Fabrik: Geschichte von Arbeit und Industrialisierung in Deutschland* (Munich: C. H. Beck, 1993) confirms both the existence of women workers in all industries and their presence in the everyday life of the factory.

mote feelings and attitudes about work best suited to turn the work community into a model of the folk community.

I

If *The Proletarian Dream* documents the emergence of the proletariat as a revolutionary class, *The Nazi Worker* examines the discursive transformation of the working class into workerdom, with the allusion to *Volkstum* (folkdom) a first indication of the romance with the volk, or people, shared by both terms. Coined in response to the radicalization of workers in the nineteenth century, workerdom sought to introduce an alternative to the Marxist analysis of capitalism and class society. From the beginning aligned with conservative if not reactionary voices, the term acquired racialized (i.e., antisemitic) meanings already during the Wilhelmine years. As a collective fantasy, workerdom provided the perfect arguments for translating socialist narratives of class, including the belief in work as an instrument of self-liberation, into racialized versions of folk and nation. With discourse defined as "practices that systematically form the objects of which they speak,"[4] the primary function of workerdom subsequently was to erase the working class as a social and political force and to make the new culture of work an integral part of Nazi society and the Nazi state. In ways that have not been fully recognized, this process of erasure involved instrumentalizing aspects of working-class culture and translating socialist values and beliefs into the language of the people and the folk.

There is a direct connection between the brutal destruction of the Weimar Left and the appearance of workerdom in Nazi propaganda, scholarship, and literary fiction. The Nazi takeover of power in 1933 meant the imprisonment of politicians from the KPD (Communist Party of Germany) and SPD (Social Democratic Party of Germany), the arrest of union leaders and banning of labor organizations, and the loss of basic worker rights; the burning of all books associated with Marxism, Social Democracy, and the workers' movement; and the forced emigration and exile of countless leftist writers, artists, and scholars. The *Gleichschaltung* (forced coordination) of cultural institutions had a devastating effect on working-class culture, from the censorship of leftist publishers and publications and the dismantling of proletarian cultural associations to the purging of Nazi Party members with socialist leanings and the creation of an entirely new infrastructure of work-based organizations and initiatives. At the same time Gleichschaltung provid-

---

4 Michel Foucault, *The Archaeology of Knowledge* (New York: Pantheon, 1972), 54.

ed new employment opportunities, institutional support structures, and well-funded official and semiofficial venues for the propagandists of Nazi ideology, including converts and opportunists, the favored representatives of high culture and the culture industry, and the countless professionals making a living at the intersection of arts, crafts, and commerce. In these contexts, the term "workerdom" functioned at once as an effective propaganda slogan, an ambitious economic program, an important tool of social control, and a compelling fantasy of unity and harmony. In offering a narrative of empowerment and participation that extended well beyond the workplace, workerdom promised the good life, with terms such as "joy," "pride," and "beauty" mapping an emotional landscape where workers were no longer exploited and oppressed, blue- and white-collar workers treated as equals, and work and life seen as integral part of the same experience of community.

Especially during the first years of the regime, the discourse of workerdom remained beholden to the legacies of proletarian culture, with the anxiety of influence evident in the thematic fixation on Weimar-era class struggles and the various attempts at imitation and containment. Meanwhile, the new culture of work, its organizational goals and biopolitical ambitions, was promoted across all art forms and mass media, including in the DAF journal *Arbeitertum*. When evoked by writers with a background in the worker's movement, workerdom proved most compelling in combination with another key term of Nazi ideology, namely folk community, with which it shared an affinity for the downtrodden and oppressed. Increasingly, this kind of romantic communitarianism became subordinated to the economic, social, and political objectives of the Nazi state, starting with disempowerment of the working class and close cooperation with German industries.

Needless to say, the habitual references to workerdom within Lingua Tertii Imperii, the language of the Third Reich examined by Victor Klemperer, reveals very little about public confidence in its promises of a new culture of work and even less about workers' experiences in the workplace. Yet even perfunctory expressions of faith in workerdom provide important insights into social imaginaries and their alternately coercive, habitual, or subversive effects – effects to be experienced by white- and blue-collar workers or to be imagined by those invested in the figure of the worker. Contradictions and hypocrisies abounded: some Nazi leaders who constantly evoked the spirit of workerdom distinguished themselves, above all, through their personal corruption and incompetence. Many factory owners used the abolishment of workers' rights after 1933 to return to pre-WWI conditions of autocratic management but refused to support new initiatives by the German Labor Front. Frustrated about longer work hours and stagnating wages, workers turned to individual acts of resistance in the form of slowdowns, absenteeism, and workplace sabotage – and that despite the obligatory references to joy and pride in countless official speeches and party pamphlets.

Understanding workerdom's appeal as a social imaginary requires close attention to its ideological sources, cultural conventions, artistic traditions, and emotional modalities. The social imaginaries organized through the figure of the worker never concealed their origins in the working-class culture of the Wilhelmine and Weimar years, beginning with the cult of muscular masculinity and the affinity for heroic and tragic registers. The workers' movements of the nineteenth century in turn drew heavily on an even older tradition of communitarianism distinguished by its belief in cultural homogeneity and ethnic distinction and organized around the overdetermined notion of *Gemeinschaft* (community). As confirmed by the countless DAF neologisms combining work and community, the term offered a convenient formula through which nation and society could be reimagined based on the unifying idea of the people – specifically, a people defined in racial and ethnic terms. Like the folk community, workerdom thus gave rise to a collective fantasy with aspirational, compensatory, and normative functions. Whereas the genealogies of folk community can be traced back to the eighteenth century and are inseparable from the critique of Enlightenment rationalism, workerdom must be examined as a product of the age of industrialization and the rise of modern class society. Populist in affect and tone, both social imaginaries relied on strategies of exclusion in order to define their boundaries and achieve their unifying effects. In the same way that the folk community in the Third Reich was predicated on the exclusion of a racialized Other, workerdom realized the often-proclaimed unity of the "workers of the forehead and workers of the fist" through the racialization of the worker and, by extension, the remasculinization of the nation.

All of these ideological narratives draw on a key distinction in modern German social thought, that between society and community, reason enough to situate this all-important term and its Nazi version of *Volksgemeinschaft* within the turbulent history of nineteenth- and early twentieth-century Germany. Translated as people's community, folk community, or racial community, the compound noun helped to channel growing opposition to the interrelated processes of modernization, industrialization, and urbanization that profoundly transformed all aspects of culture and society from the making of the German nation-state in 1871 to the founding of the first German republic in 1918. Forcing these complex processes into an essentializing narrative of class reconciliation, folk community during the Third Reich came to represent the complete opposite of the antagonistic model of society associated with Marxism. As a collective imaginary, it served two not always compatible functions: defining an ideal society before, after, or beyond class and projecting present problems into an imagined future past. The emotional appeals to folk community shared by conservative, nationalist, and *völkisch* movements built on Ferdinand Tönnies's 1887 famous distinction between community and society (*Gesellschaft*), with the second term standing for the pursuit of individual self-interest in formalized social structures and relations and the first one referring to the shared experience of rootedness and belonging in kinship-based forms of sociability. Related binaries such as modern versus traditional, open versus closed, and constructed versus organic gave additional legitimacy to a conservative critique of modernity that, through the equation of community with essential truths, ended up associating modern class society with alienation, massification, deracination, and so forth. Helmuth Plessner, in *Grenzen der Gemeinschaft: Eine Kritik des sozialen Radikalismus* (1924, The limits of community: a critique of social radicalism), was one of the first to recognize the dangerous potential of regressive social fantasies that seek to contain the forces of modernity, including its promise of individual freedom, through authoritarian solutions shrouded in the idioms of organic unity.

Folk community acquired its antidemocratic and antisemitic connotations in the context of the conservative revolution, with Werner Sombart, Max Scheler, Friedrich Meinecke, and Ernst Troeltsch providing the antiliberal, antibourgeois, and antimodern arguments that henceforth sustained the romance with communitarianism, including its fateful alliance with the authoritarian nation-state.[5] For these thinkers, folk community marked the discursive ground on which the two-front battle against liberalism and communism would be won, namely through a modern corporatism that solved class conflicts and capitalist crises by organizing society into distinct groups that, like organs, made up the body politic and through a modern authoritarianism that empowered the charismatic leader to demand endless sacrifices from his people. Whether the promises of peace, harmony, and camaraderie were fulfilled or not proved irrelevant in the end; what mattered was the unifying effect of the processes of exclusion that began with the proletarian as the embodiment of class society and ended with the Jew as the personification of finance capitalism. As Martina Steber and Bernard Gotto have shown, the racialized discourse of folk and community conveyed its aggressive undercurrents through Nazi slogans such as *Kampfgemeinschaft* (community of struggle) and *Opfergemeinschaft* (community of sacrifice) that helped to complete the reorganization of labor in the name of *Werkgemeinschaft* (work community) and *Betriebsgemeinschaft* (factory community).[6] Of special relevance to this discussion, the term

---

[5] For a short summary, see Gunther Mai, "'Arbeiterschaft' und 'Volksgemeinschaft,'" in *Staat, Gesellschaft, Wissenschaft: Beiträge zur modernen hessischen Geschichte*, ed. Winfried Speitkamp (Marburg: Elwert, 1994), 211–226.

[6] See Martina Steber and Bernhard Gotto, eds., *Visions of Community in Nazi Germany: Social Engineering and Private Lives* (Oxford: Oxford University Press, 2014).

"work community" signified equality, trust, and unanimity between blue- and white-collar workers and a harmonious relationship between employer and employees based on the Nazi *Führerprinzip* (leadership) principle.

Rejecting earlier assessments of folk community as a mere political myth invented to conceal social differences and hierarchies, a younger generation of historians has emphasized its productive qualities as a generative concept that actively shaped social reality and intervened in political processes. Influenced by the cultural turn, they have concluded that "the promise of social community and national rebirth, the end of class society and political disunity added significantly to the attractiveness of National Socialism."[7] Of course, the concept of social fantasy must not be confused with social reality; yet its emotional intensity and anticipatory quality made it seem real in often surprising and unsettling ways. To quote Frank Bajor and Michael Wildt: "In the promise, in the act of mobilization but not in the diagnosis of current conditions lay the political force of the speaking about 'folk community.'"[8] In the same way that the appeal of folk community resided in its exclusionary and inclusionary functions, the purpose of workerdom was to at once neutralize and utilize the legacies of the workers' movement. And in the same way that folk community drew on the universalizing claims of what Thomas Rohkrämer calls a single communal faith, the discourse of workerdom conjured a society beyond classes in which everyone (i. e., every man) was a worker and work the essence and destiny of the folk.[9] Awareness of the difference between fantasy and reality and the crucial role of mass deception, including self-deception, in bridging that unbridgeable gap was integral to the elaborate public rituals and political performances staged in the name of folk community and workerdom.

Many scholars locate the origins of old and new populist movements in the various fascisms that emerged in Europe during the interwar years. Beholden to conventional left-right distinctions, they rarely consider the similarities between

---

7 Frank Bajor and Michael Wildt, eds., *Volksgemeinschaft: Neue Forschungen zur Gesellschaft des Nationalsozialismus* (Frankfurt am Main: Fischer, 2009), 8. All translations from the German are mine unless noted otherwise. For an early analysis of the term, see Heinrich August Winkler, "Vom Mythos der Volksgemeinschaft," *Archiv für Sozialgeschichte* 17 (1977): 484–490. For recent scholarship, see Detlef Schmiechen-Ackermann, ed., *"Volksgemeinschaft": Mythos, wirkungsmächtige soziale Verheißung oder soziale Realität im "Dritten Reich"?: Zwischenbilanz einer kontroversen Debatte* (Paderborn: Schöningh, 2012) and Dietmar von Reeken and Malte Thießen, eds., *"Volksgemeinschaft" als soziale Praxis: Neue Forschungen zur NS-Gesellschaft vor Ort* (Paderborn: Schöningh, 2013).
8 Bajor and Wildt, *Volksgemeinschaft*, 8.
9 See Thomas Rohkrämer, *A Single Communal Faith? The German Right from Conservatism to National Socialism* (New York: Berghahn, 2007), especially chapter 6 on the Third Reich (189–247).

socialism and populism – to be more precise, the populist elements shared by socialist and nationalist movements since the late nineteenth century.[10] Jan-Werner Mueller defines populism as a fiction of the people – specifically, the belief that one part of the people is in fact *the* people and that the people represent a singular entity. Accordingly, populism's "moralistic imagination of politics"[11] departs from the conclusion that liberal democracy has failed, that it has been destroyed by old elites and new multitudes, and that is has left large groups marginalized, disenfranchised, and spiritually homeless. It is precisely this politics of grievances and resentments and its obverse, the desire for community and belonging, that make populist movements such a challenge for cultural historians beholden to ideology-critical approaches. Populist tendencies materialize in response to crises of representation in the political and symbolic sense, one reason for the importance of culture wars in the Nazi pursuit of power. Causing a crisis of interpretation as well, these developments first became apparent in the discursive scrambling of left-right, progressive-reactionary, and subversive-affirmative binaries from which new social and political movements emerged in the aftermath of World War I. In the place of interest-based party affiliations, political emotions gained ever greater relevance, as can be seen (then and now) in the eruptions of anger and fear in response to more fluid gender roles and racial hierarchies, the deep suspicion of social and economic elites and, by extension, traditional political parties, and the growing contempt for democratic institutions, scientific knowledge, and consensus politics in favor of identity-based antagonisms.

Ernesto Laclau's assertion that "constructing a people is the main task of radical politics"[12] represents an impassioned argument for a leftwing populism. His

---

10 See Peter Fritzsche, *Rehearsals for Fascism: Populism and Political Mobilization in Weimar Germany* (New York: Oxford University Press, 1990). For the continuation of this argument, including a thematic focus on the politics of optimism, see his *Germans into Nazis* (Cambridge, MA: Harvard University Press, 1999). For a summary of the scholarship, also see his "Did Weimar Fail?," *Journal of Modern History* 68.3 (1996): 629–665. For a comparative perspective through Latin American history, compare Federico Finkelstein, *From Fascism to Populism in History* (Berkeley: University of California Press, 2017).
11 Jan-Peter Müller, *What Is Populism?* (London: Penguin, 2017), 19. For a useful concise introduction, consider Benjamin Moffit, *Populism* (London: Polity, 2020).
12 The is the title of Ernesto Laclau, "Why Constructing a People is the Main Task of Radical Politics," *Critical Inquiry* 32.4 (2006): 646–680. On leftwing populism, also see Laclau, *On Populist Reason* (London: Verso, 2018) and Chantal Mouffe, *For a Left Populism* (London: Verso, 2019). On the connection between socialism and democracy, see Geoff Eley, *Forging Democracy: The History of the Left in Europe, 1850–2000* (Oxford: Oxford: University Press, 2002). For a summary of the main scholarly debates, also see his *Nazism as Fascism: Violence, Ideology, and the Ground of Consent in Germany 1930–1945* (London: Routledge, 2013), especially chapter 3 on the ideology of the folk community.

definition could also describe the Nazi Party program before 1933 and the modification of its socialist elements within the parameters of workerdom. Given the inherent instabilities of populist movements, including their tendency toward authoritarianism and their affinity with nativism and racism, it is therefore necessary to determine how oppositional voices become part of hegemonic practices and structures. Based on what Raymond Williams calls structures of feeling, individual chapters subsequently seek to identify the dominant and residual elements that made the discourse of workerdom part of an ongoing balancing act between the Nazi Party's original socialist rhetoric and the biopolitical ambitions of the racial state.[13] The strange position of community between inclusion and exclusion and the shared genealogies of socialism, nationalism, and populism are particularly important for understanding the range of emotions associated with, generated through, and projected onto the new culture of work. Its work stories and worker figures modeled normative experiences (or performances) of joy and pride in work but they also stood for the unredeemed hopes and expectations after the National Socialist revolution. In the beginning, workerdom functioned like a repository of emotions that, notwithstanding official pronouncements on the identity of worker and folk, included the recognition that there was still room for socialist positions, even if only in the form of phrases and clichés. During the war economy with its heavy dependence on women workers and forced labor, the discourse of workerdom lost much of its explanatory power and emotional appeal. Yet in the organizations and initiatives of the German Labor Front, the culture of work continued to draw on the aesthetic and emotional experiences described by Ernst Bloch an essential part of what he calls the spirit of utopia – but now fully in line with the goals of Nazi biopolitics and without any references to the proletarian legacies still traceable in the discourse of workerdom.[14]

Laying out the conceptual terrain mapped by *The Nazi Worker* requires some acknowledgment of the challenges of studying Nazi culture(s), and the culture of work in particular. The Third Reich has often been used to address larger questions of art and politics and define modern media dictatorships in relation to visuality, specularity, and performativity. The results can be seen in the numerous studies on art and propaganda, the politics of mass manipulation, and, with greater theoretical ambition, the fascist aesthetic. Most surveys of Nazi culture offer broad overviews that document the process of Gleichschaltung and analyze the Nazification of literature, art, architecture, music, film, and theater based on ideology-driven,

---

[13] The distinction between emergent, dominant, and residual is taken from Raymond Williams, "Structures of Feeling," *Marxism and Literature* (Oxford: Oxford University Press, 1977), 128–135.
[14] For the Bloch reference, see *The Spirit of Utopia*, trans. Anthony A. Nassar (Stanford: Stanford University Press, 2000).

institution-based, top-down models. Such approaches tend to validate the regime's intentionalist models of power and control as implemented by the Propaganda Ministry through the Reich Culture Chamber system and continuously revised through new dictates, decrees, and directives. As a result, the totalizing accounts of culture from the Nazi period and the theories of totalitarianism favored after World War II end up reproducing each other as if in an endless loop.[15] In less obvious ways, postwar studies on totalitarian art indirectly affirm the superiority of autonomous art in liberal democracies and use the ideological confrontation of capitalism vs. communism as a template for other highly charged divides – individualism vs. collectivism, modernism vs. realism, and so forth – as a result of which Nazi culture is forever removed from the master narratives of modern(ist) art and literature. Noting the longevity of this art-and-dictatorship model in her recent critical historiography of Nazi culture, Pamela Potter speaks of "the *postwar suppression of inconvenient truths about artistic productivity during the Third Reich*."[16] These include focusing on Nazi organizations and institutions at the expense of actual engagement with artistic works and ignoring inefficiencies within the cultural bureaucracy for the benefit of a simplistic model of ideological indoctrination. As Potter rightly notes, similar patterns of interpretation can be found in relation to the contribution of exile writers, artists, and scholars to the enduring myths of Weimar modernism and the bifurcated narratives of modernist and totalitarian art created in the context of the Cold War.

Since the 1990s, there has been a steady stream of archives-based monographs on major figures and institutions and comprehensive overviews of theater, dance, and film in particular that have both clarified and complicated earlier approaches to art and politics in the Third Reich.[17] Studies of the continued appeal of American mass culture, the mixed reception of favored Nazi writers, the political instru-

---

15 For two recent English-language overviews that offer very different accounts of the period but are equally removed from the questions addressed in this study, see Michael H. Kater, *Culture in Nazi Germany* (New Haven: Yale University Press, 2019) and Moritz Föllmer, *Culture in the Third Reich* (Oxford: Oxford University Press, 2020).
16 Pamela M. Potter, *Art of Suppression: Confronting the Nazi Past in Histories of the Visual and Performing Arts* (Berkeley: University of California Press, 2016), 3.
17 For representative English-language studies (in chronological order) Brandon Taylor and Winfried van der Will, eds., *The Nazification of Art: Art, Design, Music, Architecture, and Film in the Third Reich* (Hampshire: Winchester, 1990); Glenn R. Cuomo, ed., *National Socialist Cultural Policy* (New York: St. Martin's Press, 1995); Jonathan Petropoulos, *Art as Politics in the Third Reich* (Chapel Hill: University of North Carolina Press, 1996); and Alan E. Steinweis, *Art, Ideology, and Economics: The Reich Chambers of Music, Theater, and the Visual Arts* (Chapel Hill: University of North Carolina Press, 1996). For case studies of individual artists, also see Jonathan Petropoulos, *Artists under Hitler: Collaboration and Survival in Nazi Germany* (New Haven: Yale University Press, 2014).

mentalization of classical music, and the moderate modernism of Nazi design have drawn attention to the power of the aesthetic within and beyond ideology. The inevitable contradictions and incongruities and their often imperceivable effects on culture, society, and everyday life are acknowledged in Hans Dieter Schäfer's notion of split consciousness, Peter Reichel's coupling of beauty and violence, and similar attempts to make sense of the irredeemable otherness of Nazi culture.[18] Today there is growing awareness of the connections and continuities across the 1933 and 1945 divides and the surprising similarities to the propaganda arts of other dictatorships in Europe and beyond. The experiential quality of fascist attractions, whether defined in the language of moods, sensations, and experiences or examined through terms such as cult, ritual, or performance has resulted in a further expansion of the conceptual terrain on which to locate the intersections of the aesthetic and the affective.[19] Meanwhile, fascist aesthetics continues to serve as a testing ground for psychoanalytic, ideology-critical, and poststructuralist readings that treat both the historical phenomenon and its continuing fascination as prefigurations of contemporary concerns about the aestheticization of politics.[20]

Very different conclusions – namely, of continued bracketing – must be reached about the place of the Third Reich in the historiography of working-class culture begun by leftist exile writers and scholars returning from the Soviet Union and the United States. During the Cold War, the ideological narratives of anticommunism in the West and Marxist-Leninism in the East only allowed for one

---

[18] For references, see Hans Dieter Schäfer, *Das gespaltene Bewußtsein: Deutsche Kultur und Lebenswirklichkeit 1933–1945* (Munich: Hanser, 1981) and Peter Reichel, *Der schöne Schein des Dritten Reiches: Faszination und Gewalt des Faschismus* (Frankfurt am Main: Fischer, 1993). The greater focus in early German studies on the aesthetics of power is evident in Ralf Schnell and Martin Rector, eds., *Kunst und Kultur im deutschen Faschismus* (Stuttgart: Metzler, 1978) and Ulrich Herrmann and Ulrich Nassen, eds., *Formative Ästhetik im Nationalsozialismus: Intentionen, Medien und Praxisformen totalitärer ästhetischer Herrschaft* (Weinheim: Beltz, 1993).
[19] Several studies have highlighted this aspect, including Gudrun Brockhaus, *Schauder und Idylle: Faschismus als Erlebnisangebot* (Munich: Kunstmann, 1997) and Dieter Bartetzko, *Illusionen in Stein: Stimmungsarchitektur im Nationalsozialismus; Ihre Vorgeschichte in Theater- und Filmbauten* (Berlin: Zentralverlag, 2012). On theories of popular culture and notions of experience as useful models for the intersection of culture and propaganda in the Third Reich, also see Thymian Bussemer, *Propaganda und Populärkultur: Konstruierte Erlebniswelten im Nationalsozialismus* (Wiesbaden: Deutscher Universitätsverlag, 2000).
[20] On this question, see George Mosse, "Fascist Aesthetics and Society: Some Considerations," *Journal of Contemporary History* 31.2 (1996): 245–252; Lutz Koepnick, "Fascist Aesthetics Revisited," *Modernism/Modernity* 6.1 (1999): 51–73; and Carsten Strathausen, "Nazi Aesthetics," *Culture, Theory and Critique* 42.1 (1999): 5–19. For comparative perspectives, see the special issue on the aesthetics of fascism, ed. Jeffrey Schnapp, in *Journal of Contemporary History* 31.2 (1996) and Richard J. Golsan, ed., *Fascism, Aesthetics, and Culture* (Hanover: University Press of New Hampshire, 1992).

way of reading workerdom: as something specific to National Socialism with no connections to the "real" socialisms of the SPD, KPD, and the East German SED (Socialist Unity Party). The reclamation of working-class culture by the "workers' and peasants' state" called the German Democratic Republic (GDR) required that its precursors only be found among the proletarian-revolutionary writers and artists associated with the Weimar KPD. Meanwhile, in the homogeneous middle-class society of the Federal Republic, questions of class were summarily dismissed as obsolete and irrelevant. The student movement brought an end to the collective amnesia of the postwar years and ushered in new phase of *Vergangenheitsbewältigung* (coming to terms with the past) also in relation to the history of German socialisms. Through the rediscovery of Weimar culture and politics, the New Left of the 1960s and 1970s reclaimed the proletarian as a model of revolutionary politics and oppositional praxis. With only certain versions of working-class culture suitable for rediscovery and reclamation, however, the worker-based images and stories produced during the Third Reich were ignored – unlike the real workers who inspired numerous studies by social historians. Today the renewed interest in proletarian and fascist cultures in a national and transnational context reflects a shared sense of urgency in response to a number of developments in Germany and beyond: the disappearance of the working class and the rise of postindustrial society, the disintegration of the European Left and the influence of new social movements, and, last but not least, the combined forces of globalization, neoliberalism, and labor migration. All these developments have heightened critical awareness of the fundamental divide separating the class-based forms of political mobilization of the past from the identity-based movements of the present and, at the same time, revealed the strange connection between Marx's working men of all countries and a new kind of "workers of the world."[21] Workerdom, this book argues, represents the missing link between these two social and political imaginaries.

With the fall of communism, the crises of liberal democracy, and the problems of global capitalism, older certainties about left-right distinctions are giving way to critical inquiries into the affinities between socialist, nationalist, and populist sentiments and the strategies of appropriation and adaptation that sustain these precarious alliances. New approaches to the question of labor and the nature of work in the postindustrial age have revealed surprising continuities between the Weimar and Nazi years, especially in relation to industrial management and organizational psychology, the global history of Fordism and Americanism, the cult of in-

---

21 The reference is to the *Communist Manifesto*.

dustrial modernity, and the biopolitics of work and leisure.[22] There are even longer lines of influence that inform literary and artistic treatments of workers from the pre–World War I to the post–World War II years and make the white, male bodies of German working-class culture an integral part of the continuously evolving constellations of class, race, and nation today.

II

It is a working assumption of this study that the social identifications and political commitments created and sustained through the discourse of workerdom be reconstructed best through the different perspectives offered by various art forms, literary genres, academic disciplines, cultural practices, and media technologies. Moreover, historicization in this context requires that these vast and diverse sources be examined within the breaks and continuities that made the Third Reich part of the longer arc of German socialisms and the many forms of influence and collaboration between European fascisms. Accordingly, the individual chapters approach the discursive transformation of "proletarians" into "German workers" through the distinct modes of representation and signification associated with literary, theatrical, artistic, photographic, filmic, and scholarly works. In recognition of the unique contribution of each art form and the corresponding research field, the chosen materials are presented in line with traditional disciplinary boundaries but in full awareness of multimedia practices and intermedial effects. The roughly chronological approach reflects the considerable differences between the early years of the regime, when the meaning of socialism in National Socialism had not yet been settled, and the war years, when the culture of work spearheaded by the German Labor Front served very different functions in the context of war and genocide.

---

22 The connection between the culture of work and biopolitics would require further attention, which cannot be accomplished here. The main arguments by Michel Foucault can be found in *The History of Sexuality*, 2 vols., trans. Robert Hurley (New York: Vintage, 1990) and *The Birth of Biopolitics: Lectures at the Collège de France, 1978–79*, ed. Michel Senellart, trans. Graham Burchell (Houndmills: Palgrave Macmillan, 2008). Recent contributions include Edward Ross Dickinson, "Biopolitics, Fascism, Democracy: Some Reflections on Our Discourse about 'Modernity,'" *Central European History* 37.1 (2004): 1–48; and Roberto Esposito, *Terms of the Political: Community, Immunity, Biopolitics*, trans. Rhiannon Noel Welch (New York: Fordham University Press, 2013). For a collection of major texts on biopolitics, see *Biopolitics*, ed. Catherine Mills (London: Routledge, 2018). For a useful overview, see Thomas Lemke, *Biopolitics: An Advanced Introduction*, foreword Eric Frederick Trump (New York: New York University Press, 2011).

Chapter 1 introduces workerdom as a key concept in the Nazi appropriation of proletarian culture and socialist ideology. Offering a race-based definition of the worker, the term found its clearest articulation in the fictional, autobiographical, and critical writings of August Winnig (1878–1956), an influential but largely forgotten author who, during the 1920s, converted from Social Democracy to National Socialism and became part of a diverse group of rightwing, *völkisch*, and antisemitic thinkers. His extensive engagement with the figure of the worker makes him ideally suited to map the historical configurations within which workerdom offered a national(ist) alternative to the anticapitalism of the proletarian dream. Workerdom added a racialized perspective to the critique of bourgeois individualism and liberal democracy shared by leftwing and rightwing groups during the late Weimar years. In particular, its emphasis on class-based experiences continued to validate the socialist tradition through populist appeals to the people and the folk. In assessing this process, the chapter pursues a three-fold goal: to introduce Winnig as a major contributor to the fluid constellations of socialism, nationalism, and populism during the Weimar and Nazi years, to present his version of middlebrow literature as an important repository for collective identifications beyond the left-right divide, and to identify some of the discursive strategies involved in the Nazi appropriation of socialist tropes, symbols, and iconographies.

Chapter 2 is the first of three chapters that show the continued influence of working-class culture through the proletarian-revolutionary novel, the socialist and communist *Sprechchor* (speaking chorus), and the workers' poetry of the Weimar years. Obsessed with "1933" as a revolutionary moment, the *Bewegungsroman* (movement novel), *Arbeiterdichtung* (workers' poetry), and *Thingspiel* (choral drama) all offer conversion experiences of some sort or another: emotional healing through the discovery of the folk community, political radicalization through the unifying concept of race, and initiation into the all-male world of the Nazi movement. Significantly, these emotional scenarios always involve a religiously coded journey from darkness into light: from suffering to redemption, from alienation to belonging, from shame to pride, and so forth. Entirely forgotten today, the movement novels feature young men from the working class who, in very didactic ways, model the political journey of becoming a Nazi. The protagonists are introduced as members of militant Red Front groups, but the communist milieu invariably fails to satisfy their yearning for community. The novels (and few films) present these conversion experiences through conventional plot structures, class and gender stereotypes, and simplistic patterns of identification. In so doing, they establish an emotional template through which joining the Nazis becomes readable as an experience of self-discovery and an expression of commitment, with the latter essential for the reader's willing participation in the folk community and work community.

Chapter 3 on Weimar-era worker-poets follows a similar process of adaptation by looking at the revisions of older poems for republication after 1933. Since the 1848 Revolution, workers' poetry had been praised as an authentic voice of the working class and an effective medium of communalization. Aware of these traditions, its Nazified versions simply redefined workers' poetry as folk poetry. The 1935 reedition of a much-discussed 1928 anthology on *Das proletarische Schicksal* (Proletarian fate), edited by Hans Mühle, illustrates how minor but significant changes preserved the emotional world of being a proletarian (e. g., feelings of suffering and indignation), yet added very different interpretations of the causes of class oppression and labor exploitation. Along similar lines, the thematic continuities in the oeuvre of Heinrich Lersch and Max Barthel show how "the proletarian" became "the German worker" through a simple adjustment of poetic form and mood to the discourses of folk and, ultimately, race. Rather than treating these revisions as evidence of political opportunism, the close readings draw attention to the shared languages of communitarianism that, from the beginning, aligned workers' poetry with nationalist, *völkisch*, and populist positions. By replacing the interpretative framework of proletarianism with that of workerdom, the worker-poets of the 1930s only reaffirmed their original commitment to the fantasy of the people as one. This highly individualized identification with the workers as victims sustained workers' poetry as a memory of past suffering but also contributed to its growing irrelevance in a culture of work taken over by the DAF program of joy, pride, and beauty.

Chapter 4 examines how the Nazi-era *Thingspiel* (literally "thing play") emulated the performance of collectivity in the socialist Sprechchor and, through multimedia practices, set out to integrate the working class into the work community. Two aspects are important for understanding the rise and fall of this short-lived theatrical experiment: the thematic preoccupation with Weimar-era labor struggles as a prehistory of the communitarianism of workerdom, and the extensive debates within the Thingspiel movement about mass ritual and cultic functions and their contribution to the transformation of oppositional stances into hegemonic practices. The first part lays out some of the conceptual problems with analyzing the Thingspiel as a product of Nazi cultural policy and *völkisch* thought while ignoring the more hidden connections to nineteenth-century mass psychology and its historical double, class analysis. The second part provides an overview of the heated debates among Nazi functionaries on cultic functions and what they signified: namely, a performative approach to politics through which class differences could be dissolved into ritualized reenactments of community. The third part highlights the continued provocation of class through the thematic preoccupation with Weimar-era labor struggles and, by extension, proletarian culture. In the fourth part, the performative qualities of the Thingspiel are illustrated by scenes from two influential plays, Richard Euringer's *Deutsche Passion 1933* (German passion 1933) and Kurt Heynicke's *Neurode: Ein Spiel von deutscher Arbeit* (1935, Neurode: a play about German work), as well as various initiatives started by the Thingspiel movement (e.g., construction of outdoor theaters, organization of mass spectacles, cooperation with radio and film).

The remaining chapters concentrate on the visual arts and explore the connection between emotionalization and aestheticization through three key Nazi phrases: *Arbeitsstolz* (pride in work), *Arbeitsfreude* (joy in work), and *Schönheit der Arbeit* (beauty of labor). Once again, the heavy debts to the Weimar years are evident in the modernism of industrial photography and film and in what, during the 1930s, emerged as a decidedly transnational aesthetic of industrial modernity. At the same time, the growing involvement by Nazi organizations aligned the new culture of work more explicitly with economic rationales and political goals. Instead of Nazi functionaries and worker poets, photographers and filmmakers on corporate assignment now dominated the discourse of workerdom. In following that visual turn, chapter 5 begins with the innovations in exhibition design in the so-called *Leistungsschauen* (achievement exhibitions) used to advertise German labor and industry, followed by a brief overview of the representation of workers in painting and sculpture since the nineteenth century. Of course, the theme of pride in work in the visual arts is unthinkable without the Greater German Art Exhibitions and extensive corporate support for industry-related public art. Workers' sculpture and industrial painting played complementary roles in the momentous discursive shift from the figure of the worker to the abstract category of work. Whether made visible through working bodies or industrial technologies, feelings of "pride" compensated for workers' loss of political agency and facilitated their integration into a hierarchically organized work community. These processes are associated with two artists: known as the sculptor of the German worker, Fritz Koelle drew on his close familiarity with the miners of the Saar region to achieve an aesthetic compromise between the traces of physical effort and the look of heroic achievement. The expressive registers of working-class masculinity are central to his attempts at ideological mediation as well. By contrast, Erich Mercker, a painter who specialized in industrial landscapes, relied heavily on the sensory effects of size and scale to create monuments to German industry and, in the process, remove the worker entirely from the scene of production.

Chapter 6 continues this line of inquiry by looking at industrial photography and film and considering the role of new media in the visualization of workerdom. Organized around the theme of "joy in work," the discussion starts out with the contribution of modern work science to the psychologization of work in capitalist modernity and Nazi biopolitics. It continues with an overview of the very different approaches taken by workers' photography and industrial photography within the historical struggles between capital and labor since the Wilhelmine years. After 1933, these differences were "resolved" through their forced integration into an official iconography of workerdom, a process traceable in the DAF journal *Arbeitertum* and similar publications. The chapter's second part introduces two photobooks, Paul Wolff's *Arbeit!* (1934, Work!) and Erna Lendvai-Dircksen's *Arbeit formt das Gesicht* (1938, Work forms the face), that establish the ideal-typical face of the German worker within the corporatist fantasy of German labor and industry. The films discussed in the third part, Walter Ruttmann's *Acciaio* (1933, Steel) and Walter Frentz's *Hände am Werk* (1935, Hands at work), extend the official preoccupation with joy in work to the moving image, including through the formal possibilities of montage and narrative.

Chapter 7 at last adds an organizational perspective through the design initiatives spearheaded by the "Schönheit der Arbeit" (Beauty of Labor) Office within the German Labor Front. The overarching theme of beauty is introduced through its complete opposite, the dystopian worker-state as imagined by Ernst Jünger in his controversial 1932 essay on *Der Arbeiter: Herrschaft und Form* (The worker: domination and form). Where the worker-type in Jünger remained haunted by the experience of war and violence, Beauty of Labor created utopian spaces of work and leisure in the *NS-Musterbetrieb* (model factory) imagined in numerous books on the construction of access roads, the decoration of meeting rooms, and the design of canteen furniture, porcelain, and flatware. In the chapter's second part, the trade journal *Schönheit der Arbeit* and the last issue of the *Die Form* provide ample opportunities not only to assess the continued influence of Werkbund and Bauhaus but also to shed light on the overdetermined role of beauty in the making of Nazi biopolitics.

Approaching the Nazi culture of work as discourse, imaginary, and social practice and locating the representation of the (German) worker within a longer history of working-class culture requires at least a brief reference to the mechanisms of exclusion that make these connections and transformations possible. First, the imagination of the worker in terms that equate masculinity with universality effectively turns workerdom into an instrument of remasculinization. Almost all stories and images of the Third Reich at work revolve around men; men also dominate Nazi-era accounts of the past and future of work. The few women captured by photographers on the factory floor not only document the contribution of female workers, especially during the war years. Their presence also draw attention to the rules of inclusion and exclusion that bring forth the heroic narratives of German work, industry, and technology and that, incidentally, produce a very different gendered script when promoting the Nazi culture of leisure and consumption. Awareness of these structuring absences especially in a study dominated by working men leads to a clearer sense of the close connections among the crises of modern class society and modern masculinity, the discourse of workerdom, and the Nazi culture of work, including their resonances after 1945. The same holds true for the coupling of "German" and "worker" that completes the shift from class to race as the main language of communalization through the exclusion of the racial Other who, within the German tradition of antisemitism and ethnonationalism, is always coded as "the Jew." Again, it is documentary photography, in this case images intended for official use only, that introduces forced laborers as essential workers in the Nazi war economy. Thus, on the other side of the preoccupation with joy in work and pride in work one is confronted with the infamous motto *Arbeit macht frei* (Work sets you free) displayed on the gates of concentration camps – and yet another indication of the centrality of the culture of work to the making of the Nazi racial state.

Speaking about absences and exclusions also means acknowledging what cannot be resolved by this book: the problem of reception – that is, ideology and interpellation, in Althusserian terms – or, to put it differently, the relationship between the intentions of Nazi ideologues and the effect of their messages on workplace attitudes and behaviors.[23] Taking an interdisciplinary approach represents one way of moving beyond the facile equation of pamphlets and treatises with the world of actual workers and real working conditions. Here interdisciplinarity draws attention to the various modes of engagement, from true enthusiasm to forced participation in official events that, beyond public performances of consent, come with questions such as the following: Who were the intended and actual readers of the conversion novels and workers' poetry? Who attended Thingspiel performances and factory art exhibitions? In what ways did the representation of workers respond to widespread political needs and demands, including for a continued engagement with questions of labor exploitation and social inequality, and to what degree did the extensive focus on work serve primarily the needs of interests of writers, critics, artists, and functionaries with Nazi affiliations or sympathies? Was the culture of work actually a culture for and by workers, or did its productions speak mostly to Nazi Party members from diverse social backgrounds but with an enduring fascination with the working folk? Providing possible answers is made difficult by the lack of reliable sources that could speak to the question of mass appeal and popular success.[24] A highly contextualized interdisci-

---

23 The reference here is Louis Althusser, "Ideology and Ideological State Apparatuses," in *Lenin and Philosophy and Other Essays*, trans. Ben Brewster (London: New Left Books, 1971), 121–176.
24 For examples of studies that rely on SOPADE reports, see David Welch, "Nazi Propaganda and the Volksgemeinschaft: Constructing a People's Community," *Journal of Contemporary History* 39 (2004): 213–239 and Julia Timpe, *Nazi-Organized Recreation and Entertainment in the Third Reich* (London: Palgrave Macmillan, 2017).

plinary approach protects against facile assumptions about a unified culture of work entirely subordinate to Nazi ideology and fully aligned with the discourse of workerdom. It also indicates that it might be better to speak of different cultures of work distinguished by medium, genre, and art form (e.g., book culture, event culture, exhibition culture, visual culture) and consider the ways in which each responded to slightly different generational and institutional attachments to working-class culture and the new culture of work. The difference between the backward-looking perspective of worker poets and dramatists and the modernist sensibilities of industrial photographers, filmmakers, and designers would certainly support such a distinction. In fact, the very concept "culture of work," which includes the fine and applied arts and which extends to economy and psychology, suggests that all of Nazi culture needs to be theorized and historicized in the plural terms that recognize different institutional and organizational foundations and different locations for cultural practices and aesthetic experiences within the high-low culture divides and related distinctions between official and everyday culture. In this particular case, closer attention to the different traditions and perspectives within the Nazi culture of work might also help to better understand the complicated relationship between the social imaginaries created in the name of workerdom and the conditions of work in the factories and beyond; but this would be the subject of a very different book.

Chapter 1
From Proletariat to Workerdom, in the Name of the People

> Workers, unite against proletarianism!
> Gustav Hartz (1932)

The Nazis' ideological assault on Weimar democracy involved three very different protagonists: the workers as the embodiment of revolutionary change, the nation as the site of renewal and empowerment, and that elusive communal body called *Volk* and translated alternatively as folk, people, or populace. Though described as unified and unifying, the culture of Volk is predicated on an exclusionary model of community based on *ethnos* (rather than *demos*) and sustained through intense resentments: against the republic, against the elites, against capitalist modernity.[1] Why the Nazis considered the identity of workers and people essential to their ascent to power can be partly explained through what Claude Lefort describes as the fantasy of the people-as-one and its merging of popular sovereignty with state sovereignty.[2] However, the degree to which the integration of class discourse into race discourse remained important to Nazi ideology and determined the way in which the worker continued to functions as a stand-in for the people seems far from settled.

What is beyond dispute is the intense preoccupation with the worker as a problem and solution in the struggle over social imaginaries. At the center of these discursive struggles stood *Arbeitertum* (literally: workerdom), that untranslatable term with the decidedly nineteenth-century etymology whose distinctive otherness is preserved here in the English neologism "workerdom."[3] Its utopian

---

1 On the discourse of *Volkstum*, see Wolfgang Emmerich, *Zur Kritik der Volkstumsideologie* (Frankfurt am Main: Suhrkamp, 1971) and Jost Hermand, *Der alte Traum vom neuen Reich: Völkische Utopien und Nationalsozialismus* (Frankfurt am Main: Athäneum, 1988). The fact that *Volkskunde* has long dominated the study of working-class culture is problematized by Wolfgang Jacobeit, "Volkskunde und Arbeiterkultur—Eröffnung," in *Die andere Kultur: Volkskunde, Sozialwissenschaften und Arbeiterkultur* (Vienna: Europa-Verlag, 1982), 11–25.
2 See Claude Lefort, *The Political Forms of Modern Society: Bureaucracy, Democracy, Totalitarianism* (Cambridge, MA: MIT Press, 1986). On the social imaginary, see Charles Taylor, *Modern Social Imaginaries* (Durham, NC: Duke University Press, 2003) and, from a Marxist perspective, Cornelius Castoriadis, *The Imaginary Institution of Society*, trans. Kathleen Blamey (Cambridge: Polity Press, 1987).
3 On the etymology of *Arbeitertum*, see Cornelia Schmitz-Berning, *Vokabular des Nationalsozialismus* (Berlin: De Gruyter, 2007), 41–43. The term no longer appears in postwar editions of the Duden

qualities and disciplinary effects can be reconstructed through the writings of August Winnig who played a key role in promoting workerdom as the only viable alternative to the scourge of what Hartz in the epigraph calls proletarianism.[4] Workerdom occupied a central place within the eclectic mixture of terms, phrases, and arguments that made up the Nazified German called Lingua Tertii Imperii (LTI) by philologist Victor Klemperer.[5] As a collective fantasy – specifically, a fantasy about work and workers – workerdom facilitated the transition from the working-class culture of the Weimar years to the official culture of *Volksgemeinschaft* (folk community) and *Werkgemeinschaft* (work community) in the Third Reich. The emergence of workerdom as a normative concept and formative principle was the result of two simultaneous processes performed on the body of the working class, a deproletarization in thoughts, feelings, and identifications and a reinscription of key socialist ideas within the parameters of folk community.[6] The various definitions of *Volk* as "people," "folk," or "populace" and the elusive meanings of *Gemeinschaft* as "precapitalist community" or "postclass society" functioned like catalysts in the discursive transformation of class into race. Socialist, nationalist, and populist frameworks of reference provided the arguments for these imaginary conversions, but the most important ingredients were the intense feelings associated with being a worker before and after 1933.

Tracing the uniquely German history of these terms, the first chapter analyzes how the working class was absorbed into "the people" and the class-based proletariat reimagined as a race-based workerdom informed by Nazi racial theory and antisemitic thought. In ways to be clarified in subsequent chapters on workers' poetry, workers' sculpture, and so forth, workerdom provided a powerful ideological blueprint, identificatory model, and emotional template in the reimagining

---

dictionary. The term can be traced back to Eugen Dühring's *Die Judenfrage als Racen-, Sitten- und Culturfrage: Mit einer weltgeschichtlichen Antwort* (1881); its significance for National Socialism is confirmed by the entry "Arbeitertum" in *Meyers Lexikon*, 8th ed., vol. 1 A-bis Boll (Leipzig: Bibliographisches Institut, 1936), 498.

4 Gustav Hartz, *Die national-soziale Revolution: Die Lösung der Arbeiterfrage* (Munich: J. F. Lehmanns, 1932), 207.

5 On this point, see Karl-Heinz Brackmann, *NS-Deutsch: "Selbstverständliche" Begriffe und Schlagwörter aus der Zeit des Nationalsozialismus* (Straelen: Straelener, 1988). Also see Victor Klemperer, *The Language of the Third Reich: LTI Lingua Tertii Imperii; A Philologist's Notebook*, trans. Martin Brady (London: Bloomsbury Academic, 2013). On the language of communitarianism in particular, see Utz Maas, *"Als der Geist der Gemeinschaft eine Sprache fand": Sprache im Nationalsozialismus: Versuch einer historischen Argumentationsanalyse* (Opladen: Westdeutscher Verlag, 1984).

6 For a definition of the term from the period, see [Johann Wilhelm] Ludowici, "Entproletarisierung," in *Schaffendes Volk: Das Buch vom Adel der Arbeit: Ein Beitrag zum Wiederaufstieg des deutschen Volkes*, ed. Rudolf Ramlow (Essen: Deutsche Vertriebsstelle "Rhein und Ruhr," 1934), 137–152.

of work and class, especially during the early years of the regime. Introduced by late-nineteenth-century conservative thinkers as an alternative to the socialist genealogies of the proletariat, the neologism *Arbeitertum*, with the suffix "-tum" denoting a condition or state of being (i.e., "-dom"), defended the eternal truths of *Volkstum* (folkdom) against the destructive forces unleashed by capitalism as well as socialism. The equation of the proletariat with masculinity, a recurring theme since the early workers' movement, became an important part of the racialization of work through the privileging of productive wage labor over unpaid reproductive labor and the implicit affirmation of traditional gender roles and family structures. As Richard Euringer, one of the more fanatical Nazi authors, put it: "Not working class [Arbeiterschaft]: Workerdom will be the watchword in which everyone recognizes themselves."[7]

No author is more closely identified with the promises of workerdom than the prolific but largely forgotten August Winnig (1878–1956). A typical worker poet who was socialized into the workers' movement, he initially became active in Social Democratic circles but eventually aligned himself with the National Socialists. He built a literary career by expressing thoughts and sentiments from the perspective of the "little people" and, within the milieu of worker unions, associations, and cooperatives, styled himself as a new type of working-class intellectual. Most important for this discussion, Winnig communicated his populist message across a range of literary genres, including memoirs, novellas, and essays, that all shared one unifying element: a deeply felt sense of inferiority and need for recognition presumably shared by the author and his readers. Accessible and aspirational in ways typical of much middlebrow literature, his writings attest to the fluidity of left-right distinctions and the ideological adaptability of antiliberal, antidemocratic, and anticapitalist views and, through its chosen perspective from below, stands as a testament to the broad appeal of populist (un)reason.[8]

The "proletariat to workerdom" argument, which provided ideological scaffolding for the emotional journey to be made by the German worker, will be reconstructed in three steps. The first section locates the fantasy of workerdom in corresponding nineteenth-century discourses of socialism and nationalism that promised reconciliation through identification with the people as the embodiment of community. The second part presents Winnig's critical, fictional, and autobiographical texts as a discursive space where class-based emotions help to dissolve the boundaries between fact and fiction and break down the distinctions that de-

---

[7] Richard Euringer, "Arbeiterdichtung Ja und Nein," in *Chronik einer deutschen Wandlung* (Hamburg: Hanseatische Verlagsanstalt, 1936), 223–224.
[8] The term is taken from Ernesto Laclau's influential reflections on the possibility of leftist populism in *On Populist Reason* (London: Verso, 2005).

fine the political in the traditional sense. Building on the broader questions laid out in the introduction, the final section discusses the integration of workerdom into folkdom as a National Socialist version of what Laclau calls populist reason, a connection that draws attention to the needs and desires shared by socialist, nationalist, and populist appeals to the working class. The equation of the workers with the people in populist rhetoric can be traced back to the utopian socialists and the beginnings of Social Democracy and must be recognized as an integral part of all versions of German socialism, including National Socialism. Yet, as the example of Winnig shows, the adaptability of the populist argument to different cultures of grievance and resentment only comes into clearer view through closer attention to the class- and gender-based emotions organized through workerdom in literary fiction and critical thought.

I

In 1928, responding to the question "Why Are We Socialists?," Joseph Goebbels wrote in *Der Angriff:* "We are socialists because we see in socialism – that is, the preordained dependence of all members of the folk on each other – the only possibility for the preservation of our racial traits and, by extension, the reclamation of our political freedom and the reinstallation of the German state. Socialism is the theory of the liberation of workerdom." But without nationalism, he added, socialism "is nothing, a phantom, a theory, a chimera, a mere tome. With it, it is everything, the future, freedom, fatherland."[9] In 1934, Goebbels revisited the worker question and its agitational potential when he concluded in his diary: "Whoever has the worker has the folk, and whoever has the folk has the Reich."[10]

Two Nazi posters for the 1932 presidential election designed by the infamous Mjölnir (Hans Schweitzer, 1901–1980) can be used to illustrate the appropriation of socialist ideologies, proletarian iconographies and, most importantly, the two emotional registers that superficially connect them: abjection and rage (see figures 1.1 and 1.2). Depicting a group of downtrodden workers, "Our Last Hope: Hitler" alludes to the sense of hopelessness weaponized by leftwing artists Käthe Kollwitz

---

[9] Joseph Goebbels, "Warum sind wir Sozialisten?," *Der Angriff: Aufsätze aus der Kampfzeit*, 16 July 1928. On Nazis as revolutionaries, see Peter Fritzsche, "On Being the Subjects of History: Nazis as Twentieth-Century Revolutionaries," in *Language and Revolution: Making of Modern Political Identities*, ed. Igal Halfin (London: 2002), 161–183.

[10] Joseph Goebbels, *Tagebücher 1924–1945*, 5 vols., ed. Elke Fröhlich for Institut für Zeitgeschichte (Munich: K. G. Saur, 1987), 2/III (Oct. 1932–March 1934): 104.

Fig. 1.1: Mjölnir (Hans Schweitzer), "Unsere letzte Hoffnung Hitler" (1932), Bildarchiv Foto Marburg, www.fotomarburg.de.

and Otto Nagel in their impassioned critiques of modern class society.[11] Yet in the treatment by Mjölnir, the workers' state of abjection serves only to incite feelings

---

11 Important themes include the focus on working-class suffering and appeal to empathy and solidarity in the work of Käthe Kollwitz, the typical scenes from the proletarian lifeworld captured by Otto Nagel, and the critical perspectives opened up through modernist interventions, from George Grosz's affinity for satire and the grotesque to John Heartfield's use of photomontage in uncovering the structural inequalities in class society. Especially the artists associated with the KPD regarded the demand for representation by the poor, hungry, and unemployed as inseparable from the process of political radicalization taking place in these neighborhoods, during labor strikes, and in

Fig. 1.2: Mjölnir (Hans Schweitzer), "Schluß jetzt: Wählt Hitler!" (1932), bpk/Deutsches Historisches Museum/Arne Psille.

of anger – namely in the form of a protest vote for the National Socialists. Breaking the chains of oppression, the raging SA man in "Enough Already! Vote for Hitler" draws on the muscular masculinity favored by communist agitprop. Yet with his barrel chest and thick neck, this Nazi reincarnation of the proletarian Prometheus turns a familiar personification of revolutionary will into a performance of Aryan

---

confrontation with state authorities. Significantly, the leftist perspective rarely showed the workers at the machines—not surprising given the mass unemployment during the Great Depression and the Communist critique of the capitalist system.

masculinity. According to Gerhard Paul, Nazi propagandists used three types of worker figures to affirm the party's socialist credentials: the oppressed proletarians familiar from realist and expressionist painting, the allegorical figures associated with classical antiquity or Nordic mythology, and, after 1933, the idealized Aryan workers on regular display at the Great German Art Exhibitions.[12] Appropriating established leftwing iconographies for rightwing policies made National Socialism, in Paul's words, "a counterrevolutionary movement of images, an uprising of emotionally charged images and mythico-utopian signs against the impoverished language of democracy and rational discourse."[13] The same conclusions can be reached about propagandistic, literary, and writings about workers.

But who exactly were these workers, who played such a crucial role in the discursive struggle over class identifications? Was Goebbels appealing to workers as a social class brought forth through the structural conditions of inequality in capitalist societies? Or was he referring to a manifestation of the people that exceeded such determinations and offered shared experiences of belonging even to bourgeois intellectuals, disaffected members of the petty bourgeoisie, and those who, like Hitler in Vienna, were part of a growing precariat? Commenting on the transformations of class society during the Wilhelmine and Weimar years, Goebbels acknowledged the workers' movement as an important contributor to the culture of work that was destined to reach its full articulation under National Socialism. Above all, the *Gauleiter* of Berlin sought to weaponize the antagonistic model of class struggle embodied by the proletariat for a definition of the political based on Carl Schmitt's critique of modern liberalism and theory of the total state and expressed in his controversial definition of politics as the distinction between friend and enemy.[14] In line with the propagandistic methods developed by the Nazi movement, this meant turning the worker into a conduit for populist grievances and resentments and a projection screen for nationalist dreams of community. The emotional attachments organized through this highly symbolic figure continued to reference socialism's original demands for equality, freedom, and democracy and, in so doing, kept the legacy of the revolutionary proletariat alive – a problem that after 1933 could only be managed but never resolved through the rhetorical contortions of the "proletariat to workerdom" argument.

---

12 Gerhard Paul, *Aufstand der Bilder: NS-Propaganda vor 1933* (Berlin: Dietz, 1992), 242–252. For later studies on the connection between propaganda and popular culture, see Berthold Hinz et al., eds., *Die Dekoration der Gewalt: Kunst und Medien im Faschismus* (Gießen: Anabas, 1984) and Peter Reichel, *Der schöne Schein im Nationalsozialismus* (Munich: Hanser, 1991).
13 Paul, *Aufstand der Bilder*, 13.
14 The reference is to the 1927 essay by Carl Schmitt, available in English as *The Concept of the Political*, trans. George Schwab, intr. Tracy B. Strong (Chicago: University of Chicago Press, 2007).

A first indication of the emotional rewards – and, by extension, political benefits – to be gained from workerdom as an integrative discourse can be found in the rightwing obsession since the October Revolution with the proletariat as an object of fear and loathing but also of endless fascination. Arthur Moeller van den Bruck (1876–1925) opened an entire chapter on the proletariat in *Das dritte Reich* (1923, The Third Reich) with the bold assertion that, "proletarians are those who want to be proletarians."[15] Germany was slowly becoming a proletarianized nation, he argued, weakened by the corrosive effects of massification and industrialization and saved only through a collective expression of the German will to heal a society torn apart by class strife and social anomie. Any voluntary identification with the proletarian as a condition of abjection had to be rejected as a deeply un-German stance that would become both unnecessary and unwarranted in a future Third Reich. Making explicit the full compatibility of anticommunist and antisemitic positions, one Nazi propagandist as late as 1937 declared: "In the name of our folk community, today we sharply reject the term 'proletariat' as used by the Jew Marx."[16] Nonetheless, throughout the 1930s, new book titles such as *Proletarier! Wie wirst du Standesherr?*, *Das neue deutsche Arbeitertum*, *Vom Proletariat zum deutschen Arbeitertum*, and (most significantly) *Vom Proletariat zum Arbeitertum* by Winnig indicate that the promised transition from class- to race-based identifications remained an incomplete project and that the anxieties around the figure of the worker could not be contained through mere discursive displacements. The path to individual and collective agency is clearly spelled out in the title of Robert Ley's pamphlet *Vom Proleten zum Herrrn* (1940, From prole to master). Ley's conclusion that "our socialism has freed the German worker of the inferiority complexes of an ugly, lowly, crudely proletarian life"[17] openly acknowledges how much the biopolitical project of National Socialism was sustained by a calculated appeal to class-based emotions.

The mutually constitutive relationship between workerdom and folkdom signaled by the shared suffix can be further clarified through their respective Others, namely the Bolsheviks and the Jews. In a series of speeches and articles from the late 1920s, Gregor Strasser (1882–1934) took advantage of the two sides in an emo-

---

15 Arthur Moeller van den Bruck, *Das dritte Reich*, 2nd ed. (Berlin: Ring-Verlag, 1926), 179. "Proletarier ist, wer Proletarier sein will." See also *Jedes Volk hat seinen eigenen Sozialismus* (Oldenburg: Gerhard Stalling, 1931). Later versions of the individualism vs. collectivism argument can be found in F. A. Hayek's influential 1944 book, *The Road to Serfdom* (London: Routledge, 2006), especially Chapter 12 on the socialist roots of Nazism (171–185).
16 Fritz Mang, *Der deutsche Arbeiter in Dritten Reich* (Berlin: Propaganda-Verlag Paul Hochmuth, 1937), 6.
17 Robert Ley, *Vom Proleten zum Herrn* (Berlin: Verlag der Deutschen Arbeitsfront, 1940), n.p.

tional dynamic often employed by authoritarian regimes – the paranoid fantasy of being surrounded by enemies and the defensive enlistment of hatred as a survival strategy. The alleged victimization of the German people by the prophets of international solidarity prevented the reconciliation of the bourgeoisie and the proletariat in the name of folk community. In his Reichstag speech from 25 November 1925, Strasser therefore called for a socialism "based on the true, submissive, dutiful, and quintessentially German feeling of, will to, and sense of community. We want the social revolution to arrive as the national revolution! We want the national revolution to achieve the social revolution!!"[18] Accordingly, the Nazis presented their attacks on so-called Jewish Bolsheviks as a long-overdue response to the "songs of hatred" disseminated in the name of Marx.[19] Drawing on this kind of antisemitic rhetoric, Strasser offered a compellingly simple model for turning political emotions into actions:

> Words remain words, no matter how urgently they come from the national heart – they must arouse emotions in order to reveal their meaning. Emotions remain emotions, no matter how honest and strong their intensity of passion – they must become deeds in order to be effective! The national emotion that we all call upon must involve the liberation of German workerdom! Then, and only then, will our people be strong enough to take on the sacrifices in the national struggle for liberation.[20]

The transformative moments in Strasser's program of workerdom are easily identified: from class-based to race-based terms, from internationalist to nationalist solidarities, from collectivist to communitarian models of belonging, and from the belief in class struggle to the faith in folk community. National Socialism promised to elevate the worker to an embodiment of the people and, ultimately, of the Aryan race. As a model of identification, workerdom imbued the Nazi dream of community with the shared values of work, duty, and service. The promotion of workerdom as an alternative to the Marxist analysis of class was predicated on what many celebrated as the German ethos of *Arbeit* and *Werk* (i.e., work in the sense of process rather than product). This belief, in turn, was dependent on the projection of idyllic pasts into glorious futures found in many populist movements with millenarian tendencies. Workerdom implied the equal standing of blue- and white-collar workers. In practice, the substitution of an abstract concept for the social and historical specificity of "the worker" obscured the hierarchies

---

18 Gregor Strasser, *Hammer und Schwert: Ausgewählte Reden und Schriften eines National-Sozialisten* (Berlin: Kampf-Verlag, n. d. [c. 1928]), 17.
19 See Gregor Strasser, "Bürger und Proletarier" (1926), in *Kampf um Deutschland: Reden und Aufsätze eines Nationalsozialisten* (Munich: Franz Eher, 1932), 162–166.
20 Gregor Strasser, "Nationaler Sozialismus" (1925), in *Kampf um Deutschland*, 77.

between employer and employee and aligned the politics of labor ever more closely with the goals of the Nazi state. Continued references to the proletariat served to acknowledge the long-lasting effects of economic and social inequality and provided retrospective justification for the almost habitual attacks on (Jewish) Bolshevism and finance capitalism. Throughout, the class-based grievances first articulated within the workers' movement provided the corporeal memories and affective patterns that made these arguments at once credible and desirable. The failures of communist internationalism could subsequently be cited as proof of the superiority of nationalism and the anti-Marxist critique of capitalism be used as a conduit for (economic) antisemitism. Yet even as the proletarian was time and again vilified as the enemy of the German worker, workerdom preserved some of the oppositional energies from the dreamworld of the proletariat. The discursive loop of writing, feeling, and acting described by Strasser – and the resulting emotional intensities – sustained the Nazi obsession with the worker but, of course, also made workerdom a constant reminder of the term it was meant to replace: the proletariat.

II

August Winnig's biography does not fit easily into conventional histories of working-class literature: union organizing and political activism in the SPD, followed by involvement with the conservative revolution and *völkisch* right, support for National Socialism without actual party membership, and the turn to Christian conservatism that, after 1945, made him one of the founding members of the West German CDU (Christian Democratic Union of Germany). Expressed in the classed terms that informed the assessment of his oeuvre during the 1970s, Winnig's political positions reflect the "embourgeoisement of a worker who advances in the German workers' movement, who during a deep crisis severs his ties to the working class, and who finally achieves psychological balance through his social integration in the bourgeois upper class."[21] At the same time, Winnig resembles Gramsci's or-

---

21 Wilhelm Ribhegge, *August Winnig: Eine historische Persönlichkeitsanalyse* (Bonn-Bad Godesberg: Neue Gesellschaft, 1973), 19. For an early biography from the Nazi period, see Friedrich Gudehus, *August Winnig: Ein Mann des Wortes, der Tat und des Glaubens: Ein Lebensbild* (Berlin: Martin Warneck, 1938). On Winnig's contribution to the discursive transformation of the worker's question and the social question to an ontological question, see Hannah Vogt, *Der Arbeiter: Wesen und Probleme bei Friedrich Naumann, August Winnig, Ernst Jünger* (Grone-Göttingen: August Schönhütte, 1945), 37–52. For a postwar reclamation of Winnig as a Christian thinker and a "voice of conscience" during the Third Reich, see Wilhelm Landgrebe, *August Winnig: Arbeiterfüh-*

ganic intellectual born from the working class and actively involved in its counter-hegemonic strategies – not only by raising but by creating consciousness.[22] Ultimately, such descriptions fail to capture the most distinctive quality of his literary voice, namely its highly adaptable populism. He became a successful *völkisch* writer during the Weimar years and, after 1933, managed to make a comfortable life for himself, complete with a house in Potsdam and just enough distance from the Nazi elites to maintain an illusion of independence. The availability of his vision of workerdom to politicized and apolitical readings is evident already in the choice of publishers: the venerable Stuttgart-based Cotta'sche Buchhandlung, forever associated with the names of Goethe and Schiller, the short-lived Munich-based Milavida Verlag, which during the 1920s published books on labor-related topics, and the Hamburg-based Hanseatische Verlagsanstalt, a key player in the marketing of Nazi bestsellers. The same elusive qualities can be found in Winnig's personal connections to conservative thinkers, *völkisch* ideologues, Christian educators, and a few high-ranking Nazi functionaries. He had a private meeting with Hitler in 1932 and, in the same year, contributed to a Nazi-friendly anthology, where he argued that antisemitism was the foundation of any true national workers' movement.[23] After the war, he insisted that Christian social thought had been the only constant in his thinking; hence occasional claims by scholars that he should be considered a member of the inner emigration. A closer look at his writings in terms of major themes and motifs show that the familiar explanations, whether the exculpatory function of the quiet resistance-argument or the totalizing effect of the "protofascist" label, cannot fully capture the unique emotional dy-

---

rer Oberpräsident Christ (Lahr-Dinglingen: St. Johannis Druckerei, 1961). On his contribution to *NS-Arbeiterliteratur*, see Vanessa Ferrari, "Nazionalsocialismo e *Arbeiterliteratur*: Il lavoro e la fabbrica nella propaganda della NSDAP (1929–1938)" (PhD diss., University of Munich, 2016), esp. 172–180. A rare English-language discussion of Winnig can be found in Joan Campbell, *Joy in Work, German Work: The National Debate, 1800–1945* (Princeton: Princeton University Press, 1989), 296–300.
22 See Antonio Gramsci, "The Intellectuals," *Selections from the Prison Notebooks*, ed. and trans. Quinton Hoare and Geoffrey Nowell-Smith (London: International Publishers, 1998), 130–161.
23 August Winnig, "Der Weg zur nationalen Arbeiterbewegung," in *Was wir vom Nationalsozialismus erwarten: Zwanzig Antworten*, ed. Albrecht Erich Günther (Heilbronn: Eugen Salzer, 1932), 11–21. Similar arguments can be found in Konrad Maß, *Der Kampf um die Seele des Arbeiters* (Leipzig: Theodor Weicher, 1927) and numerous other treatises that argue for the nationalization of the worker question. The role of *völkisch* thought, including its antisemitic elements, in the emerging discourse of workerdom is difficult to evaluate. Explicit antisemitic comments are absent from Winnig's writing before 1933; their later proliferation can mean many things, including willing conversion to the primacy of Nazi racial theory.

namic of victimhood and empowerment that sustains his work beyond the 1919, 1933, and 1945 divides.

With his enduring attachment to the idea of the people, Winnig stands perhaps closest to Ernst Niekisch (1889–1967), who started his political career in the antiwar USPD (Independent Socialist Democratic Party of Germany), then made a name for himself as a leading National Bolshevik and eventually joined the conservative anti-Nazi resistance. Both writers have been neglected in standard accounts of Nazism because of their reputation as middlebrow thinkers rather than heroic intellectuals of the Jünger or Schmitt type and, closely related, their association with the free-floating populism that eludes left-right and high-low distinctions. *Der Weg der deutschen Arbeiterschaft zum Staat* (1925, The German worker's journey to the state) can be described as Niekisch's version of the workerdom argument in which the worker is hailed as the embodiment of the people but with a stronger emphasis on the state as the guarantor of popular sovereignty. After the war, Niekisch ended up in East Germany's Cultural Association and People's Chamber before moving to West Berlin following the workers' uprising of 1953.

The permeable boundaries connecting conservative, nationalist, and *völkisch* milieus during the 1920s and 1930s account for some of the difficulties in evaluating Winnig's work; the lack of a theoretical framework for assessing populist movements in their historical specificity and contemporary relevance is an additional complicating factor.[24] In studies on literature in the Third Reich, Winnig is often mentioned in the same breath as rightwing authors such as Edwin Erich Dwinger (1898–1981), Hans Grimm (1875–1959), and Hans Carossa (1878–1956). Given his thematic interests, it may make more sense to place him within the long tradition of workers' life writings and emphasize his considerable debts to *Heimat* literature and its provincial points-of-view. At the same time, Winnig must be read within a transnational culture of romantic anticapitalism and folk socialism that, especially in the Scandinavian countries, thrived on mythic elements and religious tropes and favored emotional styles wavering between existential despair and ecstatic hope. Across national literatures, these admixtures of pathos and sentimentality gave rise to the proletarian pastoral in its manifold manifestations and contributed to the enduring appeal of what Stefan Arvidsson calls socialist idealism.[25]

---

[24] A recent reference to Winnig can be found in a 2005 article by Wiggo Mann, titled "August Winnig—Ein preußischer Sozialist," showcased on the website of the "rechtsintellektuelle Zeitschrift" *Sezession*, 1 May 2005; see https://sezession.de/6708/august-winnig-ein-preussischer-sozialist.

[25] See Stefan Arvidsson, *The Style of Mythology of Socialism: Socialist Idealism 1871–1914* (London: Routledge, 2018).

Intellectual historians usually group Winnig with the main representatives of the conservative revolution: the abovementioned Arthur Moeller van den Bruck, Oswald Spengler (1880–1936), and Ernst (1895–1998) and Friedrich Georg Jünger (1898–1977). Their proposals for adapting the socialist project to what they considered special German conditions have attracted the most scholarly attention and – identified with keywords such as cultural pessimism, *völkisch* utopianism, spiritual antimaterialism, and antisemitic anticapitalism – are certainly relevant for assessing Winnig's contribution to the nationalization of socialism. Here titles such as *Preussentum und Sozialismus* (1919, Prussianism and socialism) by Spengler and *Preussischer Sozialismus* (1934, Prussian socialism) by Friedrich Schinkel confirm the easy compatibility of authoritarianism and communitarianism in the name of a distinctly Prussian ethos of order and discipline that appealed to those discontented with capitalist modernity. The role of the conservative revolution in defining this German path to socialism can be seen in the academic career of sociologist Werner Sombart (1863–1941), from his early writings on socialism as a social movement and the history of modern capitalism to his diagnosis of the end of proletarian socialism in the age of German socialism.[26] At the same time, a comparison to Ernst Jünger and his influential 1932 essay on *Der Arbeiter: Herrschaft und Gestalt* (The worker: dominion and form) highlights the difficulties of locating the affinities between fascism, nationalism, and populism beyond a shared contempt for bourgeois liberalism, a point to be picked up in this study's last chapter. What requires further attention still is how the humanistic tradition rooted in both Judaism and Christianity, which theologian Paul Tillich (1886–1965) in *Die sozialistische Entscheidung* (1933, The socialist decision) presents as one of the philosophical foundations of socialism, could in a figure like Winnig allow for antisemitic invective as part of a Christian communitarian ethos. What also might prove very productive is to explore the connection to corporatist thought that promised an alternative to liberal capitalism and communism in the form of organic-statist models emphasizing national interests and communal values.[27]

Among the bourgeois intellectuals associated with the conservative revolution, an uneducated provincial such as Winnig remained the eternal outsider. Born and raised in the small mining town of Blankenburg in the Harz region, Winnig ap-

---

[26] The relevant book titles are *Sozialismus und soziale Bewegung* (1896), *Der proletarische Sozialismus* (1924), and *Deutscher Sozialismus* (1934).

[27] The influence of corporatist models, so important to Italian Fascism and other authoritarian regimes in interwar Europe, continues to be a subject of debate; for a European perspective, see Antonio Costa Pinto, ed., *Corporatism and Fascism: The Corporatist Wave in Europe* (London: Routledge, 2019). Going forward, fascism will be capitalized whenever it refers to the specific Italian case.

proached questions of class, race, and nation from the perspective of the disempowered and dispossessed. The early death of his father, a gravedigger, left the large family financially struggling and made the boy painfully aware of his limited opportunities in life. In his autobiographical writings, Winnig openly acknowledges these childhood experiences as the source of deep feelings of inferiority. The culture of the small town with its social rituals and hierarchies continued to inform his view of collective actions and interclass relations and color his depiction of workers as modern craftsmen rather than the factory workers heroized by the KPD's proletarian-revolutionary writers. Leaving home, Winnig was radicalized during his formative years as an apprentice and journeyman, became active in the bricklayers' union, and assumed leadership roles in various Social Democratic organizations. An appointment in 1918 as the Reich's General Plenipotentiary in the Baltic States and, in 1920, as the Reich Commissioner in East Prussia could have been the beginning of a significant party career; it ended abruptly because of his support for the Kapp Putsch and subsequent expulsion from the SPD. While the personal crisis that followed may have contributed to his rightward turn, his belief in the bonds of folk and community and his hatred of cultural Bolshevism were in fact integral to his political thinking from the start.

Three books make up Winnig's contribution to the discourse of workerdom and its key role in the making of folk community, *Der Glaube an das Proletariat* (1924, Faith in the proletariat), *Vom Proletariat zum Arbeitertum* (1930, From proletariat to workerdom), which appeared in numerous editions after 1933 and was translated into French, and its Nazified sequel *Der Arbeiter im dritten Reich* (1934, The worker in the Third Reich).[28] Organized around the prepositional pairing of "from" and "to," his basic argument represents a model of populist reason, with the people introduced as a stand-in for the workers and the folk community affirmed as the *telos* of their spiritual and ideological transformation. Drawing on socialist positions, Winnig acknowledges the plight of the propertyless, the distinguishing trait of the proletariat in early (non-Marxist) definitions of the term. Yet he insists that the causes of proletarization are to be found not in the capitalist mode of production but in the eternal laws of life itself, which he elucidates through a mixture of Social Darwinist, Nietzschean, and vitalist concepts. Similarly, he recognizes the divisive effects of social and economic inequality but insists that only the alliance of proletarian and bourgeois against external enemies defined in racial (i.e., antisemitic) terms can provide a long-lasting solution and reestablish

---

28 Similar titles published after 1933 include Gustav Berger, *Das neue deutsche Arbeitertum* (1934, see discussion below); Artur Roemer, *Proletarier! Wie wirst du Standesherr?* (Kevelaer: Butzon & Bercker, 1933); and Winfried Thomsen, *Vom Proletariat zum deutschen Arbeitertum*, Leitblätter zu öffentlichen Mitarbeiterschulung im DHV (n.p., ca. 1934).

the folk as the foundation of the state. Throughout, the claims to the people as the rightful subject of history are predicated on the identification, vilification, and elimination of a racialized Other through which the process of unification can be initiated and completed. In light of these structural qualities, it must be concluded that antisemitism, even if rarely thematized, is in fact an integral part of Winnig's conception of the workers as the embodiment of the people.

From Proletariat to Workerdom received much praise during the Third Reich. Leading Nazi literary scholar Josef Nadler described it as "the völkisch culmination of Winnig's thinking: "'Collective' turns into 'community,' 'workerdom' grows out of the 'proletariat' [...] The masses that became the proletariat because they lost their standing as an estate (*Stand*) will reclaim their position and, once again, become folk. In accordance with the laws of young nations, the future belongs to workerdom because it is a 'young' estate."[29] Another reviewer evaluated the book's contribution in light of the difficult legacies of the Weimar years and noted that, "It is the tragedy of our folk that the worker could not be integrated into state and society in due time to prevent his succumbing to proletarian consciousness."[30] In a general tribute to Winnig, one contributor praised the book as the long-awaited response to a deep spiritual crisis: "The German worker suffered most under the destruction of his dignity. Now August Winnig has given us the proper word with which we can adequately and correctly identify the essence of the working German people. That word has a truly special meaning and is called workerdom."[31] How much the emotional aspects of workerdom dominated the scholarship on Winnig is evident in a 1945 dissertation by Hannah Vogt who used his description of Marxism as a revolutionary theory of hatred to establish love as the essence of the soul (*Seelentum*) of the worker.[32] Even outside literary circles, Winnig was soon recognized as "the champion of a movement that has always fought the alienation of the worker from the nation-state and the national idea, fought the advance of Marxist theory and internationalism. Winnig's lifework rests on championing the connection of the social with the national idea."[33]

Faith in the Proletariat and *From Proletariat to Workerdom* trace the rise of the workers as a new estate throughout German history and emphasize the

---

29 Josef Nadler, *Literaturgeschichte des deutschen Volkes: Dichtung und Schrifttum der deutschen Stämme und Landschaften*, 4 vols. (Berlin: Propyläen, 1938–1941), 4:242–243.
30 Werner Betke, review of *Vom Proletariat zum Arbeitertum*, *Zeitenwende: Monatsschrift* 8.1 (1932): 237.
31 Ludwig Fehler, "Fruchtbares Leben," in *Ein deutsches Gewissen: Dank an August Winnig* (Berlin: Eckart-Verlag, 1938), 74.
32 Vogt, *Der Arbeiter*, 77.
33 Originally in the NSBO journal *Der Betrieb*, quoted by Ferrari, 175.

model character of the new culture of work for other nations. Unlike the misguided proletarians, who hold on to the divisive rhetoric of class struggle, the workers transcend their hopes, fears, and resentments in the racial state and transform modern society into a true community. Drawing on the familiar distinction between class and estate, Winnig explains: "The worker is more than a class. The worker is a new estate [Stand]. Estate means more than class. [...] Estate means a community that has been founded on blood and shaped by history. [...] This new estate ushers in nothing less than a new age with new internal values and new forms of external life. I call this new estate workerdom."[34] The realization of this unifying idea, however, requires the workers' rejection of the old model of class struggle, which pits the working class against the ruling class, and their initiation into new experiences of unity, strength, and belonging organized along racial lines. In an autobiographical text from the mid-1920s, Winnig summarizes the necessary rhetorical adjustments:

> No more wage struggle without ubiquitous cries of indignation about German enslavement! No complaint about workers' suffering that does not include an indictment of German slavery! No word to foreigners that does not express the anger of the enslaved! No meeting of the unemployed without protest against enslavement by international capital! No demonstration without the battle cry "Against German slavery – for German freedom!"[35]

Published in 1930, *From Proletariat to Workerdom* draws more explicitly on antisemitic tropes to establish the people as the main protagonist in the ideological narratives of renewal and reconciliation. Winnig presents the rise of the working class as the result of explosive population growth and dramatic changes in family structures and gender relations. He cites the hidden Jewish influence in banking and industry as an important reason for the failure of the proletariat to overcome its wretched condition as a formless and directionless mass. Railing against the foreign infiltration of the workers' movement and disparaging Social Democracy as "a machine without soul," he time and again returns to the central problem of modern class society, the desire of the worker to be more than a worker. He describes the problematic in the form of an internal monologue: "The worker tries to find himself. He looks for an answer to the unspoken question: Who am I? What do I mean to this world? Why am I here? What is the meaning of my life? Do I have a goal? What is it? What should I do?"[36] Rather predictably, answering

---

34 August Winnig, *Der Glaube an das Proletariat* (Munich: Milavida, 1926), 30.
35 August Winnig, *Befreiung* (Munich: Milavida, 1926), 32.
36 August Winnig, *Vom Proletariat zum Arbeitertum* (Hamburg: Hanseatische Verlagsanstalt, 1930), 5, 10. Excerpts from the book appeared in the first issue of *Arbeitertum* 1 (1930): 8–10, the official organ of the NSBO (later DAF).

these questions involves juxtaposing the "German" Wilhelm Weitling, an early utopian socialist, and the "Jewish" Karl Marx and equating their nationalist and internationalist socialisms with two very different emotional registers. Using metaphors reminiscent of Ernst Bloch's distinction between warm and cold streams in Marxism, Winnig explains: "One [i.e., the Weitling version of socialism] was hot, the other cold. One was driven by compassion and love. The other was driven only by hatred. One wanted to create a new world. The other wanted to destroy a world. One was the early harbinger of a youthful folkdom. The other was the product of a decaying, old, educated elite."[37]

The same antagonistic logic informs Winnig's description of the proletarian in *The Worker in the Third Reich*, a summary of the first two books published after the Nazi takeover and a realignment of earlier arguments with Nazi ideology. The proletarian's entire being and feeling is now captured in one word: No – no to church and state, no to hierarchy and authority, no to tradition and convention, and so forth. Rejecting this damaging legacy of hatred through a vote for the Nazis, Germans in 1933 at long last recognized the shared interests of labor and industry and, after the difficult years of hyperinflation and Great Depression, found their true savior in Adolf Hitler. Presumably, only the charismatic leader as the personification of the people could establish workerdom as the foundation of the folk – reason enough for Winnig to profess his faith in Hitler in quasi-religious terms: "The worker's rise to participation in leadership is the fulfillment of his calling; it is the will of history, and this means the will of the living God in history."[38]

Winnig's populist conception of workerdom not only attests to the remarkable adaptability of the fantasy of the people to insurrectionist as well as authoritarian movements, it also reveals the surprising continuity in the emotional registers that require and sustain these adaptations: intense fear and loathing and exuberant hope and joy, expressions of resentment and demands for recognition, appeals to unity and calls for violence, and so forth. His psychology of workerdom offered an apolitical version of the political within then-contemporary thought that found its full realization in literary fiction. Unlike conservatives such as Spengler, or Friedrich Naumann for that matter, Winnig had little interest in promoting a strong

---

[37] Winnig, *Vom Proletariat zum Arbeitertum*, 57. The same juxtaposition of "Weitling" and "Mardochai" as representative of two kinds of socialism can be found in Kurt S. Neumann, *Die jüdische Verfälschung des Sozialismus in der Revolution von 1848* (Berlin: Junker and Dünnhaupt, 1939), 28–42. Some of the precursors of this type of German socialism (e.g., Lorenz von Stein, Wilhelm Heinrich Riehl) are presented in Erich Thier, *Wegbereiter des deutschen Sozialismus: Eine Auswahl aus ihren Schriften* (Stuttgart: Alfred Kröner, 1940).
[38] August Winnig, *Der Arbeiter im Dritten Reich* (Berlin: Buchholz & Weißwange, 1934), 46.

authoritarian state or addressing the social question through market-based solutions. But he had even less in common with "leftist folks from the right"[39] who, like the abovementioned Niekisch, sought rapprochement with the Soviet Union or who, like the Strasser brothers in the journal *Nationalsozialistische Briefe* (National socialist letters), envisioned a revolutionary National Socialism equally critical of Bolshevism and capitalism. In fact, the latter's characterization of the Nazi Party as a workers' party and their promotion of the proletarian element in the SA would have horrified Winnig whose version of the good life probably looked like his hometown Blankenburg or Potsdam, his residence during the Nazi years. More than other self-declared "socialists" in the early Nazi Party, Winnig was above all motivated by what Gregor Strasser in a Reichstag speech called the "great anticapitalist longing"[40] that had arisen in response to the profound transformations brought about by capitalist development and the industrial revolution and that had been weaponized most successfully by a new type of protest party promising to reconcile labor and capital under the strong leadership of the state.

The main ideological narrative laid out by Winnig, the transition from class to race in the name of workerdom, was neither particularly original nor profound in the larger context of *völkisch* thought. His diagnoses of the workers' loss of pride and need for recognition reproduced prevailing approaches to the problems of class society that, by explaining social struggles in psychological terms, called for a "return" to the organic communities held together by "the heart of the people" and "the soul of the folk." His success as a popular writer and populist thinker lay precisely in reducing these analyses to their experiential qualities and validating the individual's sense of alienation and desire for belonging. Combining political and religious perspectives, drawing on familiar literary formats and traditions, and using plain language to make a few basic points, Winnig appealed to his working-class and lower-middle-class readers through such simple but effective techniques of emotionalization.

Not surprisingly, Nazi propagandists paraphrased Winnig's arguments and included his books in suggestions for further reading. To give a few examples, in sev-

---

[39] The phrase is taken from Otto-Ernst Schüddekopf, *Linke Leute von rechts: Die nationalrevolutionären Minderheiten und der Kommunismus in der Weimarer Republik* (Stuttgart: Kohlhammer, 1960). For a recent contribution, see Benedikt Sepp, *Linke Leute von rechts: Die nationalrevolutionäre Bewegung in der Bundesrepublik* (Marburg: Tectum, 2013). On the larger context, also see Christoph H. Werth, *Sozialismus und Nation: Die deutsche Ideologiediskussion zwischen 1918 und 1945*, preface by Karl Dietrich Bracher (Opladen: Westdeutscher Verlag, 1996).
[40] Gregor Strasser, "Antikapitalismus," *Nationalsozialistische Monatshefte* 3 (1932): 421.

eral 1931 articles about the "suffering of workerdom,"[41] Otto Bangert heavily drew on Winnig when he predicted the absorption of proletarian and bourgeois mentalities into a shared belief in work as the meaning of community and the essence of the folk. A 1934 instructional pamphlet by Gustav Berger reproduced Winnig's basic argument all the way to the conclusion that "authentic German workerdom is the driving force behind the National Socialist struggle."[42] Only after defeating the proletariat, "an amorphous mass without shared purpose and spiritual value, [...] without structure, without leader, and without guiding idea," could the idea of workerdom be realized and the workers become part of "an achieving community [Leistungsgemeinschaft] based on living community [Lebensgemeinschaft]."[43] Last but not least, in a 1935 treatise on socialism as the foundation of the new Reich, Walter Haid called for the integration of the working class into the folk community based on "community as the foundational experience of socialism."[44] He made it very clear that its successful implementation would require the elimination of other political parties and the Nazis' complete control over all aspects of public life. Few comments better capture the importance of violence as the unifying principle behind National Socialism as populist ideology than Haid's justification of the one-party state as the enabling condition for both folkdom and workerdom. In Winnig, these connections remain hidden behind a recuperative approach in which all individual feelings are validated and all psychological wounds healed. His imitators are more outspoken in acknowledging the violence behind fantasies of unity that always require an external Other.

Winnig's autobiographical writings, which recount his personal rise from the rural proletariat to the labor aristocracy, shed additional light on the central role of emotions in mediating the socialist, nationalist, populist, and antisemitic elements within workerdom. Childhood memories provide the material for poignant observations on rural culture and small-town life, but it is through the class-specific experience of powerlessness that he, drawing on the perspective of the young adult, connects to the soul of the people and, presumably, his typical readers. In these accounts, an individual experience of exclusion is time and again projected back on the existential condition of the workers and then magically resolved

---

41 Otto Bangert, "Leidensweg des Arbeitertums," in *Deutsche Revolution: Ein Buch vom Kampfe um das dritte Reich* (Munich: Franz Eher, 1931), 32–47.
42 Gustav Berger, *Das neue deutsche Arbeitertum* (Leipzig: Eichblatt, 1934), 50. Published in a series on National Socialist education. Compare to Wolf Zeller, *Arbeiter-Mythos! Die Arbeiterbewegung, ihr Wandel und ihre Vollendung* (Berlin: Widder, 1933) and, for a national-conservative Christian perspective, the abovementioned Hartz, *Die national-soziale Revolution*.
43 Berger, *Das neue deutsche Arbeitertum*, 23–24, 38.
44 Walter Haid, *Sozialismus als Träger des neuen Reichs* (Berlin: Junker und Dünnhaupt, 1935), 12.

through their promised inclusion in the folk community. Following such a restorative logic, Winnig's novel *Wunderbare Welt* (1938, Wonderful world) tells the improbable story of an orphan boy who grows up in a poorhouse, becomes radicalized as a journeyman and labor organizer, and then, in true colportage fashion, finds out that he is the long-lost grandson of a factory owner. The various Others that function as obstacles in this socialist fairy tale are easily identified: the modern masses and their materialist needs, the Weimar party system as the enemy of true democracy, and the primitive socialisms of the past that promote meanness (*Gemeinheit*) rather than community (*Gemeinschaft*).[45]

The workers' movement started the long struggle for national liberation, Winnig concedes, but only workerdom was able to complete the process by redefining folk community along racial lines. The urgent tone with which he describes "the workers' movement as the last chance for a fundamental renewal of folkdom"[46] points to what he calls a deep crisis in confidence, the workers' "belief in the social inferiority of the working class,"[47] which could never be overcome through party programs or public policies. Once again Winnig's autobiographical writings provide further insight into the emotional foundations of this type of populist reason and its heavy dependence on blending fact and fiction in the service of psychological revisionism. In *Frührot* (1929, Dawn), he remembers a childhood haunted by the early death of his father and the family's resultant descent into poverty. He writes about his discovery of books (e.g., Nietzsche, Darwin) and the power of learning and describes his growing awareness of social and economic inequality. Throughout, his identification with the radicalized workers is based on what may be called a primal scene of populist mobilization, the perceived loss of dignity and lack of recognition. Using the first-person plural, Winnig declares: "We want to be free of the crushing feeling that we are less and worse than others." Responding to these profoundly human needs, "the task of socialism is to educate and elevate the working class, so that it is equal to other classes in their moral standards, mental faculties, public spirit, and noble ambition."[48]

These definitions recall the nineteenth-century discourse of *Bildung* as both refinement and formation, which played such a central role in Social Democratic cultural and educational initiatives, but they also draw on modern therapeutic languages and a privileging of individual self-expression that translates everything

---

45 August Winnig, "Der Schritt zur Partei," in *Wir hüten das Feuer: Aufsätze und Reden aus zehn Jahren (1923–1933)* (Hamburg: Hanseatische Verlagsanstalt, 1933), 162.
46 August Winnig, "21 Thesen zur Arbeiterbewegung," in *Wir hüten das Feuer*, 142.
47 Winnig, *Der Glaube an das Proletariat*, 22. "Glaube an die soziale Minderwertigkeit der Arbeiterklasse."
48 August Winnig, *Frührot: Ein Buch von Heimat und Jugend* (Stuttgart: Cotta, 1929), 445, 446.

into private feelings. In *Das Buch Wanderschaft* (1941, The book of wanderings), the sight of poor, starving, homeless people in the towns of the Ruhr region only inspires sentimental musings about true wealth and the meaning of life from the author:

> I began to ask myself whether one could rightfully speak of the wealth of the Ruhr region. Based on common opinion, the Ruhr was a rich land. But where was the wealth? I only saw poverty; never before had I seen so much poverty. Could one live more miserably and hopelessly than in Herne or in the grey rowhouses of these mill towns? Walking through the streets I saw no happy face and heard no laughter; once in a while a drunk staggered by. Nothing but poor people! To be sure, the owners of the mines lived somewhere, and they must be rich? Were they really rich? What is wealth anyway? Was a person rich if he had gold, silver, money, stocks? It only became true wealth when something else was added, when someone with such wealth also had a heart and soul and took pleasure in making others happy.[49]

In what ways feelings of shame and despair served as a conduit for antisemitic prejudices can be seen in the two-part novel *Arbeiter und Reich* (1937, Worker and Reich). Titled "On the Wrong Track," the first part tells the story of a young and naive cooper with the telling name Gotthold Grimm, a "typical German worker who became susceptible to the hateful spirit of Jewish world revolutionaries and allowed himself to be guided by those who could know nothing of his historical destiny." As a first step in his conversion to National Socialism, Grimm breaks with Marxist orthodoxy and angrily confronts a Jewish agitator:

> "What do you know of the worker?" he asked: "What do you have in common with the folk? Do you know these people, the stonemasons, smelter workers, wood cutters! Their hearts are burning! They have a soul! They have a conscience! Such a village is like a family! Core makers and dye casters are comrades! And the master is the oldest comrade! Woodcutter and forester also belong together! And what do you know about any of this! You destroy everything! You destroy those above and below! Destroy the entire folk! These people need comfort! Need pride! Yes, their soul is hungry and thirsty! And you give them sulfuric acid to drink! Do you know that you cannot survive a hard life without faith? You rob people of the faith in heaven and on earth! In what should people believe? In you?"[50]

The novel's second part, "The Great Ordeal," recounts the failures of the workers' movement and uses the betrayal of the workers by Social Democracy and their manipulation by foreign agitators for a final moment of personal and political reck-

---

[49] August Winnig, *Das Buch Wanderschaft* (Hamburg: Hanseatische Verlagsanstalt, 1941), 191–192. The continuation, *Der weite Weg* (1932), describes his years as a mason, party member, and union man; *Heimkehr* (1935) depicts his experiences in the Baltic States after the war.
[50] August Winnig, *Arbeiter und Reich, Vol. I: Auf falscher Bahn* (Leipzig: B. G. Teubner, 1937), 52.

oning. Disillusioned, Grimm at last makes peace with a representative of the old Prussia, a cavalry captain, and finds new strength in the conviction that Germany can only be saved by National Socialism. The ending shows him addressing a group of workers at a rally with arguments that could have been taken from one of Winnig's political treatises:

> "We are not the masters of history, but we are active participants. In order to act, we need a belief and a will. It is our belief that the worker is called upon to provide leadership to the folk. It is our will that the workers assume the leadership – assume it in a way that grants the right to leadership, namely by becoming part of the whole and serving the whole. That is the socialism that we bring. The socialism of service! The old socialism demanded: We want to have. The socialism of the Swastika declares: We want to serve! We want to serve to become worthy of our leadership role! The worker who we call upon must become the new master."[51]

III

In 1930, Hans Biallas, editor of the magazine *Arbeitertum*, answered the question of why German workers should cast their votes for the Nazis by declaring that "National Socialism will resume the building of the German workers' movement stopped by Marxism and bring it to a victorious conclusion in the new state!"[52] By 1940, the question "Why does the German worker stand with Adolf Hitler?" no longer required any reference to the problem of class to celebrate the unity of folk, nation, and Führer. To quote Hans Munter: "Now that it [workerdom] has cast off its old ideology and absorbed the idea of National Socialism [...] it stands strong and united behind the Führer of the Reich."[53] These two quotes conveniently summarize the complicated relationship between workerdom and folk community: namely, that the discourse of workerdom was based on the self-representation of the early Nazi Party as a protest party with a strong cross-class appeal, and, moreover, that the figure of the worker continued to be a source of conflicting political attachments and cultural traditions after 1933.

Discussing Winnig as a populist has accomplished two things so far: it has drawn attention to the adaptability of populist arguments made in the name of the disenfranchised and dispossessed and confirmed the unique contribution of literature (broadly defined) in mapping the discursive terrain on which the prole-

---

51 Winnig, *Arbeiter und Reich, Vol. II: Die große Prüfung*, 61.
52 Hans Biallas, *Warum muß der deutsche Arbeiter nationalsozialistisch wählen?* (Munich: NSBO, ca. 1930), 16.
53 Hans Munter, *Warum steht der deutsche Arbeiter zu Adolf Hitler?* (Berlin: Deutscher Verlag, 1940), 28.

tarians of the past could become the German workers of the future. Given the heavy dependence of populist mobilizations on political emotions, it makes sense in the third and final part to situate Winnig's "proletariat to workerdom" argument within comparable strategies of emotionalization in the writings of early Nazi politicians, including those eliminated in subsequent power struggles.

In reading workerdom as a populist discourse, it is essential to see beyond its propagandistic functions, whether in campaign promises about uniting workman and burgher against international finance capital or in philosophical diatribes against the modern culture of degeneracy, and to acknowledge the contradictory role of "the people" as both a projection screen for incompatible social imaginaries and a placeholder for changing definitions of society, nation, and state. In the late nineteenth century, the populist elements shared by nationalist and socialist movements had established the worker's suitability as an embodiment of the people and made community the preferred term for the social(ist) utopias circulating throughout working-class culture and beyond. Meanwhile, the people played a key role in the bourgeois romance with the folk as a communal body unified in language and literature, a connection first theorized by Johann Gottfried Herder in his writings on German folk, language, and nation and developed further by a diverse group of writers and thinkers throughout the nineteenth century. Drawing on both traditions, Hitler redefined nationalism and socialism in the heightened terms that established the Nazi Party's cross-class appeal, namely as the "highest service to the people, highest devotion to the people, highest struggle for the people, not for one estate, not for one class."[54] In several speeches given during the first years of the regime, he announced: "I reject the term *proletariat* because of its false distinction between manual and mental labor," and promised that the Nazis would once again make the word *Arbeiter* "the great honorific of the German nation."[55]

The identification of the workers with a position of abjection, a recurring theme in Winnig's work, provided a psychological model for the all-important distinction between class and estate in *völkisch* thought. In ways that are less apparent and more difficult to prove, it also kept alive the memory of class-based experiences of exclusion and discrimination long after their integration into Nazi racial thought. Here, the writings of two early members of the movement, Anton Drexler (1884–1942) and Gottfried Feder (1883–1941), can be used to reconstruct these socialist commitments, including through their heavy reliance on personal experience as political argument. Drexler was a Munich toolmaker who in 1919 founded

---

54 Adolf Hitler, speech of 4 March 1933 in Königsberg, quoted in Michael Schneider, *Unterm Hakenkreuz: Arbeiter und Arbeiterbewegung 1933 bis 1939* (Bonn: Dietz, 1999), 246.
55 Adolf Hitler, quoted in Fritz Meystre, *Sozialismus, wie ihn der Führer sieht: Worte des Führers zu sozialen Fragen* (Munich: Heerschild, 1935), 28, 50.

the German Workers' Party (DAP) that in 1920 became the NSDAP. With the name change, party leaders sought to offer a nationalist alternative to workers organized on the Left but frustrated by the ongoing splits between the SPD, USPD, and KPD. The appeal to a distinctly German tradition of community rooted in the people or the folk would continue to align socialist and nationalist imaginaries in ways that recognize the emotional power of political identifications. "I had to become actively involved in politics," he confessed in his frequently reprinted diary of a German socialist worker: "For someone without money, name, or purpose, and without party as I was, that was a bold decision. Everywhere I was wandering in the dark."[56] The close connection between the condition of lack marked by the preposition "without" and the restorative effect expected from collective action has already been identified as a driving force behind the populist genealogy of the workers' movement in Winnig's writings. The same holds true for the sense of betrayal that allows Drexler to magically transform the individual worker into a stand-in for the nation. "You poor hounded worker!" he cries out, drawing on the trauma of war and revolution to rewrite the story of class struggle as a new kind of race war: "Everywhere you turn, betrayal, betrayal of you, your homeland and the entire German people. They made the revolution with you – not in order to give you freedom but to establish the rule of money."[57] His closing remarks name the two steps necessary to bring together socialism and nationalism: rejection of old enmities and hierarchies and identification of the real threat to German survival. "You must find the way to the burgher," he implores his readers, "because workers and soldiers, burghers and peasants all have only one common enemy: the Jewish capitalist and his fellow travelers."[58]

The Twenty-Five Point Program of the Nazi Party, written by Gottfried Feder in 1927, similarly evokes the enemies of the German folk – the educated elites, the wealthy and powerful, and the corrupt party system – to buttress its anticapitalist, antisemitic message through emotional languages borne of fear and resentment. Feder, an early member of the DAP, affirmed the party's socialist credentials by calling for the nationalization of all trusts, profit-sharing in large industries, and new laws concerning workers' rights and corporate responsibilities. But the real targets behind his antagonistic rhetoric are identified with the three watchwords – Marxism, liberalism, and Jewish finance capital – which for him capture the destructive nature of capitalist modernity. Repeating Nazi slogans such as *Gemeinnutz vor Eigennutz* (community before the individual) and railing against the dic-

---

56 Anton Drexler, *Mein politisches Erwachen: Aus dem Tagebuch eines deutschen sozialistischen Arbeiters*, 4th ed. (Munich: Deutscher Volksverlag, 1937), 22.
57 Drexler, *Mein politisches Erwachen*, 50.
58 Drexler, *Mein politisches Erwachen*, 48.

tatorship of the so-called *Profitariat*, he draws on the deep reserves of class resentment to announce the magical transformation of the property-less proletarian into the co-owning worker under the terms of people's sovereignty established by National Socialism. Drexler and Feder knew that the political identifications developed in the workers' movement were essential to attracting new members to the movement. But as Goebbels, Ley, and others later found out, the political lessons learned through acts of resistance could never be fully contained or controlled. Revealing an anxiety of influence that would continue to haunt the Nazis culture of work, Feder first denounces Marxism for its ideology of hatred and envy, noting that "class struggle as a political principle means to preach hatred as a guiding principle. 'Expropriation of the expropriators' means to elevate envy to the foundation of the economy,"[59] only to then resort to the same politics of resentment when attacking Marxism and capitalism as part of a coordinated assault on the German people that could only be stopped through violence in the name of the people.

Given the remarkable adaptability of workerdom, it might be worthwhile to summarize its appeal as a populist fantasy through what Paul Tillich calls its three levels of articulation. The most obvious level can be described with the help of Tillich's definition of false consciousness in *The Socialist Decision* as "nothing but the will to self-assertion of older social structures that are being threatened and eroded."[60] In response to the profound transformations of society and the resultant crises of meaning, workerdom sought to preserve premodern ways of life through *ständisch* (estate-based) models of labor and industry but did so based on corporatist and technocratic solutions. Understood in that way, workerdom perfectly illustrates Louis Althusser's famous definition of ideology as "the imaginary relationship of individuals to their real conditions of existence."[61]

---

59 Gottfried Feder, *Das Programm der NSDAP und seine weltanschaulichen Grundgedanken* (Munich: Franz Eher, 1933), 56, 57. To what degree the problem of the workers remained a major point of contention among competing factions in the early Nazi Party can be seen in the 1929 proposal for a revised party program by its small, but influential social-revolutionary left. Their declaration that, "the NSDAP is a workers' party. It is committed to the class struggle of all who are productive against the parasites from all races and faiths" channels all anticapitalist elements into the antisemitic trope of the Jew as parasite. Quoted in Karl Otto Paetel, *Nationalbolschewismus und nationalrevolutionäre Bewegungen in Deutschland* (Schnellbach: Siegfried Bublies, 1999), 160. For a Communist response to National Bolshevist tendencies within the Nazi Party, see Fritz David, *Ist die NSDAP eine sozialistische Partei?* (Berlin: Internationaler Arbeiter-Verlag, 1933).
60 Paul Tillich, *Die sozialistische Entscheidung* (Berlin: Medusa, 1980), 97.
61 Louis Althusser, "Ideology and Ideological State Apparatus," in *Lenin and Philosophy*, trans. Ben Brewster, new intr. Fredric Jameson (New York: Monthly Review Press, 2001), 109.

The second layer has to do with what Tillich sees as the dangerous "connection of the revolutionary proletariat with the revolutionary groups of political romanticism."[62] This highly charged term references the eponymous 1919 book in which Schmitt first developed his notion of the political (i.e., as the distinction between friend and enemy) through a final reckoning with romanticism as the main reason for Germans' political inaction, indecision, and love of law and order. The constitutive tension between aesthetic productivity and political unproductivity associated with political romanticism also marks Winnig's own life and work after his expulsion from the SPD. His enduring popularity throughout the Third Reich, especially at the edges of official Nazi culture, offers the clearest evidence of how, by validating experiential qualities, even the minor voices functioned as important mediators of what Schmitt calls the antagonistic structure inherent in the political. The political romantic, after all, has no interest in actually changing the world. In fact, he never wants to leave the interior world of aestheticized experiences:

> The romantic wants to do nothing except experience and paraphrase his experience in an emotionally rich fashion [stimmungsmäßiges Erleben]. This is why in his case, arguments and inferences become the reverberating figures in his emotional states of affirmation and denial, emotional states that – after they have experienced the liberating and occasional stimulus of the object world – revolve around themselves in "lofty circles."[63]

A third approach to making sense of workerdom involves its mythic elements, that is, the transhistorical and transpersonal aspects that made the transition from proletariat to workerdom both imaginable and interpretable. A Nazi propagandist close to the Strasser faction described the myth of the worker in this way: "Myth pulses through the one and the many in one single stream. In the individual, myth flows as passion, fervor, and vitality. Above the many, it hovers as the archetype that still requires grappling with the last fiber of one's being."[64] Tragically familiar with this kind of turgid rhetoric, Tillich urged the leftist parties to gain a better grasp of these mythic structures and conceive of a leftist populism that could compete with the Nazis' highly effective politics of emotion. *The Socialist Decision*, which was immediately banned upon publication, was one of the first scholarly works to recognize the Nazi cult of community as both reactionary in the original sense of the word and radical in its full embrace of biopolitics. For Tillich, the usefulness of mythic structures in rewriting the narratives of class hinged on the ability of the mythic to recast collective identifications in experiential terms, a connec-

---

62 Tillich, *Die sozialistische Entscheidung*, 106.
63 Carl Schmitt, *Politische Romantik* (Munich: Duncker & Humblot, 1919), 100.
64 Wolf Zeller, *Arbeiter-Mythos: Die Arbeiterbewegung, ihr Wandel und ihre Vollendung* (Berlin: Widder, 1933), 6.

tion since then explored in numerous studies on the religious aspects and performative elements of Nazi ideology. Modern social movements, he argued, rely on mythic constructs to imagine simple solutions to the problems of advanced capitalism and the crises of liberal democracy. Myths of origins proved particularly important for a movement with a difficult relationship to the legacies of socialism and the unresolved question of class – which explains why folk community (rather than workerdom) survived as the unifying social fantasy from the Nazi Party's early beginnings to the catastrophe of World War II and the Holocaust.[65]

As this chapter has argued, the discourse of workerdom played a key role in the ongoing management of the legacies of the workers' movement within National Socialism. This discourse drew on arguments of the conservative revolution and *völkisch* right and superimposed a mythic (or mythicizing) structure and a psychological model of interpretation on the history of class struggles. The political, literary, and autobiographical writings by August Winnig indicate how the Nazis' complicated relationship to the working class, from the pre-1933 years of revolutionary fervor to the post-1933 dynamics of coercion and consent, was held together by powerful collective emotions and forms of identification. At the end of the proposed transition from proletariat to workerdom stood a complete break with liberal democracy, its ideas, values, and practices, and (at least theoretically) total submission to the leadership principle and the racial state. For Winnig and his inspirations and imitators, this required an open rejection of the promises of freedom and equality in favor of the hierarchies and exclusions established in the name of folk community. But it also meant continued confrontation, if only in the realm of prose, poetry, and drama, with the worker both as a figure of abjection and a symbol of resistance. Speculating about the "deepest, almost unconscious yearning of the worker," Nazi publications repeatedly asserted that, "at the bottom of his heart [...] he rejects democracy as homogenizing and is prepared

---

65 In that sense, the movement from proletariat to workerdom can also be described as a social myth in the sense defined by Georges Sorel as "the feelings and the ideals of the masses preparing themselves to enter on a decisive struggle: the myths are not descriptions of things but expressions of a determination to act." See Georges Sorel, *Reflections on Violence*, intr. Edward A. Shils, trans. T. E. Hulme and J. Roth (Mineola, NY: Dover, 1961), 50. In *Reflections on Violence* (1901), Sorel hailed the general strike as the most powerful expression of the will of the people. What the general strike represented for a syndicalist such as Sorel, and what the revolution did for the communists, the *Machtübernahme* became for the Nazis the only possible means to deliver on the promise of people's sovereignty in the *Volksgemeinschaft*. And what propagandists took from Sorel is that "the people" are moved by myths irrespective of historical reality—and that the kind of mythic transformation of the body politic always involves acts of symbolic violence.

to submit to leaders who convince him that they are capable of leading."⁶⁶ The preoccupation with the proletariat after 1933 reveals how and why the "from proletariat to workerdom" argument remained essential for feeding the dream of folk community and maintaining the precarious balance between nationalism and socialism in the name of the people. Expanding on some of these points with the help of the so-called *Bewegungsromane* (movement novels), the next chapter examines how individual workers during the Weimar years made the transition – in life and in fiction – from what was then called Marxist socialism to Nationalist Socialism and, in so doing, filled the idea of workerdom with new psychological and political meaning.

---

66 Quoted in Joachim Bons, *Nationalsozialismus und Arbeiterfrage: Zu den Motiven, Inhalten und Wirkungsgründen der nationalsozialistischen Arbeiterpolitik vor 1933* (Pfaffenweiler: Centaurus, 1995), 71.

Chapter 2
Conversion Stories: Turning Communists into Nazis

> We sensed and we knew that [...] if we could unite the concepts of nationalism and socialism, we would have a banner under which we could lead the German people to freedom.
> Theodor Abel, *Why Hitler Came into Power*

The injustices of the class system and the yearning for community in Nazi Germany appear everywhere in a unique essay contest organized by Columbia University sociologist Theodore Abel in 1934.[1] Offering modest cash prizes, Abel had traveled to Germany to find out why so many Germans joined the Nazi party prior to 1933. His (all-male) respondents represented various professions, generations, and geographical regions and included a large number of industrial workers. Convinced of the scientific value of life writings, Abel asked them to share their personal conversions to Nazism. Reproducing the narrative of crisis and renewal familiar from Nazi election propaganda, almost everyone drew on the language of resentment – anger, fear, and hatred – but also expressed a deep need for recognition and belonging. Many contributors mentioned the Nazi promise of eliminating all class divisions and uniting the people through shared experiences of folk community and national pride. One of the two types of conversion stories emphasizes the need for class solidarity and references the culture of socialism; the other draws on the languages of German nationalism, racism, and xenophobia. Both narratives build on the traditions of the workers' movement, which include an older romantic communitarianism rooted in the people and a more strident class antagonism familiar from KPD agitprop. In both cases, the insidious effects of Nazi propaganda are evident already in the ways that antisemitic and anti-Bolshevist tropes shift collective identifications toward an exclusionary ethnonationalism.

---

[1] Theodore Abel, *Why Hitler Came into Power: An Answer Based on the Original Life Stories of Six Hundred of his Followers*, intr. Thomas Childers (Cambridge, MA: Harvard University Press, 1986), 47. Originally published in 1938. Abel never wrote up his findings on women's responses in a separate article. For two historical studies on party membership, see Michael H. Kater, *The Nazi Party: A Social Profile of Members and Leaders, 1919–1945* (Cambridge, MA: Harvard University Press, 1983) and William Brustein, *The Logic of Evil: The Social Origins of the Nazi Party, 1925–1933* (New Haven: Yale University Press, 1996). With a special emphasis on the theme of radicalism, also see Timothy S. Brown, *Weimar Radicals, Nazis and Communist between Authenticity and Performance* (New York: Berghahn, 2009).

Combining descriptive and narrative elements, the individual responses gathered in *Why Hitler Came into Power* resemble the so-called *Bekennerbriefe* (confession letters) by recent converts to the movement published in the Nazi party newspaper *Der Angriff*.² They can also be described as miniature versions of the *Bewegungsroman* (literally: movement novel) about the early years of the Nazi movement. Scholars have all but ignored these novels because of their obvious propagandistic function and lack of literary quality.³ Written by and for ordinary people during the transitional period from 1930 to 1935, the movement novels generally avoid the heroic registers that, in a strange kind of wish fulfillment, still dominate conventional views of Nazi culture. Filled with stereotypes and clichés familiar from the colportage novel, they represent literature at its most derivative – an assessment that, rather ironically, would have been shared by many Nazi Party functionaries. Like other hyperpolitical textual practices from the early 1930s, the movement novels expose the limits of the politicization of culture even in a dictatorship, limits revealed through an excessive conventionality and intentionality. In particular, their reliance on the conversion narrative makes them ideally suited for reconstructing the Nazi Party's problematic relationship to the figure of the worker and the legacy of socialism.

This chapter starts out by defining movement novels as a vehicle for placing the individual within society, folk, and nation and, in ways familiar from the previous chapter, for moving collective identifications from class- to race-based categories.⁴ With a focus on the debts to proletarian-revolutionary literature and, to a

---

2 Confirming the appeal of conversion narratives, a (fictional?) *Bekennerbrief* by a former communist was published in *Der Angriff*, 9 April 1931 and 16 September 1931. Stories of workers who joined the Nazi movement can also be found in Hans Domeyer, *Junge Arbeiter: Erzählungen* (1934). Other conversion stories set during the Weimar years but featuring middle-class protagonists include Thor Goote's trilogy *Wir fahren den Tod* (1930), *Wir tragen das Leben* (1932), and *Die Fahne hoch!* (1933) and Hans Zöberlein's two-part bestseller *Der Glaube an Deutschland* (1931) and *Der Befehl des Gewissens* (1937). For an analysis of key themes in the Nazi discourse about Weimar, see Bernd Weyergraf, "Aspekte faschistischer Demagogie und Volkstümlichkeit," in *Kunst und Kultur im deutschen Faschismus*, ed. Ralf Schnell (Stuttgart: J.B. Metzler, 1978), 1–16.
3 Nobody seems to have read these novels since the end of World War II—aside from the occasional members of militaria forums on the internet. Most books disappeared from German libraries after the war because of the de-Nazification efforts that, in the Soviet zone, produced the *Liste der auszusondernden Literatur*, the list of banned Nazi literature, and that, at the initiative of the US Army, brought troves of Nazi books and artifacts to the United States. Today almost half of all surviving copies of these novels can be found in US libraries and archives.
4 The term "emotional scripts" is taken from the script theory of psychologist Silvan Tomkins, where it refers to the processing of affects in the form of scripts—that is, the affective responses that form emotions and the narratives that inform behavior, define personalities, and later become life stories. For an example of how these terms are applied to narrative analysis, see Dan

lesser degree, *völkisch* literature, the second part analyzes the didactive use of social types and milieus, the engagement with contemporary problems, and the affinity for what KPD critics called *Parteilichkeit* (partiality) to constitute what, in a variation on the Soviet model, might be called National Socialist realism. The third section introduces a few typical works to understand the emotional appeal of a conversion narrative released from conventional definitions of social realism and, by extension, social critique, but still heavily invested in the fantasies of the real that sustained the Nazi system of coercion and consent. Based on the proposition that history never quite escapes its origins in storytelling, the conclusion outlines how a neglected and negligible genre such as the movement novel can, in fact, open up new perspectives for social historians of the Third Reich.

Writing about what literary scholar Susan Rubin Suleiman calls authoritarian fictions, that is to say, works that seek "to persuade their readers of the 'correctness' of a particular way of interpreting the world," is difficult because the reductionist perspective shared by authors and readers makes everything appear as a manifestation of dominant ideology.[5] The didacticization of realism confirms the enduring appeal of the epistemological certainties promised by this kind of monolingualism, especially when compared to the perceived chaos and anarchy associated with the fictional worlds of cosmopolitan heteroglossia (to evoke Bakhtin). Weaponizing the illusion of one language and one voice, the rightwing (and leftwing) narratives of class, folk, and nation produced during the interwar years participated in the confrontation between nationalist and internationalist versions of socialism by basing their claims about revolution (or counterrevolution) on the exclusion and silencing of other voices. The ambitions and shortcomings of this political monolingualism are especially apparent in the countless Nazi conversion stories proliferating across literary forms and media contexts and distinguished above all by their marginal position even within Nazi Party culture.

P. McAdams, *The Redemptive Self: Stories Americans Live By*, rev. and exp. ed. (Oxford: Oxford University Press, 2013).
5 See Susan Rubin Suleiman, *Authoritarian Fictions: The Ideological Novel as a Literary Genre* (Princeton: Princeton University Press, 1992), 1. The importance of figures of identification has been examined in Heiko Luckey, *Personifizierte Ideologie: Zur Konstruktion, Funktion und Rezeption von Identifikationsfiguren im Nationalsozialismus und im Stalinismus* (Göttingen: Vanderhoeck & Ruprecht, 2008).

I

The individual conversion stories collected by Abel in *Why Hitler Came into Power* have become part of the prevailing historical explanations for the mass appeal of the Nazi Party as the "other" workers' party. Very similar convergences between history and narrative can be found in a small group of novels about the Nazi movement set during the 1920s and early 1930s and published mainly between 1932 and 1935. In one of the better-known works, the narrator describes the main protagonist's reasons for joining as follows:

> This was the time when the young National Socialist movement started to attract attention in Berlin. He made a conscious decision to join the Nazis; it was clear to him that the future belonged only to them or the Communists. Both were revolutionary and antibourgeois, and both were ready to fight for a great idea – here in the name of world domination by one proletarian class, there for a free Germany for all estates and professions. He did not hesitate for a moment and entered the ranks of the small, shunned squad of Nazi flags.[6]

The "he" in question is Horst Wessel, the most famous martyr of the Nazi movement, and the one recalling his moment of conversion is Hanns Heinz Ewers, a bestselling author otherwise known for his explorations of the fantastic and the occult.

The typical movement novel retells the struggles and triumphs of the Nazi movement through the perspective of the male worker as the driving force of narrative and history. The primary goal on the level of ideology is to present the Nazi revolution as a socialist revolution, introduce race as the new category of collective identification, and establish the terms under which the emotional labor of conversion would continue after 1933. Unsurprisingly, characters and narrators mobilize the entire range of anticapitalist, antisemitic, antidemocratic, and antibourgeois resentments, with anti-Bolshevism providing the main category of distinction against which the German worker eventually reclaims his authentic voice and rediscovers his true racial self. Like *Hitlerjunge Quex, Hans Westmar,* and *SA-Mann Brand,* three much-advertised but cheaply produced *Bewegungsfilme* (movement films) released in 1933, movement novels were part of two very different political projects: to build mass support for the new regime by presenting National Socialism as a revolutionary movement, and to use the party's struggles in the past to justify the Gleichschaltung of all areas and aspects of cultural life. Setting a pattern that would be repeated over and over again, initial enthusiasm and frantic activity were quickly followed by disillusionment and indifference. Disagreements be-

---

6 Hanns Heinz Ewers, *Horst Wessel: Ein deutsches Schicksal* (Stuttgart: Cotta, 1932), 330.

tween Joseph Goebbels's Propaganda Ministry and Alfred Rosenberg's Kampfbund für deutsche Kultur (Fighting League for German Culture) over the future direction of literature and film contributed to the equally quick banishment of literary treatments of the Nazi movement to the fringes of political and popular culture. Official explanations cited the novels' limited range of themes and lacking popular appeal. The continued preoccupation with questions of class and the palpable nostalgia for the *Kampfzeit* (literally: period of struggle) during the Weimar year may have been contributing factors.

In the typical movement novel, all narrative elements are arranged to follow the conversion of a young idealistic worker to National Socialism – sometimes from other rightwing groups, but most often from the proletarian lifeworld dominated by the KPD and Rotfront, the Red Front Fighters' League. Typical chapter headings such as "The Red Front Nest" and "Swastika or Soviet Star?"[7] conjure up a milieu of crowded tenements, dark inner courtyards, and hostile encounters in corner pubs, meeting halls, and employment exchanges. The main characters are usually young working-class men caught in the violent confrontation between the two political ideologies competing for their hearts and minds. In joining the "right" side, they are often aided by educated friends and neighbors who already identify with the Nazi cause; they are introduced to model the promised elevation of "the worker" to an honorific soon to be bestowed on all folk comrades. Often unemployed, these men make initial contact with the Nazi movement through the culture of militant masculinity shared by SA and Rotfront, the two parties' respective paramilitary units. In this aggressively male world, women only appear in the supporting roles of mother or sister (reduced to their functions within the family), the sexually threatening but also alluring New Woman (introduced as a destabilizing force), and the idealistic female companion (designated as a future partner in marriage). In going through all the stages of the conversion process, the male lead comes to personify what Germanist Ernst Jelken in 1937 called "the type of German worker who could not be estranged from his essential being by proletarian-Marxist ideologies [...] In him, the prole of the class struggle disappears and the German worker arises."[8]

At first glance, the propagandistic function of the movement novel seems almost painfully obvious: to integrate the working class into the dreamworld of National Socialism and to advertise the party's socialist values and beliefs. From the

---

[7] See the chapter headings in Josef Viera, *Utz kämpft für Hitler* (Leipzig: Franz Schneider, 1933), 5 and 15.
[8] Ernst Jelken, *Die Dichtung des deutschen Arbeiters* (Jena: Frommann, 1938), 63. A similar argument can be found in Erich Thier, *Gestaltwandel des Arbeiters im Spiegel seiner Lektüre* (Leipzig: Otto Harrassowitz, 1939).

working-class characters, settings, and situations to the heroic, melodramatic, and sentimental tones, every narrative element serves to highlight the revolutionary nature of the National Socialist Workers' Party. The climactic moments of conversion present the eventual shift from feelings to actions in experiential or performative terms. A similar process takes place at the level of ideology itself, with class converted into folk/race and the identity of socialism and nationalism proclaimed in the name of the people. Mostly through character identification, the movement novel establishes the binaries of self and other, and friend and enemy, through which older narratives of defeat and triumph, persecution and liberation, and deception and revelation could be rewritten and reclaimed for new ideological certainties. These techniques of reinscription illustrate how National Socialist realism takes an approach to social reality based not on any particular literary technique or theory but on very specific ideas – or feelings about ideas – that define what that reality should be, could become, or has always been.

Very little is known about these movement novels and their authors. Were the latter recent converts eager to share their experiences or functionaries intend on recruiting more party members? In writing dialogues and monologues, did they rely on Nazi campaign speeches and political pamphlets, or did they draw on personal accounts by fellow comrades? Were they taking advantage of the commingling of fact and fiction in political propaganda or modeling their techniques on literary reportage and colportage? Probably no more than twenty novels were published in book form, with a few more serialized in party newspapers. It can be assumed that most authors were party members, with some found among the proverbial unknown SA men, or Stormtroopers, extolled in early Nazi publications and others occupying influential positions in the German Labor Front, for example. Apart from Ewers and Schenzinger, none of these authors managed to have actual literary careers. On the contrary, Waldemar Glaser, the author of *Ein Trupp SA: Ein Stück Zeitgeschichte* (1933, An SA unit: a piece of contemporary history) used his membership in the SA and NSDAP to become a city councilman in Breslau and later get involved with broadcasting in Silesia.

Even less is known about the readers of movement novels. In a way, the participants in Abel's essay competition could be described as ideal readers – that is, disaffected, disgruntled, and downwardly mobile men mostly of the war generation (or younger) who were either already involved with Nazi groups or attracted to their paramilitary rituals. It is unlikely that apolitical workers would have bought books published by the Munich-based Franz-Eher-Verlag, the central publishing house of the Nazi Party, or read serialized novels in newspapers such as *Völkischer Beobachter* or *Der Angriff.* Today the limited circulation of these books, of which few have survived in libraries and archives, can be retraced through library stamps from, for example, a military hospital library in Kempten, a commercial lending library in Munich, a municipal library in Breslau, and a DAF-factory library in Hanover. Scholarly studies on workers' libraries during the Wilhelmine and Weimar years have shown that reading preferences tended toward travelogues, biographies, historical novels, and science books – meaning that movement novels, too, may have failed to reach their intended readership. Meanwhile, the popularity of workers' life writings around the turn of the century was driven by a decidedly middle-class interest in working people, often as part of larger debates on the social question or a prurient fascination with "those living in the shadows." There are good reasons to assume that the reading preferences of the working and middle classes did not change considerably after 1933 and that movement novels probably found their most enthusiastic readers among lower middle-class and middle-class party members.[9] In short, fictionalization may have established the parameters for a new politics of emotion but the propagandistic effects remained largely limited to self-propaganda.

A cursory look at the titles of movement novels confirms the leading role played by the Stormtroopers (or Brownshirts) as the self-styled vanguard of the Nazi movement and as living proof of its "authentic" working-class roots. A few critics at the time were so convinced of the agitational potential of these novels that they envisioned the "SA-Roman" as a literary genre in its own right.[10] *Horst Wessel: Ein deutsches Schicksal* (1932, Horst Wessel: a German fate) established the basic formula: a main protagonist who introduces his readers to a world of working-class suffering but also of mutual help and support; who shares the disappointments and frustrations experienced by countless other unemployed young men; who goes through a period of confusion and doubt that involves a brief flirtation with communism; and who, after a transformational experience, finds community, comradeship, and a new spiritual home in National Socialism. Cheap imitations of the Horst Wessel book include Waldemar Glaser's abovementioned *An SA Unit*, Hermann Reisse's *Sieg Heil SA!* (1933), Josef Viera's *SA-Mann Schott* (1933, SA man Schott), and Heinz Lohmann's *SA räumt auf!* (1933, SA cleans up!). The sudden disappearance after 1934 of novels featuring Stormtroopers can be partly explained by intensifying clashes over the meaning of class in National Socialism – a process that, in this case, culminated in the Röhm-Putsch of 8 June 1934, the infamous Night of the Long Knives. One of its intended outcomes was the consolidation of power inside the NSDAP against the more openly working-class SA

---

9 Circulation figures for the conversion novels are difficult to find; a start would be the numbers offered by Dietrich Strothmann, *Nationalsozialistische Literaturpolitik: Ein Beitrag zur Publizistik im Dritten Reich* (Bonn: Bouvier, 1960), 385–408.
10 See Hellmuth Langenbucher, *Bücherkunde, Organ des Amts Schrifttumspflege* (1939): 184–189. A rare discussion of the SA-Roman can be found in Eggersdorfer, *Schönheit der Arbeit*, 122–141.

and the further marginalization of the leftwing factions that included Gregor and Otto Strasser and, for a brief time, Joseph Goebbels.

The few novels that continued to take the perspective of the workers were written by members of the German Labor Front who were eager to promote its Beauty of Labor program und leisure organization Kraft durch Freude (KdF, Strength through Joy). For instance, in *Parteigenosse Schmiedecke: Ein Zeitroman* (1934, Party comrade Schmiedecke: a novel of the times), Alfred Karrasch, a self-declared "confidant of the workers,"[11] uses the observations of a veteran worker socialized in the workers' movement to promote the new values of *Werkgemeinschaft* on two fronts: against opportunistic careerists in the factory administration who want to preserve class hierarchies and against older workers who resist technological progress through random acts of sabotage. Praising the book as a real workers' novel, a reviewer in *Arbeitertum*, perhaps aware of the Marxist debates on tendency and partiality, concluded that "the book breathes National Socialist spirit from beginning to end. It is free of any tendency."[12] For *Hilfsarbeiter Nr. 50000* (1938, Unskilled worker no. 50,000), Eugen Hadamovsky, head of national broadcasting and author of an influential study on *Propaganda und nationale Macht* (1933, Propaganda and national rule), even went undercover in an industrial plant to gain firsthand knowledge of the workers' attitudes toward National Socialism. Arriving at Continental Tires in a blue overall, he explains to the puzzled managers: "I am not here to schedule tours and walk-throughs or to work in the office. [...] I want to be a worker in the factory, and I want to be hired and treated like every other worker."[13] Meanwhile, for *Brandelmann auf grosser Fahrt* (1936, Brandelmann going to sea), DAF press secretary Gerhard Starcke used the fictional setting of a KdF-organized Norwegian fjord cruise to show how vacationing workers learned that socialism represented "the highest expression of an ideal of community that, rather than making all people the same, seeks to put everyone in the place assigned to them."[14] Standing on the deck of the infamous *Wilhelm Gustloff*, the title character at last understands that, "the choices made during the past days were the right ones. His mind now only had to confirm it. Indeed, community is everything. [...] But it was not enough just to recognize these connections. You

---

[11] Ute Haidar, "Alfred Karrasch, der Vertraute der Arbeiter," in *Dichter für das "Dritte Reich": Biografische Studien zum Verhältnis von Literatur und Ideologie*, ed. Rolf Düsterberg, 2 vols. (Bielefeld: Aisthesis, 2003), 2:107–142.

[12] Karl Halbritter, "Das Buch des deutschen Arbeiters," review of *Parteigenosse Schmiedecke*, *Arbeitertum* 4.13 (1934): 9.

[13] Eugen Hadamovsky, *Hilfsarbeiter Nr. 50000* (Munich: Franz Eher, 1938), 24.

[14] Gerhard Starcke, *Die Deutsche Arbeitsfront: Eine Darstellung über Zweck, Leistung und Ziele* (Berlin: Verlag über Sozialpolitik, 1939), 11.

have to draw the necessary conclusions, sever all ties to the wrong ways of the past, and direct all steps toward the truth. After all, the realm of truth exists already in this world."[15] In the approving words of a reviewer from *Der Angriff*, "Brandelmann *experiences* what he, until that point, has only heard or read about."[16] The book's conclusion neatly sums up the larger political project in two sentences: "In the factories the fate of nations is being decided. Germany's rise and fall lies in the hands of the German workers."[17]

The movement novels created a new reality based on the discourse of workerdom and its prevailing patterns of identification and forms of attachment. The mythification of the Nazi movement during the Weimar years established the emotional template for the all-important first years of the regime, which was depicted as a time of challenges and opportunities in the DAF-themed novels. Writing far removed from the literary establishment with its well-established rituals, venues, and circles, the Nazi authors took part in a profound redefinition of the political as an experiential category organized through public spectacles, rituals, and symbols. In identifying the emotions best suited to this kind of symbolic politics, writers and readers needed to look no further than the minister of propaganda himself. In his political memoir, titled *Kampf um Berlin: Der Anfang* (1934, The struggle for Berlin: beginnings), Goebbels describes his first years as *Gauleiter* of Berlin as a single-minded effort at breaking the emotional hold of the leftwing parties over the best-organized working class in the country.[18] In fact, *The Struggle for Berlin* can be read as a continuation of his own conversion story from troubled humanities student to master propagandist, which is recounted in sometimes lurid detail in the semiautobiographical novel *Michael* (1929). "His [i.e., Michael's] grappling

---

15 Gerhard Starcke, *Brandelmann auf grosser Fahrt: Der Roman einer unverhofften Freude* (Berlin: Büchergilde Gutenberg, 1939), 170. DAF produced several short films about the KdF cruises, including *Schiff ohne Klassen* (1938) on occasion of the maiden voyage of the *Wilhelm Gustloff*.
16 Schie., review of *Brandelmann auf großer Fahrt*, *Der Angriff*, 7 August 1939. An excerpt from the novel was reprinted in *Arbeitertum* 6.12 (1936): 15 under the title "Brandelmanns Fahrt in die unbekannte weite Welt."
17 Eugen Hadamovsky, *Hilfsarbeiter Nr. 50000* (Munich: Zentralverlag der NSDAP, 1938), 234.
18 Joseph Goebbels, *Kampf um Berlin: Der Anfang* (Berlin: Franz Eher, 1936). On Nazi autobiographies, see Alan Rosen, "Autobiography from the Other Side: The Reading of Nazi Memoirs and Confessional Ambiguity," *Biography* 24.3 (2001): 553–569. For a historical perspective on the culture of violence and militancy, see Eve Rosenhaft, *Beating the Fascists? The German Communists and Political Violence 1929–1933* (Cambridge: Cambridge University Press, 1983) and Dirk Schumann, *Political Violence in the Weimar Republic: Fight for the Street and Fear of Civil War* (New York: Berghahn, 2009).

with the soul of the German worker"[19] was based on the firm belief in the primacy of the political over the economic and the simultaneous rejection of class as a valid category of analysis. To quote the narrator: "The community of workers is not a class. Class comes from economics. The community of workers has its roots in politics. It is a historically specific estate." With these words, the emphatic appeal by Goebbels's alter ego to some workers "to free the German people both internally and externally"[20] perfectly captures the political and psychological project of the movement novel as a whole.

In declaring the failure of liberal democracy, its system of compromises and hypocrisies, the conversion stories return time and again to the early years of the Nazi movement to affirm the party's connections to the workers' movement. In most cases, socialist credentials are established through the sons of the working class who, like the Communist-Youth-turned-Hitler-Youth Heini Völker of Karl Aloys Schenzinger's bestseller *Der Hitlerjunge Quex* (1932, Hitler Youth Quex), reject the class-based solidarities of their fathers in favor of a nationalist reclamation of folk and community. Highlighting the cross-class appeal of National Socialism, a less common generational script revolves around the offspring of the middle class who, like the son of the small business owner in Heinz Lohmann's *SA räumt auf!* (1933, SA cleans up!), begin their political journeys by flirting with communism. "I, son of a merchant, wanted to belong to the proletarians"[21] – this is how the main character in that novel later explains his foolish choices to his new Nazi friends.

Movement novels rely heavily on the language of workerdom as they transfer the terms of attachment from the antagonistic structures of class to the exclusionary categories of race. This requires that the "proletariat," together with the revolutionary role assigned to it by Marx and Engels, be eliminated from the heroic narratives of German labor and industry and replaced by the work comrade (*Arbeitskamerad*) and work community. While traditional socialist values such as unity, solidarity, and camaraderie are still promoted, specific Marxist positions (e.g., internationalism) are rejected through the equation with Bolshevism and, later, the Soviet Union. In organizing these antagonisms, writers rely heavily on the clichéd figure of the Jewish functionary from Moscow but abstain from dismissing the original project of socialism when showing individual KPD and Rot-

---

19 Walter Vogel, preface to the reprint from *Michael* in Joseph Goebbels, *Student, Arbeiter und Volk* (Frankfurt am Main: Diesterweg, 1934), n.p.
20 Joseph Goebbels, *Michael: Ein deutsches Schicksal in Tagebuchblättern* (Munich: Franz Eher, 1929), 118. *Michael* was serialized in *Der Angriff* in the fall of 1930.
21 Heinz Lohmann, *SA räumt auf! Aus der Kampfzeit der Bewegung* (Hamburg: Hanseatische Verlagsanstalt, 1933), 10.

front men in a sympathetic light. Similarly, they disparage communist women for their liberated sexuality but venerate proletarian mothers for their service to the folk. In the words of Nazi propagandist Hans Schemm, creating an authentic German socialism meant for each German to decide in favor of "man or machine, spirit or matter, God or devil, blood or gold, race or mongrel, folk song or jazz, family or collective, National Socialism or Bolshevism,"[22] with the choice of the first term inseparable from the defense of traditional gender roles and family structures and the full acceptance of the racial laws, norms, and values of the Nazi state.

II

The personal accounts collected in *Why Hitler Came into Power* and the movement novels published during the 1930s contain rich source material for analyzing the Nazis' reliance on emotions as an explanatory lens and mobilizing force. Both Abel's working-class informants and the novels' fictional characters admit to intense feelings of shame, despair, and resentment as they describe the pervasiveness of discontent during the hyperinflation and world economic depression. Actual and fictional workers draw on the same emotional scripts whenever they explain their conversions to themselves and others. They speak of feelings of humiliation after the traumatic loss of the war and the punitive terms of the Treaty of Versailles and share their sense of betrayal by political and economic elites, including the Social Democrats. And all of them acknowledge the sheer excitement generated by the Nazi movement, its rituals and symbols, and its unique qualities as a mass phenomenon.

Relying on political emotions as expressions of authenticity and truth raises a number of difficult methodological questions: Are these dreams of community created to mobilize recent and prospective converts or to support the ongoing Nazification of institutions and imaginaries known as Gleichschaltung? Do the references to class society offer corroborating evidence of the Nazis' selective appropriation of communist rhetoric, or do they point to the enduring appeal of premodern and antimodern visions of community? Do conversion stories provide access to the mass psychology of political movements, or do they speak to larger trends in modern mass culture toward emotionalization? The problem with intentions and effects introduces even more questions about the relationship between political fantasy and social reality: Are Nazi authors and their readers reproducing the

---

22 Hans Schemm, *Der rote Krieg: Mutter oder Genossin?* (Bayreuth: Nationalsozialistischer Kulturverlag, 1931).

formulaic explanations circulated by party propagandists during the 1920s? In other words, is ideology the ultimate point of reference? Or are the real Nazis modeling their political biographies on the characters in the stories? To phrase it differently, is narrative the key mechanism of political subject formation?

To begin with, the relationship between narrative and ideology in the movement novel must be treated as mutually constitutive. The boundaries separating fact and fiction remain forever porous, fluid, and contested; the same can be said about the dynamic between past struggles and future triumphs that informs the narrativization of the (Nazi) present. In the typical movement novel, the experience of conversion is depicted as both radicalizing and essentializing. Promising a final reckoning with the despised Weimar system, the authors establish this basic narrative structure either against the backdrop of major historical events or in the context of street battles in working-class neighborhoods. The elements that lead up to the conversion experience include mentors and opponents, testimonies and temptations, as well as initiation rites and cults of martyrdom. Joining the Nazi movement is unvaryingly depicted as a process of self-discovery, which means a return to the presumed essence of race. For the individual worker, this involves a redemptive journey from isolation and alienation to the rewards of community. The transformation begins with nagging doubts about leftwing orthodoxies and the nature of class society. The convert first learns of National Socialism through fliers and pamphlets that open up very different perspectives on the problems of Weimar society. Anxious excursions into unknown territory are followed by long discussions with Nazi propagandists and initial exposures to a new kind of ethnic solidarity. Yet it is an almost religious experience based on cult and ritual – singing the Horst Wessel song or seeing the swastika flag – that prompts the main protagonist finally to declare "I believe" and join the movement: not in order to reject the promises of socialism but to realize them under the conditions of ethnonationalism.

The proliferation of conversion stories during the early years of the Nazi regime points to internal conflicts and tensions that seem to require ongoing adjustments. For that reason, conversion must not just be read in individual psychological terms but also in the expanded sense of conversion as transformation of the very terms that define politics in relation to fantasies and feelings. Recent literary studies have shown how the language of conversion can be identified with assimilation as well as resistance to the dominant culture; how the narrativization of conversion remains haunted by ambiguity and contradiction; and how its affective qualities offer useful models for translating the political into the spiritual and the social into the cultural.[23] Read in that sense, Nazi conversion stories not only utilize anti-Bolshevist and antisemitic rhetoric to establish binary categories through which claims to the ideological truth are established. They also take full advantage of the similarities between National Socialism and communism in order to preserve the revolutionary energies behind Nazi visions of community.

If there is one figure that embodies these contradictions within Nazi fictions of self and other, it is the proletarian whose continuous presence – as type, symbol, and cipher – attests to the enduring legacy of the nineteenth-century workers' movement and the continued political threat posed by the workers' state in the Soviet Union. As the previous chapter has shown, extricating the proletarian from the Nazi body politic was considered essential to the discursive processes of aligning socialism with nationalism. Cognizant of the power of language, movement novels choose to recognize this proletarian Other only in its abbreviated, derogatory form as the prole (*Prolet*), the kind evoked by Nazi cultural functionary Willi Lorch when he asserted that "the worker is not a culture-despising prole but the bearer of a new folk culture."[24] Almost ritualistically, this shadow figure of the prole is introduced to legitimate the techniques of othering favored by all authoritarian movements, starting with contempt for political enemies and disdain for those already defeated. Accordingly, the novel "Proletenglück" (Happiness of the proles) by Marie Diers, which was serialized in *Der Angriff* in the spring of 1931, ends with the narrator impersonating the communists with an air of faux indignation: "Worker against worker. That is the proletarian happiness brought to us by Marxism!"[25] The narrator in *SA Man Schott* assumes a similar attitude of mocking superiority when he declares that "as long as there are class-conscious proletarians, there will be capitalist exploiters. Long live the proletariat! Long live the capitalist!"[26]

The narrators' condescending tone prefigures the sense of mastery presumably awaiting all Germans on the other side of the conversion experience. Nonetheless, the fascination with communism continues to feed the anxieties of influence that motivate the many excursions into proletarian lifeworlds. The aura of authen-

---

23 On the discourse of conversion, including its religious aspects, see Gauri Viswanathan, *Outside the Fold: Conversion, Modernity, and Belief* (Princeton: Princeton University Press, 1998) and Guiseppe Giordan, ed., *Conversion in the Age of Pluralism* (Leiden: Brill, 2009). For a comparative literary perspective, Michael Ragussis, *Figures of Conversion: "The Jewish Question" and English National Identity* (Durham, NC: Duke University Press, 1995).
24 Willi Lorch, *Was soll ich lesen* (1938), quoted in Ine Van linthout, *Das Buch in der nationalsozialistischen Propagandapolitik* (Berlin: De Gruyter, 2012), 189.
25 Marie Diers, "Proletenglück: Ein Roman aus unseren Tagen," *Der Angriff*, 7 Mai 1931.
26 Josef Viera, *SA-Mann Schott* (Leipzig: Franz Schneider, 1933), 33.

ticity associated with the working class holds a particular appeal for the sons of the bourgeoisie. In a telling scene from the film adaptation of the *Horst Wessel* novel, titled *Hans Westmar* (1933), the former corps student decides to become a taxi driver in order to disprove those who claim that "only the prole understands the prole." Other characters return time and again to communist groups to immerse themselves in an uncannily familiar otherness. In *Sieg Heil, SA!*, the observations of a Stormtrooper during a KPD meeting at once deepen his aversion to those "subhumans" and harden his resolve to resist the empty promises of proletarianism. Toward the end of the meeting, the workers jump up and spout communist slogans, supported by stock characters from the anticommunist imagination such as the hysterical woman revolutionary and the Jewish party functionary. This is how the nightmarish scene looks from a Nazi perspective:

> Now a three-time "Red Front!" burst forth from rough, alcohol-fueled proletarian throats. With their shrill voices, the women joined in. "Hitler, croak! Death to fascism!" they all screamed. One "antifascist" jumped on the table. A short hunchback with a large nose, dark, greedy eyes, and black curly hair. "Proletarians!" he began and they pricked up their ears. "The brown plague is becoming more impertinent every day. We cannot allow these provocations to continue. The proletariat has to counter the attacks by these minions of capitalism with all means available. With all means!"[27]

The role of proletarian otherness in establishing the National Socialist point of view is even more pronounced in Alfred C. Schröder's *Prolet am Ende* (1935, The end of the prole). Defending its lurid sensationalism, one contemporary reviewer called the novel an important lesson for the present: "All of this seems miserable and depressing today – and still: it is necessary once in a while to remember this boiling caldron of pain, suffering, shamelessness, agitation, and resentment."[28] The unemployed Christian Doneleit, the doomed prole of the novel's title, first has to fall for the lies propagated in the name of world revolution in order to become a warning example to others. Communism, after all, always betrays the workers: "Wanting to see all lives, all events only from one side, only from a predetermined point of view, was not working out. Proletarians, [...] proletarian points of view [...]

---

[27] Hermann Reisse, *Sieg Heil SA!* (Berlin: Nationaler Freiheitsverlag, 1933), 29. The only scholarly discussion of the genre can be found in Rainer Stollmann, "Das Nazi-Selbstbildnis im SA-Roman," in *Kunst und Kultur im deutschen Faschismus:* Literaturwissenschaften und Sozialwissenschaften 10, ed. Ralf Schnell and Martin Rector (Stuttgart: Metzler, 1978), 191–215.

[28] Anon., review of *Prolet am Ende, Thüringer Fähnlein: Monatshefte für die mitteldeutsche Heimat* 4.6 (1935): 378.

with these phrases, they [i.e., the communists] beat everything to death."²⁹ Fortunately, the Nazi agitator Franz Soternes is able to show Doneleit that National Socialism is creating an entirely new reality based on the feelings that forever "eliminate class hatred and class struggle from the German world, the German world of pure concepts."³⁰

III

The reduction of fictional experiences and imaginary identifications to ideological positions, the approach taken by many literary scholars working on the Third Reich, distracts not only from the role of political emotions in mass mobilizations but also from the self-mythification of the Nazi movement, especially during the first years of the regime. For that reason, it might be more productive to think of conversion stories also as a discursive template for practices of media convergence – namely, the dissolution of the distinction between fictional and nonfictional writing, the new admixtures of political agitation and literary trash, and the ascendancy of a decidedly modern politics of emotion across literary genres and media platforms. In other words, conversion stories cannot be examined outside the fundamental reorganization of the institution of literature that, after the infamous book burnings starting in May 1933, brought new publications and publishing houses as well as new types of authors and readers. Taking advantage of the growing concentration in media ownership and the expanded possibilities for media conversion, several movement novels were first serialized in party dailies and weeklies. Bestsellers such as Schenzinger's *Hitler Youth Quex* were adapted to the screen and marketed through extensive advertising campaigns. The Horst Wessel novel and film became part of elaborate annual events commemorating the slain SA man's martyrdom. Under these conditions, the differences between, say, sensationalist novels and journalistic reportages like Wilfrid Bade's *SA erobert Berlin* (1933, SA conquers Berlin) became increasingly irrelevant. Already by the end of 1933, the patterns were so well established that the narrative formulas shared by fictional and nonfictional texts could be mixed and matched and repro-

---

29 Alfred C. Schröder, *Prolet am Ende* (Berlin: Holle, 1935), 9. For two movement novels that confirm the continuities between Freikorps and Nazi movement, see Friedrich Barthel's *Sturmgeschlecht: Zweimal 9. November* (1934) and Hans Zöberlein's *Der Befehl des Gewissens* (1937). On the *Freikorps* novels and the psychosexual history of fascism, see Klaus Theweleit, *Male Fantasies*, 2 vols., trans. Chris Turner, Stephen Conway, and Erica Carter (Minneapolis: University of Minnesota Press, 1987).
30 Schröder, *Prolet am Ende*, 106.

duced *ad infinitum*. In one single year, Josef Viera, who later specialized in colonial novels, published three movement novels with the Leipzig-based Franz Schneider Verlag: *Utz kämpft für Hitler* (Utz fights for Hitler), an imitation of the Schenzinger novel, *Horst Wessel*, a version of the Ewers novel, and *SA-Mann Schrott*, yet another contribution to the cult of the unknown SA-man. This development proved so worrisome – which also means, so revealing of the political principle of endless multiplication – that some commentators denounced these novels as *Konjunkturliteratur*, trashy novels known as colportage. After Law for the Protection of National Symbols, which forbade the treatment of Nazi symbols in an undignified fashion, passed in May 1933 even the youth novel *Utz Fights for Hitler* was placed on a list of banned books.

Like all propagandistic literature, movement novels borrowed heavily from a wide range of cultural traditions and literary precursors, but always in a very superficial, mechanical way. Because of its penchant for endless reproduction, National Socialist realism in that regard stands closer to the postmodern aesthetics of simulation and appropriation than any conventional realist notions of narrative and authorship. For the conversion scenes, movement novels authors usually draw on a wide range of Christian themes and motifs, from revelation to redemption, all of which confirm the enduring power of religiosity as a political script. Addressing middle-class readers, they model their stories on the bildungsroman (i.e., educational novel) in which a young man, after initial opposition to prevailing norms and beliefs, eventually finds his place as a responsible member of society. Focusing on this aspect, Hans Günther notes that the narrative strategies of the bildungsroman, originally meant "to demonstrate the self-realization and social integration of an individual," in the totalitarian versions end up legitimizing the "gradual submission of the individual to existing organizational ideological structures."[31]

Movement novels also borrow extensively from Weimar *Zeitromane* (topical novels about contemporary problems) which use typical stories about ordinary people to reflect on profound transformations caused by modernization, industrialization, and urbanization, but without the critical perspectives offered by most of the writers associated with New Objectivity. In predictable ways, movement novels instead reproduce the nationalist and militaristic attitudes familiar from

---

[31] Hans Günther, "Education and Conversion: The Road to the New Man in the Totalitarian *Bildungsroman*," in *The Culture of the Stalin Period*, ed. Hans Günther (Houndsmills: Palgrave Macmillan, 1990), 205. He makes the point by comparing Schenzinger's *Hitler Youth Quex* to Nikolai Ostrovsky's *How the Steel Was Tempered*. For a reading of the socialist bildungsroman that also applies to Nazi conversion stories, see Benjamin Kohlmann, "Toward a History and Theory of the Socialist Bildungsroman," *Novel* 48.2 (2015): 167–189.

rightwing literature and the writings of Freikorps men.[32] Less obvious are the structural similarities with the politicization of literature advocated by the Bund proletarisch-revolutionärer Schriftsteller (BPRS, League of Proletarian-Revolutionary Writers). In a recent study on the worker in popular literature of the late 1920s and early 1930s, Michaela Menger draws attention to these similarities by tracing narrative schemata and images of self and other across the left-right divides and by identifying shared themes such as sacrifice, heroism, martyrdom, and cult of community.[33] Regardless of their diatribes against cultural Bolshevism, not a few Nazi authors emulated the KPD program of weaponizing literature and set out to become *völkisch* versions of what Stalin once called engineers of the human soul. After all, in their respective narratives of revolution, both the BPRS authors and their Nazi imitators emphasized the failures of modern capitalism and liberal democracy and used antidemocratic and antibourgeois positions to foster contempt for the rule of law, denounce compromise as weakness, and promote violence as a legitimate political means. In Nazi Germany as well as Stalinist Russia, the redefinition of realism aimed at a complete reconceptualization of social reality based on specific ideas, attitudes, and feelings about a new society in the process of becoming. Notwithstanding profound differences, socialist realism thus found a strange doppelgänger in National Socialist realism – a much less influential, less successful, and less transformative version, but just as revealing about the reversals of fantasy and reality weaponized in the name of two very different kinds of worker states.

The doctrine of socialist realism, according to Slavicist Leonid Heller, made three demands on the conventional realist narrative: ideological commitment, party-mindedness (or partisanship), and national or popular spirit. These categories represent an integral part of the master narrative of communism after the October Revolution and distinguish literary practices in the Soviet Union from those in France, Italy, and Germany where, at least in his view, stronger neoclassicist tendencies prevailed.[34] In fact, Soviet socialist realist and National Socialist realist novels share many characteristics, starting with the focus on ordinary people

---

32 On the Weimar *Zeitroman*, see Michael Hahn, *Scheinblüte, Krisenzeit, Nationalsozialismus: Die Weimarer Republik im Spiegel später Zeitromane (1928–1932/33)* (Bern: Peter Lang, 1995). On the *Zeitroman* after 1933, see Rolf Geissler, *Dekadenz und Heroismus: Zeitroman und völkisch-nationalsozialistische Literaturkritik* (Berlin: De Gruyter, 2010).
33 See Michaela Menger, *Der literarische Kampf um den Arbeiter: Populäre Schemata und politische Agitation im Roman der späten Weimarer Republik* (Berlin: De Gruyter, 2016).
34 Leonid Heller, "A World of Prettiness: Socialist Realism and the Aesthetic Categories," in *Socialist Realism Without Shores*, ed. Thomas Lahusen and Evgeny Dobrenko (Durham, NC: Duke University Press, 1997), 51–75.

and extraordinary leaders, the preoccupation with labor, industry, and technology, and the celebration of male heroism and collective sacrifice. The most successful literary genres during the Nazi years, which include the war, colonial, scientific, and industrial novel, would fit perfectly into Heller's list of criteria based on their realignment of conventional techniques of literary realism and reportage with Nazi definitions of partisanship and popularity (or *Volkstümlichkeit*). This connection becomes even clearer through Katerina Clark's insistence on paying closer attention to the didactic model function of socialist realism in creating what she calls "the official repository of state myths."[35] If the main purpose of the socialist realist master plot was to turn the novel into "a sort of parable for the working-out of Marxism-Leninism in history," she concludes, one of the most significant consequences for the organization of everyday life was to provide workable "myths for maintaining the status quo."[36] In a study on book publishing in the Third Reich, Ine Van linthout makes a surprisingly similar point when she defines National Socialist realism less as a representational category than an active intervention into reality, "a method through which literature is supposed to oblige the reader to partisanship for what is presented as 'right' or 'true.'"[37]

IV

Most movement novels narrativize the shift from proletariat to workerdom through stories of individual workers who join the movement after witnessing the healing powers of the folk community. Two examples, starting with *Hitler Youth Quex*, will suffice to illustrate how the hatreds, resentments, and prejudices organized through antisemitism helped to establish the mythical communitarianism at the heart of National Socialist realism. Karl Aloys Schenzinger, a physician dabbling in travel writing, had been asked by Baldur von Schirach to write a novel about, and for, the Hitler Youth. Using the religious motif of self-sacrifice and

---

[35] Katerina Clark, *The Soviet Novel: History as Ritual* (Bloomington: University of Indiana Press, 1981), xii. On the related debates, also see Régine Robin, *Socialist Realism: An Impossible Aesthetic*, trans. Catherine Porter, foreword Léon Robert (Stanford: Stanford University Press, 1992) and Thomas Lahusen, *How Life Writes the Book: Real Socialism and Socialist Realism in Stalin's Russia* (Ithaca, NY: Cornell University Press, 1997).
[36] Clark, *The Soviet Novel*, 9 and 10.
[37] Van linthout, *Das Buch*, 319. On literature as part of popular culture in the Third Reich, see Carsten Würmann and Ansgar Warner, eds., *Im Pausenraum des "Dritten Reiches": Zur Populärkultur im nationalsozialistischen Deutschland* (Berne: Peter Lang, 2008). For a cultural studies approach to these questions, see Thymian Bussemer, *Propaganda und Populärkultur: Konstruierte Erlebniswelten im Nationalsozialismus* (Wiesbaden: Deutscher Universitätsverlag, 2002).

turning it into a sign of German racial superiority, he delivered a paean to the life of Herbert Norkus (Heini Völker in the film), a sixteen-year-old Hitler Youth member stabbed by communists while distributing fliers in Berlin-Moabit. A phenomenal success, the novel was immediately adapted to the screen by Hans Steinhoff, an experienced Weimar-era film director. Early in the story, two groups of youngsters are leaving Berlin for a weekend excursion in the surrounding woods: a uniformed, disciplined, and cheerful Hitler Youth unit and a disorderly, rowdy, lewd group of communist boys and girls, including Heini. Repulsed by his comrades' behavior, he runs away and soon comes upon a mysterious light in the darkness (17:00 – 19:00'):

> The glow became brighter. Again, he heard singing, very clearly now; it had to be very close to him. It was a marching song that took hold of his legs. He ran up the hill, stumbling over roots and tangling with twines. His breathing was labored, with sweat running down his nose. Having reached the top, he suddenly saw a blazing flame. He was blinded by the strong light and stopped breathing. He did not dare to move. He stood still and stared. Slowly his eyes adjusted to the brightness. About a thousand boys, or perhaps only a hundred, were standing around a burning pile of wood. It appeared as if this circle of a hundred human beings extended until the end of the world. [...] Silently they all looked toward the fire. A tall man appeared and was speaking to them. He was obviously giving a speech. Heini only heard individual words, he heard "movement" and "leader," and he understood half a sentence: "every individual life for the others." As he was listening and thinking of moving closer in order to hear more clearly, he was overcome by a great fear. "Germany, Germany above all," it rolled over him like a wave in a thousand voices. I am a German, too, he thought, and this insight hit him like a powerful shock like never before in his life [...] This was German soil, German forest, these were German boys, and he saw that he stood apart, alone, helpless, and he didn't know what to do with this overwhelming feeling.[38]

The free indirect discourse in the novel finds a filmic equivalent in the point-of-view shots depicting Nazi flags, torches, and rituals. But these do not fully capture the emotional significance of the scene and require the addition of a later dialogue between his father and the *Bannführer* (squad leader). Triggered by the latter's

---

38 Karl Aloys Schenzinger, *Der Hitlerjunge Quex* (Berlin: Zeitgeschichte, 1932), 39–40. The novel was serialized in *Völkischer Beobachter* in January and February of 1933; it inspired a wave of Hitler Youth novels. Walter Schönstedt, in the Rote-Eine-Mark novel *Kämpfende Jugend* (1932), describes a very similar milieu from the Communist perspective. Written in exile, his *Auf der Flucht erschossen* (1934) tells the story of one SA Man disillusioned with Nazi demagoguery. For a reading of the Schenzinger novel that focuses on the conversion theme, see Daniel Stahl, "Literature and Propaganda: The Structure of Conversion in Schenziger's *Hitlerjunge Quex*," *Studies in Twentieth Century Literature* 12.2 (1988): 129–147. On the Nazi cult of martyrdom more generally, see Jay W. Baird, *To Die for Germany: Heroes in the Nazi Pantheon* (Bloomington: Indiana University Press, 1990), with chapters on Horst Wessel (73–107) and Herbert Norkus (108–129).

probing question – "Where does a boy belong?" – their exchange (57:00–58:00') redefines political commitment in terms of racial identity and, as a consequence, connects the trajectory from working-class family to Nazi movement outlined for Heini to the larger promise of reconciliation to be made to all workers and, by extension, all Germans:

> Father: I am a simple man. I am a prole [...] And where I belong, that is where the boy belongs. With his class comrades.
> Leader: You mean the International?
> Father: Yes, indeed, the International.
> Leader: And where were you born?
> Father: In Berlin.
> Leader: And where is that?
> Father: On the Spree.
> Leader: On the Spree, yes. But where? In what country?
> Father: In Germany.
> Leader: In Germany, yes, in *our* Germany. Think about that.

Hitler Youth Quex, just like *Horst Wessel*, overlays its *Zeitroman* elements – that is, typical figures and typical scenes of Berlin working-class life – with an essentializing concept of belonging (i. e., Germany) that, in this scene, gives the unemployed father an immediate sense of pride and self-worth. Ultimately, the two novels and their screen adaptations remain constrained by the external pressure of turning their real-life model into martyrs to the cause. The opposite is true for Max Barthel's *Das unsterbliche Volk* (1933, Immortal folk), where the conversion story becomes part of virulent anti-Bolshevik and anti-Soviet polemics that revive old antagonisms with a view toward future military confrontations. Not unlike his protagonist, Barthel (1893–1975), whose contribution to workers' poetry will be discussed in the next chapter, had worked as an unskilled laborer and joined Spartakus, KPD, and SPD after the war. During the world economic crisis, he became an ardent National Socialist who pledged full allegiance to Hitler in 1933.[39] Josef Nadler, in his literary history based on German tribes and landscapes, praises Barthel for transcending all class distinctions and singles out *Immortal Folk* for showing the "political conversion of the German workers from the class struggle to the German Reich."[40]

The Immortal Folk tells the story of two members of the Bundschuh family, long displaced from their ancestral home, whose improbable reunion ends up con-

---

[39] Max Barthel, "Aufruf an die Schriftstellerkollegen," *Der Angriff*, 9 June 1933.
[40] Joseph Nadler, *Literaturgeschichte des Deutschen Volkes: Dichtung und Schrifttum der deutschen Stämme und Landschaften*, 4 vols. (Berlin: Propyläen, 1941), 4:341.

necting the Nazi dream of the folk community with the search for *Lebensraum* in the East. Jacob Bundschuh is a Black Sea German peasant who, faced with the threat of collectivization after the October Revolution, rediscovers his love for the "old homeland" and its "immortal folk." Meanwhile Eugen Bundschuh, an unemployed toolmaker, moves to Berlin from the provinces and soon joins the communists in conspiratorial meetings and skirmishes with the police. Time and again his new commitments are tested by unscrupulous functionaries from Moscow, free-spirited seductive young women, and bored bourgeois intellectuals sprouting revolutionary slogans. Once again, it is the designation "proletarian" that, by failing to capture the essence of the German worker, allows Eugen to make sense of his growing disillusionment with the communists. As one of his former comrades, now active in the Nazi movement, explains: "You are for the dictatorship of the proletariat. What is the proletariat? An invention of your leaders who want to perpetuate these conditions in order for their rule to last forever! [...] If you knew, Eugen, what we want, you would join us. Why are you still in your party?" [41] Despite growing doubts, he travels to the Soviet Union as part of a KPD delegation and, through a series of coincidences, meets the Black Sea Germans who have just been evicted from their farms as a result of forced collectivization. A young woman named Anna beseeches Eugen to speak to her about Germany and the Germans. In being asked to reclaim his ethnic identity, he not only discovers his true allegiances but also decides (together with Anna as his future wife) to return home, back to the Reich:

> Germany was no longer just a geographic term. More than a battleground for classes and estates, the homeland at last was becoming a *Lebensraum* (living space) with living people and things. Germany! [...] Here in Perlowka [near Moscow], the worker Eugen Bundschuh met his fate and, for the first time, recognized the community of fate that characterized the entire folk beyond classes, estates, and other differences. [...] Reason and emotion belonged together, just like man and woman belonged together.[42]

V

One of the opening questions in this chapter has revolved around the usefulness of movement novels in locating the figure of the worker within Nazi ideology and social policy. It is beyond the scope of this study to address the situation of actual workers in the Third Reich, a topic that has inspired a large amount of research

---

[41] Max Barthel, *Das unsterbliche Volk: Roman* (Berlin: Büchergilde Gutenberg, 1933), 195.
[42] Barthel, *Das unsterbliche Volk*, 188–189.

and heated debates among social historians.[43] Nonetheless, the similarities between literary fiction and history as narrative can be used in closing to think more expansively about political emotions, their adaptability to vastly different ideologies, their compatibility with competing identifications, and their convertibility into different emotional scripts, including the necessary adjustments after 1933 from the revolutionary habitus of the Nazi movement to the dynamic of coercion and consent in the Nazi dictatorship. An expanded definition of conversion – in the sense of turning communists into Nazis and blurring the boundaries between fact and fiction – has been used to shed light on the ideological fantasy at the heart of both aspects, namely, that National Socialism was a movement fully committed to the workers and, by extension, to the fantasy of socialism. The implications can be summarized as follows: First, conversion stories attest to continuing anxieties over the prevailing narratives of class that made the worker a necessary but problematic link between socialism and nationalism. Second, in modeling the shift from class to race as the main category of identification, conversion stories rely heavily on leftwing literary genres and class iconographies from the Weimar years. And third, the theme of conversion takes part through a process of emotionalization that blurs the boundaries between reality and fantasy in literature and politics; the result in this case has been called National Socialist realism.

Both the movement novels of the early 1930s and the historical scholarship on German workers after 1933 draw on basic elements of storytelling: main protagonists and supporting characters, crises and turning points, assumptions about cause and effect, attributions of collective and individual agency, and most importantly, dispositions, attitudes, motivations, and aspirations. In creating mises-en-scène for conversion experiences, the novels offer veritable templates of ideologi-

---

[43] Important studies (in chronological order) include Max H. Keele, *Nazis and Workers: National Socialist Appeals to German Labor, 1919–1933* (Chapel Hill: University of North Carolina Press, 1972); Eberhard Heuel, *Der umworbene Stand: Die ideologische Integration der Arbeiter im Nationalsozialismus* (Frankfurt am Main: Campus, 1989); Francis Ludwig Carsten, *The German Workers and the Nazis* (Aldershot: Scholar Press, 1995); Conan Fischer, ed., *The Rise of National Socialism and the Working Classes in Weimar Germany* (Providence: Berghahn, 1996); Joachim Bons, *Nationalsozialismus und Arbeiterfrage: Zu den Motiven, Inhalten und Wirkungsgründen nationalsozialistischer Arbeiterpolitik vor 1933* (Pfaffenweiler: Centaurus, 1995); William Brustein, *The Logic of Evil: The Social Origins of the Nazi Party, 1925–1933* (New Haven: Yale University Press, 1996); and Michael Schneider, *Unterm Hakenkreuz: Arbeiter und Arbeiterbewegung 1933 bis 1939* (Bonn: Dietz, 1999). For a Marxist analysis that emphasizes the appeal to the ruling class, see Donny Gluckstein, *The Nazis, Capitalism and the Working Class* (London: Haymarket, 2012). On the condition of industrial labor in particular, see Rüdiger Hachtmann, *Industriearbeit im "Dritten Reich": Untersuchungen zu den Lohn- und Arbeitsbedingungen in Deutschland 1933–1945* (Göttingen: Vanderhoeck & Ruprecht, 1989).

cal interpellation – as works of fiction and as historical documents. Two insights follow from this observation: that the Nazi fantasy of the worker must be separated from the problem of the worker in the Third Reich, and that literary fiction and political ideology played equally important but not identical roles in the imagination of a racial community beyond class.

Since Theodore Abel's 1934 study *Why Hitler Came into Power*, narrative structures and strategies have played a key role in the history and historiography of workers during the Third Reich. Regarding the elusive meaning of "socialism" in National Socialism, two explanations for the Nazi rise to power have proven influential: the crises of global capitalism and the problems of modernization, on the one hand; and the breakdown of traditional class structure and the rise of modern mass society, on the other. For a long time, doubt about the Nazis' socialist beliefs and exaggerated faith in the democratic values of the working class contributed to widespread assumptions that support for the party was most prevalent among the lower-middle classes and resistance to the regime most pronounced among those previously involved with the SPD and KPD. As a result, the search for another, better Germany led by the exploited and oppressed of the past became part of the official historiography of socialism in East Germany and long sustained the romance with the working class among members of the West German New Left.

Timothy Mason's probing question from the 1980s – "Why did that class in German society which suffered greater disenfranchisement, greater persecution and greater oppression than any other not mount at least one major challenge to the regime?"[44] – has since been answered by case studies that take regional peculiarities, generational experiences, religious affiliations, gendered perspectives, and differences between prewar and wartime years into close account. Drawing on a wide range of methodologies, this research has shown that workers, especially handicraft, agricultural, and white-collar workers, in fact joined the Nazi Party in significant numbers. Disproving early claims that the party was primarily a lower-middle-class party, recent studies have highlighted its broad cross-class appeal evidenced by strong support among university students, members of the educated bourgeoisie, workers in small towns, and the rural population in general. Others have used the party's promise of economic growth, social mobility, and respect for manual labor to explain growing support for the Nazis especially during the early 1930s. Most scholars today agree that the post-1933 dynamic has to be ex-

---

44 Timothy W. Mason, *Nazism, Fascism, and the Working Class: Essays by Tim Mason*, ed. Jane Caplan (Cambridge: Cambridge University Press, 1995), 234. Also see his *Social Policy in the Third Reich: The Working Class and the "National Community"* (Oxford: Oxford University Press, 1997) and, for a wealth of historical documents, *Arbeiterklasse und Volksgemeinschaft: Dokumente und Materialien zur deutscher Arbeiterpolitik 1936–1939* (Opladen: Westdeutscher Verlag, 1975).

amined as part of a longer process of deproletarianization that started during the Weimar years when the rise of white-collar society and modern mass culture weakened the bonds of working-class culture and the world economic crisis intensified fears of proletarianization among members of the petty bourgeoisie. Along similar lines, newer studies on workers after 1933 document continued problems in the reorganization of labor, despite lower levels of unemployment and ambitious public works projects. Many structural problems persisted or increased after the Nazi seizure of power, from longer working hours and declining wages to wartime food shortages and dependency on women workers. Localized strikes and work slowdowns, both expressions of what Alf Lüdtke calls *Eigensinn* (obstinacy, stubbornness), were not uncommon but often remained unpublicized.[45]

A 1999 study by Michael Schneider on the working class in the Third Reich provides a good summary of the complex political, social, and economic issues that the conversion stories sought to resolve through the sheer power of new emotional attachments.[46] On the workers' side, one could find expressions of dissent as well as consent, idealism as well as opportunism, and, on the regime's side, a strategic back and forth between terror and violence, concessions and incentives. Writing on the difficulties of resistance, Mason in fact early on reminded his readers that, "only those whose loyalties and judgments were firmly rooted will have been able to withstand the blandishments of Nazi cultural flattery of workers, and to distinguish consistently, for example, between productionist Nazi icons and the lost representations of worker pride, or between Nazi comradeship and socialist solidarity."[47] A fictional dialogue from 1933 between Heini, the son of a Communist worker, and Fritz, the Hitler Youth member from an upper-middle-class family, confirms this diagnosis from the perspective of a fictional problem and solution. In the novel *Hitler Youth Quex*, the title figure asks: "What can I contribute?" His new friend answers: "What can you contribute? To be a good comrade [Kamerad]."[48] It is the ambiguity of the term, brought out by the reverse translation of the English "comrade" as either *Genosse* or *Kamerad*, that attests

---

[45] Alf Lüdtke, *Eigen-Sinn: Fabrikalltag, Arbeitererfahrungen und Politik vom Kaiserreich bis in den Faschismus* (Münster: Westfälisches Dampfboot, 2015). For a contribution to the history of emotions, compare his "Macht der Emotionen. Gefühle als Produktionskraft: Bemerkungen zu einer schwierigen Geschichte," in *Rausch und Diktatur: Inszenierung, Mobilisierung und Kontrolle in totalitären Systemen* (Frankfurt am Main: Campus, 2006), 44–55. On the question of resistance, also see Alf Lüdtke, "The Appeal of Exterminating 'Others': German Workers and the Limits of Resistance," *The Journal of Modern History* 64 (Dec. 1992): 46–67.
[46] See Michael Schneider, *Unterm Hakenkreuz: Arbeiter und Arbeiterbewegung 1933 bis 1939* (Bonn: Dietz, 1999), especially chapter 3.5.
[47] Mason, *Nazism, Fascism and the Working Class*, 256.
[48] Schenzinger, *Der Hitlerjunge Quex*, 55.

to the continuous influence of socialism in the language of nationalism. Yet it is the unequal power relationship between the young working-class boy and the future leader figure that aligns the Nazi position with narrative authority and establishes conversion as an experience of empowerment as well as submission. Heini rejects the grand narrative of class struggle for the dream of community offered by National Socialism. As movement novels demonstrate, becoming part of "us" in the way defined by Fritz required much more than an initiation into Nazi rituals and beliefs; it involved the work of subjectivization that depended so heavily on political emotions and their reaffirmation in the making of old and new antagonisms. In this particular instance, Fritz's casual antisemitism, including a remark about international finance capital, makes the proposed transition from the discourses of class to race at once necessary, desirable, and imaginable. It is with these larger developments in mind that this chapter has used the movement novels to examine the conversion of communists into Nazis – in fiction and beyond. The logics of substitution that allowed worker poets to replace "proletarian" with "German worker" and achieve similar conversion effects will be the subject of the next chapter.

Chapter 3
The Revisionist Project of Workers' Poetry

> As part of the general labor front, the poets are organized in a poetic labor front. [...] Only members of the poetic labor front are allowed to write poems. [...] Every poet has to hand over his honoraria to a "mutual trust" whose "lyrical socialism" guarantees equal distribution.
>
> Wilhelm Stapel

In literature, it sometimes takes little more than adding an adjective or changing a noun to realign the social imaginaries of class and nation and give collective identifications new meaning and direction. By attaching "German" to "worker," the *Arbeiterdichter* (worker poets) of the 1920s and 1930s made the literary traditions of the workers' movement available to the (counter)revolutionary project of National Socialism – and did so quite literally with the stroke of a pen. To quote a 1935 dissertation on the topic, "worker poets [are] the designated heralds of a new form of being that finds its living likeness in German workerdom."[1] On the level of language, the disappearance of class analysis involved the kind of erasures performed by Arthur Mellon, who in 1935 changed the title of his 1929 poem "Proletarian Child" to "Worker's Child (*Arbeiterkind*)."[2] The replacement of *Proletarier*, including its Latin roots and French origins, with the German(ic) *Arbeiter* signaled the end of internationalist solidarities and established the nationalist version of socialism as the only acceptable one in literature and beyond. Existing interpretations of workers' poetry after 1933 have focused on writers' political allegiances and questions of (self-)censorship. These revisionist tendencies bring into view something often ignored or underestimated – namely, the populist sensibilities that informed workers' movements and socialist parties from the beginning and that resonated in the poetic imaginings of community, folk, and the people. During the transition from the Weimar Republic to the Third Reich, the inevitable contradictions are particularly noticeable in a literary subgenre with a strong investment in the power of language: *Arbeiterdichtung* (workers' poetry).

With or without the attribute "German," the *Arbeiter* of workers' poetry played a key role in the communalization, nationalization, and, ultimately, racial-

---

[1] Johannes Razum, *Wesensformung des deutschen Arbeiters: Darstellung seines Bildungsstrebens an Hand der Arbeiterdichtung* (Frankfurt am Main: Schramberg, 1935), 2.
[2] Arthur Mellon, "Proletarierkind," in Hans Mühle, *Das proletarische Schicksal: Ein Querschnitt durch die Arbeiterdichtung der Gegenwart* (Gotha: Leopold Klotz, 1929), 117, and "Arbeiterkind," in Hans Mühle, *Das Lied der Arbeit: Selbstzeugnisse der Schaffenden; Ein Querschnitt durch die Arbeitsdichtung der Gegenwart*, with preface by Robert Ley (Gotha: Leopold Klotz, 1935), 82.

ization of the working class during the interwar years. This transformative process drew heavily on the languages of grievance and resentment established in the early workers' movement and, notwithstanding categorical denials by Nazi authors, empowered by a Marxist analysis of class. As established worker poets revised older poems and published new ones, they seemed to fall in line with what Stapel above mockingly describes as a fully coordinated poetic labor front. Writing paeans to the German worker henceforth meant eliminating the proletarian from the history of social struggles and replacing calls for revolutionary change with dreams of folk and nation. Nonetheless, even these diminished and compromised versions of the literary genre most closely associated with the working class kept alive the utopian dream of equality, unity, and fraternity first articulated in the workers' songs of the Vormärz years.

Many of these changes played out on the level of terminology. The majority of original worker poets preferred subject matter far removed from the workplace, as evident in their many paeans to nature, love, family, and faith. Nonetheless, the long shadow of labor exploitation and class oppression continued to frame the popular reception of workers' poetry and almost routinely endow worker poets with oppositional sensibilities. Only now, after 1933, the introduction of the anachronistic *Arbeitsmann* (working man) alongside the more gender-neutral *Arbeiter* helped to absorb the *Arbeiterklasse* (working class) as a social group into *Arbeit* as a process-based category and contributed to the mythification of (manual) labor as part of the ongoing masculinization of folk and nation. Some Nazi critics sought to mark the distance from the radicalized worker poets of the past by replacing the designation *Arbeiterdichtung* (workers' poetry) with *Arbeitsdichtung* (poetry of work). Others proposed opening up *Arbeiterdichtung* toward *Volksdichtung* (folk poetry) and explained: "When we say 'Arbeiterdichtung,' we do not mean poems and novels that deal with workers but a type of poetry that arises from the folk as it is today [...] For us, workers are German folk comrades who have understood the following: the German folk community is the product of everyone's untiring effort to fulfill their duty in the place where the community has placed them."[3]

Inseparable from the history of the workers' movement, workers' poetry has been described as the most authentic expression of class-based feelings, ranging from the humiliations of unemployment to the thrills of collective action. *The Proletarian Dream* has traced these qualities through the poetic and performative

---

[3] Helmut Jahn, "Arbeiterdichtung wird gebraucht," *Der Deutsche*, 8 July 1934. Quoted by Vanessa Ferrari, "Nationalsocialismo e *Arbeiterliteratur:* Il lavoro e la fabbrica nella propaganda della NSDAP (1929–1938)," (PhD diss., University of Munich, 2016), 233. Ferrari proposes calling the work published after 1933 *NS-Arbeiterliteratur.*

qualities of workers' poetry and workers' song and, to give one example, pointed to their shared ability to emulate the rhythms of factory work through rhyme and meter. While the authors could be called conventional in their choice of forms and styles, they took full advantage of the agitational potential of heroic, melodramatic, and sentimental registers. Rejecting bourgeois notions of interiority, the worker poets were much more interested in exploring alternative experiences by evoking collective agency. In the words of Germanist Heinz Ludwig Arnold, workers' poetry replaced the first-person singular of the poetic voice (*das lyrische Ich*) with the first-person plural (*das solidarische Wir*) of lived solidarity.[4] "Renouncing the I and consciously moving toward the we," as Hellmuth Langenbucher in 1939 defined the main goal in surprisingly similar ways, indeed proved integral to the imagination of a community of work sustained by "the natural rootedness of the poet in the life of the folk."[5]

Claiming the worker for an ethnic definition of the folk/nation, workers' poetry relied heavily on populist tropes, sentiments, and attitudes to integrate the iconographies of class into the mythologies of folk. The revisions can be read as both a manifestation (or performance) of hegemonic practices and a symptom of official anxieties over the continued appeal of oppositional voices. Meanwhile, the apparent ease with which writers and, presumably, readers as well made the language of workerdom their own must be seen as a first indication of the primacy of group emotions over any particular ideology. The feelings described, expressed, and validated by workers' poetry reveal very little about the fundamental reorganization of labor and industry and of work and life in the Nazi dictatorship. Yet as archives of emotions, these poems shed important light on the nonsimultaneities that kept the proletarian dream alive, even in its Nazi incarnation in the German worker.

The decision to add, delete, and replace ideologically contaminated terms in previously published works can be (and has been) read as proof of an author's political conversion, acquiescence, or opportunism. Yet even with such a focus on individual writers, poetic mood and tone added layers of meanings that evoke what Raymond Williams calls the residual and Ernst Bloch the nonsimultaneous.[6] The

---

4 See Heinz Ludwig Arnold, "Im Lesebuch unserer Gesellschaft kaum zu finden," in *Arbeiterlyrik 1842–1932*, ed. Heinz Ludwig Arnold (Berlin: Parthas, 2003), 206–214.
5 Hellmuth Langenbucher, "Volk und Dichter," reprinted in Sander L. Gilman, ed., *NS-Literaturtheorie: Eine Dokumentation*, preface Cornelius Schnauber (Frankfurt am Main: Athenäum, 1971), 18 and 20.
6 The term residual is taken from Raymond Williams, "Dominant, Residual, Emergent," in *Marxism and Literature* (Oxford: Oxford University Press, 1977), 121–127. Ernst Bloch introduces the notion of "the simultaneity of the non-simultaneous" in *Heritage of Our Times*, trans. Neville

proliferation of revisions speaks to the Nazis' dependency on the class-based identifications that sustained workers' poetry from the very beginning. Clearly, the emotional energies channeled through poetic means were considered an important resource in the official promotion of workerdom. The minimal efforts involved corroborate the strong affinities between socialist, nationalist, and populist imageries that, channeled through the affective tonalities of poetry, made the German worker the embodiment of the people (*Volk*) – in the sense of folk and race, the common or simple man, and the modern masses.

The chapter's epigraph by Wilhelm Stapel, a national conservative and self-proclaimed antisemite, is taken from a 1934 journal article about what its title ironically describes as the "Centrally Planned Reconstruction of German Poetry."[7] Like other members of the educated bourgeoisie, Stapel denounced the politicization of culture by the Nazis (and, before them, the Bolsheviks) as a coordinated assault on the creative individual and the autonomous work of art. After 1933, poems by and about workers could be found everywhere, from poetry collections and anthologies to workers' calendars, daily newspapers, illustrated magazines, and *Werkzeitungen* (company newspapers). Nonetheless, in terms of popular appeal and political relevance, the moment for this kind of poetry seemed to have passed. Stapel's nightmare of a poetic labor front never became reality. Even the Nazi *Kampflieder* (fight songs) seemed to provide little inspiration, compared to the close bonds between workers' poems and workers' songs forged during nineteenth-century struggles for freedom, equality, and democracy. All well-known worker poets began writing during the Wilhelmine and Weimar years, and often inside the cultural organizations of the workers' movement. Accordingly, their activities after 1933 can be seen as either the culmination of long-held *völkisch* and nationalist convictions or the full realization of the populist nature of this particular version of socialism. Indicative perhaps also of the diminished standing of literature in the Nazi media dictatorship, a new generation of worker poets socialized inside the Nazi Party failed to take their place – in contrast to the ambitious young artists and architects recognized through massive official support for the visual arts.

Since the mid-nineteenth century, the communalization and, ultimately, racialization of class discourse has had a profound effect on the representation of work and workers across artistic forms, genres, and practices. Intellectual histories have

---

and Stephen Plaice (Cambridge: Polity, 1991); *Ungleichzeitigkeit* is translated either as nonsynchronicity or nonsimultaneity.

7 Wilhelm Stapel, "Planwirtschaftlicher Wiederaufbau der deutschen Lyrik" (1934), quoted by Erhard Schütz, "Sänger der Autobahn oder dienstbare Dichtung: Lyrik als Propaganda," in *Kunst im NS-Staat: Ideologie, Ästhetik, Protagonisten*, ed. Wolfgang Benz, Peter Eckel, and Andreas Nachama (Berlin: Metropol, 2015), 155.

shown how the terms "worker" and "proletarian," with their very different connotations, allowed socialist, communist, liberal, and conservative writers to signal their positions on the worker question and align their analyses of class society and capitalist modernity with the alternatives of reform or revolution. The fact that these terminological choices continued to haunt Nazi literature after 1933 should not be surprising, given the party's aggressive claims on the socialist tradition, whether through appropriation or elimination. However, what is surprising is how much the emotional attachment to the worker as a figure of abjection survived the obligatory heroization of manual labor and sustained a subgenre heavily promoted by Nazi scholars, largely ignored by the reading public, and widely dismissed by postwar Germanists because of its literary shortcomings and political entanglements.[8]

Because of its failures as a vehicle for Nazi ideology, workers' poetry proves ideally suited for reconstructing the emotions channeled through the worker as a conduit of competing social, racial, and national imaginaries. Consequently, this chapter uses select poems written during the 1920s and rewritten after 1933 to identify the populist elements that transformed the worker into a representative of the folk but also preserved the emotional legacies of the worker's movement in modified and diminished form. The first part examines this systematic elimination of all things "proletarian" by looking at the updated 1935 edition of a much-discussed 1928 poetry anthology on *Das proletarische Schicksal* (Proletarian fate) and the post-1933 changes made by Heinrich Lersch to some of his signature poems from the Wilhelmine and Weimar years. The second part establishes the historical context in which workers' poetry assumed such a significant role within the workers' movement by focusing on the psychological back and forth between resignation and indignation, suffering and pride, solidarity and resentment, despair and hope, and so forth. In the third part, the blind spots of scholarship informed by ideology critique will be used to consider the political adaptability of

---

8 For an introduction to workers' literature in the Third Reich, see Wolfgang Eggerstorfer, *Schönheit und Adel der Arbeit: Arbeiterliteratur im Dritten Reich* (Berne: Peter Lang, 1988). For general overviews, see Horst Denkler and Karl Prümm, eds., *Die deutsche Literatur im Dritten Reich: Themen Traditionen Wirkungen* (Stuttgart: Reclam, 1976); Ernst Loewy, *Literatur unterm Hakenkreuz: Das Dritte Reich und seine Dichtung* (Frankfurt am Main: Fischer, 1983); Uwe-Karsten Ketelsen, *Völkisch-nationale und nationalsozialistische Literatur in Deutschland 1890–1945* (Stuttgart: Metzler, 1976); and Uwe-Karsten Ketelsen, *Literatur und Drittes Reich* (Vierow bei Greifswald: SH-Verlag, 1992). For an institutional perspective, also see Jan-Pieter Barbian, *Literaturpolitik im "Dritten Reich": Institutionen, Kompetenzen, Betätigungsfelder* (Frankfurt am Main: Buchhändler-Vereinigung, 1993) and *Literaturpolitik im NS-Staat: Von der "Gleichschaltung" bis zum Ruin* (Frankfurt am Main: Fischer, 2010). For an English-language overview by the same author, see *The Politics of Literature in Nazi Germany: Books in the Media Dictatorship* (London: Bloomsbury, 2013).

workers' poetry as evidence of its long-standing commitment to what Ernesto Laclau calls populist reason and what invariably contains its Other, namely unreason.[9]

I

Worker poets after 1933 relied heavily on textual revisions to express their support for the idea of folk community and, at the same time, conceal their ties to the workers' movement.[10] In 1929, Hans Mühle published *Das proletarische Schicksal: Ein Querschnitt durch die Arbeiterdichtung der Gegenwart* (Proletarian fate: a cross-section of contemporary workers' poetry); in 1935, an updated edition appeared as *Das Lied der Arbeit: Selbstzeugnisse der Schaffenden* (The song of work: testimonies by working people). Mühle was ideally suited for such a revisionist project, having just written a Sprechchor titled *Vaterunser der Arbeit* (1934, The Lord's Prayer of work) that infused the socialist mass spectacle with Christian imagery and *völkisch* terminology. Even more importantly, he was well versed in populist phrases such as the power of the people or the unity of the folk and used them as cover for his rabid anticommunism and nascent antisemitism.

In the introduction to *The Song of Work*, Mühle proudly introduces the chosen poems as models for an "experience of work liberated from class hatred and committed to Germany. [...] This is how workers' poetry opens up to become poetry of work."[11] In the earlier *Proletarian Fate*, his sympathy for *völkisch* thought already finds expression in the praise for worker poets who, untouched by "the disease of intellectualism," promote the unity of workers and folk as a valid solution to the divisions in modern class society. Through these poets, he concludes, "the people who created language and legend, fairy tale and folk song are once again singing from their own hearts. These sounds of the heart, originating in the immediacy of experience, break through from the subconscious of the national psyche and, more forcefully in lyric verse than in prose, become the providential voices of the worker's soul."[12] Mühle in 1929 still draws on familiar socialist rhetoric as he recognizes

---

9 The reference is to Ernesto Laclau, *On Populist Reason* (London: Verso, 2005).
10 Revisionism is an overdetermined term in the history of Marxism referencing at once the abandonment of the revolutionary project in favor of gradual reforms and the reinterpretation of world history, including the history of communism, according to (new) Marxist theories and political exigencies.
11 Hans Mühle, introduction, in *Das proletarische Schicksal*, viii.
12 Mühle, introduction, v.

"the subterranean smoldering of hatred and revolutionary defiance" and conjures the elusive "spirit of a new time arising from the depths."[13] His language may recall communist agitprop, but the revolutionaries are now the Nazis. More specifically, his celebration of the ability of the folk to turn present misery into future glory is predicated on the denunciation of the social and economic elites of the Weimar Republic and driven by the same antidemocratic resentments found in Nazi treatises on the culture of degeneracy.

The Song of Work can be described as an adaptation of *Proletarian Fate* to political realities that require the erasure of the proletarian as a figure of identification. Already the red and black Gothic lettering and the hammer and wheat wreath icons on the 1935 cover announce the new focus on new industrial and artisanal workers. Both editions include poems by Max Barthel, Karl Bröger, Gerrit Engelke, Alfons Petzold, and the abovementioned Heinrich Lersch; missing now are communist authors Kurt Kläber, Oskar Maria Graf, and Bruno Schönlank, along with the frontispiece of a mourning mother by Käthe Kollwitz. The most noticeable changes involve the deletion of lines or stanzas that use the language of class struggle and the adjustments in tense and mood that relegate the realities of class oppression to a distant past. How the integration of working-class voices into the coming folk community was to be imagined can be discerned from a poem by Hans Brüssow, a Berlin lead caster, that recalls the *Kampfzeit:* "We called to battle, and they marched with us, / And the night, it must shine bright. / Prole of Berlin, because you joined in! / Comrade, be prepared, / Now our time has come / And Germany must be ours!"[14]

The early 1930s saw the publication of several anthologies of workers' poetry and collections of individual poets that advanced an ever more racialized definition of workerdom. If literature, to take a definition from 1942 by Heinz Kindermann, functioned as the mirror of a nation, and if work represented the essence of Germanness, then it was the task of workers' poetry to reconcile the perspectives of class and nation by celebrating the communal nature of work.[15] "After years of a folk-destroying obsession with class, the new Germany has finally discovered the value and dignity of work and embraced it as the foundation of the national will to life," concluded Peter Diederichs in his afterword to a small 1933 an-

---

13 Mühle, introduction, xvi.
14 Hans Brüssow, "Weddinglied," in Mühle, *Das Lied der Arbeit*, 191. Wedding refers to a working-class neighborhood in Berlin.
15 See Heinz Kindermann, "Vom Sinn der Arbeit in tausend Jahre deutscher Dichtung," in *Ruf der Arbeit* (Berlin: Nordland, 1942), 5–93. The study of literature for him belonged to the "volksunmittelbaren Wissenschaften." See his introduction to *Kampf um die deutsche Lebensform: Reden und Aufsätze über die Dichtung im Aufbau der Nation* (Vienna: Wiener Verlagsgesellschaft, 1941), 5.

thology titled *Volk an der Arbeit* (The folk at work), which features poems by Bröger, Lersch, Barthel, Petzold, Engelke, and others.[16] His argument that literary quality is less important than the authenticity of experience indirectly confirms the role assigned to workers' poetry as a laboratory of emotions – and dovetails nicely with concurrent attempts by literary scholars to develop an aesthetics of reception unconstrained by formal considerations. The sudden faith shared by writers and scholars in the formative power of emotions finds expression in various stylistic registers, including the ecstatic tone with which Hermann Claudius introduces the National Socialist "We!" as the voice of the old and the new: "When we walk side by side / And sing the old songs / And the forests echo them. We feel everything must succeed: / With us, a new time arrives."[17] Similarly, the genre's constitutive tension between transgressive moments and disciplinary effects is modeled perfectly by Lersch who, in "Arbeiterlied" (Workers' song), summons his readers, "Brothers in labor, may we be united in / A holy passion" but also reminds them that "Struggle is work, work love, / In struggle, we set ourselves free!"[18]

Heinrich Lersch (1889–1936), who appears in both editions of the Mühle anthology, undertook significant efforts after 1933 to resolve the tension between class and folk that had haunted his writing from the start and made it so appealing to readers from the lower classes. A boilersmith from the Rhineland with close ties to the Catholic workers' movement, Lersch was an enthusiastic convert to National Socialism and joined the eighty-eight writers who signed an oath of allegiance to Hitler in October 1933. Contemporaries hailed him as a "poet of the people," with qualifications: "Yes! But no 'worker poet' who only wanted his work to serve an uprooted proletarian class and who knew nothing but privation and misery, insurrection and damnation, accusation and cry for redemption."[19] Hans Eiserlo, in his 1937 dissertation, described Lersch as someone who "feels instinctively that the victory of Marxism will forever destroy what is good and divine in human beings: the yearning for greatness and beauty."[20] During the war years, the infa-

---

16 Peter Diederichs, afterword, *Volk an der Arbeit, Gedichte* (Jena: Eugen Diederichs, 1933), 62.
17 Hermann Claudius, "Wir," *Volk an der Arbeit*, 58.
18 Heinrich Lersch, "Arbeiterlied," *Volk an der Arbeit*, 5. The song was reprinted frequently, including in the DAF magazine *Arbeitertum* 3.7 (1933): 19. An early assessment of Lersch as a new type of worker poet can be found in Asta Südhaus, "Von Heinrich Lersch bis H.W. Leuchter: Deutsche Arbeiterdichtung," *Arbeitertum* 3.26 (1933): 8–10.
19 Ernst Wilhelm Balk, *Heinrich Lersch* (Munich: Deutscher Volksverlag, 1939), 4. For a recent assessment, see Steffen Elbing, "Heinrich Lersch—der Arbeiterdichter," in *Dichter für das Dritte Reich: Biografische Studien zum Verhältnis von Literatur und Ideologie*, ed. Rolf Düsterberg (Bielefeld: Aiesthesis, 2009), 133–158.
20 Hans Eiserlo, *Heinrich Lersch, ein deutscher Arbeiterdichter* (Würzburg: Konrad Triltsch, 1937), 37. Lersch also wrote *Die Pioniere von Eilenburg* (1934), a novel about the early workers' movement.

mous Joseph Nadler proclaimed that "through Lersch, the German workers completed the transition from world citizenship to fatherland, from class society to folk community, from state to Reich."[21] Interestingly, the equation of workers' poetry with a position of ambivalence would be revived in a much later comment by Martin Walser, then still a man of the New Left, for whom Lersch's life story exemplifies "how someone cannot become a proletarian" because of his religious faith and patriotic pride, with the implications for a scholarly assessment of his oeuvre far from clear.[22]

Lersch's self-editing (or self-censorship) illustrates how the substitution of "workerdom" for "proletariat" was meant to reconcile socialist and populist elements in the name of nationalism and resolve their competing claims on the worker as the embodiment of the people. Sometimes his revisions involve nothing more than a single adjective or noun. For instance, "Wir sind die Soldaten der neuen Armee" of 1930 begins with "We are the soldiers of the new army" and ends with "We are the loving proletariat, / The original brothers of the world." In the 1934 version, the newly Nazified lines read (with changes in italics): "We are the soldiers of the *brown* army" and "We are the soldiers of the *working folk*, / The *hammering* brothers of the world!"[23] Elsewhere a reference to "God's earth" in the 1918 version of "Wir Werkleute" (We workmen) becomes "German soil" in the 1934 version.[24] In all such cases, the revisionist process involves two sets of equivalencies, between "German" and "worker" and between "worker" and "National Socialist," that magically overcome the social and political divisions of the past and, with ecstatic tones reminiscent of utopian socialism, imagine the worker of the future as the personification of collective joy, pride, and nobility.

Despite these revisions, the voices of the workers continued to be haunted by the inequities and injustices of class society. On the one hand, Lersch depicts the workers' journey from powerlessness to empowerment in the essentializing terms that present their suffering as an integral part of the human condition. On the

---

21 Josef Nadler, *Literaturgeschichte des Deutschen Volkes: Dichtung und Schrifttum der deutschen Stämme und Landschaften*, 4 vols. (Berlin: Propyläen, 1941), 4:321.
22 Martin Walser, afterword to Heinrich Lersch, *Hammerschläge: Ein Roman von Menschen und Maschinen* (Frankfurt am Main: Suhrkamp, 1980), 267. The novel was first published in 1930.
23 Heinrich Lersch, "Wir sind die Soldaten der neuen Armee," in *Ausgewählte Werke in zwei Bänden*, ed. Johannes Klein (Düsseldorf: Diederichs, 1965), 1:370 and "Soldaten der braunen Armee," in *Mit brüderlicher Stimme: Gedichte* (Stuttgart: DVA, 1934), 179–180. Italics added for emphasis. The 1930 version was printed with sheet music in *Werkgesang: Lieder des Werkvolkes* (Cologne: Werkjugendsekretariat, 1930), 8–9. "Brown army" refers to the SA.
24 Lersch, "Wir Werkleute all," in *Deutschland! Lieder und Gesänge von Volk und Vaterland* (Berlin: Eugen Diederichs, 1918), 91 and "Wir Werkleute all," in *Mit brüderlicher Stimme*, 176. In the 1933 collection *Volk an der Arbeit*, the term is still "Gottes Erde."

other, he introduces new distinctions based on ethnic identities in order to enlist the old dream of community in a very different struggle for *Lebensraum* bound to end in war and genocide. At the end of World War I, Lersch still draws on Marxist and Christian terminology when he confesses to his readers that "Like you I am a mere servant, / A prole by the grace of God."[25] Sixteen years later, all references to the struggle of the workers are replaced by hackneyed clichés involving the spirit of the folk. His new definition of the worker poet as someone who "dream[s] about miracles and about beauty / in the land of yearning called your soul"[26] explains why psychologization became the preferred strategy of retreating from the political demands of the workers' movement. The transformation of socialism into a spiritual phenomenon henceforth defined the conditions through which the problem of class was to be translated into racialized terms. Whereas emotions in nineteenth-century workers' poetry often functioned as a radicalizing force, their effect after 1933 amounted to the exact opposite: the complete separation of work from its social and economic conditions. The experience of community became reduced to the individualizing terms that, as the KPD-affiliated writers rightly pointed out about their Nazi colleagues in the making, precluded any analysis of its compensatory function in revolutionary struggles.

Lersch's extensive self-editing can be studied exemplarily in "Es kommt dein Tag" (Your day cometh), a poem first published in 1918 and republished in 1934. The main exhibit in scholarly discussions on the ideological adaptability of workers' poetry, the original version is often referred to by the opening lines "What Causes Your Pain, Prole?" The promise made to the worker at the end of the original version reads as follows: "When the world one day understands you and your deed, / You are redeemed. *Your day cometh, prole!*" In the 1934 version, this pledge becomes a statement of fact: "When your deed serves as a model throughout the lands, / You are redeemed. *You are no longer a prole!*"[27] Despite this promise of closure, class resentment survives the editing process in the allusion to past strug-

---

25 Lersch, "Selbstbildnis," in *Deutschland!*, 138.
26 Lersch," Arbeiterdichter," in *Mit brüderlicher Stimme*, 57.
27 Lersch, "Was schafft dir deinen Schmerz, Prolet?," in *Deutschland!*, 128 and "Es kommt dein Tag," in *Mit brüderlicher Stimme*, 130. Italics added for emphasis. An early version of "Was schafft dir deinen Schmerz," titled "An die Arbeiter," can be found in the 1916 anthology *Schulter an Schulter: Gedichte von drei Arbeitern* (Jena: Bernard Vopelius, 1916), 25. "Es kommt dein Tag" is also included in a luxury edition produced for Robert Ley's fiftieth birthday, titled *Arbeiter Bauern Soldaten*, ed. Reichsamt Deutsches Volksbildungswerk (Berlin: Buchdruckwerkstätte, 1940), n.p. Perhaps as an homage to the DAF organization, *Werkmann* has been replaced with *Werkleute*. Interestingly, a West German collection of Lersch's poems includes the Nazi-era version, and not the Weimar original; see Johannes Klein, ed. and intr., *Heinrich Lersch* (Düsseldorf: Eugen Diederichs, 1965), 448–450.

gles. Here Lersch's assertion that "for this world of the masters, you were and will forever be a prole" functions like a traumatic memory evoked time and again to confirm the superiority of the nationalist version of socialism. His closing declaration that "one day, you will be a free man in a free land of work"[28] implies that the National Socialist revolution eliminated the artificial distinction between manual and mental labor by instituting a shared ethos of work embodied by the folk community. The substitution of the archaic *Werkmann* (workman) in the 1934 version for the Communist *Prolet* of the 1918 version indicates that the state of redemption required a backward-looking social imaginary modeled on the guilds and crafts of feudal societies. To underscore this point, the entire first stanza is cited here with the original lines in brackets:

> Workman, what is the cause of your pain? [What causes your pain, prole?]
> That you, with all of your body and soul,
> Has given yourself completely to work, to labor,
> In courageous duty with a full heart: [Sustaining it with your soul:]
> And that nothing of you is resurrected through it,
> That caused you bitter pain. [That causes your pain, prole!][29]

Mensch im Eisen: Gesänge von Volk und Werk (1925, Man of iron: songs about folk and work), Lersch's best-known work, represents his most ambitious attempt at claiming the proletarian for a *völkisch* genealogy and of reconciling socialist and nationalist positions in the language of populism. Drawing on religious themes of suffering and salvation, he insists on the unity of individual and collective voices in a dream of community at once retrospective and anticipatory. First, he addresses his working-class reader as an equal – "Like you, I was a prole and worked for bread" – and speaks to shared experiences of labor exploitation and traumatization during the war years. Then he translates the Marxist call for self-emancipation into Christian terms – "Oh proletarian folk, why are you loudly flocking together? God wants you to redeem yourself" – and integrates the workers into an organic model of community – "mother of my people: the proletariat!" – no longer confined by the antagonistic structures of class society but still held back by the divisiveness of Marxist rhetoric.[30]

The Germanization of the worker in Lersch is inseparable from the masculinization of work and, by extension, of radical politics, a connection forged in the

---

28 Lersch, "Es kommt dein Tag," 130 (128 in the 1937 edition).
29 Lersch, "Was schafft dir deinen Schmerz, Prolet?," in *Deutschland!*, 128 and "Es kommt dein Tag," in *Mit brüderlicher Stimme*, 199. Italics added for emphasis.
30 Heinrich Lersch, *Mensch im Eisen: Gesänge von Volk und Werk* (Stuttgart: DVA, 1925), 7, 43, and 199.

trenches of World War I and exploited by rightwing narratives about military defeat, national humiliation, and republican betrayal. The abjection of the working man subsequently came to stand in for the fate of the German people as a whole, which Lersch at that time described in crudely sexualized terms: "Once proud! German! Brave! Wild! Filled with lust for battle and for death! / Now: Diligent and gutless! Obedient! / A large, a cheap whore, a poor, starving street whore who offers her holiest for a piece of bread! / There you are, proletariat, my fate, / from you, I came, to you, I return."[31] As part of a thus defined project of re-masculinization, the fight for the future of the German nation inspired an equally sexualized spectacle of work involving the mythical figure of the blacksmith: "Between hammer and anvil / When they become one through the strike of my arm, / Currents, as between man and woman, / Work-semen, between hammer and anvil – / Shivers of unification passing through and through. Mythical moment! Reverberating screams of conception! / Sounding man and woman, sounding hammer and anvil."[32]

About a decade later, the *völkisch* teleology of workerdom found full articulation in *Mit brüderlicher Stimme* (1934, With a brotherly voice). "All of us working people, under the blue cloth, have a soul like you," Lersch now declares, "All of us working people weld together a new folk in proud freedom."[33] However, such a glorious future is imaginable only in the heightened terms that transform the socialist critique of capitalism into a triumphalist narrative of folk and race, complete with public performances of joy and pride. The result is a compensatory fantasy that reduces the original provocation of agitational poetry written since 1848 to mere eruptions of ecstatic communitarianism: "In millions of human hearts, / Faith joyfully takes up residence: / What the hands of the folk create, / Should be owned by the folk. / Land and freedom our possession, / Human dignity our right! / Strength shall yield to weakness. / In brotherly terms: no one the master and no one the slave."[34] Even in his wretched appearance as a despised prole, the proletarian from then on could no longer be part of any celebratory "Morning Song of the New Worker." Now the racial state brought into being through the new terms of exclusion determined the symbolic function of work and worker – reason enough in the next section to consider the role of literary scholarship in making sense of these discursive realignments.

---

31 Lersch, *Mensch im Eisen*,145–146. The quote appears on 150–151 in *Das dichterische Werk* (Stuttgart: DVA, 1934).
32 Lersch, *Mensch im Eisen*, 193 (199 in the 1934 version).
33 Lersch, "Wir Werkleute all," in *Mit brüderlicher Stimme*, 176. "Blue cloth" refers to the *blaue Bluse*, the traditional work shirt worn by industrial laborers.
34 Lersch, "Morgenlied der neuen Arbeiter," in *Mit brüderlicher Stimme*, 174.

II

Numerous dissertations written during the Nazi years examined the image of the worker in German literature, an indication both of heightened scholarly interest in the topic and of the Nazification of *Germanistik* as an academic discipline. All sought to clarify the subgenre's precarious status as *völkisch* literature during the Wilhelmine and Weimar years and evaluate its contribution to the discourse of workerdom. Ernst Jelken restated existing positions by calling workers the embodiment of the people; the poems, he concluded, are expressions of the "unspent, unrestrained force, the immediacy and original strength of the worker's feelings."[35] Through the new type of worker, "the prole of the class struggle is defeated at last, and the German worker begins."[36] Locating workers' poetry within a historical struggle for freedom and equality, Eleonore Tinnefeld boldly declared that the Nazi takeover of power created the conditions for the self-abolition of workers' poetry. In her words, "the historical integration of the worker as a new estate, which in the life of the folk has now reached an end and a new beginning, must also find an end in poetry."[37] In 1932, Minna Loeb had taken a very different sociological approach and analyzed the worker poets' individualistic solutions as typical manifestations of false consciousness. Her hope "that the working class will gain political power and cultural significance and that the petty-bourgeois interclass will eventually complete the transition to the proletariat on the level of consciousness"[38] would soon be disproven by the realities on the ground. Predictably, Hans Hermann Schulz in 1940 denounced Loeb's interpretation as obviously "Jewish" and countered her argument for the importance of critique with two key terms from the toolbox of Nazi *Germanistik*, *Volkstumserlebnis* (experience of the folk) and *Werkverbundenheit* (connection to the work) that foreground the emotional quality of literature.[39] A firm believer in the transformative power of literature, Adolf Bartels, an influential *völkisch* thinker, declared as late

---

35 Ernst Jelken, *Die Dichtung des deutschen Arbeiters* (Jena: Frommann, 1938), 5 and 20.
36 Jelken, *Die Dichtung des deutschen Arbeiters*, 63.
37 Eleonore Tinnefeld, "Der soziale Kampf in der deutschen Arbeiterdichtung" (PhD diss., University of Leipzig, 1938), 74. The same year saw the publication of Arno Mulot, *Der Arbeiter in der deutschen Dichtung unserer Zeit* (Stuttgart: Metzler, 1938).
38 Minna Loeb, "Die Ideengehalte der Arbeiterdichtung" (PhD diss., University of Giessen, 1932), 195.
39 See Hans Hermann Schulz, *Das Volkstumserlebnis des Arbeiters in der Dichtung von Gerrit Engelke, Heinrich Lersch und Karl Bröger* (Würzburg: Konrad Triltsch, 1940).

as 1943 that Nazi literature was still in the process of becoming and moving toward "an era when literary and political greatness will be one."[40]

In many German literary histories, workers' poetry is rightly recognized as the most significant literary expression of the workers' movement, with the poets associated with the 1848 Revolution (Georg Weerth, Georg Herwegh, Friedrich Freiligrath, Heinrich Heine) and the founders of Social Democracy (Ferdinand Lassalle, Wilhelm Hasenclever) cited as important influences. The countless poems written by, for, and about workers since the early years of the industrial revolution functioned as an integral part of working-class culture, its associations, anniversaries, festivities, publications, and forms of sociability: in short, the beginnings of what has been called an oppositional or alternative public sphere. Poems were regularly published in the daily newspapers and cultural journals of the Social Democratic Party press and included in the popular *Arbeiterkalender* (workers' almanac) marketed annually since the 1880s as a socialist version of the *Volkskalender* (people's almanac) – a first indication of the full compatibility of class and folk in the poetic imagination. The astonishing appeal of workers' poetry can be measured by the voluminous collections put together by new publishing houses associated with the SPD and, later, the KPD. A particularly ambitious undertaking, *Deutsche Arbeiter-Dichtung*, first appeared in 1893 and grew into five thick volumes featuring poems and songs by Wilhelm Hasenclever, Karl Frohme, Adolf Lepp, and many others.[41]

Several factors contributed to the popularity of poetry as the voice of the oppressed. Poems required little time commitment or formal education from readers and could be enjoyed in contemplative private moments as well as festive public events. Especially when combined with music to become workers' songs, the subgenre drew on community-based folk traditions in ways that the novel as the quintessential genre of bourgeois interiority could not. Moreover, the diverse body of work categorized as workers' poetry covered a wide range of class-specific topics and drew on various established formats. The popularity of older verse forms such as ballads and hymns points to the enduring influence of the oral traditions, dialogic formats, and didactic uses of literature prevalent in precapitalist societies. Meanwhile, the penchant for allegory and mythology and the affinity for heroic and sentimental modalities reveal a heavy debt to German Romanticism and its cherished fantasy of the people as one. Last but not least, the endurance of the proletarian pastoral and other examples of socialist kitsch speak to a continuing

---

[40] Adolf Bartels, *Geschichte der deutschen Literatur* (Berlin: Georg Westermann, 1943), 768.
[41] See the anthology *Deutsche Arbeiter-Dichtung: Eine Auswahl Lieder und Gedichte deutscher Proletarier*, 5 vols., vol. 1: *Wilhelm Hasenclever*, vol. 2: *Jacob Audorf*, vol. 3: *anon.*, vol. 4: *Max Kegel*, vol. 5: *Andreas Scheu* (Stuttgart: Dietz, 1893).

desire for escaping the oppressive conditions of wage labor through compensatory scenarios involving nature; the same could be said about the many poems about women, children, and romantic love.

The various terms of self-identification – worker or proletarian, class or estate – available throughout the late nineteenth century left plenty of room for patriotic, nationalist, and *völkisch* sentiments that ignored left-right distinctions and combined Marxist terminology with older languages of belonging. For instance, "Die Arbeitsmänner" (The working men), written in 1870 by the socialist-turned-anarchist Johann Most and later chosen by the KPD as one of their fight songs, moves effortlessly between the ethnonationalist and internationalist perspectives represented by the "working men" and the "proletariat," respectively. With surprising ease, the descriptive tone of "They are the working men, the proletariat!" in the opening line first becomes the exhortative "Awaken, you working men! Up, proletariat!," then explodes into the imperative "To battle, you working men! Up, proletariat!," and concludes with the declarative "Then you triumph, working men, the proletariat!"[42]

During the prewar and war years, workers' poetry continued to service two very different emotional registers in working-class culture, the register of resistance, with its occasional eruptions of rage and defiance, and the register of accommodation, with its almost obligatory expressions of suffering and resignation.[43] The following examples confirm that these two sides cannot be equated with specific parties such as the revolutionary KPD or reformist SPD but must be seen as manifestations of the many nonsimultaneities, including the debt to religious traditions and the influence of folk culture, that made workers' poetry a repository of experiences of discrimination and oppression but also of unity and solidarity. Mapping a course of empowerment, Paul Gent's "Arbeiterpsyche" (1910, The psyche of the worker) opens with painful memories of being called "the least and the last in the hierarchy of classes" known as "lowly proles" and "dirty plebs" but ends with a passionate appeal to the workers to embrace such derogatory labels and turn them into political weapons: "We're proud of it! We make demands – and do not beg! – / For us the same respect! For us the same

---

[42] Johannes Most, "Die Arbeitsmänner," in KPD and KJD, eds., *Kampflieder* (Berlin: Vereinigung internationaler Verlagsanstalten, 1923), n.p.

[43] Emotional regime is a term coined by William M. Reddy to describe the particular mode of emotional expression prevalent in a particular historical time or social milieu. Emotional community is Barbara Rosenwein's term for analyzing the social basis of shared norms and forms of emotional expression. See William M. Reddy, *The Navigation of Feelings: A Framework for the History of Emotions* (Cambridge: Cambridge University Press, 2001) and Barbara Rosenwein, *Emotional Communities in the Early Middle Ages* (Ithaca, NY: Cornell University Press, 2006).

rights! / For us culture, too! The treasures of the earth / For all of humanity."⁴⁴ Drawing on Christian imagery, Michael Friedrich Eisenlohr, in "Das Gebet des Tagelöhners" (1912, Prayer of the day laborer) takes a very different approach when he summons his readers to find solace in righteousness: "We have been created by the same God, / Yet he created me in robes of dust / And you in full abundance / And me with a beggar's hand."⁴⁵ Intent on nationalizing the worker question, Friedrich Wilhelm Weber, in "Arbeit" (1919, Work) introduces the qualifier "German" to turn what he treats as an existential truth, "To be a worker – we all must do it. / To be a worker – we all know it" into a unifying idea, namely, "That only work, leading out of need and night, / Can bring the German folk into the light."⁴⁶

Workers' poetry is often described in generational terms, with the two choices available around the turn of the century – renewal or decline, revolution or reform, innovation or tradition – reflected in the class habitus of its main representatives. Lersch, Bröger, and Barthel were all born during the 1880s and 1890s, grew up among impoverished craftsmen and tradespeople, worked as apprentices and factory laborers, became involved in various workers' groups, and suffered traumatic injuries in World War I, with the decisions to write for a living as much an economic necessity as an artistic choice. The larger forces of industrialization and urbanization and the individual experiences of discrimination and exploitation established the historical backdrop against which they channeled workers' fears, hopes, and desires into presumably universal themes, starting with the equation of man with mankind. Yet unlike the members of the KPD's BPRS, whose main goal was to advance the idea of class struggle, the worker poets sought to assert their sense of self against these structural inequalities, explore the spiritual dimension of work as national service, and validate pain and suffering as part of the human condition.

The career of Max Barthel corroborates how class-based grievances and resentments could be entirely compatible with changing political allegiances from SPD to KPD to NSDAP. Like many men of his generation, Barthel was radicalized by war and revolution, disillusioned with the Left during the world economic crisis, and reenergized by the Nazi promise of a strong, unified Germany. *The Immortal Folk*, a movement novel discussed in the previous chapter, draws extensively on his own experience of political conversion. The Nazis, in turn, saw Barthel's con-

---

44 Paul Gent, "Arbeiterpsyche," in Rudolf Broda and Julius Deutsch, *Das moderne Proletariat: Eine sozialpsychologische Studie* (Berlin: Georg Reimer, 1910), 171.
45 Michael Friedrich Eisenloh, "Das Gebet des Tagelöhners," *Des deutschen Arbeiters Herz- und Hammerschläge* (Mönchengladbach: Volksvereins-Verlag, 1912), 72.
46 Friedrich Wilhelm Weber, "Arbeit," in *Arbeiter: Das deutsche Volk im Werktagsgewand und was seine Kraft schaffen und tragen kann*, ed. Ernst Weber (Munich: Callwey, 1919), 5–6.

frontational tone as a welcome alternative to the miserabilist depictions of working-class life associated with Social Democracy. "Fellows! Worker poets!" he proclaimed in 1914: "Do away with the ditties! / No more declarations of suffering in verses" and then demanded: "Compose songs that are alive!"[47] Barthel's increasingly aggressive attitude can be traced in the titles of poetry collections such as *Die Faust* (1920, The fist) and *Lasset uns die Welt gewinnen!* (1920, Let us conquer the world!) and the confrontational tone throughout *Arbeiterseele* (1920, Worker's soul). "We are coming, the slaves, claiming our power, / Making wishes and dreams come true," he declared and issued a clear warning to anyone putting up resistance: "When we proletarians march through the cities, everything bends to our will."[48] In the KPD's *Rote Fahne*, even Gertrud Alexander cited Barthel's *Worker's Soul* as a model for working through the contradictions of proletarian culture of being at once partisan in its revolutionary stance and universal in its humanist message.[49] Ten years later, the critics of the KPD's *Linkskurve* called the formal shortcomings of workers' poetry evidence of its complete ideological corruption. Now Johannes R. Becher accused its representatives "of softening up the proletariat through lyrical means and, through 'aesthetic moods,' making them accept their fate at the conveyer belt and the machine."[50] For KPD author Rudolf Braune, little was left to say about "those clowns known as worker poets."[51]

---

[47] Max Barthel, "Kerls, Arbeiterdichter," *Der Strom* 4.5 (August 1914): 129. For an example of the treatment of Barthel in leftist scholarship, see Martin Rector, "Über die allmähliche Verflüchtigung einer Identität beim Schreiben über das Problem des 'Renegatentums' bei Max Barthel," in *Kunst und Kultur im deutschen Faschismus*, ed. Ralf Schnell (Stuttgart: Metzler, 1978), 261–284. For a recent biography written by his son, see Karl Wolfgang Barthel, *Der Dichter und die Diktatoren: Eine Biografie* (Berlin: Kramer, 2011).
[48] Max Barthel, "Rebellion" and "Aufbruch," in *Arbeiterseele: Verse von Fabrik, Krieg, Landstraße, Wanderschaft und Revolution* (Jena: Eugen Diederichs, 1920), 16 and 132.
[49] Gertrud Alexander, review of *Arbeiterseele*, *Die Rote Fahne*, 26 August 1920.
[50] Johannes R. Becher, "Vor dem 2. Weltkongreß der revolutionären Literatur," *Linkskurve* 2.10 (1930): 14.
[51] Rudolf Braune, "Arbeiterliteratur," *Die literarische Welt* 5.28 (1929): 4. Weimar-era anthologies of workers' poetry with modern or modernist sensibilities include Kurt Offenburg, ed., *Arbeiterdichtung der Gegenwart* (Frankfurt am Main: Mittelland, 1925); Karl Bröger, ed., *Jüngste Arbeiterdichtung* (Berlin: Arbeiterjugend-Verlag, 1929), and Otto Schulz, ed., *Im Takte der Maschinen: Gedichte vom Rhythmus der Arbeit* (Breslau: Ferdinand Hirt, 1932).

III

About forty years later, these worker poets were rediscovered by the proponents of *kritische Germanistik* who, on the one hand, claimed their voices for a forgotten history of working-class culture and, on the other, used the poems' deficiencies to work through questions of ideology and aesthetics within the larger debates consuming the West German New Left. Since then, ideology critique in the broadest sense has played a decisive role in analyzing how the Nazis during the first years of the regime established cultural hegemony in the Gramscian sense. In the case of literature, it has proven fairly easy to reconstruct the processes by which key ideas about work and community not only became normative but also naturalized – that is, considered real and true despite evidence to the contrary. What has not been examined is how workers' poetry contributed to these processes by drawing on emotional registers – the despair of powerlessness, the demand for recognition, the yearning for belonging – established during the late nineteenth century and increasingly at odds with the obligatory performances of joy and pride orchestrated by the German Labor Front.

Far removed from the mass spectacles that have come to signify the aestheticization of politics in fascism, workers' poetry after all belonged to a very different politics of emotions that, traceable across a range of literary forms and practices, favored two equally passive modalities: suffering under the conditions of inequality *and* blind trust in the inevitability of change, existential loneliness and despair *and* paeans to harmony and unity, and, to express it in explicitly political terms, acceptance of the defeat of the working class *and* belief in the final coming of a society beyond classes. With its main themes and motifs well-established since the Wilhelmine years, workers' poetry after 1933 continued to provide a space to express discontent even after the deletion of proletarian signifiers, proof that aesthetic experiences are above all an effect of the elusive connections formed between words and meanings. The resultant mixture of class antagonism, utopian socialism, and political defeatism was animated by populist sentiments not always compatible with the new program of "beauty of labor" and "strength through joy," to cite two well-known initiatives of the German Labor Front. At the same time, it was precisely populist reason that had sustained the nonsimultaneous traditions in workers' poetry from the beginning.

The importance of reading workers' poetry as a repository of political emotions comes into clearer view through a brief look at the literary scholarship of the 1970s and 1980s that has become as obsolete as its subject of inquiry. Two tendencies can be identified: the analysis of workers' poetry as an expression of petty-bourgeois consciousness and the treatment of socialism and nationalism as incompatible ideologies. By ignoring the populist tendencies within workers' poetry, scholars have been able to concentrate on its compromises, failures, and betrayals. In a later overview of literature in the Third Reich, Uwe-K. Ketelsen rightly cautions against using programmatic statements from the times as evidence of ideological and aesthetic conformity, treating the Gleichschaltung of the institution of literature as proof of the existence of a fascist poetics complete with specific themes and styles, and reading the continuities in the representation of the workers as signs of a successful appropriation of socialist topoi rather than as evidence of the ongoing need for accommodation.[52]

Ketelsen's comments also describe the conditions under which West German scholarship on workers' poetry came to function as an integral part of the larger project of ideology critique and the concomitant search for examples of politically engaged literature. The rediscovery of workers' poetry occurred in the shadow of the New Left fascination with the revolutionary proletariat and its potential model character for oppositional voices and counterpublics. More often than not, critical assessments of the literary texts replicated Marxist and Leninist theories from the 1920s and 1930s and referenced key ideas about the dialectics of Enlightenment and the utopian potential of the aesthetic examined by the Frankfurt School. In less obvious ways, the placement of workers' poetry at the margins of the literary canon reproduced the aesthetic tastes of a postwar generation that remained suspicious of provincial sensibilities and religious modalities and equated democratic subjectivities primarily with modernist registers.

Measured by evaluative criteria that privilege literary technique and stylistic innovation, workers' poetry indeed offers few aesthetic pleasures and rewards. Aside from the ecstatic tones and spiritual ambitions of expressionist poetry, the historical avant-gardes had little impact on the formal and thematic choices of a group of writing workers born during the 1880s and far removed from the various experiments in modernism. The machine aesthetic of Erich Grisar remained the exception in a subgenre that looked to the precapitalist past even when celebrating technology and industry and that favored experiential intensities over the interventionist strategies modeled by Bertolt Brecht in a very different kind of workers' poetry titled "Fragen eines lesenden Arbeiters" (1935, Questions of a reading worker). Interestingly, Grisar ended up publishing his short stories in DAF's *Schönheit der Arbeit* journal (to be discussed in chapter 7).

Literary scholars associated with the New Left have read workers' poetry along rather predictable lines that include a discussion of the failures of the Old

---

52 See Uwe-K. Ketelsen, *Literatur und Drittes Reich* (Schernfeld: Süddeutsche Hochschul-Verlagsgesellschaft, 1992), 28–71; on the latter point, 286–304. For the larger context, see Sebastian Graeb-Könneker, *Autochtone Modernität: Eine Untersuchung der vom Nationalsozialismus geförderten Literatur* (Opladen: Westdeutscher Verlag, 1996).

Left in the face of the Nazi threat and the postwar transformation of the public sphere through new social movements. Arguments about definitions have played a crucial role in the resultant struggle over interpretations. Some Germanists have rejected the characterization of workers' poetry as poetry by, for, and about workers and proposed a more dynamic description based on the transformation of the worker from a victim of capitalist exploitation to an agent of revolutionary change. Assessing the contribution of individual poets, other scholars have weighed questions of literary quality against those of social relevance and excused any lapses in political judgment with reference to all-important messages about the necessity of social change. Questions of historical continuity have proven particularly relevant in attempts to either claim worker poets for a new history of German literature written from below or make them prime exhibits for the petty-bourgeois dispositions that inevitably turn prefascist tendencies into fascist commitments.

To give a few examples: Bernd Witte contributed to the search for suitable literary precursors when he likened early workers' literature to a "poetry of opposition."[53] By contrast, Jürgen Rühle dismissed the writings of Lersch and others as a "Social Democratic lyricism of uplift [and little more than] republican anniversary poetry,"[54] with truly radical voices only found among the authors organized in the BPRS. Early on, Helmut Lethen and Helga Gallas formulated what would become the standard complaint – namely, that the worker poets (to paraphrase) were nothing but peddlers in pseudo-emancipation, apologists for alienated labor, and promoters of the fascist ideology of work; their greatest failing, however, seems to have been "their infatuation with the self that turns everything external into mere material for feelings."[55] Drawing on traditional class analysis, Christoph Rülcker added a sociological perspective when he characterized workers' poetry as an mechanism of integration and explained its defeatist, quietist habitus with reference to the downward mobility experienced by "proletarianized petty-bourgeois families."[56] Professing his political revulsion and aesthetic disgust, Rainer Stollmann concluded that "the historical workers' poetry is trash – aesthetically

---

53 Bernd Witte, "Literatur der Opposition: Über Geschichte, Funktion und Wirkmittel der frühen Arbeiterliteratur," in *Handbuch zur deutschen Arbeiterliteratur*, ed. Heinz Ludwig Arnold (Munich: edition text + kritik, 1977), 12.
54 Jürgen Rühle, *Literatur und Revolution: Die Schriftsteller und der Kommunismus* (Cologne: Kiepenhauer & Witsch, 1960), 180.
55 Helmut Lethen and Helga Gallas, "Arbeiterdichtung—Proletarische Literatur: Eine historische Skizze," *Alternative* 9.51 (1966): 158.
56 Christoph Rülcker, *Ideologie der Arbeiterdichtung 1914–1933: Eine wissenssoziologische Untersuchung* (Stuttgart: Metzler, 1970), 26.

and politically."⁵⁷ In an attempt to rescue at least some viable elements for then-contemporary debates about oppositional voices in literature, Wolfgang Eggerstorfer modified the distinction between workers' literature and literature of work from the Nazi period in order to better separate the culture of critique associated with the former from the forms of interpellation modeled by the latter.⁵⁸

Scholarly assessments of workers' literature in the wider sense have furthermore been troubled by a continued unwillingness to recognize its considerable debt to nationalist, *völkisch, and* populist representations of the people and, closely related, to take seriously those writers for whom socialist commitments were entirely compatible with nationalist identifications. The leftist romance with the organized workers of the big cities, large factories, and modern industries rarely extended to the world of small-town craftsmen and rural workers and the traditions associated with the preindustrial guild system. The resultant blind spots have been made worse by approaches to periodization that neatly separate the historical "aberration," alternatively called Nazi literature or literature in the Third Reich, from broader developments in Weimar, exile, and postwar literature. Most studies on workers' poetry simply end in 1932/33 – despite the continuities that assured many worker poets at least some role in the reimaginings of workerdom during the Nazi years.⁵⁹

Confirming the fluidity of nationalist and socialist identifications, the revisionist strategies employed by the worker poets can in fact be read as a symptom of what Bloch calls the nonsimultaneities (*Ungleichzeitigkeiten*) of capitalist development, including their resonances in hegemonic *and* counterhegemonic practices. Such nonsimultaneities draw attention to the continued influence of regional, rural, and provincial culture and the forgotten voices, vanishing traditions, and peripheral sensibilities preserved in these geographic and conceptual hinterlands. Moreover, thinking of workers' poetry as an archive of political emotions means mapping the diminished relevance of nineteenth- and early twentieth-century poetic registers of sentiment and pathos and their increasingly limited ability to articulate working-class grievances and resentments across the ideological divides of

---

57 Rainer Stollmann, *Ästhetisierung der Politik: Literaturstudien zum subjektiven Faschismus* (Stuttgart: Metzler, 1978), 11.
58 See Wolfgang Eggerstorfer, *Schönheit und Adel der Arbeit: Arbeitsliteratur im Dritten Reich* (Frankfurt am Main: Peter Lang, 1988).
59 Rülcker's *Ideologie der Arbeiterdichtung* and Günter Heintz's annotated collection *Deutsche Arbeiterdichtung 1910–1933* (1974) take different starting points but both end in 1932/33; the same is true for Heinz-Ludwig Arnold's later volume on *Arbeiterlyrik* (2003). Because of considerations of space, the East German perspective on workers' poetry cannot be considered here; see Friedrich G. Kürbisch, *Anklage und Botschaft: Die lyrische Aussage der Arbeiter seit 1900* (Berlin: Dietz, 1969).

the early twentieth century. Bloch, who had a keen understanding of the power of populist movements and popular cultures, coined the term "nonsimultaneities" partly to make sense of the incomplete nature of modernization in "the classical land of nonsimultaneity" (i.e., Germany) and draw attention to the enduring viability of practices grounded in precapitalist times and structures. In similar ways, the simultaneity of nonsimultaneities haunts the emotional registers of (dis)empowerment that sustained workers' poetry before and after 1933 and today makes it a useful case study for tracking the slow disappearance of working-class culture throughout the twentieth culture.[60]

As regards the study of old and new populisms, reading workers' poetry as a repository of emotions not only safeguards against timeworn assumptions about (leftist) political critique and (modernist) literary form but also raises important questions about the historically specific function of the national and regional in relation to working-class literature, including in the context of international developments and internationalist sentiments. Furthermore, closer attention to the genealogies of populism as an oppositional habitus not only extends the dreams of community from the Vormärz period to the Third Reich and beyond but also introduces a possible model for rereading from the perspective of precarity in the postindustrial, postnational age of globalization.[61]

In short, approaching workers' poetry as a laboratory and archive of emotions means paying special attention to populism as a fantasy of the people that depends on essentialist definitions of class, nation, and community in order to continuously redraw the boundary between the fantasy of the people as one and the specter of a threatening Other. Worker poets after 1933 set out to adapt and preserve the qualities that had made poetry such an important vehicle for marginalized, silenced, and excluded voices. Through their efforts and their failures, they turned the German worker into an important conduit from the antagonism inscribed in class discourse to the externalization of otherness in race discourse. Workers' poetry after 1933 developed its unique brand of literary revision(ism) under conditions that included its active promotion by Nazi scholars, its reduced status in the culture of the Third Reich, and its subsequent exclusion from the histories of socialist literature

---

60 See Ernst Bloch, "Nonsynchronism and the Obligation to its Dialectics," trans. Mark Ritter, *New German Critique* 11 (1977): 22–38. "Nonsynchronous" is an alternative translation of the term.
61 On the first point, see Patrick Eiden-Offe, *Die Poesie der Klasse: Romantischer Antikapitalismus und die Erfindung des Proletariats* (Berlin: Matthes & Seitz, 2017). For a comparative European approach, see Magnus Nilsson and John Lennon, eds., *Working-Class Literature(s): Historical and International Perspectives*, 2 vols. (Stockholm: University of Stockholm, Press, 2017–2020). On contemporary definitions of working-class writing beyond class, also see Perera Sonali, *No Country: Working-Class Writing in the Age of Globalization* (New York: Columbia University Press, 2014).

and workers' literature. The Thingspiel, another failed experiment modeled on Weimar-era socialist traditions, attempted something very similar on the level of cultic practices. Here the absorption of the worker into the fascist mass spectacle promised to shatter traditional genre categories and explore the possibilities of public performance, spectacle, and ritual. Once again, the figure of the worker stood at the center of sustained official efforts at what could be called suppression through appropriation.

Chapter 4
The *Thingspiel* and the Performance of Class

> Herald: Tell what you saw, and proclaim what you believe
> So that we may profess what we want to believe.
> Eberhard Wolfgang Möller, *Die Verpflichtung*

Few scenes from the Nazi-era *Thingspiel* (choric theater or choral play) capture the performative quality of political emotions better than the herald's instructions on believing or, rather, wanting to believe.[1] The "You" in *Die Verpflichtung* (1935, The covenant) is called "All" in the dramatis personae, a multitude still lacking form and direction. Yet an unnamed "We" is about to come into existence through this public declaration of faith, a "We" henceforth called folk community.[2] Significantly, it is the workers who complete the transition from a divided class society to a unified folk community, reason enough to look more closely at the overdetermined function of class-based categories in the staging of Germany's rebirth.[3] That means paying closer attention to the role of mass performance and, more generally, symbolic politics in repurposing the figure of the worker. It also means recognizing the institutional challenges and intermedial possibilities of mass mobilization (e.g., architecture, broadcasting) and treating the Thingspiel as an important step toward the full convergence of performance, spectacle, and politics achieved by Leni Riefenstahl in *Triumph des Willens* (1935, *Triumph of the Will*).

Like workers' poetry, the Thingspiel is obsessed with scenes of interpellation: their social dimensions, cultic elements, and emotional effects. Coined by Cologne theater scholar Carl Niessen, the term alludes to the *Thingplatz* (place or space)

---

1 Eberhard Wolfgang Möller, *Die Verpflichtung* (Berlin: Albert Langen/Georg Müller, 1935), 7. Möller wrote what is generally regarded as the most famous Thingspiel, *Das Frankenburger Würfelspiel*, which premiered at the 1936 Olympic Games.
2 The large body of research on the notion of Volksgemeinschaft includes Michael Wildt, *Hitler's Volksgemeinschaft and the Dynamics of Racial Exclusion*, trans. Bernard Heise (New York: Berghahn, 2012).
3 Other Thingspiele that restage the struggles of the *Systemzeit* include (in chronological order) Gustav Goes's *Aufbricht Deutschland: Ein Stadionspiel der nationalen Revolution* (1933) and *Opferflamme der Arbeit: Ein Freilichtspiel* (1934), Julius Maria Becker's *Deutsche Notwende: Epischer Sprechchor in zwei Teilen* (1933), Hans Jürgen Nierentz's *Symphonie der Arbeit* (1934), Max Barthel's *Das Spiel vom deutschen Arbeitsmann* (1934), Kurt Eggers's *Das große Wandern: Ein Spiel vom ewigen deutschen Schicksal* (1934), Erich Müller-Schnick's *Soldaten der Scholle* (1935), Heinrich Zerkaulen's *Der Arbeit die Ehr': Ein deutsches Weihespiel für die Freilichtbühne* (1935), and Kurt Eggers, *Schüsse bei Krupp: Ein Spiel aus deutscher Dämmerung* (1937) about the violent clashes on 31 March 1923 between French troops and Krupp workers.

used by the Germanic tribes for public assemblies and religious practices; it refers to outdoor performances with ritual qualities and propagandistic aims. Alternative terms such as *chorisches Gedicht* (choral poem), *Weihespiel* (consecration play), *Aufmarschspiel* (marching play), and *Werkspiel* (work or factory play) indicate a formal eclecticism that confirms the primary emphasis on cultic functions. Combining poetic, dramatic, and musical forms, taking elements from military parades, church liturgies, and mass sports, and utilizing the spatial effects of architecture and light design, the Thingspiel was all about forming, moving, and controlling multitudes on and off the stage. Instead of psychologically motivated characters and realistic stage settings, performances offered up (simulations of) participation in the folk and the ethos of work. Intent on making this new type of theater a model of communalization in public life, writers, directors, architects, and party bureaucrats joined forces to overcome the traditional distinction between actors and audiences and integrate the staging of community into other performances of the political.

Under these circumstances, what does it mean to demand declarations of faith without mentioning any shared values or beliefs? Do the acts of "proclaiming" and "professing" create the very commitments that these instructions demand? Does the process not reduce community to mere ritual acts and cultic functions? If these questions are answered with "yes," how can such paradigmatic scenes be used to make sense of the Thingspiel's peculiar obsession with the Weimar working class? Are these moments part of an emerging event culture that aligns socialist legacies and national(ist) policies with mass cultural practices? How can these performances shed light on one of the more puzzling aspects of Nazi culture, the simultaneous elimination of the working class from the social imaginary and its reappearance in these ritualized evocations of workerdom? And to extend this inquiry to the relationship between mass culture and political culture, how does the failure of the Thingspiel complicate widespread assumptions about the ecstasies of the folk?[4]

At first glance, the dialogue from *The Covenant* reads like a typical example of interpellation, of being hailed in the Althusserian sense. The final declaration "We believe in the God. / [...] We believe in the land. / [...] We believe in the folk"[5] ref-

---

4 On the discussion on mass culture as a critical category, see the special issue on "The Origins of Mass Culture: The Case of Imperial Germany 1871–1918," in *New German Critique* 29 (1983). On the new cultural history of politics, see Thomas Mergel, "Überlegungen zu einer Kulturgeschichte der Politik," *Geschichte und Gesellschaft* 28.4 (2002): 574–606, and Kathleen Canning, "Culture of Politics—Politics of Culture: New Perspectives on the Weimar Republic: The Politics of Symbols, Semantics, and Sentiments in the Weimar Republic," *Central European History* 43 (2010): 567–580.
5 Möller, *Die Verpflichtung*, 13.

erences key Nazi concepts such as the leadership principle and the myth of blood and soil and confirms their formative roles in aligning the fantasy of the people with the goals of the racial state. For audiences to be moved in the emotional and political sense, however, these performances of community have to designate those who, in the making of We, are to be excluded from the original group of All. In predictable ways, these exclusions establish German identity in racial(ized) terms and confirm antisemitism as the new master narrative. Moreover, the introduction of a unified, empowered We is predicated on the selective appropriation of socialist iconographies that advance masculinist versions of class and community. "We," in other words, stands for the promise of Aryanizing and masculinizing the nation. The overdetermined figure of the worker aligns both processes by keeping alive the memory of class struggles within the new culture of work.

All of the Thingspiele set during the Weimar years revolve around workers as the main subjects and subject matter. Time and again the workers are called upon to reenact the liberation of the people from the false promises of Marxism and embrace National Socialism as the only protection against the double threat of (finance) capitalism and Bolshevism. Enthusiastic declarations of collective will, "Wir sind bereit" (We are willing/ready), announce their imminent transformation into "soldiers of work" ready to join performances of community that invariably extend beyond the stage. The integration of memories of class struggle into this nationalist version of socialism depends heavily on the ability of cultic functions in redefining the political as an emotional experience – reason enough to pay special attention to the cultic as a unique product of the historical convergence of mass culture and political culture.

This chapter extends the class-to-race argument of the previous chapters into performative terms by considering the contribution of the Thingspiel to the transformation of the workers into the people – what one Nazi scholar called the *Volkswerdung des Arbeitertums* (racialization of workerdom).[6] Performance in this context involves a range of concepts and debates: performative politics and performing politics, political theater and the theatricality of politics, and, most importantly, the relationship between performative populism and performative socialism. In reconstructing these dynamics, the chapter first addresses the problems with analyzing the Thingspiel as a product of Nazi cultural policy and ideology alone and ignoring the more elusive connections to mass discourse and its historical double, that of class analysis. The second part provides an overview of the official discussions among Nazi writers and functionaries on cultic elements and

---

6 Erich Trunz, *Deutsche Dichtung der Gegenwart: Eine Bildnisreihe* (Berlin: Georg Stilke, 1937), 36. The phrase comes from a chapter on Heinrich Lersch.

what they were supposed to achieve: namely, a performative approach to politics through which class differences could disappear into ritualized reenactments of community. The chapter's third part addresses the continued provocation of class through the thematic preoccupation with the Weimar years and, by extension, the socialist legacy. Finally, the fourth part draws on scenes from Richard Euringer's *Deutsche Passion 1933* (1933, German passion 1933) and Kurt Heynicke's *Neurode: Ein Spiel von deutscher Arbeit* (1935, Neurode: a play about German work) to show how the workers continued to function as both a source of instability and an instrument of integration. Given the multimedia ambitions of the Thingspiel initiative, it is only logical that the chapter concludes with the Reichsarbeitsdienst (Reich Labor Service, RAD) sequence from *Triumph of the Will*, Riefenstahl's famous film about the 1934 Nazi Party rally in Nuremberg.

I

Despite high expectations, the Thingspiel remained the outlier in a state-subsidized theater culture centered in the big cities and, after the modernist experimentation of the Weimar years, preoccupied with the canon of great works and beholden to the demand for well-made plays.[7] By most standards, the Thingspiel movement can

---

7 In addition to the excellent overview offered by Strobl (*The Swastika*), English-language introductions to the Thingspiel can be found in William Niven, "The Birth of Nazi Drama? Thing Plays," in *Theatre under the Nazis*, ed. John London (Manchester: Manchester University Press, 2000), 54–95, and Erika Fischer-Lichte, *Theatre, Sacrifice, Ritual: Exploring Forms of Political Theatre* (London: Routledge, 2005), 122–158. For general overviews of theater in the Third Reich, see (in chronological order) Joseph Wulf, *Theater und Film im Dritten Reich: Eine Dokumentation* (Gütersloh: Sigbert Mohn, 1964); Boguslaw Drewniak, *Das Theater im NS-Staat: Szenarium deutscher Zeitgeschichte 1933–1945* (Düsseldorf: Droste, 1983); Konrad Dussel, *Ein neues, ein heroisches Theater? Nationalsozialistische Theaterpolitik und ihre Auswirkungen in der Provinz* (Bonn: Bouvier, 1988); Glen W. Gadberry, ed., *Theatre in the Third Reich, the Prewar Years: Essays on Theater in Nazi Germany* (Westport, CT: Greenwood, 1995); Thomas Eicher, Barbara Panse, and Henning Rischbieter, eds., *Theater im Dritten Reich: Theaterpolitik, Spielplanstruktur, NS-Dramatik* (Seelze: Kallmeyer, 2000); and John London, ed., *Theatre under the Nazis* (Manchester: Manchester University Press, 2000). On Nazi festival culture and historical spectacle, also see Stefan Schweizer, *"Unserer Weltanschauung sichtbaren Ausdruck geben": Nationalsozialistische Geschichtsbilder in historischen Festzügen* (Göttingen: Wallstein, 2007). For a comparative perspective, also see Günter Berghaus, ed., *Fascism and Theatre: Comparative Studies on Aesthetics and Politics in Europe, 1925–1945* (Providence: Berghahn, 1996). On comparable developments in Fascist Italy, see Jeffrey T. Schnapp, *Staging Fascism: 18 BL and the Theater of Masses for Masses* (Stanford: Stanford University Press, 1996).

be described as a failed cultural and political experiment. The first years of the regime saw a flood of new initiatives: ambitious plans for the building of four hundred open-air theaters throughout the Reich, playwriting competitions resulting in countless submissions by enthusiastic folk comrades, and much-hyped public performances with tens of thousands of participants. Concerns about a lack of literary quality and declining public interest after 1935 did not stop Germanists from promoting the Thingspiel as evidence of the successful transformation of the *Schaubühne* (literally: viewing stage) into a *Versammlungsraum* (assembly space) and a first step toward the complete merging of theater and politics in the name of that mysterious essence called *Rassenseele* (racial soul).[8] Interestingly, it was growing opposition to the cultic elements that, in 1937, resulted in the withdrawal of all official support from the Thingspiel movement. In the end, only forty *Thingstätten* (Thing sites) were ever built. Whereas the plays and their authors have since been forgotten, several amphitheaters are still in use: the Waldbühne in Berlin, originally built for the 1936 Olympic Games for large concerts and events, the Kalkberg Stadium in Bad Segeberg for the annual Karl May Festival, and the Thingstätte in Heidelberg (until 2017) for unofficial Saint Walpurgis Night celebrations. The rest of this architecture of community has become part of the ruins of the Third Reich.

Defying conventional definitions, the Thingspiel contributed to the continuous blurring of the boundaries separating mass politics, performance, and spectacle and produced what Möller called a new kind of *Erlebnistheater* (theater of experience) built around the "cultic expression of mass feeling."[9] Indeed, the term "experience" captures best the aspirations of the entire Thingspiel movement: the rejection of the proscenium stage in favor of more open and dynamic relationships between performers and audiences, the introduction of the collective subject in the form of group choruses and allegorical figures, the reliance on parable and ritual as preferred didactic modalities, the exploration of the social, spatial, and multimedia potentialities of theater as a (surrogate) public space, and, above all, the emotional appeal of such performances of community irrespective of any specific content or context.

---

8 For example, see Bruno Nelissen Haken, "Erfahrung an Thingspielmanuskripten," *Bausteine zum deutschen Nationaltheater* 3 (1935): 136–141. By the same author, see "Das Volks- und Thingspiel," in *Hochschule und Ausland* 13.8 (1935): 55–65.
9 Eberhard Wolfgang Möller, "Die Verwandlung des deutschen Theaters," *Hochschule und Ausland* 13.4 (1935): 48. Describing German theater as an *Erlebnisgemeinschaft* was a common theme; compare Carl Maria Holzapfel," Aufbruch zum Nationaltheater," in *Bausteine zum deutschen Nationaltheater* 2.4 (1934), 115–117. On dramatic theory, also see Uwe-Karsten Ketelsen, *Heroisches Theater: Untersuchungen zur Dramentheorie des Dritten Reiches* (Bonn: Bouvier, 1968).

A thus-defined theater of experience is difficult to evaluate through conventional literary criteria. Yet like the historical failure of the Thingspiel movement, this difficulty also opens up the conceptual framework toward the significance of collective emotions as both product and producer in the new constellations of political spectacle and mass entertainment. The following questions can thus be used to clarify the underlying issues: Is the Thingspiel a secular version of the passion play or an early manifestation of what has been termed postdramatic theater (Hans-Thies Lehmann)? Must the reliance on choric speaking be seen as retrograde and derivative or as a first step toward what would become the society of the spectacle (Guy Debord)?[10] Does the Thingspiel participate in what Walter Benjamin describes as the aestheticization of politics under fascism or amount to little more than what Gerwin Strobl poignantly calls "ecstatic amateurism"?[11] Did these performances remain marginal to the fundamental restructuring of private and public life undertaken in the name of fascist biopolitics? Or did the blurring of boundaries between the political, the cultic, and the performative profoundly change the relationship between mass culture and political culture and lay the ground for entirely new types of collective experiences in the postliberal public sphere? Last but not least, can the official promotion and, only four years later, demotion of the Thingspiel be read as evidence of the limits of Nazi cultural policy or as a first step in the expansion of performative politics toward modern mass media such as broadcasting and film?

These questions can be answered by locating the cultic functions of the Thingspiel within a longer history of staging the people. Any superficial similarities with the theater of ancient Greece, including the semicircular amphitheater form, should not distract from the very different functions of choral speaking as public commentary in Athenian democracy and as social control in the Nazi dictatorship. Instead, the theatricalization of politics must be traced along two concurrent developments since the Wilhelmine years, the national ceremonies and anniversaries promoted as part of an official Prussianized imperial culture and the calendar of events, festivals, and conventions created within Social Democracy

---

10 The references are to Guy Debord, *The Society of the Spectacle*, trans. Donald Nicholson-Smith (New York: Zone Books, 1999) and Hans-Thies Lehmann, *Postdramatic Theatre*, intr. Karen Jürs-Munby (London: Routledge, 2006).
11 Gerwin Strobl, *The Swastika and the Stage: German Theater and Society, 1933–1945* (Cambridge: Cambridge University Press, 2007), 78. The Benjamin reference refers to the famous Art Work Essay, "The Work of Art in the Age of Its Technological Reproducibility. Second Version," in *The Work of Art in the Age of Its Technological Reproducibility and Other Writings on Media*, ed. Michael W. Jennings, Brigid Doherty, and Thomas Y. Levin (Cambridge, MA: Harvard University Press, 2008), 19–55.

as part of an emerging working-class culture. The various reform movements of the turn of the century assigned theatrical practices a special place in the proposed renewal of German culture and society. In the context of the avant-gardes, new performance practices developed around the emotional intensities of expressionist theater and the physical expressiveness of modern German dance, or *Ausdruckstanz*. Meanwhile, the public support for *Freilichtbühnen* (open-air theaters) as part of a conservative critique of big city life provided important organizational structures for preserving or reclaiming folk traditions within the contested spaces of modernity. The ways in which the building of Thingstätten also provided much-needed resources for regional infrastructures and professional organizations should not be underestimated, a point confirmed by the activities of the Reichsbund der deutschen Freilicht- und Volksschauspiele.[12] The participation of German Labor Front and Reich Labor Service units in Thingspiel performances and Thingstätten construction projects confirms their attractiveness as work creation schemes.

Scholars have examined the Thingspiel's performances of community along two lines of inquiry, their place within the history of festival culture and their contribution to performances of the political. In both cases, the preference for comprehensive overviews and the reliance on writings about the Thingspiel (rather than close readings of select works) have produced findings that tend to follow a familiar top-down approach to Nazi culture and ignore the differences between hyperbolic official pronouncements and actual theatrical practices. In delineating patterns of influence, literary scholars have pointed to an older tradition of theater as moral instruction, from the Jesuit play of the Counterreformation to the Baroque drama of ideas, that has always sought to convey a *Weltanschaung*, a distinct world view. Others have noted similarities with the didactic tone of Bertolt Brecht's *Lehrstücke* (teaching plays) and, more generally, the confrontational style of communist agitprop.[13] Modern staging practices such as Max Reinhardt's Theater of Five Thousand and modernist experiments such as Erwin Piscator and Walter Gropius's plans for a Total Theater are sometimes mentioned as part of a continuous

---

12 See the comprehensive study by Rainer Stommer, *Die inszenierte Volksgemeinschaft: Die "Thing-Bewegung" im Dritten Reich* (Marburg: Jonas, 1985).
13 On the Thingspiel and the (Brechtian) teaching play, see Johannes M. Reichl, *Das Thingspiel: Über den Versuch eines nationalsozialistischen Lehrstück-Theaters (Euringer-Heynicke-Möller)* (Frankfurt am Main: Dr. Mißlbeck, 1988). The first close readings can be found in Klaus Sauer und German Werth, *Lorbeer und Palme: Patriotismus in deutschen Festspielen* (Munich: dtv, 1971), 170–224. The similarities between the cult of community in the socialist Sprechchor and fascist Thingspiel are one reason why GDR research on proletarian theater during the Weimar Republic mostly ignores the former.

opening toward performance as a Gesamtkunstwerk. To give a few examples, the set designer and director Traugott Müller (formerly of the leftist Piscator Theater) became actively involved in the Reichsfestspiele in Heidelberg. The rediscovery of Handel oratories by Hanns Niedecken-Gebhard during the Weimar years and his minimalist staging of mass spectacles during the Nazi years also attest to continuities, as do the explorations of movement and rhythm as expressions of the collective body in the choreographic work of Rudolf Laban and Mary Wigman.

The Weimar-era Sprechchor and its movement-based variant, the *Bewegungschor* (movement chorus), are usually cited as the most important influence on the Thingspiel because of their similar experiments with choral speaking and mass choreography. Both introduce the working class as a historical and dramatic subject and use collective identifications to turn audiences into political actors. Nonetheless, there are distinct differences between the confrontational stance in Sprechchor productions sponsored by SPD- and KPD-affiliated organizations that demand social equality and call for revolutionary action, on the one hand, and the hierarchical structures and exclusionary practices that place the communities of the Thingspiel in relationship to the leader figure, on the other. This gradual process of subjectification-turned-subjection can be traced from the rousing experience of solidarity in, say, Hendrik de Man's *Wir! Ein sozialistisches Festspiel* (1932, We! A socialist festival) to the ritualized scenarios of submission staged by Riefenstahl and Speer in *Triumph of the Will.*[14]

Representing the second line of inquiry, cultural historians have pointed to comparable communal practices and, in the process, greatly expanded the conceptual framework toward theories of performativity and spatiality. To mention a few examples, sports historian Henning Eichberg, situates the Thingspiel within an international event culture that includes the Olympics.[15] By coining the term "mood architectures," architectural critic Dieter Bartetzko draws attention to the experiential qualities shared with other spatial practices and acknowledges the impor-

---

14 For a discussion of the socialist *Sprechchor*, see chapter 11 on "Social Democracy and the Performance of Community" in *The Proletarian Dream*; the gendered habitus of communist agitprop is discussed there in chapter 13, "Taking a Stand: On the Habitus of Agitprop." For an example of continuities, see Richard Noethlichs, *Der Sprechchor: Eine Anleitung für den Chorführer* (Stuttgart: Franck'sche Verlagshandlung, 1934).
15 See Henning Eichberg, "Thing-, Fest- und Weihespiele in Nationalsozialismus, Arbeiterkultur, und Olympismus," in Henning Eichberg, Michael Dultz, Glen Gadberry, and Günther Rühle, eds., *Massenspiele: NS-Thingspiel, Arbeiterweihespiel und olympisches Zeremoniell* (Stuttgart: Friedrich Frommann-Holzboog, 1977), 19–180 and the short English version translated by Robert A. Jones in "The Nazi *Thingspiel*: Theater for the Masses in Fascism and Proletarian Culture," *New German Critique* 11 (Spring 1977): 133–150.

tance of ambience and atmosphere for staged experiences of community.[16] In her recent study on National Socialist mass performances as an "elementary school of theater," theater historian Evelyn Annuß offers a sophisticated analysis of the attendant processes of *Vergemeinschaftung* (communalization) and their social and political implications.[17] What still awaits further examination are the considerable debts to religious pageantry, especially by choral poems that emulate the ritual structure of appeals, oaths, and sanctifications. And beyond a few passing comments by Egon Menz on the Thingspiel as a conduit for working-class grievances, there has been surprisingly little discussion of the class-specific experiences channeled by these performances of collectivity.[18]

The appearance of workers as a collective subject before and after 1933 is of course inseparable from the asymmetrical power structures in which they performed their significatory functions. Important ideological and institutional differences separated the Thingspiel as a product of official Nazi culture from the oppositional stance of the socialist Sprechchor tradition. Nonetheless, even the most racialized versions of communalization continued to draw on the forms and styles developed in the workers' movement. The preoccupation with community as the main dramatic subject, whether conceived in class- or race-based terms, reflected the unique historical configurations in Germany that had made these encounters between theater, dance, festival, and sports culture possible. Spectacle, performance, and ritual came to play a key role in defining what Erika Fischer-Lichte calls the "self-organizing and self-organized community."[19] What is more difficult to measure is the authenticity of emotions generated in the enactment of collective identities and identifications. Beyond the confident claims in Nazi writings on the Thingspiel, one can only speculate about the degree to which audiences participated enthusiastically in breaking the fourth wall and the ways in which these performances of collectivity were perceived as obligatory and experienced as little more than empty public rituals. Instead of showing the process of becoming a social class or political movement, which requires both self-reflection and self-cultivation, the Thingspiel, after all, merely asserted the existence of the folk commu-

---

16 Dieter Bartetzko, *Illusionen in Stein: Stimmungsarchitektur im deutschen Faschismus; Ihre Vorgeschichte in Theater- und Filmbauten* (Reinbek: Rowohlt, 2012).
17 See Evelyn Annuß, *Volksschule des Theaters: Nationalsozialistische Massenspiele* (Munich: Wilhelm Fink, 2019).
18 Egon Menz, "Sprechchor und Aufmarsch: Zur Entstehung des Thingspiels," in *Die deutsche Literatur im Dritten Reich: Themen—Traditionen—Wirkungen*, ed. Horst Denkler and Karl Prümm (Stuttgart: Reclam, 1976), 330–346.
19 Erika Fischer-Lichte, *Theatre, Sacrifice, Ritual: Exploring Forms of Political Theatre* (London: Routledge, 2005), 240.

nity by equating its empowerment with willing submission to the Führer principle, a contradiction that is particularly noticeable in post-1933 reenactments of working-class struggles set during the Weimar years.

From the perspective of contemporary debates on performativity, politics, and identity, the Nazis' experiments with the theatricalization of politics draw attention to the shared languages of socialism, nationalism, and populism that sustained the promise of communalization and, in ways examined in earlier chapters, attest to the central role of the worker in maintaining these elusive configurations. If one wants to avoid the circular logic of aesthetics as ideology as aesthetics, which continues to haunt much scholarship on Nazi culture, identifying the key terms that made the Thingspiel "the theater of ideology" and the Thingspiel movement part of the Nazification of culture is necessary but not sufficient.[20] New approaches cannot rely solely on literary criteria such as the dramatization of social conflicts or the presentation of social types since they tend to reduce theater to its representational functions. Instead, it is the cultic element, starting with the equation of the experiential with the performative, that opens up a new perspective on the formative role of workers in the Nazi dream of community and what it tries to suppress, namely the continued provocation of class.[21] The previous chapter introduced the Blochian notion of nonsimultaneity to characterize workers' poetry as a repository of those voices that survived the destruction of the workers' movement. Similar nonsimultaneities sustained the chorus of workers in the Thingspiel – namely, as a witness to the anticapitalist Nazi rhetoric of the Weimar years and as a herald, so to speak, of the reorganization of work in the Nazi state.

II

The extensive writings about the Thingspiel can be described as a veritable primer on performative politics as they spell out the underlying assumptions about collective identities and identifications. All offer heady pronouncements on the ability of literature to birth an authentic folk community out of the ravages of modern class society. Building on Möller's call for a theater of experience, Wolf Braumüller from the Amt Rosenberg (Rosenberg Office) spoke for many when he described the

---

[20] Bruce H. Zortman, "The Theater of Ideology in Nazi Germany," *Quarterly Journal of Speech* 57.2 (1971): 153.

[21] The German *kultisch* does not translate well into "cultic," given the latter's prevailing association with "cult." The connotation of *Kult* is broader than "ritual" and includes the communal aspects not always present in "performance."

Thingspiel as "communal experience and experienced community."²² Its main task, he declared, was "the cultivation of the creative power of folkdom, the formation and representation of German faith, and the symbolization of the public sphere as such."²³ As early as 1928, Hanns Johst, author of the well-known Nazi play *Schlageter* (1933), characterized the coming theater as a cultic form destined to bring about the "rebirth of a community of faith" through the writer as the voice of the folk.²⁴ Ten years later, such definitions were repeated ad nauseam by scholars such as Erich Trunz, who hailed the German writer as the "Führer of the soul" and praised German literature as an expression of "community as the truth of faith."²⁵ In aligning literary analysis with anthropological (i.e., racial) categories and what Heinz Kindermann called folk-based (*volkshaft*) humanities scholarship, the Thingspiel movement played a not insignificant role.²⁶ For it promised nothing less than to turn theater into a mechanism for "fortifying hearts, stealing wills, building strengths, and elevating the power of faith over that of feeling, will, and strength,"²⁷ to quote Josef Buchhorn from the Reichsschriftumskammer (RSK, Reich Literature Chamber).

How did the Thingspiel produce these emotional effects? Its most important techniques of communalization involved choral speaking: from the sameness in tone, volume, pace, and pitch to the calculated use of rhyme, verse, repetition, and parataxis. The heavy reliance on oration with its declaratives and imperatives and the repeated use of call and response as a simulation of free and open debate produced highly choreographed mass performances that could be experienced as either empowering or oppressive, exhilarating or monotonous. The intended outcome in both cases was a repudiation of the belief in individual subjectivity shared by Weimar classicism and European modernism and a move away from the nuclear family as the primary focus of identifications on and in front of the stage. As would be expected, the replacement of individuals with collectives sometimes caused problems for audiences used to the cathartic structure of classical Aristo-

---

22 Wolf Braumüller, *Freilicht- und Thingspiel: Rückschau und Forderungen* (Berlin: Volkschaft-Verlag, 1935), 45.
23 Wolf Braumüller, "Die Landschaftsbühne: Wesen und Wege einer neuen Theaterform," *Bausteine zum deutschen Nationaltheater* 2.7 (1934–35): 211.
24 Hanns Johst, "Vom neuen Drama," in *Ich glaube! Bekenntnisse* (Munich: Albert Langen, 1928), 36.
25 Trunz, *Deutsche Dichtung der Gegenwart*, 37 and 64.
26 Heinz Kindermann, *Dichtung und Volkheit: Grundzüge einer neuen Literaturwissenschaft* (Berlin: Junker and Dünnhaupt, 1937), 31–56. For a collection of source texts and an overview of the scholarship during and after the Third Reich, see Klaus Vondung, *Völkisch-nationale und nationalsozialistische Literaturtheorie* (Munich: List, 1973).
27 Josef Buchhorn, "Sinn und Sendung des Theaters," *Deutscher Kulturwart* (September 1935): 375.

telian theater since the lack of individual agency and psychological motivation could only partially be compensated for by a surfeit of communal feeling.

All cultic practices rely on reenactment in constituting and maintaining the group of believers. Cultic functions arise from the performance of specific rites and gestures and the use of distinct symbols and objects in designated public spaces with the explicit goal of affirming the covenant.[28] The cultic, by definition, is event- and performance-based; it is formative as well as normative, at once egalitarian and hierarchical. Just as cultic practices in religious contexts define the relationship between the community of believers and the deity or divine principle, the Nazi movement from the beginning relied on cultic practices to maintain mass support for the regime: by creating political symbols and rituals (e.g., swastika flag, Hitler salute), introducing an annual calendar of celebrations (e.g., National Labor Day, Reich Thanksgiving Festival), and commemorating the movement's early struggles and martyrs (e.g., March on the Feldherrnhalle).

The cultic functions shared by Thingspiele and party rallies were not limited to the theatrical use of objects, symbols, and costumes, in combination with highly choreographed movements, postures, and gestures. Writers and critics actively promoted the experiential qualities of such performances, especially their ability to inspire pride and joy – in short, to function as a laboratory of political emotions. Whether these performances actually increased popular support for the regime, provided intense but ultimately fleeting experiences of belonging, or amounted to little more than obligatory events for party members cannot be said. Warning against the automatic equation of propagandistic aims, methods, and results, Eichberg rightly asks: "To what extent do those behavioral patterns portrayed in the Thingspiel reveal information about the political attitudes of that period?"[29] Even more elusive than political convictions are the social imaginaries that, channeled through the figure of the worker, were appropriated to visualize what Nazi scholars, given their steadfast belief in the power of the simulacrum, described as the full convergence of fantasy and reality through cultic means and effects.

---

28 This definition of cultic function is based on the entry on "Kult," in *Ästhetische Grundbegriffe: Historisches Wörterbuch in Sieben Bänden,* ed. Karlheinz Barck et al. (Stuttgart: Metzler, 2010), 3:489–510. For an early study of the primacy of cult in Nazism, see Hans-Jochen Gamm, *Der braune Kult: Das Dritte Reich und seine Ersatzreligion: Ein Beitrag zur politischen Bildung* (Hamburg: Rütten & Loening, 1962). On the importance of rituals from a sociological perspective, see also Simon Taylor, "Symbol and Ritual under National Socialism," *British Journal of Sociology* 32.4 (1981): 504–520.
29 Eichberg, "The Nazi Thingspiel," 138. He developed these ideas further in *Bodily Democracy: Toward a Philosophy of Sport for All* (London: Routledge, 2011).

To a large degree, the different views on the Thingspiel reflected the significance attributed to its cultic functions. Support for the community-building effects of performance as public practice, in turn, linked up with concurrent debates on German(ic) art and literature, including on expressionism as an acceptable kind of modernism. Describing theater as "political world-view building," in 1933 the dramatist Paul Beyer openly championed cultic functions as he called for a national dramaturgy freed of the legacies of Aristotle and Lessing and inspired by a tradition of the choric that completed the unification of will and idea in the gestus of the folk.[30] Reinhard Schlösser, the Reich Dramaturge in the Propaganda Ministry, similarly emphasized the transformative potential of cult and ritual when he characterized the Thingspiel as an integral part of "the education of the German people in the ways of mass assembly."[31] Last but not least, the journalist Wilhelm von Schramm used conceptual binaries such as individual versus type and dialogue versus chorus to identify the formal features through which the Thingspiel, by validating the second term, could keep alive the spirit of the estates through dramatic reenactments of community. He conceded that such expectations were not always compatible with official demands for a "public representation of the power and unity of the new state."[32] For one, the cultic validated the mythical elements that, through themes of martyrdom and sacrifice, revealed a continued dependency on the symbolic practices of Christianity, a connection examined by Bill Niven in an article on apocalyptic scenarios and messianic figures in the Thingspiel.[33] For another, revisiting the struggles of the Weimar years may have reminded audiences of the long history of class-based grievances and perhaps encouraged them to look critically at the actual solutions available in the present. As Fischer-Lichte has shown, thematizing the relationship between folk and leader highlighted the tension between the democratic community and authoritarian leadership principle in ways that validated deliberative democracy even if the ritual qualities of such exchanges now aligned political agency exclusively with the leader figure.[34]

---

30 Paul Beyer, *National-Dramaturgie: Ein "erster Versuch"* (Berlin: Theater-Tageblatt, 1933), 8.
31 Rainer Schlösser, *Das Volk und seine Bühne: Bemerkungen zum Aufbau des deutschen Theaters* (Berlin: Albert Langen, 1935), 40.
32 Wilhelm von Schramm, *Neubau des deutschen Theaters: Ergebnisse und Forderungen* (Berlin: Schlieffen, 1934), 39 and 40.
33 Bill Niven, "Apocalyptical Elements in National Socialist 'Thingspiele' and in the Drama of the Weimar Republic," *German Life and Letters* 48.2 (1995): 170–183. On the larger context, see Klaus Vondung, *Deutsche Wege zur Erlösung: Formen des Religiösen im Nationalsozialismus* (Munich: Wilhelm Fink, 2013).
34 Erika Fischer-Lichte, "Revival of Choric Theatre as Utopian Visions," in *Choruses, Ancient and Modern*, ed. Joshua Billings, Felix Budelmann, and Fiona Macintosh (Oxford: Oxford University Press, 2013): 347–362.

The contested status of cultic functions and their connection to the unresolved question of class were a major reason for repeated changes in the official Nazi position on the Thingspiel. Early on, Joseph Goebbels promoted the Thingspiel as "a theater of the fifty and one hundred thousand,"[35] capable of casting a spell even over doubtful and indifferent folk comrades. Soon the Propaganda Ministry established an approval process for all plays worthy of the designation, partly to stem the flood of submissions and gain some clarity on the cultic question.[36] The terms most frequently used to identify the main problem were pomp and bombast. After attending the 1935 performance of Heynicke's *Der Weg ins Reich* (1935, The path to the Reich), Goebbels felt compelled to issue a clear warning against "conceptualizing cultic 'acts' in a vacuum and indiscriminately using terms such as 'cult,' 'Thing plots,' and so forth."[37] Starting in 1936, Thingspiel performances at party events were no longer permitted; in 1937, Goebbels withdrew the predicate *reichswichtig* (important to the Reich) and, with it, all official support for the Thingspiel movement. In 1938, even Hitler spoke out against the obsession with cult spaces and cult places and concluded that "National Socialism in its organization may be a folk movement but under no circumstances is it a cultic movement."[38]

Scholars have explained these reversals with reference to the competing institutional goals pursued by the Rosenberg Office, the German Labor Front, and the Propaganda Ministry. The inconsistencies of Nazi aesthetic theory reflect this instrumentalized view of culture; they also point to the performative function of discourse with its own rules of engagement separate from artistic practices. According to Alfred Rosenberg, founder of the Fighting League for German Culture and author of an often cited but rarely read tome, *Der Mythus des 20. Jahrhunderts* (1930, The myth of the twentieth century), the Thingspiel suffered from too much cult (of the Christian kind) and too little culture (of the Germanic kind) and was incapable of establishing the racial soul as the foundation of National Socialism. Nonetheless, some of the fiercest advocates for the Thingspiel, including

---

35 Goebbels, 8 May 1933 speech to theater professionals, reprinted in Gerd Rühle, ed., *Das dritte Reich: Dokumentarische Darstellung des Aufbaus der Nation; Das erste Jahr 1933* (Berlin: Hummel, n.d.), 89.

36 On this point, see "Schutz des Thingspiels" (1934), reprinted in Wulf, *Theater und Film im Dritten Reich*, 167–169. For a list of approved works, see Werner Kurz, "Genehmigte Thingspiele," *Bausteine zum deutschen Nationaltheater* 3 (1935): 148.

37 Joseph Goebbels, quoted by Klaus Vondung, *Magie und Manipulation* (Göttingen: Vandenhoek & Ruprecht, 1971), 42.

38 Adolf Hitler, *Der Parteitag Großdeutschland vom 5.–12. September 1938: Offizieller Bericht über den Verlauf des Reichsparteitages mit sämtlichen Kongreßreden* (Munich: Franz Eher, 1938), 81. Hence the later change in terminology from *Kultstätte* to *Volkshallen* for official places of assembly.

those promoting the construction of outdoor theaters, were located in the Rosenberg Office. Meanwhile, for those active in the German Labor Front, the Thingspiel offered a perfect vehicle for honoring workers, not least through the inclusion of DAF and RAD units in public performances – even if such appearances amounted to little more than official endorsements without any dramatic function. Last but not least, Goebbels's early sympathies for the leftist Strasser faction and his Catholic appreciation for all things cultic may have contributed to his initial support for the Thingspiel. But soon the Reich Minister of Public Enlightenment and Propaganda recognized that radio and film were much better suited to achieving the full compatibility of mass culture and political culture. The result: the Thingspiel as a theatrical practice disappeared but its underlying assumptions developed further in other media contexts, most notably film.

III

The debates on cultic elements remain mystifying as long as they are not connected to a source of great anxiety among the proponents of the Thingspiel – that is, its heavy debt to Weimar proletarian culture and the resultant need to integrate its legacies into the discourse of workerdom. During the first years of the regime, mass events explicitly addressed the workers and their demands for symbolic representation. The first Day of National Labor on Berlin's Tempelhofer Feld, which established Speer's credentials as a political events organizer, appropriated the socialist tradition of May Day and, by bringing together elements of rally, parade, and ceremony, turned the entire city square into a performance space. According to Inge Marszolek, the Nazification of May Day can be read as a prefiguration of the political project behind later performances of the culture of work: the nationalization of labor as an alternative to the Marxist class struggle, the celebration of work as a source of national pride, the apotheosis of German industry, and the militarization of work in all of its aspects.[39]

Despite effusive statements about a new German theater based on race as the sole criterion, the Thingspiel never broke free of the models of class solidarity developed in the workers' movement and brought to the stage by theater groups associated with the SPD and KPD. Acknowledging the similarities between Sprech-

---

[39] See Inge Marszolek, "Vom Proletarier zum 'Soldaten der Arbeit': Zur Inszenierung der Arbeit am 1. Mai 1933," in *Arbeit im Nationalsozialismus*, ed. Michael Wildt and Marc Buggeln (Munich: Oldenbourg, 2014), 215–228.

chor and Thingspiel, Hellmuth Langenbucher, a member of Rosenberg's Fighting League, and Franz Moraller, the managing director of the Reich Chamber of Culture, initially welcomed these influences in the name of (National) Socialism.[40] Specifically, they sought to harness the energies of the Sprechchor as a repository of grievances and resentments while separating the figure of the worker from the Marxist critique of class. The proposed shift from workers as a historical subject to work as a prerequisite for membership in the folk community, however, came with its own challenges since the abstract concept of work on the stage still had to be embodied by working-class characters. Through these holdovers from the socialist imaginary, the contradictions of performed ideology remained ever present despite repeated attempts at linguistic containment, which produced the short-lived alternative term *nationaler Sprechchor*. Given such patterns of influence, the liberating message of the Sprechchor could at any point become an obstacle to the disciplining effect of the Thingspiel. Bruno Nelissen-Haken, in a review of the first performance of *German Passion 1933*, diagnosed this problem as too much Sprechchor and too little Thingspiel, which really meant too many similarities with socialist and communist precursors and not enough attention to the racial question.[41]

Both the Sprechchor and the Thingspiel promised radical solutions to the worker question and conceived of their performances of class and community as part of a broader critique of liberalism and capitalism. The anxiety of influence haunting the Thingspiel after 1933 is reflected in the large number of plays set during the late Weimar years when the Nazi movement came into its own. In Nazi rhetoric, "Weimar" meant the tragedy of the loss of World War I, the humiliation of the Versailles Peace Treaty, the economic crises of 1923–24 and 1929–32, and, above all, the insidious effects of social and economic disintegration and moral and racial degeneracy traceable on the body of the German worker.[42] With their conventional three-part structure, most plays restage the exploitation of workers in the capitalist system, show their deception by Marxist ideology, and conclude with triumphant conversions to National Socialism. Two basic dramatic formulas can be distinguished. Relying on allegorical figures and didactic modalities, Euring-

---

[40] Hellmuth Langenbucher, *Nationalsozialistische Dichtung: Einführung und Übersicht* (Berlin: Junker & Dünnhaupt, 1935), 43–44. Also see Franz Moraller, "Der Sprechchor in der nationalsozialistischen Feiergestaltung," *Unser Wille und Weg* 6 (1936): 118–121.
[41] Bruno Nelissen-Haken, review of *Deutsche Passion 1933*, *Die Neue Literatur* 35 (1934): 653.
[42] On Weimar society and crisis discourse, see Moritz Föllmer and Rüdiger Graf, eds., *Die "Krise" der Weimarer Republik: Zur Kritik eines Deutungsmusters* (Frankfurt am Main, 2005) and Rüdiger Graf, *Die Zukunft der Weimarer Republik: Krisen und Zukunftsaneignungen in Deutschland 1918–1933* (Munich: Oldenbourg, 2008).

er's *German Passion 1933* uses the suffering of the German people after World War I to diagnose the problem of class as a failure of nationalism. Drawing on the conventions of the social drama, Heynicke's *Neurode* takes a 1930 mining accident in Silesia to "prove" that the workers find justice only when they become part of the people. The endings in both plays model how the class struggles of the past can be overcome through an ecstatic vision of community.

The preoccupation with Weimar-era labor conflicts is also noticeable in the similar languages of mass mobilization – with the demands for discipline and sacrifice reminiscent of KPD versions of the Sprechchor and the expressions of suffering and despair familiar from SPD-funded productions. For instance, the confrontational tone used by Gustav von Wangenheim in *Chor der Arbeit* (1924, Chorus of work) – "Pay attention, proles / We bring clarity / Pay attention, proles! / We speak the truth! / We Communists!"[43] – could also, with the necessary revisions, appear in comparable Nazi performances of political militancy. And the rapturous pledge at the end of Max Barthel's *Aufmarsch* (1930, Rally) that "the world be perfect / We stand together / That it be joyful and free, / We stand in flames [...], / to build a new world"[44] would fit perfectly in any Thingspiel promoted by the Rosenberg Office but was in fact commissioned by the SPD-affiliated Deutsche Arbeitersängerbund (German Worker Singing Association). The same can be concluded about the mass choreographies that, by equating motion with emotion, transformed the classed body into the body of the folk. Accordingly, the "'heroic' German bodily movements" in Lotte Wernicke's choric dance play *Die Geburt der Arbeit* (1934, The birth of work) relied on the same equation of moving bodies with movement politics as the 1928 performance of "Arbeitslose" (Unemployed) by the leftist Volksbühne's movement chorus under the direction of Berthe Trümpy and Vera Skoronel.[45] Both productions point to Laban's concept of kinesthesia as an important

---

[43] Gustav von Wangenheim, "Chor der Arbeit" (1924), in *Deutsches Arbeitertheater 1918–1933*, 2 vols., ed. Ludwig Hoffmann and Daniel Hoffmann-Ostwald (Munich: Rogner & Bernhard, 1976), 1:141. A performance still of the Volksbühne production can be found in *Der Sturm* 18.12 (1928): 181. On the continuities between Social Democratic and National Socialist traditions of mass theater, see Hannelore Wolff, *Volksabstimmung auf der Bühne? Das Massentheater als Mittel politischer Agitation* (Frankfurt am Main: Peter Lang, 1985). On the difficulties of theorizing performance beyond established political categories, see Kimberly Jannarone, ed., *Vanguard Performance beyond Left and Right* (Ann Arbor: University of Michigan Press, 2015).
[44] Max Barthel, *Aufmarsch: Werk für gemischten Chor, Sprecher und Blasorchesterbegleitung*, with Hans Tiessen (Berlin: Deutscher Arbeiter-Sängerbund, 1930), 24 (and slightly different on 13–14). His contribution to the Thingspiel includes *Das Spiel vom deutschen Arbeitsmann* (1934).
[45] The quote is taken from Karl Eric Toepfer, *Empire of Ecstasy: Nudity and Movement in German Body Culture, 1910–1935* (Berkeley: University of California Press, 1997), 315. On the Nazis' debt to Weimar festival and body culture, see Carole Kew, "From Weimar Movement Choir to Nazi Com-

influence in the making of *Erlebnisgemeinschaft* (community of experience) and what Möller and others at the time praised as the unique (per)formative qualities of the Thingspiel.

All of these patterns of influence eventually came up against the institutional contexts in which the Thingspiele were written and performed. As a contribution to the new culture of work – that is, as an integral part of Nazi ideology and cultural policy – the Thingspiel turned critique into affirmation as it celebrated the new covenant of service, sacrifice, and sacrament in plays such as Gerhard Schumann's *Feier der Arbeit* (1936, Celebration of work), as well as Herbert Böhme and Erich Lauer's *Volk der Arbeit* (1936, Folk of work). The performance of Weihespiele and Aufmarschspiele as part of public works projects, and, in the case of Herbert Molenaar's *Schwert und Flamme* (1933, Sword and flame), of Day of National Labor celebrations dramatically expanded the opportunities for theatrical events. Industrial plants in Berlin-Siemensstadt and elsewhere provided a setting for amateur performances of Werkspiele such as Anthes Kiendl's *Aufbruch 1933* (1934, Arise 1933) that presented workers, engineers, and managers as equal partners in the work community and further blurred the boundaries between work as performance and the performance of work.[46] More aggressive scenarios of national self-assertion first appeared with the figure of the worker-soldier in Hans-Jürgen Nierentz's *Symphonie der Arbeit* (1934, Symphony of work) and Erich Müller-Schnick's *Soldaten der Scholle: Ein chorisches Spiel aus deutscher Geschichte* (1934, Soldiers of the soil: a choral play from German history), two plays that advocated the complete militarization of German society.

---

munity Dance: The Rise and Fall of Rudolf Laban's 'Festkultur,'" in *Dance Research: The Journal of the Society for Dance Research* 17.2 (1999): 73–96 and, more generally, Nadine Rossol, *Performing the Nation in Interwar Germany: Sport, Spectacle, and Political Symbolism, 1926–1936* (Houndsmills: Macmillan, 2010). On the legacies of modern German dance, also see Susan Manning, *Ecstasy and the Demon: The Dances of Mary Wigman* (Minneapolis: University of Minnesota Press, 2006) and Lilian Karina and Marion Kant, *Hitler's Dancers: German Modern Dance and the Third Reich* (Oxford: Berghahn, 2004).

46 For definitions, see Heinz Riecke, "Laienspiele, Werkspiele, Thingspiele," *Ostdeutsche Monatshefte* 17 (1936/37): 83–87, and Anthes Kiendl, "Werkspiel," *Autor* 9.10 (1934): 11–12. Examples of the *Werkspiel* include Erich Müller-Schnick's *Die Zeitenwende: Ein Chorspiel vom Kampf um die Arbeit* (1935), Ferdinand Oppenberg's *Hämmer schwingen—Fahnen flattern: Ein Spiel der Arbeitsmannschaft* (1935), and Hans Brüssow's *Die Weggestellten* (1936). A photograph from the performance of *Aufbruch* in Berlin-Siemensstadt can be found in *Das deutsche Volksspiel* 1 (1933/34). Kiendl was in charge of organizing *Werkspiele* as part of the short-lived Reichsbund Volkstum und Heimat. *Werkspiele* were part of the expansion of the cultural front into the factories, including through art exhibitions and literary education; on the *Werkszeitschriften*, see Vanessa Ferrari, "Nazionalsocialismo e *Arbeiterliteratur*: Il lavoro e la fabbrica nella propaganda della NSDAP (1929–1938)" (PhD diss., University of Munich, 2016), 283–326.

As a work-creation scheme, the Thingspiel initiatives participated actively in the reorganization of labor in the corporatist state. By introducing SA, RAD, and DAF units as dramatis personae, Erich Müller-Schnick's *Zeitenwende: Ein Chorspiel vom Kampf um die Arbeit* (1935, Turning point: a choral play about the fight for work) and Gustav Goes's *Opferflamme der Arbeit: Ein Freilichtspiel* (1934, Sacrificial flame of work: an open-air play) made the identity of political and theatrical actors an integral part of the new culture of work. In less visible ways, these productions offered professional opportunities for unemployed or underemployed writers, actors, directors, lighting technicians, set designers, and stagehands. The banning of labor unions and socialist parties in 1933 had eviscerated the workers' movement and paved the way for the reorganization of labor and industry. Ambitious public works projects were launched in part to reduce mass unemployment and jumpstart the national economy. Once more, cultural bureaucrats relied on organizational structures established during the Wilhelmine and Weimar years. These included professional associations such as the precursor of the abovementioned Reichsbund, the kind of cultural networks created by the SPD-affiliated Kulturkartelle, and the Voluntary Labor Service introduced on the national level as early as 1931. Soon, local communities competed in the site selection process for Thingstätten to be built throughout Germany. Well-known architects such Hans and Wassili Luckhardt, Fritz Höger, and Wilhelm Kreis submitted proposals to architectural competitions. Fritz Schaller and Ludwig Moshamer ended up designing several of the sites completed with the help of local craftsmen and artisans as well as unskilled RAD units. Not unlike the Reichsautobahn project, the Thingspiel movement often promoted these work-creating schemes in the name of region-branding and cultural tourism and as part of propaganda campaigns in contested border regions.

The problem of unemployment had been a pressing one not only for stage designers and theater actors. For some members of what Max Weber called the academic proletariat and what even Braumüller referred to as the artistic proletariat, involvement in the Thingspiel movement brought an end to long years of professional disappointments.[47] Born during the 1900s and early 1910s, Richard Euringer, Kurt Heynicke, and others had lived through Weimar culture as their own generational trauma. Whereas the worker poets had been socialized into the workers' movement, these middle-class men became writers only after they joined *völkisch* and nationalist groups. Forced to abandon university studies after the hyperinflation period, Euringer (1891–1953) tried his hand at various menial jobs before he

---

47 Braumüller, *Freilicht- und Thingspiel*, 14. The Weber reference comes from "Wissenschaft als Beruf."

started writing for the *Völkische Beobachter*.⁴⁸ In 1935, this true believer was rewarded for his party loyalty with the directorship of the Essen public library. Born in Liegnitz, in Lower Silesia, Heynicke (1891–1985) dabbled in expressionist poetry, had some success as a screenwriter for the Ufa studio, and after World War II withdrew to the Black Forest to focus on Alemannic folk plays.⁴⁹ Described best as a political opportunist, he later claimed ignorance about the propagandistic goals of the Thingspiel, a self-serving assertion quickly disproven by his characters' full command of Nazi phraseology in *Neurode* and *The Path to the Reich*.

IV

The emotional intensities organized through the workers in the Thingspiel can be captured through exemplary scenes that at once acknowledge past struggles and lay out the new rules of belonging. In psychological terms, Euringer's *German Passion 1933* restages the trauma of Weimar through key elements of the passion play and its familiar trajectory from suffering to redemption (see figure 4.1). This process involves several encounters between an unemployed worker and a dead soldier as victims of the coordinated assault on German nationhood by internal and external enemies. From the outset, the worker's shame and self-loathing is presented as inseparable from his disillusionment with socialism. "I am just ooze. The prole, / to be devoured by trusts and capitalists / [...] a man without God or fatherland / kicked, mistreated, enslaved, robbed. Let me be. I believed in you *once*," he shouts at the communist agitator.⁵⁰ Eventually the unemployed

---

48 On Euringer, see Jürgen Hillesheim, *"Heil Dir, Führer! Führ uns an!" Der Augsburger Dichter Richard Euringer* (Würzburg: Königshausen & Neumann, 1995), especially the chapter on *Deutsche Passion* (60–76). His conception of class as a subjective experience (rather than objective structure) can be reconstructed through the curious change in title of *Die Arbeitslosen* (1930), a novel set in the Ruhr region, for its republication in 1932 as *Metallarbeiter Vonholt: Der Tag eines Arbeitswilligen* (1932).
49 On the author and his contribution to the Thingspiel, see Magdalena Maruck, *Kurt Heynicke (1891–1985), ein Dichter aus Schlesien zwischen Revolte und Opportunismus: Eine rezeptionsgeschichtliche Studie* (Dresden: Neisse, 2015) and Sven Behnke, "Kurt Heynicke: Trivialität oder Programm?," in *Ästhetik und Ideologie 1945: Wandlung oder Kontinuität poetologischer Paradigmen in Werken deutschsprachiger Schriftsteller*, ed. Detlef Haberland (Berlin: De Gruyter, 2017), 129–146.
50 Euringer, *Deutsche Passion 1933: Hörwerk in sechs Sätzen* (Berlin: Gerhard Stalling, 1933), 20–21. On productions *of Deutsche Passion 1933* in Heidelberg and Halle, see Annuß, 237–251. For a comparative fascist/antifascist reading of Euringer's *Deutsche Passion* and Heiner Müller's *Germania*, see Leah Hadomi, *Dramatic Metaphors of Fascism and Antifascism* (Tübingen: Max Niemeyer, 1996), 98–114.

Fig. 4.1: Richard Euringer, *Deutsche Passion 1933*, Theater des Volkes Berlin, 1935, set design by Traugott Müller, photograph by René Fosshag. Institut für Theaterwissenschaft der FU Berlin, Theaterhistorische Sammlungen Nachlass Traugott Müller.

worker and the fallen soldier come together in the Chorus of the Workers and the Chorus of the Dead and, through their shared suffering and longing for redemption, create the conditions for a new kind of solidarity based on racial criteria. Their willing sacrifice, in turn, makes the appeal to those still committed to Marxist ideas all the more compelling:

> And you who today goes begging,
> You class fighter and prole!
> Step out of your cloud!
> Be once again folk from the folk!
> Free yourself of the madness of politics!
> Do not curse workshop and factory!
> Work, work is not bondage,
> Work is solace. Work is reward.
> Work saves the land.[51]

---

51 Euringer, *Deutsche Passion 1933*, 35.

Euringer's 1934 theses on the Thingspiel read like a commentary on *German Passion 1933* and further clarify the heavy reliance on cultic forms in the new culture of work. Like Möller, Euringer emphasizes its experiential qualities and insists that "cult, not art is what the Thingspiel is about."[52] To the question posed by an unnamed interlocutor, he responds: "There are no spectators. There are no good seats. There is nothing but the folk." Eager to distinguish the Thingspiel from its socialist precursors, he explains that "choruses are not collectives. Choruses presume folk and leader as the foundation of the body politic. We no longer know any masses. Group (*Mannschaft*) and man (*Mensch*), not 'the mass of men,' will henceforth be the message."[53]

Taking a different approach, Heynicke in *Neurode* draws on elements of the social drama to address the threat of finance capitalism and the failure of liberal democracy (see figure 4.2). Once again, the workers are introduced as the powerless and dispossessed through which the Nazi promise of renewal gains emotional urgency and political legitimacy. Initially, a solution to the problem of unemployment seems within reach when one of the workers is hired by the owners of a struggling mine. Announcing, "A man has work," the chorus delivers a rousing paean to work as the most powerful bond between individual and community and evidence of the need for recognition shared by manual and mental workers. This new feeling of community, they declare, can be experienced everywhere

> Where someone raises his hands,
> Where someone shakes up the minds,
> Where someone scatters the young seed,
> Where someone harvests the mature hay,
> Where someone moves wheel and shank,
> Where someone hammers and another one writes,
> Where someone works deep in the mine,
> Where someone stays awake with books,
> Where one man moves by the force of destiny
> guides his people to victory –
> There, there is work! Sing praise
> Praise all in the service of duty![54]

These testimonies to joy in work are put to the test with the arrival of an agent of finance capital who declares the mine no longer profitable. Comparable to the *deus*

---

52 Richard Euringer, "Thingspiel-Thesen," in *Chronik einer deutschen Wandlung* (Hamburg: Hanseatische Verlagsanstalt, 1936), 233.
53 Euringer, "Thingspiel-Thesen II," in *Chronik*, 237 and 238.
54 Kurt Heynicke, *Neurode: Ein Spiel von deutscher Arbeit* (Berlin: Volkschaft-Verlag, 1935), 22. On the staging of Neurode, see Annuß, 251–260.

ex machina in ancient Greek theater, a mysterious stranger appears during the subsequent public auction and helps the miners take ownership of the mine themselves. Like the fallen soldier in *German Passion 1933*, this savior figure functions as a personification of Germany. "Work is the heartbeat of the new Reich," he proclaims and implores the workers, "Close the ranks / All of Germany is the goal! / The man of the forehead, the man of the fist, / March when the oath swells loudly: / And if the road is rocky, / We are forever unified, / All of Germany marches with us!"[55]

Fig. 4.2: Thingstätte auf dem Brandberge, Halle (Saale), Sammlung Katharina Bosse, reprinted in *Thingstätten: Von der Bedeutung der Vergangenheit für die Gegenwart* (Bielefeld: Kerber, 2020), 92. With permission of the author.

German Passion 1933 was originally conceived as a radio play and broadcast on Maundy Thursday, the Thursday before Easter. Its Thingspiel version was first performed in July 1934 during the annual Reichsfestspiele in Heidelberg. *Neurode*, too, started out as a radio play before its premiere at the June 1934 opening ceremony for the first Thingstätte built on the Brandberge near Halle (see figure 4.2). The affinity of the Thingspiel for medialization may have been initially necessitated by the requirements of sound amplification in outdoor performances but quickly

---

55 Heynicke, *Neurode*, 53 and 56.

opened up other possibilities, starting with the promotion of Thingspiele as radio plays. The technical advances in broadcasting, in turn, created auditory communities beyond the limitations of time and space and facilitated experiences of what Annuß calls acoustic communalization.[56]

In a roundabout way, expanding the cultic function toward the world outside the theater meant returning to a very different space of collective dreaming, namely the motion-picture theater. From the beginning, Thingspiel authors and directors sought to offer communal experiences beyond the spatial constraints of the conventional stage: first through the construction of open-air theaters, then through the means of sound amplification and radio transmission, and, eventually, through the introduction of Thingspiel principles into fully mediated performances of the political. Otto Laubinger, the first president of the Reich Theater Chamber, saw the connection early on when he called the Thingspiel "a political demonstration turned theater."[57] Arriving at the same conclusion from the other side of these equivalencies, Braumüller described the party rallies as "the *Thing* idea incarnate."[58] Along similar lines, the radio pioneer Eugen Kurt Fischer referred to Nazi Party rallies as an exemplary "dramaturgy of reality"[59] that took full advantage of the slide toward performative and experiential categories in the convergence of mass culture and political culture. For that reason, *Triumph of the Will* could in fact be described as a filmic version of the Aufmarschspiel. To quote a 1935 article that enthusiastically discussed Riefenstahl together with the above mentioned Möller: "Reality and formation (*Gestaltung*) become one – reality not just as the reality of the image but also as the manifestation of the political will."[60]

---

56 See Evelyn Annuß, "Vom Gemeinschaftssound zur vergemeinschafteten Vogelperspektive," in *Kunst im NS-Staat: Ideologie, Ästhetik, Protagonisten*, ed. Wolfgang Benz, Peter Eckel, and Andreas Nachama (Berlin: Metropolis, 2015), 191–217. On the soundscapes of the Nazi cult of community, see Carolyn Birdsall, *Nazi Soundscapes: Sound, Technology, and Urban Space in Germany, 1933–1945* (Amsterdam: Amsterdam University Press, 2012), especially the chapter on "the festivalisation of the everyday" (65–102). On the multimedia aspects, also see Uwe-Karsten Ketelsen, "Theater-Hörspiel-Thingspiel: Versuch eines medialen *crossing over* im Theater der frühen dreißiger Jahre," in *Literatur intermedial: Paradigmenbildung zwischen 1918 und 1968*, ed. Wolf Gerhard Schmitt and Thorsten Valk (Berlin: De Gruyter, 2009), 247–265. On the role of broadcasting, and the Weimar era radio plays produced for and by the unemployed, see Hans Jürgen Krug, *Arbeitslosenhörspiele 1930–1933* (Frankfurt am Main: Peter Lang, 1992).
57 Otto Laubinger, unpublished ms., quoted by Strobl, *The Swastika*, 76.
58 Braumüller, "Weltanschauliche Glaubensgestaltung auf der Heidelberger Thingstätte," *Deutsche Bühnenkorrespondenz*, 24 July 1935.
59 Eugen Kurt Fischer, *Dramaturgie des Rundfunks* (Heidelberg: Vowinckel, 1942), 165.
60 Karl Schwarz, "Wir kämpfen um den Ausdruck unserer Zeit," *Hochschule und Ausland* 13.6 (1935): 30.

Fig. 4.3 and 4.4: *Triumph des Willens* (1935) Reichsarbeitsdienst sequence (c. 38'), screen captures.

Aware of these connections, Laubinger was more than ready to leave behind the labor struggles of the Weimar years when he summarized the goals of the Thingspiel movement with a clear view toward more confrontational stances in the future. "In contrast to the nationalisms of the past," he reiterated, "we are not content with filling the German people only with a national feeling but also with a national will, fully in line with National Socialism."[61] The hidden message in his statement – namely, the fact that "will" inevitably means war – is spelled out loud and clear in the Reich Labor Service sequence (approx. 31:00 – 36:00') from *Triumph of the Will* (see figures 4.3 and 4.4). The roll call involving 52,000 RAD men is the first major event shown after the speeches of opening night and begins with a series of long shots along marching worker soldiers. "Here we stand. We are ready to carry Germany into a new era," they declare and lower their spades to the ground: "Germany!" The call-and-response sequence that follows first connects individual men and then, in accordance with the principles of choral speaking, encompasses the entire group. The closeups of their faces are shot from below and in profile, emphasizing their youthful masculinity and soldierly resolve. To the question "Comrade, where are you from?" they answer: "From Friesland." "And you, comrade?" "From Bavaria." "And you?" "From the Kaiserstuhl." Hailing from rural areas and border regions, the RAD men are brought together through their public pledge to "One folk, one Führer, one Reich, Deutschland!" Soon their voices, separately and jointly, become louder and stronger. The montage of young, earnest faces that make up the working folk in the Riefenstahl film draws on the same ritual elements as the choreography of worker bodies in the Thingspiel. The powerful sense of phys-

---

61 Laubinger, quoted by Stommer, *Die inszenierte Volksgemeinschaft*, 31.

Fig. 4.5: Kurt Heynicke, *Der Weg ins Reich*, Reichsfestspiele 1935, Thingstätte auf dem Heiligen Berg Heidelberg, set design by Traugott Müller, photograph by René Fosshag. Institut für Theaterwissenschaft der FU Berlin, Theaterhistorische Sammlungen Nachlass Traugott Müller.

ical proximity and emotional intimacy indicates why early discussions about the cultic found their logical continuation in the media-specific qualities of film:

> We are all at work together. In the turf marches. And we in the furnaces. In the furnaces. And we in the quarries. In the quarries. We are reclaiming the North Sea [...] We are planting trees [...] rustling forests. We are building roads [...] from village to village, from town to town. We are making new fields for the farmers. Forests and fields, land and bread for Germany.

Their pledge of allegiance ends with the signature song "We Are the Men from the Peasant Estate" and an extensive traveling shot along the first row of worker soldiers. Taking advantage of the cultic function of repetition, the next sequence uses the same formal principle to take on the difficult legacies of the past. Too young to have served in World War I, the RAD men present themselves a new kind of soldier: "With our hammers. Axes. Mattocks. Pickaxes. Shovels. We are the Reich's young company." As in *German Passion 1933*, their identification with the fallen of the movement – "You are not dead. You are alive. You are Germany!" – transforms their commitment to work into a force of both (spiritual) renewal and (territorial) aggression. At last, Hitler announces their deliverance from the trauma of Weimar through the new culture of work in the Nazi state: "You, [i. e., the workers] represent a great idea. And we know that for millions of our folk comrades, work will from now on no longer be a dividing concept but one that unites us all."

The sequence in *Triumph of the Will* could have ended with the main chorus from Heynicke's *The Path to the Reich* (see figure 4.5): "The work needs soldiers, / Soldiers of the new time, / With pick and with spade, / Ready for youthful service. / [...] Through work we become victors / Victorious over suffering and strife. / We all are warriors / Fighting for a new time."[62] In light of such affinities, the RAD sequence completes the transformation of the workers into the people modeled by the Thingspiel and continues the redefinition of the political through its cultic functions and experiential qualities. However, the convergence of mass culture and political culture through new forms of public performance and new technologies of medialization also greatly expanded the possibilities for the performance of politics and for the performative politics conjured in Erhard Schütz's description of the Third Reich as a media dictatorship.[63] How these developments opened up a space for redefining the relationship between work and workers in image-based practices – painting, sculpture, photography, and film – will be discussed in the next two chapters.

---

62 Kurt Heynicke, *Der Weg ins Reich* (Berlin: Volkschaft-Verlag, 1935), 34.
63 See Erhard Schütz, *Mediendiktatur Nationalsozialismus* (Heidelberg: Winter, 2019).

Chapter 5
Pride in Work: On Workers' Sculpture and Industrial Painting

> Art is the only truly eternal investment of human labor power.
> Adolf Hitler

Room 12 at the 1940 Große deutsche Kunstausstellung (GDK, Great German Art Exhibition) featured twelve artworks on the theme of labor and industry that showcased the regime's commitment to the new culture of work. Among them were two bronze statues, a miner and a raftsman, by Fritz Koelle and four industrial landscapes by Erich Mercker, including the large-scale *Aus Deutschlands Schmiede* (From Germany's forge).[1] Eager to fill the new Reich Chancellery, Adolf Hitler made five purchases in that room alone: two Mercker paintings about the construction of the chancellery plus three others by Franz Gerwin about the blast furnace at Reichswerke Hermann Göring in Salzgitter. At least for the Führer, the veneration of art as "the only truly eternal investment of human labor power" seemed entirely compatible with such mundane subject matter.[2] For the other buyers, the Hauptamt für Technik in Munich run by Fritz Todt, the Krupp AG in Rheinhausen, and the Benzol Association in Bochum, which purchased Koelle's *Der Bergmann* (The Miner), the traditional arts were an integral part of their corporate branding strategies. At the time, Koelle was known as the foremost sculptor of the German

---

[1] The two artists in question were well represented in room 12, Koelle with *Der Bergmann* and *Der Isarflößer* and Mercker with *Bau der Reichskanzlei, Marmor für die Reichskanzlei, Aus Deutschlands Schmiede,* and *Tirol baut auf.* Koelle had a total number of eight works in the exhibition, including a plaster of *Der erste Mann vom Blockwalzwerk.* Other works on display were (in alphabetical order) Franz Gerwin's *Reichswerke Hermann Göring, Hochöfen im Bau,* and *Reichswerke Hermann Göring, Hochofenanlage*; Otto Geigenberger's *Im Industriehafen*; Richard Gessner's *Hüttenwerk* and *Hochofen*; Wenzel Gröll's *Neubau*; Walter Hemming's *Im Thomasstahlwerk*; Ewald Jorzig's *Hochofenabstich am Abend*; Leonhard Sanrock's *Werftarbeiter*; Hans Schlereth's *Hufschmied*; Rudolf Schmalfuß's *Hochofenabstich* and *Thomasstahlwerk*; Elisabeth Schmitz's *Industriestilleben*; Richard Schreiber's *Im Walzwerk*; Robert Seyfried's *Neubau der Mainzer Bahnhofshalle*; and Friedrich August Weinzheimer's *Eisengießerei.* For more information, see the excellent online research tool gdk-research.de. On the history of the GDK, see Ines Schlenker, *Hitler's Salon:"The Große Deutsche Kunstausstellung" at the Haus der Deutschen Kunst in Munich 1937 – 1944* (Oxford: Peter Lang, 2007).

[2] This often-quoted passage is from a speech given by Adolf Hitler on 9 September 1936 during the NSDAP's Kulturtagung in Nuremberg. "Die einzige wahrhaft unvergängliche Anlage der *menschlichen Arbeitskraft* ist die *Kunst!*" The use of a Marxist concept such as *Arbeitskraft* is noteworthy. Published in *Hitler: Reden und Proklamationen, 1932 – 1945* (Leonberg: Pamminger, 1988), 639.

worker, and Mercker recognized as the most prolific painter of technical subjects. Largely forgotten today, both were included in many Great German Art Exhibitions and heavily promoted through art books, journals, and postcards. Far removed from what often counts as Nazi art today, Koelle and Mercker played a key role in visualizing the Nazi culture of work – even if through very different means and to very different effects.

The art pieces exhibited in room 12 of the GDA were an important part of museum and exhibition culture during the Third Reich and contributed to the aestheticization of work promoted by party officials, industry representatives, and anyone associated with the Beauty of Labor initiative.[3] By visualizing workerdom, artists became an integral part of the mechanisms of exclusion and exploitation that defined the culture of work in the Nazi dictatorship. Idealized workers appeared on large-scale murals and stained-glass mosaics in the new model factories just as organized workers faced arrest, deportation, and harassment. Monuments to the working man were put in public parks and corporate headquarters, while labor organizations were banned, and labor laws rewritten. Large, commissioned works celebrated the heroism of the industrial age and commemorated those killed in the struggle over steel and coal, while forced laborers died from the inhumane working conditions in the armament factories. As the two case studies will show, the relationship between the visible and the invisible and the conditions of visibility and invisibility proved essential to the celebration of work in official Nazi art and, by extension, its contribution to the discourse of workerdom.

Hitler's purchase selections offer a first glimpse of what Benjamin's aestheticization of politics under fascism looked like on the ground – in this particular case, as part of the new culture of work. No new genres, forms, styles, and techniques but their adaptation to the greatly expanded role of art as symbolic politics. No emerging young artists working in a recognizable fascist style but the growing influence of large corporations and party organizations as patrons of the arts. And no overarching ideological project in line with National Socialism but the enlistment of iconographic traditions and artistic conventions in the celebration of industrial modernity. The Nazi cult of labor and industry relied heavily on emo-

---

3 For a comprehensive overview, see the only monograph on the subject, Peter Schirmbeck, *Adel der Arbeit: Der Arbeiter in der Kunst der NS-Zeit* (Marburg: Jonas, 1984) and, for the larger context, Klaus Türk, ed., *Arbeiter und Industrie in der bildenden Kunst: Beiträge eines interdisziplinären Symposiums* (Stuttgart: Franz Steiner, 1997). An international perspective can be found in Valerie Mainz and Griselda Pollock, eds., *Work and the Image II: Work in Modern Times* (London: Routledge, 2018). For overviews of the representation of the worker in the arts, see Paul Brandt's two-volume *Schaffende Arbeit und bildende Kunst* (1928); his *Kunst und Arbeit: Ein Bilderbuch für die deutsche Jugend* (1929) was intended to teach appreciation for manual labor in the schools.

tions for integrating class-based identifications into the new narratives of work and community. In ideology-critical terms, the results could be described as an obscuring of the conditions of production and, by extension, the structures of domination. However, the enlistment of art in redefining the relationship between capital, labor, and the state not only vastly expanded the possibilities of aestheticizing work. It also introduced slogans such as pride and joy in work as aesthetic categories and expanded the modalities through which work could be described, represented, and (presumably) experienced. These mutually constitutive processes, in turn, remained heavily dependent on the emotional attachments organized through the worker as the personification of the coming folk (or work) community.

Today there exists broad agreement that Nazi culture was a visual culture – that is, a culture of images and imaginaries, defined by conditions of visibility and visuality, and essential to the dynamics of coercion and consent. What still requires closer attention are the characteristics of official Nazi art, Nazi kitsch, and the vast but largely unexplored spheres of commercial and amateur art. Once again revealing continuities with the Weimar years, the diverse visual practices focused on industrial themes offer a good case in point. Even a brief look at the range of topics, themes, and styles included in the Great German Art Exhibitions and in the leading Nazi art journals and books disproves widespread claims about a distinct fascist aesthetic (i.e., heroic, monumental, neoclassicist) associated with names such as Albert Speer, Arno Breker, and Leni Riefenstahl. Most studies on Nazi art treat industrial painting as a negligible phenomenon, perhaps because of its formal limitations and role in corporate self-promotion. By contrast, workers' sculpture after 1933 is usually discussed as a residue of prewar socialist traditions and the artistic expressions by miners seen through the lens of heritage culture.

Questions of labor and industry do not fit into conventional accounts that equate Nazi art with hypermasculine warriors, idealized female nudes, medieval settings, idyllic landscapes, and kitschy family scenes. Peasants and craftsmen dominated the look of the working folk displayed at the Great German Art Exhibitions and promoted by popular art journals with programmatic titles such as *Kunst und Volk* (Art and people) and *Kunst dem Volk* (Art for the people).[4] Meanwhile, industrial workers became a favorite subject in photojournalism and documentary film, evidence that, given the divisions of labor between old and new visual media, nostalgia for the folk was entirely compatible with the cult of tech-

---

[4] The most important art journals during the Third Reich included the openly political *Kunst und Volk* (1935–1937), the popular monthly *Kunst dem Volk* (1938–1944), and the quasi-official *Die Kunst im Dritten Reich* (1937–1944, since 1939 called *Die Kunst im Deutschen Reich*). The Munich-based *Die Kunst für Alle* (1885–1944) was strongly invested in a preindustrial vision of work as a craft.

nology. Far removed from the art works commissioned to glorify party and state, the visual practices discussed in the next three chapters – painting and sculpture, film and photography, and architecture and design – played equally significant but complementary roles in the visualization of workerdom. Each practice drew on established conventions and traditions, responded to new demands and purposes, addressed specific audiences and settings, and promised unique pleasures, sensations, and experiences. Throughout, the production and distribution of images remained inseparable from the rules of the market that made art a commodity in capitalist societies and the new horizons of interpretation that defined art as propaganda in the Third Reich. The resultant contradictions are especially pronounced in painting and sculpture, where bourgeois notions of quality and classical definitions of style continued to compete with the ideological demands of workerdom.

Koelle and Mercker were part of these larger configurations, the one through his preoccupation with the body of the worker and the other through his fascination with large industrial complexes. Their respective contribution will be examined using a highly contextualized approach: the thematic continuities in the depiction of labor and industry since the nineteenth century, the influence of socialist traditions and artistic conventions, and the close connection between aestheticization and emotionalization in relation to workerdom. The latter point, in turn, will be reconstructed through a specific work-related feeling, attitude, and disposition – *Arbeitsstolz* (pride in work) – that in its aesthetic manifestations helped to coordinate the new imaginaries of industrial labor with their corresponding ideological narratives. Like *Arbeitsfreude* (joy in work), the term introduced in the next chapter, pride in work was an important Nazi propaganda slogan, a buzzword in new work initiatives, and a subject of inquiry for psychologists, sociologists, and *völkisch* thinkers.[5]

Within the linguistic universe of Nazism, "pride in work" referred to the shared sense of achievement and advancement brought about by National Socialism. Specifically, the term identified "typical" German attitudes and behaviors underlying the renewed appreciation for work as a sociopolitical project. Not to be equated with (calls for) increased productivity, pride in work implied consent if not submission to the work community and, by extension, folk community. Its main discursive function was to separate the experience of work from its foundation in the economy (and, in the final analysis, capitalism) and reorient its social organization toward psychological criteria and aesthetic effects. In that sense, "pride" aimed at a complete rewriting of the class-based narratives in which

---

5 For a typical article, see "Arbeitsstolz und Arbeitsfreude—Bausteine nationalsozialistischer Sozialpolitik," *NS-Sozialpolitik* 4 (1937): 194–197.

wage labor invariably meant alienated work under capitalist conditions of exploitation. Associated most closely with the German Labor Front but traceable across a range of artistic, literary, and theatrical practices, pride in work was seen as one of the distinguishing traits of the German worker. Introduced during the Weimar years in the context of industrial psychology and scientific management, the term played a key role in reconciling three seemingly incompatible aspects of workerdom: its socialist origins, *völkisch* beliefs, and corporatist ideas.

In Koelle, a thus defined pride in work found privileged expression in the physical body of the worker, the observable traces of his exertion, exhaustion, and expertise. Mercker chose a more indirect approach in which pride was made visible through the size and scale of production facilities and their overdetermined function as symbols of technical progress and industrial might. In visualizing workerdom, both artists contributed to what one critic at the time called a new religion, more truthful and more inspiring than the gloriole in medieval art: the nobility of manual labor.[6]

I

Any discussion of images of work and workers after 1933 must begin with an acknowledgment of the devastating impact of the Gleichschaltung, which eliminated all critical perspectives on capitalism and class society.[7] With the creation of the Reichskammer der bildenden Künste (Reich Chamber of the Visual Arts) came immediate dismissals, expulsions, and imprisonments for countless artists associated with the Weimar Left. Attacks on the representatives of "cultural Bolshevism," campaigns against modern art as "degenerate" art, and so-called *Malverbote* (painting bans) for those choosing "inner emigration" followed suit. In 1933, Käthe Kollwitz resigned from the Prussian Academy of Art. George Grosz, John Heartfield, and Gerd Arntz were forced into exile and their works removed from muse-

---

6 Hermann Hieber, "Schaffende Arbeit in der Kunst," *Kunst der Nation* 2.10 (1934): 5.
7 For exhibition catalogues and anthologies that reflect the changes in scholarship over the past forty years, see (in chronological order) Janos Frecot et al., eds., *Zwischen Widerstand und Anpassung: Kunst in Deutschland 1933–1945* (Berlin: Akademie der Künste, 1978); Georg Bussmann, ed., *Kunst im 3. Reich: Dokumente der Unterwerfung* (Frankfurt am Main: Zweitausendeins, 1980); Ulrich Krempel and Jörn Merkert, eds., *Skulptur und Macht: Figurative Plastik im Deutschland der 30er und 40er Jahre* (Berlin: Akademie der Künste, 1983); and Silke von Berswordt-Wallrabe, Jörg-Uwe Neumann, and Agnes Tieze, eds., *"Artige Kunst": Kunst und Politik im Nationalsozialismus* (Bielefeld: Kerber, 2017). On questions of historiography, see Pamela M. Potter, *Art of Suppression: Confronting the Nazi Past in Histories of the Visual and Performing Arts* (Berkeley: University of California Press, 2016).

um collections. Fellow leftists such as Otto Nagel, Otto Griebel, and Curt Querner remained in the country and retreated to painting apolitical subject matter.

Much has been written about the Nazi campaigns against modernism and, more recently, the terms under which modernist elements continued in the registers of what scholars call Nazi modern, Nazi modernism, or Nazi Sachlichkeit.[8] Coordinated by the Propaganda Ministry, the antimodernist forces came together in the infamous 1937 Degenerate Art Exhibition that, with slogans such as "'Art' Preaches Class Struggle" and "Marching Plan of the Cultural Bolshevists," explicitly equated modernist tendencies with communist positions.[9] There is no doubt that the rhetoric of antimodernism served important discursive functions as a placeholder for anticommunism and antisemitism. At the same time, the defense of expressionism as an authentically German contribution to modernism and the changes in modernist styles during the 1930s point to more fluid constellations. In the end, expanding on an existing art historical term (i.e., by treating Nazi Sachlichkeit as a continuation of New Objectivity) does not necessarily make it easier to evaluate the contribution of Koelle, Mercker, and others.[10] Given the coexistence

---

8 For reassessments of Nazi art along these lines, see James A. van Dyke, *Franz Radziwill and the Contradictions of German Art History, 1919–1945* (Ann Arbor: University of Michigan Press, 2010); Gregory Maertz, *Nostalgia for the Future: Modernism and Heterogeneity in the Visual Arts of Nazi Germany* (Stuttgart: ibidem, 2019); and, from the German perspective, Volker Böhnigk and Joachim Stamp, eds., *Die Moderne im Nationalsozialismus* (Bonn: University Press, 2006). In relation to photography, also see Brian Stokoe, "The Landscape Photobook in Germany: From Neue Sachlichkeit to Nazi Sachlichkeit," *History of Photography* 42.1 (2018): 78–97.
9 On the Degenerate Art Exhibition, see Stephanie Barron, ed., *"Degenerate Art": The Fate of the Avant-Garde in Nazi Germany* (New York: Harry N. Abrams, 1991). For overviews of the Gleichschaltung of art after 1933, the place of art between accommodation and resistance, and the challenges of writing Nazi art history, see (in chronological order) Hildegard Brenner, *Die Kunstpolitik des Nationalsozialismus* (Reinbek: Rowohlt, 1983); Jonathan Petropoulos, *Art as Politics in the Third Reich* (Chapel Hill: University of North Carolina Press, 1996); and Uwe Fleckner, ed., *Angriff auf die Avantgarde: Kunst und Kunstpolitik im Nationalsozialismus* (Berlin: Akademie, 2007).
10 The scholarly debates on New Objectivity, from the difficulty with definitions to the question of continuities, started during the 1980s. For early contributions that focus on the cult of industry and technology, see Helmut Kriedel and Ingeborg Güssow, ed., *Kunst und Technik in den 20er Jahren: Neue Sachlichkeit und Gegenständlicher Konstruktivismus* (Munich: Städtische Galerie im Lenbachhaus, 1980) and Adam C. Oellers, "Zur Frage der Kontinuität von Neuer Sachlichkeit und Nationalsozialistischer Kunst," *Kritische Berichte* 6.6 (1978): 41–54. Most surveys of New Objectivity limit the selection of works to the Weimar period. For contributions that move beyond these limitations, see Olaf Peters, *Neue Sachlichkeit und Nationalsozialismus: Affirmation und Kritik 1931–1947* (Berlin: Dietrich Reimer, 1998) and Sprengel Museum exhibition catalog *"Der stärkste Ausdruck unserer Tage": Neue Sachlichkeit in Hannover*, ed. Christian Fuhrmeister (Hildesheim: Georg Olms, 2001). The interdisciplinary orientation of recent scholarship on New Objectivity in painting, photogra-

of classicist, historicist, regionalist, modernist, and art deco styles within the Nazi culture of work, it might be more productive to focus on contextual factors such as the function of fine and applied arts in relation to different art markets, exhibition practices, forms of patronage, and so forth. After all, Mercker's impressionistic corporate panoramas have little in common with Carl Grossberg's almost surrealist depictions of a steam boiler, oil refinery, or spinning mill.

For the proletarian imaginaries shaped in the early workers' movement and developed further within the divided leftist politics of the Weimar SPD and KPD, the year "1933" meant a complete rupture and total erasure. Certain kinds of images simply disappeared from view and, by extension, from public consciousness. Beginning in the late nineteenth century, the politically charged iconographies of class had emerged alongside workers' struggles for the right to assemble, protest, and strike. The range of topics included depictions of unemployment, homelessness, and the destitution produced by capitalist exploitation and social marginalization. Making working-class experiences invisible did not automatically eliminate the proletarian as a problem, however. The socialist legacies of the Nazi Party remained a source of internal struggles, with different factions arguing whether to preserve, abandon, or utilize the label "socialist" in the party's name. As earlier chapters have shown, the discourse of workerdom gave worker poets and Thingspiel authors critical tools for separating positive and negative feelings about work from class analysis. Painters, sculptors, photographers, and filmmakers, too, integrated existing iconographies of industrial work into the new imaginaries of work community. Yet unlike the novels, poems, and plays with their Nazi terms and phrases, most of these artworks would be difficult to place if encountered outside their historical contexts. Understanding their contribution consequently requires close attention to the publication venues, exhibition practices, and organizational settings that, taken together, expanded the meaning of work toward emotional and experiential terms – namely, through the languages of joy, pride, and beauty.

There is no doubt that the Nazi regime created unprecedented new opportunities for artistic treatments of industrial modernity. Major corporations such as Krupp, Siemens, and Thyssen, and large public works projects such as those overseen by the Organization Todt commissioned artists to celebrate the unity of industry, party, and state. Paintings of industrial complexes in the Saar region, Alsace-Lorraine, and Upper Silesia supported the Reich's territorial ambitions pursued through referendum, annexation, or military invasion. Meanwhile, sculptures of

---

phy, literature, and film has contributed to a shift from formal and thematic concerns to broader social phenomena captured in terms such as mentality and attitude.

steelworkers placed in front of factory gates and vocational schools made sure that class identifications were integrated into the larger *völkisch*-populist-nationalist project. Traveling exhibitions about work-related themes, art exhibitions in factories, and industrial fairs known as Leistungsschauen relied heavily on the visual arts to advertise the accomplishments of the regime. Reviewing the 1937 Great German Art Exhibition, Kurt Eichelberger emphasized this point when he concluded that the aestheticization of work entailed much more than creating images of peasants and workers. His admonition that "the artist should not invent heroic man but himself join the columns of the Labor Service"[11] confirms that the blurring of the boundaries between artist and worker was as important to the "Gesamtkunstwerk of work" as any listing of formal characteristics.

The Nazi culture of work promised a fundamental shift from the primacy of production, whether as process, relation, or condition, to the emotional and aesthetic experiences made possible through participation in the work community. However, the aestheticization of work had to appear egalitarian as well as hierarchical and be inclusive even when exclusionary. Only then could the Nazi program of *Kunst für Alle* (Art for everyone), to cite the title of a popular art journal, fully realize its prefigurative and performative functions. This expanded meaning of work in art and work as art can be traced in the numerous exhibitions organized to showcase the accomplishments of the Nazi regime. Fordist terms such as productivity and rationality gave way to evocations of joy and pride in work, and calls for beautiful workplaces replaced Taylorist demands for better workflow design. The political significance attributed to these art exhibitions is evident in the close attention to all aspects of exhibition design, from the selection of exhibits and the design of catalogs to the choice of cities in the case of traveling exhibitions. Some exhibitions, such as the 1936 *Die Straßen Adolf Hitlers in der Kunst* (The Reichsautobahn in art), which included two paintings by Mercker, took a traditional approach by focusing on artistic treatments of the largest public works project begun during the Third Reich.[12] Organized by the NS-Kulturgemeinde, the 1936 exhibition *Lob der Arbeit* (Praise of work) showcased the new spirit of hope and pride, including through a piece by Koelle. Last but not least, the German Labor Front put together the 1937 exhibitions *Schönheit der Arbeit* (Beauty of labor) and the related *Die Arbeit in der Kunst* (Work in art) to demonstrate how the aestheticization of work grew organically out of the values of the racial state. As Ernst

---

11 Kurt Eichelberger, "Dem Volke Arbeit—Neue Aufgaben der Kunst," *Arbeitertum* 7.14 (1937): 20.
12 See the 1936 traveling exhibition *Die Straßen Adolf Hitlers in der Kunst* and the eponymous book and catalogue. On the mythification of the Reichsautobahn, see Erhard Schütz and Eckhard Gruber, eds., *Mythos Reichsautobahn: Bau und Inszenierung der "Straßen des Führers" 1933–1941* (Berlin: Christoph Links, 1996).

Wichert, one of the organizers, explained: "In contrast to the 'poor people' paintings of the past and the proletarian distortions of the postwar years, this exhibition is designed to give expression to the value of work, the beauty of its strength, the pride of its achievement, and the satisfaction of its execution."[13] As a guide to organizing such exhibitions explained, the goal was "to defeat the materialism of the decades-long Marxist workers' education."[14]

Taking full advantage of the connections between modernism and modernity, early Nazi propaganda shows drew heavily on the formal innovations of the Bauhaus. For the 1934 *Deutsches Volk-deutsche Arbeit* (German folk-German work) exhibition in Berlin, Herbert Bayer designed the catalogue, Lilly Reich and Mies van der Rohe worked on some of the displays, and Carl Grossberg contributed a large fresco.[15] Confident in the formative effect of good design, the various exhibits chosen for *German Folk-German Work* promoted the close cooperation of industry, agriculture, and traditional crafts as a precondition for social unity and economic growth. The 1937 *Schaffendes Volk* (Working folk) exhibition in Düsseldorf was even more ambitious in its proposals for merging art, work, and life when it included a model housing estate for ordinary workers and corporate managers.[16] Here the organizers drew on regional building styles and premodern social imaginaries, like the one evoked by a group of sculptures called *Die Ständischen* (The estates), to show the full compatibility of old and new communitarianisms. At least conceptually, these exhibitions offered guidelines for realizing the biopolitical goals of what the 1938 DAF exhibition *Gesundes Leben, frohes Schaffen* called "healthy life" and "happy work." The systematic blurring of the boundaries sepa-

---

13 Ernst Wichert, ed., *Lob der Arbeit: Kunst-Ausstellung 25 November – 20 Dezember 1936* (Berlin: NS-Kulturgemeinde, 1936), 5.
14 *Der Arbeiter und die bildende Kunst: System und Aufgabe der Kunstausstellungen in den Betrieben* (Munich: NS- Gemeinschaft "Kraft durch Freude," 1938), 48.
15 See the catalogue *Ausstellung Deutsches Volk deutsche Arbeit, Berlin 21.4 – 3.6.1934* (Berlin: n.p., 1934). On Nazi exhibition design, see Michael Tymkiw, *Nazi Exhibition Design and Modernism* (Minneapolis: University of Minnesota Press, 2018).
16 On this exhibition, see Stefanie Schäfers, *Vom Werkbund zum Vierjahresplan: Die Ausstellung Schaffendes Volk, Düsseldorf 1937* (Düsseldorf: Droste, 2001). One of the sculptors featured in *Die Ständischen* group was Hans Breker, Arno's brother. On the emphasis on work in Nazi propaganda shows, see Christoph Kivelitz, "Der 'schaffende Mensch' und die 'Veredelung der Materie': Der Begriff der Arbeit in Propagandaausstellungen im Nationalsozialismus," in *Arbeit und Industrie in der bildenden Kunst: Beiträge eines interdisziplinären Symposiums*, ed. Klaus Türk (Stuttgart: Franz Steiner, 1997), 119–130.

rating art and life confirmed what Ernst Jünger, in the dystopic language of *The Worker*, describes as "art as forming of the work-world."[17]

Koelle and Mercker benefitted greatly from the heightened significance accorded to public art in the Third Reich. They contributed to the discourse of workerdom by celebrating the dignity and nobility of the workers and naturalizing the conditions of work in the process. Koelle drew on socialist traditions as he made the worker's body the measure of all human effort and, hence, a vehicle for race-based identifications. By contrast, Mercker removed workers from the sites of production and compensated for their absence with an aestheticizing perspective on industry and technology. Both Koelle and Mercker were determined to find a formal solution to what Anson Rabinbach describes as the continued dematerialization of labor power, "the disappearance of the systems of representation that placed the working body at the juncture of nature and society."[18] The transition, in Rabinbach's terms, from the conception of the body as machine to a more complicated motor/energy model can be traced from the crisis of representation diagnosed by the historical avant-garde to the return of mimetic styles in the heroic realisms of the 1930s to which Koelle and Mercker contributed through their respective artistic forms and means.

II

Embodiment provided a powerful mechanism of class identification in the making of proletarian culture during the Wilhelmine and Weimar years. Not surprisingly, proletarian residues after 1933 survived in an artistic practice sometimes neglected in the histories of modern art because of its continued faith in the mimetic impulse: figurative sculpture. The conservative nature of figurative sculpture, according to Martin Damus, was inseparable from its historical role in public displays of power, a tradition on full display in the government architecture of the Reich.[19] At the same time, the continued faith in embodiment – which also means, the bodily traces of past struggles – made working-class bodies open to identifications still beholden to the master narratives of socialism. Yet how exactly were collective iden-

---

17 Ernst Jünger, *The Worker: Domination and Form*, ed. Laurence Paul Hemming, trans. Bogdan Costeda (Evanston, IL: Northwestern University Press, 2017), 126.
18 Anson Rabinbach, *The Human Motor: Energy, Fatigue, and the Origins of Modernity* (Berkeley: University of California Press, 1992), 295 and 300.
19 Martin Damus, "Gebrauch und Funktion von bildender Kunst und Architektur im Nationalsozialismus," in *Kunst und Kultur im deutschen Faschismus*, ed. Martin Rector and Ralf Schnell (Stuttgart: Metzler, 1978): 87–128.

tifications channeled through men made of granite, marble, or bronze? Were these figures perceived as embodiments of class, folk, or nation? Or just as personifications of the human condition and the eternal nature of work?

In the most general sense, figurative sculpture during the Third Reich involved translating notions of class, gender, and race into the solids and spaces through which the so-called *Leibgestalt* (bodily gestalt) could materialize the unity of body and soul and, by extension, the essence of the folk. Accordingly, the hypermasculine bodies favored by Arno Breker were presented as allegories of the Nazi state (e.g., The Party and The Army) and manifestations of its racial foundations (e.g., The Fighter, The Victor, The Genius). Breker, the most famous sculptor of the Third Reich, created bulked-up male bodies inspired by classical Greek sculpture. Josef Thorak monumentally enlarged their size and proportion, including in his unrealized *Monument of Work*.[20] On view at the Great German Art Exhibitions and elsewhere, sculptures with titles such as coal miner, foundry worker, blast furnace operator, and hammer mill operator functioned very differently because of their reference to specific job descriptions and, by extension, social types. Little known sculptors such as Gustav Adolf Bredow, Ernst Kunst, Otto Winkler, Robert Propf, Bernd Hartmann (Wiedenbrück), and Hans Breker (later pseud. Hans van Breek) drew on neoclassical, symbolist, expressionist, and naturalist elements to mediate between the social specificity of working bodies and the presumed universality of work-related emotions.[21] Franz Iffland's elegant worker figurines, Gerhard Adolf Janensch's miniature foundry workers, and Hans Scholter's small desk bronzes, which were given to model factories in recognition of their beautification efforts, translated these artistic homages to workerdom into the small-scale formats of Nazi kitsch.

---

20 For this aspect of the fascist body politics (in a global context), see the two volumes edited by James Anthony Mangan, *Shaping the Superman—Fascist Body as Political Icon: Aryan Fascism* (London: Routledge, 2013) and *Superman Supreme—Fascist Body as Political Icon: Global Fascism* (London: Routledge, 2014). The standard study on the subject is George L. Mosse, *The Image of Man: The Creation of Modern Masculinity* (Oxford: Oxford University Press, 1996), especially the chapter on "The New Fascist Man" (155–180). On Nazi body politics more generally, see Paula Diehl, ed., *Körper im Nationalsozialismus: Bilder und Praxen* (Munich: Ferdinand Schöningh, 2006) and Elke Frietsch and Christina Herkommer, eds., *Nationalsozialismus und Geschlecht: Zur Politisierung und Ästhetisierung von Körper, Rasse und Sexualität im Dritten Reich* (Bielefeld: transcript, 2009).

21 For a selection of workers' sculpture in general, see the catalogue edited by Klaus Türk, *Sculptures of Workers: Figures from the Grohmann Museum at Milwaukee School of Engineering* (Milwaukee: MSOE Press, 2009). On the political role of statuary in the twentieth century, also see Sergiusz Michalski, *Public Monuments: Art in Political Bondage 1870–1997* (London: Reaktion, 1998), 93–106.

Fritz Koelle, the leading representative of workers' sculpture, has been characterized as "the creator (*Gestalter*) of the worker," to cite the title of a comprehensive study on the artist.[22] His legacies have been subject to probing questions about Germany history and museum culture, as evident by a recent exhibition by the Kunstsammlungen und Museen Augsburg. During the Nazi period, critics celebrated him as a champion of "the unknown worker,"[23] a reference to the unknown soldier in Nazi rhetoric, and called his sculptures "allegories [Sinnbilder] of work and the readiness for work."[24] Born in Augsburg, Koelle (1895–1953) trained as a metal worker and then studied applied arts in Munich. Through his wife Elisabeth, a fellow artist and the daughter of a miner from St. Ingbert in the Saar region, he became fascinated with the lifeworld of ordinary miners. Working exclusively in bronze, Koelle ended up devoting much of his artistic career to two iconic figures, the coal miner and the steelworker. In 1927, he (together with Kollwitz) participated in a group exhibition at the Prussian Academy of Arts in Berlin and, praised for his expressive style, first gained greater recognition. However, a prospective professorship in Munich never materialized because of the Nazi rise to power and, for a brief moment, charges of Bolshevist tendencies against the artist.

After 1933, Koelle sought to reach an artistic compromise between the worker as a representative of his class and a visualization of workerdom. This meant mediating between the habitus of suffering and its corollary, empathy, a frequent choice in socialist treatments of the figure, and the attitude of pride and belief in the nobility of work, a key feature of the racialized treatments favored by the Nazis. In personal recollections written after the war, Koelle described himself as an apolitical artist who, despite occasional threats, resisted cooptation by the regime; the similarities with Winnig would be worth exploring further. Included in all Great German Art Exhibitions, he was successful enough to maintain a studio in Geiselgasteig near Munich where he worked until his death. He never joined the

---

22 The reference is to Eva-M. Pasche, *Fritz Koelle (1895 bis 1953), der Gestalter des Arbeiters: Leben und Werk* (Essen: Glückauf, 2001). On the reception of Koelle, see Eva-M. Pasche, "Vom Kulturbolschewisten zum völkischen Gestalter des Arbeiters: Der Bildhauer Fritz Koelle," in *Machtergreifung in Augsburg: Die Anfänge der NS-Diktatur 1933–1937*, ed. Michael Cramer-Fürtig and Bernhard Gotto (Augsburg: Wißner, 2008): 214–225. For a local perspective, see Gudrun Opladen, "Plastiker der Arbeit. Der Augsburger Bildhauer Fritz Koelle: Ein Leben zwischen Anpassung und Verfemung," *Augsburger Zeiten* 18 (2007/8): 16–19. On the Nazi years, also see Schirmbeck, *Adel der Arbeit*, 51–59. On the East German years, see Béatrice Vierneisel, "Fritz Koelle—Der Gestalter des deutschen Berg- und Hüttenarbeiters," *Kunstdokumentation SBZ/DDR 1945–1990: Aufsätze Berichte Materialien*, ed. Günter Feist, Eckhart Gillen, and Béatrice Vierneisel (Cologne: DuMont: 1996), 191–201.
23 Ernst Kammerer, *Fritz Koelle* (Berlin: Rembrandt, 1939), 5.
24 Edgar Schindler, "Denkmale der Arbeit," *Die Kunst im Dritten Reich* 2.5 (1938): 139.

Nazi Party and endured occasional Gestapo visits but still received prestigious prizes and lucrative commissions (e. g., by MAN in Augsburg and Saarbergwerke in Reden).[25] A large version of *Betender Bergmann* (1934, Praying miner) was acquired by Hitler for the Reich Chancellery, and a rendition of his *Saarbergmann* (Miner from the Saar) appeared on an official coin commemorating the 1935 Saar plebiscite.

After the war, his close ties to the Nazi elites made Koelle once again ineligible for a professorship at the Munich Art Academy. Even better opportunities opened up after he joined the Bavarian KPD and offered his services to the East German SED (Socialist Unity Party) as a longtime champion of the working class. In 1948, the SED, at the initiative of Otto Grotewohl, purchased a small version of *Hüttenarbeiter* (1931, Mill worker) for the Central Committee's main meeting room. Through these new contacts, Koelle was soon appointed to teaching positions at art academies in Dresden and (East) Berlin-Weißensee. In a sworn affidavit written after the war, he explained: "My workers are no Hellenistic rulers with imperial poses, but they are also no figures from the underworld of dives as others like to show them. Instead, they are workers with a nascent class consciousness, aware of their power! That is true proletarian nobility! That is the nobility of work!"[26] Whereas terms such as "class consciousness" and "proletarian" boosted his socialist credentials, "nobility of work" came straight from the Nazi discourse of workerdom – evidence to the degree that his worker figures, too, were adaptable to changing ideological pressures.

The fact that Koelle created busts of Nazi "martyr" Horst Wessel (1936) and Karl Marx (1952) should be seen less as evidence of political opportunism than of the populist attitudes that from the beginning sustained his classed bodies across the right-left divide. The organizing principle guiding all of his formal and thematic choices was the passionate belief in *Volksnähe* (closeness to the people) as the most effective strategy for being at once popular and populist. Confirming this point, a private photograph shows Koelle in an embroidered peasant frock, and a 1940 bronze bust of the artist features him with a worker's cap. Whether "authentic" or not, Koelle's identification with the "working folk" and his connection to regional culture establish the interpretative framework within which his sculptures have continued to be exhibited and evaluated since the postwar years. Museums in St. Ingbert and Augsburg have hosted his only solo shows,

---

25 On Koelle's relationship to the regime and the various interpretations given by the artist and his defenders after the war, see Schlenker, *Hitler's Salon*, 167–174.
26 Koelle, quoted in Pasche, *Fritz Koelle*, 181.

and the latter's municipal museum, the Schaezlerpalais, holds the largest collection of his work.[27]

Koelle's worker figures inspired widely divergent interpretations during the first years of the Nazi regime. As in the case of workers' poetry, they tend to reproduce the opposing views on German art taken by the Propaganda Ministry under Goebbels, the German Labor Front under Ley, and the NS-Kulturgemeinde under Rosenberg.[28] Moreover, these positions express the competing competencies (or lack thereof) of the institutions responsible for public art and art policy after 1933, including on the local level. In September 1933, Koelle's life-size bronze *Der Blockwalzer* (1929, The block mill worker) was removed from Munich's Karl-Preis-Platz (then called Melusinenplatz), only four years after it had been installed as part of a new public housing estate. According to the city councilmen arguing for removal, "the treatment of the worker's body showed typical Bolshevist traits and the worker's head and posture lacked all nobility of work. In fact, it amounted to a clear provocation, an invitation to class struggle."[29] Wearing a leather apron and protective shoes, with muscular arms attesting to the physical demands of his job, the block mill worker is leaning heavily on a lifting and pouring shank, the kind used to handle molten ore. His sunken cheeks and weary eyes convey a sense of being at once damaged and distinguished by such a dangerous assignment. His exhaustion – which also means, his resistance to heroizing interpretations – can be read as either recognition of the realities of labor exploitation or proof of his commitment to the grand project of industrialization (see figure 5.1). Alternatively, it may be described as a prototypical performance of pride in work.

Only one year later, a reviewer of the 1934 Great Munich Art Exhibition praised Koelle's *Der Hammermeister* (1932, The hammer mill worker) as a perfect example of "the self-confident German worker who regards his creating, fighting, and suffering as part of a sacrificial service to the folk and finds his service ennobled through his belief in the future of Germany."[30] On the pages of the *Völkische Beo-*

---

27 The two Koelle exhibitions confirm this point, the 2003 Augsburg exhibition "Fritz Koelle zum 50. Todestag" at the Maximilianmuseum and the 2003/04 exhibition "Fritz Koelle, der Bergmann von der Saar" at the Heimatmuseum in St. Ingbert. On the city of Augsburg and the Fritz Koelle estate, see https://kunstsammlungen-museen.augsburg.de/koelle.
28 On this point, see Thomas Mathieu, *Kunstauffassungen und Kulturpolitik im Nationalsozialismus: Studien zu Adolf Hitler, Joseph Goebbels, Alfred Rosenberg, Baldur von Schirach, Heinrich Himmler, Albert Speer, Wilhelm Frick* (Saarbrücken: PFAU, 1997).
29 Hans Flügge, quoted in Pasche, *Fritz Koelle*, 95.
30 Gerd Buchheit, quoted in Pasche, *Fritz Koelle*, 107. *Der Hammermeister* was shown at the 1937 *Schönheit der Arbeit* exhibition, together with two other works. A small version of *Der Hammermeister* was included at the 1941 GDK exhibition. Koelle also featured prominently in *Schönheit*

138 — Chapter 5 Pride in Work: On Workers' Sculpture and Industrial Painting

Fig. 5.1: Fritz Koelle, *Der Blockwalzer* (1929, 190 cm), Melusinenplatz (today: Karl-Preis-Platz), Munich. Public domain, Wikimedia Commons.

Fig. 5.2: Fritz Koelle, *Der Hammermeister* (1932, 200 cm), in Ernst Kammerer, *Fritz Koelle* (Berlin: Rembrandt, 1939), 36.

bachter, the figure still inspired tirades against "a pathos of ugliness that exceeds all standards of naturalness"[31] and amounted to an attack on all German ideals (see figure 5.2). The actual two-meter bronze features a bare-chested worker standing upright, wearing a leather apron and work boots, with one hand holding a pole and the other raised in what looks like a warning gesture. Significantly, the apron displays rich surface textures, whereas the upper body has been smoothed out and looks younger and stronger, compared to the 1929 *Block Mill Worker*. The question remains how to interpret these features: As a momentous shift from the diagnosis of exploitation to the idealization of work? As a change in artistic focus, away from the suffering of the physical body of class toward the protective armor provided by the idea of folk community? Or as evidence of broader artistic trends throughout Europe that included a general preference for more streamlined bodies? In one of the first articles on the artist, Ernst Kammerer acknowledged Koelle's artistic debt

---

der Arbeit 4.1 (1939), where two of his sculptures illustrate an article by Wilhelm Lotz on "Kunst im Betrieb" (50–59); his Bergmann appears on the cover of 4.2 (1939).
31 Anon., quoted by Schirmbeck, 77.

to Auguste Rodin and Aristide Maillol, both known for their explorations of expressive physicality, but insisted that the former was committed to restore the dignity of work by casting his worker figures exclusively in bronze.[32] Despite growing recognition, official anxieties about socialist tendencies remained, which may be one reason why the reviewer of a 1936 exhibition in the Augsburger Kunstverein felt compelled to assure visitors that they were faced not with "the tendentiously conceived representatives of an international proletariat but were looking at German workers, self-sufficient, self-confident members of the folk community with an open gaze and head raised high."[33] In the first monograph on the sculptor, Kammerer insisted that Koelle was only interested in the ideal type, "*the* man at the blast furnace, *the* coal miner, *the* ancestor" – all to be defined in racial terms.[34] Impressed by Koelle's use of scale, another critic called on all artists to overcome the limitations of realism and strive toward a higher realm of symbolization; in his words: "[The figures'] dimensions – they are as tall as three meters – and the force of artistic treatment, which is especially evident in the unusual take on muscle formation, turn them into symbols of work and the willingness to work."[35]

The irresolvable tension between the discourses of class and race and, closely related, between social type and political allegory can be clarified through a closer look at several Koelle sculptures from the late 1920s and late 1930s. Some are distinguished by an expressive realist style that emphasizes the worker's physical features; others use a smooth art deco style that hides the body under protective clothing. There is no question that Koelle modeled his approach to embodiment on Meunier, the first to develop a rich social typology that values the worker's contribution to industrial modernity. Emphasizing the dignity of the laboring class, both artists treat classed bodies as physical bodies and not as mere abstractions. A comparison of *The Hammer Mill Worker* to Meunier's *Le marteleur* (1886, The hammer man) confirms their shared attention to the tools and attires of working people. The noticeable shift toward neoclassical sensibilities in *The Hammer Mill Worker* must therefore be explained through broader trends in the aestheticization of labor and industry also found in the statuary of the WPA (Works Progress Administration) Federal Art Project during the New Deal era. In studies on the art

---

32 Ernst Kammerer, "Die Kunst der Bronze: Der Bildhauer Fritz Koelle," *Die Kunst für Alle: Malerei, Plastik, Graphik, Architektur* 51.4 (1936): 94–99.
33 Anon., quoted in Schirmbeck, *Adel der Arbeit*, 71.
34 Ernst Kammerer, *Fritz Koelle* (Berlin: Rembrandt, 1939), 13. My emphasis. The book appeared in a series titled *Die Kunstbücher des Volkes*; an earlier book, Alfred Hentzen's *Deutsche Bildhauer der Gegenwart* (1934), also contains a section on Koelle.
35 Edgar Schindler, "Denkmale der Arbeit," *Die Kunst im Dritten Reich* 2 (1938): 138. The work in question could be *Betender Bergmann*.

of the machine age, elongated lines and smooth surfaces are often connected to the liberating effects of mobility and adaptability in a democratic society. In the Third Reich, the same formal elements prompted very different interpretations, but that does not mean that the promise of greater recognition for industrial workers could not have inspired a comparable formal expression of dynamism.

Fig. 5.3: Fritz Koelle, *Hochofenarbeiter* (1935, 200 cm), in Kammerer, *Ernst Koelle*, 44.

Fig. 5.4: Fritz Koelle, *Hochofenarbeiter* (1938, 420 cm), in Kammerer, *Ernst Koelle*, 60.

Over the course of four years, Koelle created seven versions of the iconic figure called either *Hochofenarbeiter* or *Der erste Mann am Hochofen* (Blast furnace worker).[36] Of various sizes, all show the blast furnace operator with the customary

---

36 They are *Der Hochofenarbeiter* (1935, 200 cm, GRK Sterkrade Oberhausen), *Der Hochofenarbeiter* (1935, 61 cm), *Der erste Mann am Hochofen* (1936, 46 cm), *Der erste Mann am Hochofen* (1937, 225 cm, Hochschule für Technik und Wirtschaft Saarbrücken), *Der erste Mann am Hochofen*

flame-retardant leather apron and gloves, steel-toed boots, and wide-brimmed felt cap. In an early version (1935), he is raising his arms in almost dance-like fashion and displaying the pleats of his tunic in ways reminiscent of Greek statuary (see figure 5.3). In later versions (1936, 1937, 1938), both hands rest on the stoking rod used to control the molten iron. From his upright posture to the central placement of the tool, all elements are aligned to convey an impression of strength, toughness, and, ultimately, pride in work. How closely pride is correlated with scale can be seen in the 4.2-meter-high bronze sculpture on a marble base commissioned in 1938 by the MAN machine factory in Augsburg to serve as a memorial for the fallen of World War I. During World War II, that company became the largest manufacturer of diesel engines for submarines and tanks (see figure 5.4).

In the only monograph on the worker in Nazi art, Peter Schirmbeck interprets Koelle's turn to neoclassical and monumental styles that "elevate and animate mere physical semblance through the realization of its ideal form" as a response to growing political pressures. By leaving behind the constraints of naturalism and realism, he argues, Koelle and others contributed to "the image- and meaning-making of an attitude toward life that was now becoming visible in all areas of *völkisch* life."[37] What speaks against this diagnosis of aesthetic and ideological accommodation is Koelle's continued interest in the steelworker as a distinct physical type with a particular class habitus. Many of the large-scale pieces created after 1933 feature workers with attitudes that find individual expression in their relaxed ways of standing. *Bergarbeiter, sich die Hemdsärmel aufkrämpelnd* (1936, Miner rolling up his sleeves) captures a small gesture that seems incongruous with the timeless qualities of bronze as an artistic medium. *Der Bergmann von der Saar* (1937, The Miner from the Saar) wears casual clothing and keeps his hands in his pockets. *Der Walzmeister* (1939, The rollerman), shown at the 1940 GDK as *Der erste Mann vom Blockwalzwerk* (The first man from the blooming mill), wears low-rise pants held up only by the tilt of his hips. Given Koelle's continued interest in individual types, these experiments with the streamlined modern style could be seen as an attempt to distinguish himself from the more static styles associated with Breker and Thorak and to maintain some connection to class-based and region-specific sensibilities.

(1937, 136 cm, Lenbachhaus München), *Hochofenarbeiter* (1938, 420 cm, MAN Augsburg), and *Der erste Mann am* Hochofen (1939, 135 cm). This information is taken from http://www.koelle-online.de/Pages_fk/fk_7_werkverzeichnis_1.html.

37 Schirmbeck, *Adel der Arbeit*, 104. A similar argument about Koelle's turn toward monumental scales can be found in Eric Michaud, *The Cult of Art in Nazi Germany*, trans. Janet Lloyd (Stanford: Stanford University Press, 2004), 199–200.

One way of moving beyond the normative categories that continue to trouble surveys of Nazi art involves paying more attention to the emotions associated with (in this case) workers' sculpture. Whereas scholars today often focus on aesthetic strategies such as heroization to place totalitarian art in a comparative context, Nazi art historians approached questions of form through anthropologically based categories that allowed them to judge an artist's ability to convey ethnically based feelings and attitudes. In the words of Wilhelm Pinder, good art involved "the enlistment of ethnic traits in a pictorially convincing self-portrayal of one's own folk."[38] How did Koelle (not) fit into a framework that located the aesthetic within a dialogic process between subjects and objects and, more specifically, an emotion-based process of self-identification? He repeatedly spoke about the negative emotions that had become associated with the working class and explained his evolving views with a desire to move beyond the miserabilist tradition perpetuated by Weimar-era artists sympathetic to the workers' movement. From the beginning, he insisted that his identification with coal miners and steelworkers was not compassion, a sentiment he associated with Kollwitz, but a decidedly masculine expression of "respect, love, and esteem."[39] Given the heavy emphasis on authenticity as a key aspect of workerdom, it would be problematic to draw on the distinction between authentic gesture and artificial pose, which plays such a key role in racial theory, to speculate about Koelle's artistic intentions. Max Imdahl's overly neat distinction – "Gesture is bodily self-expression. Pose, on the other hand, is an expression of the Other [Fremdausdruck]"[40] – may be useful in formalist analyses and iconological studies. But the underlying assumption about authenticity becomes problematic when applied to forms of embodiment and practices of figuration that assert their presumed essence only through and against a racialized Other. Moreover, the ideological possibilities of embodiment are inseparable from the logics of absence and presence that make the disappearance of the worker from representation as revealing as his changing expressive faculties.

III

Convinced of the artistic and critical potentialities of realism, nineteenth-century artists Jean-François Millet, Gustave Courbet, Wilhelm Leibl, and, above all, Con-

---

38 Wilhelm Pinder, *Wesenszüge deutscher Kunst* (Leipzig: E. A. Seemann, 1940), 59. Pinder's model for ideal German art is the Naumburg Master.
39 Fritz Koelle, quoted in Pasche, *Fritz Koelle*, 40.
40 Max Imdahl, "Pose und Indoktrination: Zu Werken der Plastik und Malerei im Dritten Reich," in *Nazi-Kunst ins Museum?*, ed. Klaus Staeck (Göttingen: Steidl, 1994), 87.

stantin Meunier were the first to treat the worker as a subject worthy of artistic interest. They used scenes of manual labor – first involving farm laborers and, increasingly, factory workers – to show the strength, resilience, and dignity of working people. Depicting craftsmen, artisans, and peasants allowed them to measure the dramatic changes brought about by the industrial revolution and document the attendant processes of urbanization and modernization. Industrial workers symbolized man's mastery of nature and triumph over the machine and, at the same time, personified the exploitation of an emerging working class. Especially the spectacle of coal and steel inspired realist, naturalist, and impressionist treatments and invited allegorizing, mythologizing, and romanticizing interpretations. In the process, the figure of the worker became linked to two very different emotional registers, the pain and suffering caused by the inequities of modern class society and the promise of social mobility linked to the historical convergence of capitalism and democracy. Women and children assumed center stage when the detrimental effects of the industrial revolution were examined through familiar melodramatic and sentimental modalities. Youthful, muscular masculinity predominated in approaches that tied industrialization to narratives of progress and growth, including in nationalist terms.

Within these gendered divides, the steel mill assumed a special place in national(ist) iconographies of industrial modernity. Adolph Menzel's monumental *Eisenwalzwerk / Moderne Zyklopen* (1875, Iron rolling mill / modern cyclops), with its dramatic interplay of light and darkness, established the standard for visualizing the productive and destructive effects of industrialization. Max Liebermann's *Flachsscheuer in Laren* (1886, Flax barn in Laren), an impressionistic study of women and children spinning flax, can be described as the protoindustrial (female) counterpart to the heroic spectacle of fire and steel that henceforth captured the aspirations of nationalists as well as socialists. In the decades that followed, artistic treatments of industry and technology inspired either heroic apotheoses of masculinity, as in Arthur Kampf's various versions of *Walzwerk* (1901, Rolling mill), formally innovative critiques of alienated labor, as in Gerd Arntz's didactic woodcuts from the 1920s, or emotionally detached studies of beautiful machines without workers, as in the New Objectivist paintings of Grossberg.[41]

---

[41] On the difficulties with the Nazi label, see Andreas Schroyen, "'NS' ist nur drin, wenn 'NS' draufsteht? Die Rezeption der Arbeitsdarstellungen von Arthur Kampf im 3. Reich und ihre Aufarbeitung in der Kunstgeschichte nach 1945," in *Arbeit und Industrie in der bildenden Kunst*, 110–118. Baluschek was included in the 1933 and 1934 Great Berlin Art Exhibitions but also shown at the 1937 Degenerate Art Exhibition. And the continuities in Grossberg's work before and after 1933 have been examined in Michael Hasenclever, ed., *Carl Grossberg: Bilder von Architektur und Industrie der Zwanziger und Dreissiger Jahre* (Munich: Galerie Hasenclever, 2006).

The 1930s and early 1940s were the golden age of industrial painting – and the period during which workers either disappeared from the sites and processes of production or, as in industrial photography, became types in highly staged and carefully framed encounters between man and machine. Recent studies have clarified how the look and feel of what has been called reactionary, fascist, or Nazi modernism must be evaluated as part of larger developments in the culture of work before and after 1933.[42] This includes the machine aesthetic as an expression of the corporatist principles that, translated into aesthetic categories, turned the industrial complex into yet another kind of laboring body. Largely forgotten today, a surprising number of artists specialized in painting factories, workshops, and construction sites, returning time and again to the founding site of industrial modernity: the blast furnace.[43] Franz Gerwin created atmospheric scenes of industry set in the Ruhr region, Richard Gessner continued to indulge his fascination with construction sites, Carl Theodor Protzen documented the building of the *Reichsautobahn*, and Ria Picco-Rückert, a rare woman in that group, did commissions for MAN, Siemens, and Reichswerke Hermann Göring.[44] Combining naturalist, impressionist, and realist elements, their paintings can be described as exercises in reauratization: of the industrial plant, the conditions of production, and

---

[42] The references are to Jeffrey Herf, *Reactionary Modernism: Technology, Culture and Politics in Weimar and the Third Reich* (Cambridge: Cambridge University Press, 1984) and Peter Fritzsche, "Nazi Modern," *Modernism/Modernity* 3.1 (1996): 1–22. For the prevailing argument since the 1980s, see Roger Griffin, "The Modernism of Nazi Culture," in *Modernism and Fascism* (London: Palgrave Macmillan, 2007), 279–309 and "Modernity, Modernism, and Fascism: A Mazeway Resynthesis," *Modernism/ Modernity* 15.1 (2008): 9–24. For a recent overview of historical debates, see Mark Roseman, "National Socialism and the End of Modernity," *American Historical Review* 116.3 (2011): 688–701. From the perspective of the literary avant-garde, see Andrew Hewitt, *Fascist Modernism: Aesthetics, Politics, and the Avant-Garde* (Stanford: Stanford University Press, 1993). From an art historical perspective, see Mark Antcliff, "Fascism, Modernism, and Modernity," *The Art Bulletin* 84.1 (2008): 148–169. On the complicated relationship between fascism and modernism, see Lynn Kellmanson Matheny, "Reactionary Modernism and Fascist Aesthetics: National Socialist Visual Culture and the Appropriation of Modernism" (PhD. diss., University of California at Los Angeles, 1999).

[43] During the interwar years, the blast furnace emerged as an icon of industrial modernity in democratic as well as totalitarian societies; see *Blast Furnaces, Night* (c. 1920) by the British Edwin Butler Bayliss, *Blast Furnace No. 1 at Kuznetsk* (1931) by the Soviet Pytor Kotov, and *Blast Furnace, Great Lakes Steel Corporation* (1947) by the Cuban-American Carlos Lopez.

[44] On Ria Picco-Rückert, one of the few women artists of the Third Reich, see Klaus Ollinger, *Kohle und Stahl: Leben und Werk der Industriemalerin Ria Picco-Rückert* (Püttlingen: Merziger, 2007). On Erna Wagner-Hehmke, a woman photographer who specialized in industrial photography, also see Ilsabe und Gerolf Schülke, ed., *Erna Wagner-Hehmke: Industriefotografien der 30er bis 50er Jahre* (Düsseldorf: Bahnhof Eller, 1989).

the relationship between (absent) man and (ubiquitous) machine.⁴⁵ The iconic status of the blast furnace, the drama of the steam engine, and the arrangement of gears, cylinders, and cogwheels – all these topoi can also be found in the art and photography of Fascist Italy, Stalinist Russia, and New Deal America. The technological imagination of the interwar years played a key role in redefining the relationship between industry, labor, and the state, but the discourse of workerdom made sure that this relationship assumed very specific meanings in the German context, where the question of race was always present even in its absence.⁴⁶ Confirming this point, one might mention local artists who developed an interest in miners and craftsmen as part of political commitments to *Volkstum* (folklore) and *Heimatschutz* (protection of the heritage) and who often ended up working for DAF and other Nazi organizations. To give two examples, Karl Reineke-Altenau, an artist and writer from the Upper Harz area, created murals at the Rammelsberg near Goslar, and Hermann Ketelhöhn produced etchings and drawings that acknowledged the hard work of the miners in the Ruhr region.⁴⁷

Far removed from the artistic and political movements of his time, Erich Mercker (1891–1973) worked in an almost industrial fashion. An autodidact, he painted countless industrial complexes and construction sites – approximately three thousand over the course of his career – in order to create what one critic at the time called "*the heroic landscape of engineering* in a renewed Germany."⁴⁸ A few courses in civil engineering taken before the war gave him a basic understanding of the functioning of an industrial plant. And a small inheritance from his mother allowed him early on to paint full time and eventually support his family through sales and commissions – in fact, quite well if prices are any indication.⁴⁹ While not associated with a particular school or group, Mercker was part

---

45 For an early article on the machine aesthetic after 1933, see Adam C. Oellers, "Zur Frage der Kontinuität von Neuer Sachlichkeit und nationalsozialistischer Kunst," *Kritische Beiträge* 6.6 (1978): 42–54. For the broader context, see Olaf Peters, *Neue Sachlichkeit und Nationalsozialismus: Affirmation und Kritik 1931–1947* (Berlin: Dietrich Reimer, 1998).
46 The similarities cannot be adequately addressed here. As in Nazi Germany, heroic worker sculptures from Fascist Italy or Stalinist Russia cover the entire range from socialist realist and neoclassical to *streamline moderne* styles. However, one significant difference involves the greater gender equality found in Soviet painting and sculpture.
47 See Kai Gurski, "Schlägel, Eisen und Hakenkreuz—Das Thema Bergbau im Werk des Malers Kal Reineke-Altenau," (PhD diss., Hochschule für Bildende Künste Braunschweig, 2008).
48 Fritz Alexander Kauffmann, *Die neue deutsche Malerei* (Berlin: Deutscher Verlag, 1941), 51.
49 This biographical information is taken from Volkmar von Pechstaedt, *Erich Mercker: Landschafts-, Industrie- und Städtemaler* (Göttingen: Hainholz, 2003) and the book by Jung and Stahnke. Sales prices for works shown at the Greater German Art Exhibitions are available on the gdk-re-

of the art community in Munich, where he lived most of his life. He regularly showed new work in the annual exhibitions of the conservative Munich Art Association (MKG). Early works such as *Abend am Hochofen* (1920, Evening at the blast furnace) and *Eisenhütte* (1920, Large steel mill) still feature the *impasto* technique (i.e., with a palette knife) that signals a creative will toward abstraction and expression. In the early 1930s, Mercker developed brush techniques better suited for accurate renderings of industrial structures. At the same time, he added impressionistic effects – muted colors, soft outlines, climatic flourishes – that made his presentation of two Duisburg-based companies, the yellowish-green *August Thyssen Hütte* (1939, August Thyssen iron and steel works) and the greyish-yellow *Im Reiche der Hochöfen/Rheinhausen Stahlwerke* (1940, In the realm of blast furnaces), look just like his idyllic Alpine landscapes and Mediterranean seascapes, a favorite subject matter since the postwar years.

After joining the Nazi Party in spring 1933, Mercker benefitted greatly from his personal acquaintance with Fritz Todt, Inspector General of German Roadways. Several early *Reichsautobahn* paintings, featuring bridge constructions, showcased his artistic technique and close attention to detail. He quickly made a name for himself as a skilled painter of technical subjects. His inclusion in several exhibitions (Essen in 1928, Dresden in 1939, and Dortmund in 1942) on the theme of "art and technology" confirms his close association with the vast Nazi bureaucracy responsible for the reorganization of labor and industry. Mercker's selection for the German pavilion at the 1937 Exposition Internationale des Arts et Techniques dans la Vie Moderne in Paris, his participation in all Great German Art Exhibitions, and the reproduction of major works in popular art magazines contributed to his growing prominence. Like Picco-Rückert, he continued to produce industrial paintings for West German corporations after the World War Two. Today the largest number of his works can be found in the Grohmann Museum at the Milwaukee School of Engineering, where his paintings (and countless similar works) are displayed according to technical subject matter.[50]

Nazi-era industrial painting resists facile comparisons to New Objectivity, despite a shared preoccupation with the object world, an affinity for surface effects, and an almost photographic attention to detail. Whereas the latter often includes some reflection on physical reality as a conduit to critical analysis, the former re-

---

search.de. website. The reference to the Wolff book can be found in Jung and Stahnke, *Erich Mercker and Technical Subjects*, 29.

50 For a catalogue of this collection, see Klaus Türk, *Man at Work: 400 Years in Paintings and Bronzes; Labor and the Evolution of Industry in Art* (Milwaukee: MSOE Press, 2003). Like the museum, the catalogue is organized according to process-based categories such as metalworking (furnaces and forges), mining (steel mills and rolling mills), and glass and textile production.

mains committed to, of constrained by, the certainties of mimesis – that is, to depict the machine or factory in accordance with the interests of corporate clients. For the same reason, it would be unproductive to overemphasize the similarities with socialist realism, for instance as part of a totalitarian art argument. Some early accounts of art in the Third Reich made no distinction between the art produced in the "brown" and "red" dictatorship, whereas others rejected such comparisons with reference to their different political ideologies.[51] More productive are comparative approaches that take into account the larger culture of industrialization and consider the role of images as part of electrification campaigns and public works schemes. Whereas Soviet paintings of constructions sites and power plants, especially if examined as part of the regional architectures of collectivism, cannot be examined without reference to the socialist fixation on productivity and the fetishization of the plan, Nazi industrial painting remains beholden to capitalism as the system most conducive to industrial and artistic production, an external constraint that accounts for its aesthetics of concealment.[52] Socialist realists aimed to capture the truth of the phenomenon, whereas industrial painters during the Third Reich could never escape the terms of obfuscation and commodification introduced through the artist-client relationship.

The definition of industrial painting as genre painting goes a long way in revealing the underlying tensions between the appearance of realism and the effect of its unreality. Drawing on established techniques and iconographies, genre paint-

---

51 For the respective positions, see Martin Damus, *Sozialistischer Realismus und Kunst im Nationalsozialismus* (Frankfurt am Main: Fischer, 1981) and Berthold Hinz, *Die Malerei im deutschen Faschismus: Kunst und Konterrevolution* (Munich: Carl Hanser, 1974).

52 Whether or not the highly theoretical debates on socialist realism can add to a better understanding of realism in Nazi-era painting as some form of hyperreality or mythical realism would require a different discussion. The affinity for the monumental and the heroic, the emphatic appeal to the people, the cult of masculinity in the New Man, and the performance of optimism (or joy) are all part of visualizations of the collective in which the arts are used not to reflect reality but to form it actively. For major contributions, see Igor Golomstock, *Totalitarian Art*, trans. Robert Chandler (London: Abrams, 2012) and *Totalitarian Art and Modernity*, ed. Mikkel Bolt Rasmussen and Jacob Wamberg (Aarhus: Aarhus University Press, 2010). For two exhibition catalogues that take a comparative perspective, see Dawn Ades, Tim Benton, David Elliott, et al., eds., *Kunst und Macht im Europa der Diktaturen von 1930 bis 1945* (Berlin: Deutsches Historisches Museum, 1995); and Hans-Jörg Czech and Nikola Doll, eds., *Kunst und Propaganda: Im Streit der Nationen 1930–1945* (Dresden: Sandstein, 2007). For a recent contribution that emphasizes the transnational, global reach of the visual culture of fascism, see Julia Adeney Thomas and Geoff Eley, eds., *Visualizing Fascism: The Twentieth-Century Rise of the Global Right* (Durham, NC: Duke University Press, 2020). For a comparative study on Third Reich and GDR before and after 1945, see Andreas Beaugrand, Ilse Lindau, and Manfred Strecker, eds., *Totalitäre Kunst—Kunst im Totalitarismus? Beispiele aus dem NS-Staat und der DDR* (Bielefeld: Pendragon, 1997).

ing is usually concerned with types and typologies; it is beholden to the conventions of academism. Art historian Berthold Hinz describes genre painting as an articulation of total immanence that "focuses exclusively on what already exists and has been achieved; it is not capable of opening new vistas."[53] The ability of genre painting to compartmentalize experience and paralyze consciousness, to paraphrase Hinz, seems at first glance to have little to do with the transformative power of art compulsively evoked by Nazi theorists but rarely put into practice.[54] Offering a conceptual workaround, Fritz Alexander Kauffmann in 1941 described industrial painting as the beginning of an entirely new kind of art. In his words,

> Our readiness to affirm the world of today and our reappreciation for endeavors of the greatest magnitude has given rise to something truly new in the field of genre painting, namely the heroic landscape of engineering in a renewed Germany. […] These artworks openly glorify enterprises that are possible only through the free cooperation of all estates under one leadership; in so doing, they glorify the newly structured German folk as such.[55]

This raises the question of visibility – that is, how to recognize what is missing or, more precisely, removed from view. Walter Horn offered a telling explanation for the absence of workers in many paintings of factories: "The measure of all things is no longer man or machine but *Volk* and community."[56] Having overcome the early romance with heroic labor and the later cult of technology as secular religion, the main task of the contemporary artist after all was to visualize the place of work "without making the worker visible"[57] – for instance, by expressing attitudes about work through point of view, scale, and composition. Rather than reinscribing class divisions through what Werner Rittich denounced as "proletarianizing poor people painting," the artists of the Third Reich must "give expression to our position, our will, and our pride."[58] Patrick Jung, the author of the only English-language study on Mercker, draws on the notion of the technological sublime to de-

---

[53] Berthold Hinz, *Art in the Third Reich*, trans. Robert and Rita Kimber (New York: Pantheon, 1979), 72.
[54] The connection between the new German art and the racial aspects of being *kulturschaffend* is analyzed in Hans Biallas, "Der Kulturwille des schaffenden deutschen Volkes," *Arbeitertum* 10.11 (1940): 2–5.
[55] Fritz Alexander Kauffmann, *Die neue deutsche Malerei* (Berlin: Neuer Verlag, 1941), 51.
[56] Walter Horn, "Kunst und Technik," *Die Kunst im Deutschen Reich* 6.2 (February 1942): 45. Also see Horn's review of the *Die Straßen Adolf Hitlers in der Kunst* exhibition in "Die heroische Landschaft unserer Zeit," *Kunst und Volk* 5.5 (1937): 129–133, where he describes the age of the total state as "the age of great political painting."
[57] Werner Rittich, "Bilder der Arbeit," *Kunst und Volk* 5.1 (1937): 30. The article is a review of the 1937 *Lob der Arbeit* exhibition in Berlin.
[58] Rittich, "Bilder der Arbeit," 4.

scribe the beauty, fear, and wonderment to be experienced in the face of such splendor and magnitude.[59] It remains subject to debate to what degree the terrifying qualities of modern industry are not in fact neutralized through Mercker's impressionistic techniques of veiling and therefore better described in terms of sublime's aesthetic Other, namely the picturesque. After all, once the struggle between man and machine, *the* classic topos in realist painting, is removed from view, all that remains is beauty and harmony – and, not to forget, pollution.

Mercker produced countless variations on a limited number of themes defined by technical function, mechanical process, and name of corporation. Interested neither in the myth of the romantic artist nor in the autonomous work of art, he approached these commissions like a craftsman who creates quality pieces in acceptable styles. To maintain his high-volume output, he rarely did sketches on location and instead relied on auxiliary materials (e. g., photographs, drawings) provided by the commissioning companies. His workbooks, according to Jung, indicate that he sometimes also used photographs, including by Emil Otto Hoppé and Paul Wolff, to produce an accurate rendition of different sections of a steel plant. Mercker benefitted from the conviction expressed by many Nazi ideologues that originality had no part in a *volkstümlich* art rooted in community. At the same time, his artistic method promoted a version of workerdom that subordinated the workers, including the artist as worker, to the corporation by making everything and everyone part of the work community.

Mercker's paintings stand out not only through their large formats, linear perspectives, and aerial points of view but also through the near complete absence of workers from the scenes and sites of production. The technological sublime (or picturesque), it seems, was incompatible with social reality; the recognition of human toil only distracted from the spectacle of German technology. *From Germany's Forge*, a panorama of Vereinigte Stahlwerke in Gelsenkirchen, can be used to consider the broader implications (see figure 5.5). Here, railroad tracks establish the diagonals around which furnaces, chimneys, and chutes are arranged to create a highly structured compositional space. Spatial depth is achieved through repetitions along these diagonals. At the same time, the high horizon line adds to an unsettling sense of spatial flattening. The grey and brown tones and the plumes of white steam convey a mood that can be described as either serene or somber. The overall sense is that there is no world beyond production and productivity, further confirmation that industrial painting pursues its documentary ambitions through techniques that are far from objective.[60]

---

59 Jung and Stahnke, *Erich Mercker and Technical Subjects*, 25.
60 During the postwar years, Mercker painted a similar version with a different title.

Fig. 5.5: Erich Mercker, *Aus Deutschlands Schmiede* (1940), VG Bild-Kunst, Bonn 2022.

As the allegorical title of *From Germany's Forge* indicates, verisimilitude should not be confused with the absence of ideological framing. On the contrary, Mercker's work from the period can be used as a primer on how to absorb workers into the category of workerdom. Two rather typical paintings thematizing the industrial revolution help to clarify the changing relationship between man and machine and, later, labor and capital involved in this elusive process of allegorization. The first paintings of factories (e.g., Karl Eduard Biermann's 1847 *Borsigsche Maschinenbau-Anstalt*) either celebrate the arrival of the factory in the landscape or show the destruction of nature by untrammeled growth. Early twentieth-century renditions (e.g., Hans Baluschek's 1920 *Arbeiterstadt*) often connect industrialization and urbanization by placing the factory right next to the tenement as the site of revolutionary ferment. The aerial or frontal views favored by Mercker bracket all social commentaries and turn the industrial landscape into a quasi-natural phenomenon. Similarly, the consequences of industrialization are veiled, quite literally, by layers of clouds, fumes, and rays of light. At first glance, Mercker's comments on his motivation behind *In Germany's Forge* seem puzzling: "Here

I wanted to show that one only needs to open one's eyes to find something eternally beautiful in these places of work. Last but not least, I was impressed by the kind of people who labor in tireless, hard work. Meanwhile, I wanted to make the worker aware of how much unseen beauty surrounds him every day."[61] The key to his reasoning lies in the reintroduction of the worker not as an active participant in but a mere consumer of the spectacle of work. The fact that most of Mercker's paintings, purchased by government agencies and displayed in administrative buildings, hung far removed from the shopfloor makes such explanations sound naïve or disingenuous. Yet from the perspective of workerdom, his statement makes perfect sense, for it offers a new collective narrative that reinserts the workers into scenes of work created precisely to facilitate their disappearance.

Fig. 5.6: Erich Mercker, *Abend am Hochofen* (1920). Courtesy of Collection of the Grohmann Museum at Milwaukee School of Engineering, Milwaukee, Wisconsin.

---

61 Erich Mercker, "Wie ich Industriemaler wurde," *Das Werk: Monatsschrift der Vereinigte Stahlwerke Aktiengesellschaft* 20 (1940): 200.

Mercker's approach to the subject matter can be further clarified through the allegorizing tendencies alluded to in the title of *Riesen der Arbeit* (Giants of work), which was displayed at the 1938 Great German Art Exhibition and chosen by one critic as proof of the artist's exemplary *Arbeitskraft* and *Arbeitslust* (drive and desire for work).[62] The flames of the blast furnace and the surrounding smoke and steam suggest an almost mythical scene of generativity. With its warm reds, browns, oranges, and yellows, *Giants of Work* captures the transformation of matter into energy involved in the smelting of iron ore. In a gesture toward the Prometheus myth, including its socialist versions, fire is celebrated as the source of man's triumph over nature and the tool of his self-liberation (see figure 5.6). Confirming the highly conventional nature both of this visual motif and its allegorical potential, Mercker used roughly the same composition and color scheme across a forty-year time period, from *Abend am Hochofen* (1920, Evening at the blast furnace) to *Im Reich der Hochöfen* (1942, In the realm of blast furnaces) to *Hochöfen an der Ruhr* (1962, Blast furnaces on the Ruhr River), three works now in the Grohmann Collection (see figure 5.7). Their descriptive titles lack the allegorical elements still foregrounded in *Giants of Work* and *In Germany's Foundry* through references to Wayland the Smith from the Old Norse sagas and Hephaistos, the Greek god of fire and metallurgy. Yet this does not mean that such additional layers of meaning have disappeared. Allegories, after all, require conventions to make them comprehensible and communicable. These conventions include an established iconography or mythology and a clear connection between images and ideas – in this case, the transformative effects of fire and heat, the energies required in the making of steel, and the immense possibilities for nation-states in putting that steel to work in realizing their expansionist plans. Tracking Mercker's blast furnaces across the decades confirms that the surplus of meanings generated by these scenes of production was entirely dependent on the contexts – Third Reich or Federal Republic – in which the paintings were shown. Without those contexts, industry and technology could appear free of ideology, which of course only indicates yet another layer of ideological framing.

As the case studies on Koelle and Mercker and the larger debates on work and art have shown, the preoccupation with the body of the worker and his simultaneous elimination from the site of production draw attention to the fundamental transformations initiated through the aestheticization of labor and industry after 1933. Indicative of the grand ambitions of Nazi ideology but difficult to put

---

[62] On this work, see Paul Weiglin, "Die Industrie in der Kunst: Zu dem Gemälde 'Riesen der Arbeit' von Erich Mercker," *Daheim* 74.5 (4 November 1937): 9. On industrial painting as a new genre, also see R. Kutsch, "Das deutsche Industriebild," *Das Werk: Monatsschrift der Vereinigte Stahlwerke Aktiengesellschaft* 20 (1940): 191–198.

Fig. 5.7: Erich Mercker, *Im Reiche der Hochöfen* (1942). Courtesy of Collection of the Grohmann Museum at Milwaukee School of Engineering, Milwaukee, Wisconsin.

into practice, these transformations were at once marginal to what is generally known as Nazi art and central to a relatively self-contained sphere or environment, namely the culture of work. Mediating between corporate and corporatist interests and expressing pride in work through different aesthetic forms and techniques, workers' sculpture and industrial painting played complementary roles in promoting this new culture of work. The enlistment of the arts in advancing what Ley at one point called the "process of refining humankind" and establishing "the foundation for a new culture in the organization of work" make perfectly clear in what ways these perspectives could coexist "productively" within the collective imaginaries of workerdom.[63] In the next chapter, the portraits of workers in photobooks by Paul Wolff and Erna Lendvai-Dircksen and in industrial films by Walter Ruttmann and Willy Zielke will shed light on the growing significance of new visual media in the emotionalization of work, this time through the theme of joy in work.

---

63 Robert Ley, Preface, *Führer durch die Ausstellung Schönheit der Arbeit und Die Arbeit in der Kunst: Munich, 16 Oktober 1937 bis 6 November 1937* (Munich: Deutsche Arbeitsfront, 1937), 5.

Chapter 6
Joy in Work: On Industrial Photography and Film

> Life is work; work is happiness.
> Robert Ley

Paul Wolff's photobook *Arbeit!* (1934, Work!) does not offer the sweeping panoramas summoned by Mercker in his painterly tributes to German industry and technology. Constrained by a camera held at eye level, the photographer never captures the *Werk* (factory or work) in its totality. Yet inside the coke ovens and rolling mills, the chemical laboratories and assembly lines, the spectacle of German labor becomes once again visible through the intimate relationship between man and machine. Through two hundred images accompanied by descriptive captions, Wolff makes the workers part of a public performance that links the physical and psychological aspects of work to the larger ideological project of workerdom. Assuming the role of documentarian, he captures the workers fully absorbed in their tasks and seemingly unaware of the presence of a camera (see figures 6.1 and 6.2). As in the portrait of the Silesian smelter, their faces are lined but their eyes are "young, bright, and joyous." It would not be far-fetched to imagine a hallway nearby that displays the slogan "Those who want to create, must be joyful!"[1]

Wolff's portrait of the smelter and the picture from a *NS-Musterbetrieb* (National Socialist model factory) offer a good introduction to the theme of *Arbeitsfreude* (joy in work), a feeling or attitude considered essential to increased productivity and good labor relations by the proponents of *Arbeitswissenschaft* (work science), a mixture of ergonomics, organizational psychology, and industrial science. Joy in work entered German debates about the modern workplace via a new academic discipline that combined elements of work psychology, including its vitalist origins and socialist credentials, with what American researchers, in line with their greater interest in measurable effects, called psychotechnics. Of equal concern to corporate management and organized labor, joy in work during the 1920s and 1930s was discussed as a right and an obligation, a habitus to be adopted by the worker in exchange for continued employment. Lack of joy was consequently seen as a symptom of disorganization and disintegration and treated like a cancer on the body politic. Establishing the new culture of joy, however, required the extension of work-related matters into the psychological domain – that

---

[1] The phrase comes from a poem by Theodor Fontane; the photograph (dated 1938) was taken in the NS-Musterbetrieb Holzbau R. Mecklenburg. Credited to Walter Tröller, it was published by Raumbild-Verlag Otto Schönstein in a two-volume 1937/38 book on *NS-Musterbetriebe*.

Fig. 6.1: Paul Wolff, *Arbeit! 200 Tiefdruckbildseiten.* Text by Paul Georg Ehrhardt (Berlin: Volk und Reich, 1937), 168. Courtesy of Dr. Paul Wolff & Tritschler, Historisches Bildarchiv, D-77654 Offenburg.

Fig. 6.2: "Wer schaffen will, muß fröhlich sein!" Courtesy bpk/Deutsches Historisches Museum, Raumbild-Verlag Otto Schönstein/Walter Tröller.

is, of feelings, attitudes, and behaviors. Henceforth, images and stories, and symbolic practices more generally, provided the social imaginaries through which a new culture of work could be created, practiced, and put into the service of the corporatist state, with industrial photography and film assuming ever greater significance during the Nazi years.[2]

From the start, joy in work was conceptualized in relation to *deutsche Arbeit* (German work), that unique manifestation of national character that, as its proponents argued, had sustained the preindustrial world of crafts and trades and been a factor in the making of the protestant work ethic. In order for joy in work to become part of an ideological narrative about work and community, its constitutive

---

2 *Arbeitswissenschaft* incorporated different analyses and approaches, including the system of scientific management developed by Frederick Winslow Taylor, Joseph Winschuh's writings on the role of the *Werkgemeinschaft* in the restoration or preservation of *Arbeitsfrieden*, the studies on work-related fatigue by Emil Kraepelin, new approaches to the social question by Heinrich Herkner and Adolf Levenstein, the psychotechnics of Hugo Münsterberg and Fritz Giese, the initiatives started by organizations such as DINTA (Deutsches Institut für technische Arbeitsforschung), and the focus on industrial management in the writings of Goetz Briefs and others.

elements had to be defined and its underlying assumptions spelled out. All agreed that the "soul of the worker" (in the language of the times) was as important for productivity and efficiency as workplace design, factory architecture, and organizational structure. Yet work psychology, with its emphasis on individual motivation and behavior, was not enough to support the reorganization of labor after 1933. Just as the aestheticization of politics in fascism expanded the boundaries of the political, the aestheticization of work propagated by DAF and other organizations redefined the relationships among capital, labor, and the state. New visual media such as photography and film played a key role in establishing the emotional registers most conducive to the reimagining of work as an expression of community. Comparable to the role of "happiness Soviet style" in Stalinist industrialization campaigns, the rhetoric of joy supported what could be called a National Socialist version of productivism – that is, a new approach to efficiency, productivity, and labor relations without improvements in worker rights or changes in the class structure.[3] Instead aesthetic experiences gained heightened relevance in modeling attitudes and behaviors: during work and leisure time, in public and private life, and through individual needs and desires. In the words of Heinrich Härtle from the Amt Rosenberg, "We not only work in order to live, we also live to work. And after doing our duty at work, we want to experience a noble joy in life."[4]

Few of the workers in Wolff's book are smiling, and it would be a mistake to equate joy in work with conventional expressions of happiness, notwithstanding the catchy slogan by DAF leader Robert Ley in the epigraph.[5] On the contrary, the joy to be experienced is measurable, above all, in the men's physical effort, intense concentration, and clear sense of purpose; inner satisfaction might therefore be a more fitting term. As labor educator Richard Gothe explained, *Arbeitsfreude* in the narrow sense was available only to a privileged few, but "there are thousands of occasions for the worker to gain inner satisfaction from his work because he experiences what he is creating with his sweat and his hands."[6] Through the asso-

---

[3] For a comparative perspective on happiness in Stalinist Russia, see Maya Turovskaya, "Easy on the Heart: Or 'Strength though Joy,'" trans. Jesse Savage, in *Petrified Utopia: Happiness Soviet Style*, ed. Marina Balina and Evgeny Dobrenko (London: Anthem, 2011), 239–262 and Anna Toropova, *Feeling Revolution: Cinema, Genre, and the Politics of Affect under Stalin* (Oxford: Oxford University Press, 2020). On the German-Italian connections behind the culture of joy, see Daniela Liebscher, *Freude und Arbeit: Zur internationalen Freizeit- und Sozialpolitik des faschistischen Italien und des NS-Regimes* (Cologne: Böhlau, 2009).
[4] Heinrich Härtle, quoted by Joan Campbell, *Joy in Work, German Work: The National Debate* (Princeton: Princeton University Press, 1989), 334.
[5] Robert Ley, in *Taschenbuch Schönheit der Arbeit*, ed. Anatol von Hübbenet, preface by Albert Speer (Berlin: Verlag Deutsche Arbeitsfront, 1938): 218.
[6] Richard Gothe, *Der Arbeiter und seine Arbeit* (Berlin: Die Runde, 1934).

ciation of joy in work with unalienated labor and, by extension, sense of community, the ideological functions of industrial photography and film come into closer view as well: first through their ability to visualize feelings about work in dialogue with other representations of workerdom and, second, through their participation in public displays of joy that can be described as either voluntary or coercive – but always performative. In all cases, the collective identification with the figure of the worker and the experience of work proved essential to the aesthetic and emotional modalities of Nazi Sachlichkeit that found foremost expression not in painting or sculpture but in industrial photography and film.

That the machine aesthetic was compatible with nostalgic visions of the folk, that the habitus of cool detachment coexisted with Nazi pathos and sentimentality, and that the coupling of European fascism and modernism produced some of the most interesting art during the interwar years is no longer disputed in the scholarship. By contrast, the overdetermined role of images of workers in reconciling socialist, nationalist, and populist elements remains far from clear, starting with the heavy debt to proletarian iconographies, documentary traditions, and modernist sensibilities from the Weimar years. Was the aestheticization of work nothing but mythification, intended to distract from growing problems with long working hours and stagnant wages? Alternatively, was the emphasis on vision and visuality part of broader processes in which experiences of the political were increasingly based on identifications, as Christopher Webster van Tonder suggests?[7] And, closely related, must the legacies of Weimar, its socialisms and modernisms, be seen as integrative or disruptive to the ascendancy of a thus defined symbolic politics? This chapter addresses these questions by using the representation of the worker in industrial photography and film to track larger and often invisible changes in the culture of work, starting with the heightened significance accorded to feelings, mentalities, and attitudes. A brief summary of the scholarly debates on joy in work establishes the historical context in which the emotionalization of work became both necessary and possible. The second part of the chapter uses two photobooks, Paul Wolff's *Arbeit!* (1934, Work!) and Erna Lendvai-Dircksen's *Arbeit formt das Gesicht* (1938, Work forms the face), to identify the visual conventions involved in placing the worker within a corporatist fantasy of German labor and industry. The films discussed in the third part, Walter Ruttmann's *Acciaio* (1933, Steel) and Walter Frentz's *Hände am Werk* (1935, Hands at work), continue this argument by examining in what ways modernist techniques, from the equation of work with rhythm to the affinity of industry with montage, foreground the tensions between

---

7 Christopher Webster van Tonder, *Photography in the Third Reich: Art, Physiognomy and Propaganda* (London: Bloomsbury, 2020), 202.

Nazi modernity and retrograde visions of community and reveal the difficulties of establishing joy in work as a sustainable collective fantasy.

I

Whether used as racial or social types, icons or allegories, the workers in Nazi-era industrial photography and film functioned as personifications of workerdom and, by extension, of folk community. In the rhetoric of the times, these "heroes of work" embodied the uniquely German nature of work through their gendered performances of expertise, competence, and mastery. Moreover, they modeled the ethical dimension of work, that is, service to a greater good, by demonstrating their commitment to company and community. Within these parameters, joy in work functioned as a signifier and a signified – namely, by announcing the end of class struggle and begin of a new culture of work beyond the old antagonisms between employer and employee. In the language of the times, by visualizing *Werkgemeinschaft* (work community), the workers' faces and bodies gave form to the *Schaffensgemeinschaft* (productive community) and *Leistungsgemeinschaft* (achievement community) that, within the new order of *Führung* (leadership) and *Gefolgschaft* (followership), established the values of communitarianism in all areas of public and private life. Another term for this approach would be biopolitics.

Two factors contributed to the profound changes in the nature of work from the late nineteenth to the early twentieth century: the working conditions in new industries and bureaucracies and the social, cultural, and psychological impact of these changes. Using the metaphor of the human motor, Anson Rabinbach notes a momentous shift from the conception of work in moral, if not theological terms to a conception of labor power "emphasizing the expenditure and deployment of energy as opposed to human will, moral purpose, or even technical skill."[8] As energy conservation became the new standard for measuring and coordinating work, references to the sin of idleness no longer offered useful explanations or solutions. According to the proponents of work science, the growing problem of fatigue or, in the language of the times, neurasthenia was caused by the shocks of modernization and their deleterious effect on individual performance and well-being. Managing the social and economic consequences required closer cooperation between industry and science, as well as state and industry. As histories of labor struggles show, the metaphor of the human motor proved of little use in make sense of

---

[8] Anson Rabinbach, *The Human Motor: Energy, Fatigue, and the Origins of Modernity* (New York: Basic Books, 1990), 4.

changing attitudes toward work, whether in capitalist or communist societies. In Stalinist Russia, the program of rapid industrialization was promoted through the Stakhanovite movement, which, in addition to celebrating high-performing "heroes of work," offered moral rules on work and life for the New Soviet Man and Woman. Meanwhile, advanced industrialized nations such as Fascist Italy or Nazi Germany focused increasingly on leisure time in order to secure the consent of their citizens and make consumption an integral part of new disciplining regimes. As *Arbeitskraft* (labor power) lost its explanatory value, functionaries and propagandists increasingly turned to *Arbeitsfreude* in promoting the new culture of work and establishing the representational modalities of Nazi biopolitics.

In a 1989 study, Joan Campbell has documented the German history of joy in work and identified the underlying assumptions that, since the nineteenth century, connected attitudes about work to national character, starting with the adage that "to be German means to do something for its own sake."[9] The pairing of "German" and "work" in turn drew on the Christian conception of work as an expression of faith and release from original sin. The workers' movement, Marxist theory, and Social Democracy based their political demands on the critique of labor exploitation and class oppression but affirmed work as an act of self-emancipation and integral part of the fight for socialism and democracy. Throughout, categories of gender and race proved essential to hegemonic and counterhegemonic iconographies of labor; the same can be concluded about the distinctions between manual and mental work. Assertions regarding the ennobling qualities and redemptive effects of work, the contribution of manual workers to the building of nation and empire, and the place of workers within the hierarchy of classes and estates can be found in arguments and findings across the disciplines. Early on, the ethnographer Wilhelm Heinrich Riehl, in *Die deutsche Arbeit* (1861, German work), bemoaned the growing divide between proletarian and bourgeois and proposed a model of reconciliation based on the uniquely German culture of work.[10] In *Die protestantische Ethik und der Geist des Kapitalismus* (1905, The protestant ethic and the spirit of capitalism), the sociologist Max Weber famously argued that the validation of work as a spiritual activity in Pietism and the rhetoric of duty to self and community in Protestantism made possible the profound transformations in the meaning

---

9 For a comprehensive overview, see Campbell, *Joy in Work*; my summary in the next paragraph relies heavily on her work.

10 Wilhelm Heinrich Riehl, *Die Deutsche Arbeit* (Stuttgart: Cotta, 1861), especially the chapter on "Die Arbeiter" (275–278). For a reflection on terminology, see Jörn Leonhard and Willibald Steinmetz, "Von der Begriffsgeschichte zu historischen Semantiken von 'Arbeit,'" in *Semantiken von Arbeit: Diachrone und vergleichende Perspektiven*, ed. Leonhard and Steinmetz (Cologne: Böhlau, 2006), 9–62.

and nature of work under capitalism and contributed to the parallel projects of social mobility and national liberation throughout the nineteenth century. With *Die Bedeutung der Arbeitsfreude* (1905, The meaning of joy), Heinrich Herkner became one of the first economists to emphasize the importance of turning *Arbeitslast* (burden of work) into *Arbeitslust* (pleasure of work). Despite (or because of) his Marxist leanings, he faulted the workers' movement with failing to address workers as full human beings. For its leaders, "the modern worker was supposed to be a proletarian and nothing else,"[11] content with finding emotional release through the heroic myth of Prometheus.

The demise of the guild system, the rise of unskilled labor, the pressures of piecework and shift work, and the low pay, long hours, and unsafe workplaces contributed to what became known as the *Arbeiterfrage* (worker question) or, euphemistically, the social question. During the first and second industrial revolutions, socialists as well as industrialists began to address these problems through a range of solutions. The Taylor system and the program of Fordism cast the debate on rationalization and its discontents in decidedly Americanized terms; the same is true for the industrial sociologists who addressed the dangers of rationalization through the sciences of human behavior, including behaviorism.[12] Alternative approaches developed out of case studies on unskilled workers, women workers, and young workers, various attempts to improve labor relations through workplace design and welfare programs, and, by Marxists such as Alfred Adler and Karl Korsch, a fundamental rethinking of the relationship between work, individual, and society. As an integral part of these debates, joy in work came with a long-overdue recognition of the psychology of work – after years of an exclusive focus on physical and physiological aspects. The study of joy as a productive force introduced a corrective or supplement to the standard socialist argument about work as exploitation, meaning devoid of any positive experiences. In offering alternative narratives for industrial modernity, joy in work drew on a wide range of intellectual traditions: leftwing and rightwing nostalgia for the precapitalist era, romantic anticapitalism and vitalist organicism, the bourgeois faith in self-improvement, the socialist utopia of unalienated labor, and last but not least, the organizational dream of

---

11 Heinrich Herkner, *Die Bedeutung der Arbeitsfreude in Theorie und Praxis der Volkswirtschaft* (Dresden: Zahn & Jaensch, 1905), 24. For a historical overview, see Peter Hinrichs, *Um die Seele des Arbeiters: Arbeitspsychologie, Industrie- und Betriebssoziologie in Deutschland* (Cologne: Pahl-Rugenstein, 1981). With a special focus on the German Labor Front, also see Karl Heinz Roth, *Intelligenz und Sozialpolitik im "Dritten Reich": Eine methodisch-historische Studie am Beispiel des Arbeitswissenschaftlichen Instituts der DAF* (Munich: Saur, 1993).
12 Interestingly, Rexford B. Hersey's *Workers Emotions in Shop and Home* (1932) was translated into German in 1935, with an introduction by Robert Ley.

fascist biopolitics. The broad appeal of this kind of emotionalization can be seen in popular books such as *Arbeit bringt Freude!* (1927, Work brings joy!) that include motivational quotes by famous poets and thinkers on the joys of working.[13]

During the first decades of the twentieth century, emerging disciplines such as sociology and psychology and various social reform initiatives proposed more systematic approaches. Scientific management and psychotechnics in particular gave scholars new tools for dealing with work-related problems in a holistic fashion. Emil Kraeplin's publications on work fatigue, Karl Bücher's observations on work and rhythm, and Fritz Giese's behaviorist approach to vocational training point to growing awareness of the psychological problems caused by the acceleration of work in modern industries and bureaucracies. Some researchers were influenced by Catholic social doctrine and cultural Protestantism, some embraced the quantitative methods of industrial management and psychology, and yet others were active in workers' education and union organizing. Guenter Krenzler's political science dissertation *Arbeit und Arbeitsfreude* (1927, Work and joy in work), which built on the work of Wilhelm Wundt and Eduard Spranger, and Ernst Horneffer's philosophical treatise *Der Weg zur Arbeitsfreude* (1928, The path to joy in work) outlined in what ways joy in work could play an important role in the psychologization of the social question – namely, as a first step toward the politics of emotion perfected by the Nazi regime.[14] In the terminology of the times, *Arbeitsfreude* promised a perfect solution to the diagnosed lack of *Arbeitsfriede* (labor peace). In his appropriately titled *Der Kampf um die Arbeitsfreude* (1927, The struggle for joy in work), even Hendrik de Man, an influential voice among European socialists before his conversion to fascism, insisted that joy in work, one of the basic human instincts, represented a natural state to be experienced by all workers.[15] Rejecting the economic determinism of orthodox Marxism, he called for a new culture of socialism based on unity, harmony, and solidarity – in short, the positive feelings flowing from real and imagined experiences of "we" at the workplace and beyond. The Catholic social philosopher Götz Briefs, too, expressed concerns about the negative effects of mechanization and rationalization and

---

13 See *Arbeit bringt Freude! Worte großer Dichter*, illus. with *Festzug der deutschen Arbeit* by Willy Planck (Königstein: Langewiesche, 1927).
14 See Günther Krenzler, "Arbeit und Arbeitsfreude" (PhD diss., Albert-Ludwigs-Universität Freiburg, 1927) and Ernst Horneffer, *Der Weg zur Arbeitsfreude* (Berlin: Reimar Hobbing, 1928). Similar debates took place in Austria after annexation; see Erich Ernst Köllinger, "Die Arbeitsfreude" (PhD diss., University of Innsbruck, 1939).
15 See Hendrik de Man, *Der Kampf um die Arbeitsfreude: Eine Untersuchung aufgrund von Aussagen von Industriearbeitern und Angestellten* (Jena: Diederichs, 1927). De Man also wrote *Zur Psychologie des Sozialismus* (1927), discussed in *The Proletarian Dream*, 226–230.

found many "objective signs for the disappearance of joy in work and pride in work."[16] His proposed solutions, formulated right before his American exile, were based on a conservative anticapitalism and faith-based communitarianism realized within a democratic political system.

Work psychology after 1933 continued to engage with socialist arguments but did so increasingly in *völkisch* terms. August Winnig, who called work satisfaction a human right, revealed his own change of mind when he concluded that real improvements would not occur through any changes in property relations but only through the lived experience of work community. What matters was "the spiritual connection," his term for what others called joy in work.[17] The growing influence of racial theory on academics can be traced in *Der Arbeitsethos: Der Mensch und seine Arbeit* (1933, The work ethic: mankind and work) and *Völkische Arbeitseignung und Wirtschaftssystem* (1939, Völkisch aptitude for work and economic system) that equate different races with different work habits and treat racial inferiority as a major cause of economic backwardness. According to the author of the second book, the innate desire to master the conditions of production presumably made German workers immune to Marxist calls for ownership of the means of production.[18] In *Unsere Arbeit ist Glaube* (1942, Our work is our faith), blood-and-soil writer Friedrich Griese made a similar point when he described the German work ethic, rooted in the village and the crafts, as a secular religion that contributed to the defeat of the proletarian world revolution.[19] Most relevant for this discussion, the convergence of racial science and work science also inspired a series of photobooks on the physiognomy of German labor, starting with the programmatically titled *Arbeiter der Stirn und Faust: Ein nationales Besinnungsbuch* (1934, Worker of the forehead and fist: a national book of contemplation). Its combination of poems and quotations (e.g., by Kurt Gerlach and Gustav Hermann) and portraits of typical workers and famous Nazis (e.g., of Hitler, Goebbels, and Göring) established the three main phenotypes: famous writers, scholars, businessmen,

---

16 Götz Briefs, *Betriebsführung und Betriebsleben in der Industrie: Zur Soziologie und Sozialpsychologie des modernen Großbetriebes in der Industrie* (Stuttgart: Ferdinand Enke, 1934), 23.
17 August Winnig, *Der Glaube an das Proletariat* (Munich: Milavida, 1927), 27. "seelische Bindung." A 1933 propaganda pamphlet on the German Labor Front cited Winnig as arguing for the compatibility of joy and duty; see Helmut Stellrecht, *Der deutsche Arbeitsdienst* (Berlin: E. G. Mittler, 1933), 3.
18 For examples, see Werner Fritzsche, *Der Arbeitsethos: Der Mensch und seine Arbeit* (Bad Homburg, Siemens, 1936) and Hermann Textor, *Völkische Arbeitseignung und Wirtschaftssystem* (Berlin: Impert, 1939), 11–50. Interestingly, Textor uses a critique of the division of labor in the Taylor system to justify the division between mental and physical work according to racial characteristics.
19 See Friedrich Griese, *Unsere Arbeit ist Glaube* (Berlin: Friedrich Eher, 1940).

and party leaders; simple working men rooted in the soil (e.g., peasant from the Black Forest, fisherman from the Baltic Sea, carpenter from the Upper Rhine); and industrial workers identified by their vocation but without discernible regional affiliation (e.g., welder, printer, metal worker).[20]

II

Among the visual arts, photography has always had a special connection to the working class, given the medium's affinity for physical reality and, by extension, realism and its corresponding usefulness as a means of political agitation and information. For that reason alone, the discourse of workerdom and the two books by Wolff and Lendvai-Dircksen cannot be separated from the historical role of photography in visualizing the relationship between man and machine and what it references in its changing configurations: questions of labor and class, attitudes about industry and technology, and the grand narratives of capitalism, nationalism, and so forth. Historically the photographic representation of work developed along two lines: in relation to the spectacle of industry, including the cult of technology, and in relation to the conditions of production in capitalist societies. The visual medium seemed ideally suited to capture processes of industrialization and spark the technological imagination. Used in time-motion studies, cameras proved essential to establishing Taylorism as one of the key components of scientific management. Modern industries put photography in the service of corporate branding, local boosterism, and good labor relations. Starting around the turn of the century, companies began to rely heavily on photography to advertise their consumer products, showcase their model factories, and manage their large workforces.[21] All of these practices were made possible by the introduction of smaller 35 mm cameras such as Leica and Rolleiflex. Serving similar functions, the Askania Z became the preferred camera for documentary filmmakers during the 1930s.

Within these parameters, representing the workers became inseparable from the hegemonic discourses of the visible that during the nineteenth century extended from the social typologies used in political caricature and product advertising to

---

20 Erich Matthes, ed., *Arbeiter der Stirn und Faust: Ein nationales Besinnungsbuch* (Leipzig: Matthes, 1934).
21 A good example is Lieselotte Kugler, ed., *Die AEG im Bild* (Berlin: Nicolaische Buchhandlung, 2000); this is an exhibition catalog produced by the Technikmuseum Berlin. On the role of photography in representing all aspects of workers' lives, see Sigrid and Wolfgang Jacobeit, *Illustrierte Alltags- und Sozialgeschichte Deutschlands 1900–1945* (Münster: Westfälisches Dampfboot, 1995).

the physiognomic categories shared by modern criminology and racial theory. Working-class photography introduced alternative or oppositional perspectives, from group portraits of singing associations and gymnastics clubs to photo reportages about labor strikes and political demonstrations. Social photographers during the 1910s and 1920s helped to raise public awareness about the hardships of factory work and the miseries of tenement housing. Heinrich Zille's milieu studies of working-class Berlin, Walter Ballhause's scenes of depression-era Hannover, and photomontages about working-class life in the KPD's *Arbeiter-Illustrierte Zeitung* (*AIZ*, Workers' illustrated newspaper) confirm that images of workers performed important functions within the proletarian lifeworld: as means of information and discovery, expressions of empathy and solidarity, and tools of social critique and political radicalization.[22] In fact, the KPD's own worker photographers, on the pages of *Arbeiter-Illustrierte-Zeitung* and *Der Arbeiter-Fotograf* (The worker photographer) relied on innovative montage techniques and text-image relations to turn photography into a weapon in the class struggle.[23]

During the Weimar years, photobooks emerged as a preferred medium for capturing what was then called the face of the times, to reference August Sander's famous 1929 book *Antlitz der Zeit* (Face of our time).[24] According to photo historians Pepper Stetler and Daniel Magilow, the popularity of photobooks at the time can be explained with regards to the epistemic potential of social photography and the explanatory power of narrative inscribed in the book format.[25] Whether focusing on urban settings and industrial landscapes, social classes and ethnic cultures, or familiar and unfamiliar scenes of everyday life, photobooks trained new ways of seeing, reading, and experiencing industrial modernity; this included the con-

---

22 For a comprehensive overview, see Richard Hiepe, *Riese Proletariat und große Maschinerie: Zur Darstellung der Arbeiterklasse in der Fotografie von den Anfängen bis zur Gegenwart* (Erlangen: Kunstpalais, 1983). For a comparative account focused on the nineteenth century, see Sabine Friese-Oertmann, *Arbeiter in Malerei und Fotografie des 19. Jahrhunderts: Deutschland, Großbritannien, USA* (Berlin: Dietrich Reimer, 2017). With a greater focus on the factory as the central site of industrialization, see Wolfgang Ruppert, *Die Fabrik: Geschichte von Arbeit und Industrialisierung in Deutschland* (Munich: C. H. Beck, 1993).
23 John Heartfield used the slogan "Use Photography as a Weapon" in a display of his photomontages at the 1929 Film and Foto Exhibition in Stuttgart.
24 The reference is to Sander's unfinished Citizens of the Twentieth Century project, which began with the publication of August Sander, *Antlitz der Zeit: Sechzig Aufnahmen deutscher Menschen*, preface Alfred Döblin (Munich: Schirmer Mosel, 2018).
25 See Pepper Stetler, *Stop Reading! Look! Modern Vision and the Weimar Photographic Book* (Ann Arbor: University of Michigan Press, 2015) and Daniel H. Magilow, *The Photography of Crisis: The Photo Essays of Weimar Germany* (University Park: Pennsylvania State University Press, 2012). For a comprehensive overview, see Manfred Heiting and Roland Jaeger, eds., *Autopsie: Deutschsprachige Fotobücher 1918–1945*. 2 vols. (Göttingen: Steidl, 2012).

nection between capitalist development, technological innovation, and the political project of national renewal. The overall purpose of photobooks after 1933 was spelled out in the preface to *Der große Auftrag* (1937, The great task) – that is, to give proof "of the primordial force with which National Socialism swept hopelessness out of every corner, cleared the air of despair, and showed its faith and will."[26] Read in that way, the overview of coal and steel industries in Max Paul Block's *Der Gigant an der Ruhr* (1928, The giant on the Ruhr) may look like an impartial contribution to urban geography but serves in fact as a patriotic call for an empowered Germany. National(ist) perspectives can be traced from E. O. Hoppé's *Deutsche Arbeit: Bilder vom Wiederaufstieg Deutschlands* (1930, German work: images from the rebirth of Germany) to Eugen Diesel's *Deutschland arbeitet: Ein Bildbuch zum Kampf um die Arbeit* (1934, Germany works: a picture book on the struggle over work).[27] Friedrich Heiß's *Deutschland zwischen Nacht und Tag* (1934, Germany between night and day) specifically draws on the reality claims of press photography to compare Germany before and after the National Socialist revolution and advertise the Third Reich as a thoroughly modern society. In this version of *Werkfotografie* (factory or work photography), the names of the photographers are often an afterthought – unlike those of the corporations and organizations whose points of view are reflected in the selection of images and texts. Credited in the Heiß photobook, Wolff and Lendvai-Dircksen worked in both traditions, the anonymous *Werkfoto* preferred by many company publications and the more artistic *Lichtbild* (literally: light image).

The contradictions of industrial photography between workers' photography, machine aesthetics, and corporate branding are on full view in *Das Werk: Technische Lichtbildstudien* (1931, The work: technical photo studies) put together by Eugen Diesel.[28] The frontispiece by Wolff still presents "Der deutsche Arbeiter"

---

26 Friedrich Heiss, *Der große Auftrag: Vier Jahre deutsche Werkarbeit 1933–1936* (Berlin: Volk und Reich, 1937), 11.
27 The steel industry published illustrated histories such as *Deutscher Stahl*, vol. 1, *Bilder aus der Geschichte der deutschen Eisen- und Stahlerzeugung*, vol. 2, *Vom Eisenerz zum Stahl* and *Stahlfibel*, (Düsseldorf: Industrie-Verlag, 1934). A longer discussion of the obsession with steel as the quintessential material of industrial modernity would point to surprising similarities across political ideologies; hence the photobooks *Métal* (1928) by Germaine Krull, *The Story of Steel* (1928) by Margaret Bourke-White, and *Eisen und Stahl* (1931) by Albert Renger-Patzsch (1931). The same phenomenon can be observed in the industrial films celebrating steel companies during the 1930s; examples include the Australian *Symphony in Steel* (1932) released by British Pathé and *The Rhapsody in Steel* (1934) produced by the Ford company.
28 The reference is to Eugen Diesel, ed., *Das Werk: Technische Lichtbildstudien* (Königsstein im Taunus: Karl Robert Langewiesche, 1931). The book was published in the well-known Blaue Bücher series and reprinted in 2002, with a preface by Franz-Xaver Schlegel.

Fig. 6.3: Eugen Diesel, ed., *Das Werk: Technische Lichtbildstudien* (Königstein im Taunus: Karl Robert Langewiesche, 1931), frontispiece.

(complete with gear shaft) as the central character of industrial modernity (see figure 6.3). Yet on the remaining pages, the workers are already reduced to silhouettes in the background, displaced by engines, tools, and machine parts. The decision by the editor to remove the workers from the sites of production can be interpreted as a celebration of the technological age or a comment on its dehumanizing tendencies. Meanwhile, for the photographers, technology becomes a subject of aesthetic contemplation – in line with the motto "the world is beautiful," to cite Albert Renger-Patzsch.[29] Exploring the beauty of the machine is predicated on specific strategies of detachment – of the product from the process, of technology from work, and of the conditions of production from the terms of visual pleasure. The celebration of modern industry and the cult of objectivity and factuality frequently align with corporate perspectives. The resulting aestheticization of German industries can be traced from the pictures of the Zollverein in Essen taken by an unknown like Anton Meinholz during the 1920s to the commissioned work done by

---

29 The reference is to *Die Welt ist schön*, intr. Carl Georg Heise (Munich: Kurt Wolff, 1928).

Renger-Patzsch for various Ruhr-era companies during the 1930s. In photobooks with an explicit artistic or political message, the proponents of New Objectivity cover the entire range from beautifully composed close-ups of machine parts as in Renger-Patzsch's *Eisen und Stahl* (1931, Iron and steel) to the reportage format chosen by Heinrich Hauser for *Schwarzes Revier* (1930, Coal mining region).

Whether in the name of nationalist boosterism or steely romanticism, cool modernist sensibilities continued to dominate the look of industrial photography in the Nazi dictatorship.[30] The close connection between what Todt called the beauty of technology and the cult of the folk found perfect expression in the monumental Reichsautobahn project and its hypervisibility across all media platforms; similar observations can be made about the representation of other construction projects such as housing estates and training facilities.[31] Meanwhile, the formal and thematic similarities with New Deal photography (e.g., Margaret Bourke-White, Berenice Abbott, Charles Sheeler, Lewis Hine) and 1930s Soviet photography (Alexander Rodchenko, Dmitri Debabov, Arkady Shaikhet) indicate that the spectacle of industrial work animated social imaginaries across the totalitarian-democratic divide. In Fascist Italy, these patterns of influence extended to the use of photography in coordinating work and leisure, a point to be pursued further in the discussion of Beauty of Labor in the next chapter.[32]

One way of understanding the relationship between industrial photography and worker photography is through the anxiety of influence surrounding questions of class. The sense of urgency with which the Nazis emulated communist approaches to "photography as a weapon in the class struggle" is on full display in *Arbeit in Bild und Zeit* (*ABZ*, Work in image and time). This cheap Nazi imitation

---

30 On the modernist commitments of industrial photography, see Michael Jennings, "The Agency of Things: Infrastructural Space in Weimar Industrial Photography," *Monatshefte* 109.2 (2017): 282–291 and "Agriculture, Industry, and the Birth of the Photo-Essay in the Late Weimar Republic," *October* 93 (2000): 23–56.
31 Fritz Todt used photographs by Lendvai-Dircksen to argue for what his essay calls "Schönheit der Technik," *Die Kunst im Dritten Reich* 2 (January 1938): 8–15. For the Weimar origins of this concept, see Hanns Günther, *Technische Schönheit* (Zurich: Orell Füssli, 1929).
32 For comparative perspectives involving the Soviet Union, see Patrick Rössler, "Bilder im Machtkampf der Systeme: *USSR im Bau* vs. *Freude und Arbeit*," in *Bilder, Kulturen, Identitäten: Analysen zu einem Spannungsfeld visueller Kommunikationsforschung*, ed. Stephanie Geise and Katharina Lobinger (Cologne: Halem, 2014), 50–77. On propaganda and political posters, also see Victoria E. Bonnell, *Iconography of Power: Soviet Political Posters under Lenin and Stalin* (Berkeley: University of California Press, 1997), 20–63. For the Italian perspective, see Katharina Schembs, *Der Arbeiter als Zukunftsträger der Nation: Bildpropaganda im faschistischen Italien und im peronistischen Argentinien in transnationaler Perspektive (1922–1955)* (Cologne: Böhlau, 2018) and Vanessa Rocco, *Photofascism: Photography, Film, and Exhibition Culture in 1930s Germany and Italy* (London: Bloomsbury, 2020).

of the KPD's *AIZ* was founded in early 1933 and ceased publication after a few issues.[33] The official journal of the German Labor Front *Arbeitertum* (Workerdom) emulated the layout of the influential *Berliner Illustrirte Zeitung* (*BIZ*) and, with its mixture of propaganda pieces, photo reportages, book reviews, drawings and cartoons, and the obligatory serialized novel, proved a great popular success. Started in 1931 by the union-busting National Socialist Factory Cell Organization (NSBO), the journal was founded "to promote National Socialism among worker comrades who continue to avoid us."[34] Under the editorship of Reinhold Muckow and, later Hans Biallas, DAF's biweekly illustrated magazine functioned as a showcase for new work-related policies and initiatives and, after 1939, a propaganda vehicle in support of the war effort. With a print run that grew from two to four million, *Arbeitertum* celebrated industrial workers as the foundation of the Nazi Party and the exemplar of the work community. Photographed at their places of work, during recreational activities, and as part of mass rallies, these workers not only represented the more than twenty-three million DAF members but, with their signature caps and overalls, also came to stand for the changing alliances formed during the war years: with white-collar workers, Wehrmacht soldiers, and women workers (see figures 6.4, 6.5, and 6.6).

III

The workers' photographers of the Weimar years, the New Objectivist cult of technology, and the photojournalism of *Arbeitertum* established the conventions against which more artistic photobooks like *Work!* and *Work Shapes the Face* defined their contribution to the physiognomy of work. Wolff and Lendvai-Dircksen combined elements of art photography and commercial photography, drew on expressionist and New Objectivist styles, and used text-image relations to naturalize the face of work in line with the *völkisch* aspects of workerdom. It would be easy to connect their attention to faces to the popularity of physiognomy as a pseudoscience, but that would ignore the conventions of social portraiture, especially in

---

[33] On the *ABZ*, see Hartwig Gebhardt, "Nationalsozialistische Werbung in der Arbeiterschaft: Die Illustrierte *ABZ-Arbeit in Bild und Zeit*," *Vierteljahreshefte für Zeitgeschichte* 33.2 (1985): 310–338. On the role of illustrated magazines in supporting notions of folk community more generally, see Jeanine P. Castello-Lin, "Identity and Difference: The Construction of *das Volk* in Nazi Photojournalism, 1930–33" (PhD diss, University of California at Berkeley, 1994).
[34] Originally published in *Der Betrieb*, quoted by Vanessa Ferrari, "Nazionalsocialismo e *Arbeiterliteratur:* Il lavoro e la fabbrica nella propaganda della NSDAP (1929–1938)" (PhD diss., University of Munich, 2016), 142.

Fig. 6.4: *Arbeitertum* 6.10 (1937), cover.   **Fig. 6.5:** *Arbeitertum* 9.13 (1939), cover.   **Fig. 6.6:** *Arbeitertum* 10.34 (1941), cover

relation to the categories of class, profession, and occupation established by Sander and others. At the same time, their preference for individual portraits does not necessarily promote the values of individualism – rather, the opposite is true. For the figure of the worker, reduced to an icon or symbol, functions also as a measure of the process of deindividualization. How much the readability of these images is predicated on the discourse of German work, including its racial underpinnings, can be seen in an ode to joy in work written by Karl Bröger in 1919: "Rip off the gilded grimace [i. e., of unproductive alienated labor under capitalism] that for so long deformed the divine, solemn face of the creative spirit. Work wants to regain its human face, the face in which the deity recognizes itself."[35]

Striking the right balance between the worker as a social type, a representative of the folk, and a participant in the new culture of work proved essential to the visualization of workerdom. Predictably, the worker portrayed in *Work!* and *Work Shapes the Face* are distinguished by professional attire, grooming, and appearance. Many are young, athletic, short-haired, and clean-shaven; older men are included to show generational continuity.[36] The few group pictures capture moments of apprenticeship and collaboration; here, a mood of respect for authority or camaraderie prevails. Wolff's and Lendvai-Dircksen's insistence on formal consistency, recognizable in their preference for close-ups and medium shots, as well as

---

35 Karl Bröger, *Vom neuen Sinn der Arbeit* (Jena: Eugen Diederichs, 1919), 11.
36 On the body politics of National Socialism, see Paula Diehl, ed., *Körper im Nationalsozialismus: Bilder und Praxen* (Munich: Ferdinand Schöningh, 2006) and Elke Frietsch and Christina Herkommer, eds., *Nationalsozialismus und Geschlecht: Zur Politisierung und Ästhetisierung von Körper, Rasse und Sexualität im Dritten Reich* (Bielefeld: transcript, 2009).

neutral backgrounds or technical settings, and their decision to organize photographs according to trades, crafts, and professions recall Sander's Citizens of the Twentieth Century project. Their penchant for chiaroscuro lighting and its ability to dramatize individual faces and hands points to an expressionist sensibility also found in Erich Retzlaff's *Menschen am Werk* (1931, Men at work) and Helmar Lerski's *Köpfe des Alltags* (1931, Everyday heads). Retzlaff soon thereafter started taking nondescript official portraits of Nazi leaders, whereas the Jewish Lerski used close-up faces of settlers in Palestine to perfect his mastery of light and shadow.[37]

Wolff and Lendvai-Dircksen came to the discourse of workerdom from very different backgrounds. An enthusiastic promoter of the small-format Leica camera, Dr. Paul Wolff (1887–1951) during the 1930s and 1940s produced numerous photobooks that captured the look and feel of modern life, whether in the new housing estates in Frankfurt am Main, at the Olympic Games in Berlin, during travels in Greece and Italy, or through experiments with early color photography.[38] He put together jubilee publications for corporations, worked on design exhibitions, supplied images for annual calendars, contributed to illustrated magazines, and created advertisements for all kinds of consumer products. Together with Alfred Tritschler, he owned a small Frankfurt-based photo agency that specialized in industrial and commercial photography. Extremely well-connected and an inveterate self-promoter, he had superior technical skills and a brilliant sense of composition

---

37 Other physiognomies of labor can be found in two Swiss projects, Werner Graeff's *Menschen an der Arbeit*, a multivolume project started in 1934 that organized images according to professions such as baker, printer, or blacksmith, and Jakob Tuggener's *Fabrik: Ein Bildepos der Technik* (1943), which focuses on the entire work environment.

38 Paul Wolff, *Arbeit! 200 Tiefdruckbildseiten*, text by Paul Georg Ehrhardt (Berlin: Volk und Reich, 1937). A discussion of *Arbeit!* can be found in Schirmbeck, *Adel der Arbeit*, 164–172. It would be interesting to compare *Arbeit!* to *Fabrik* by Tuggener. On his work during the Third Reich, see Kristina Lemke, "Konform mit der Zeit? Dr. Paul Wolff während des Nationalsozialismus," in *Dr. Paul Wolff and Tritschler: Licht und Schatten—Fotografien 1920–1950*, ed. Hans-Michael Koetzle (Heidelberg: Kehrer, 2019), 344–370. In addition to the comprehensive catalog, see Edward S. Schwartzreich, *The Photo Books of Dr. Paul Wolff: An Annotated Bibliography* (Waterbury: Digital Works, 2015) and Kristina Lemke and Manfred Heiting, eds., *The Photo Publications of Dr. Paul Wolff and Alfred Tritschler* (Göttingen: Gerhard Steidl, 2020)—in particular, Thomas Weigand, "Photobooks for the Industry: Between Art and Propaganda," 488–507. For a short summary, see Hanna Koch, "Erfahrungen mit der Leica: Fotobücher von Dr. Paul Wolff & Tritschler," in *Autopsie: deutschsprachige Fotobücher 1918 bis 1945*, ed. Manfred Heiting and Roland Jaeger, 2 vols. (Göttingen: Steidl, 2017), 2:447–475. For a discussion of new photography and inner emigration in the case of Renger-Patzsch, also see Daniel H. Magilow, "The Mystery of Albert Renger-Patzsch," in *The Absolute Realist: Collected Writings of Albert Renger-Patzsch, 1923–1967*, ed. and trans. Daniel H. Magilow (Los Angeles: Getty Research Institute, 2022), 174–189.

reminiscent of Renger-Patzsch. His approach to photography draws on the cultural mentalities of New Objectivity and the formal explorations of New Vision, but always within a clear view toward their commercial uses. Wolff's belief in photography as the quintessential modern mass medium is evident in his promotion both of color photography as a new technology and of amateur photography as an easy school of seeing. Bringing his skills to a range of venues, he influenced the look of illustrated magazines such as *Berliner-Illustrirte Zeitung* and *Die Woche* as well as the Wehrmacht publication *Signal*. He contributed to several photobooks on German industries published after 1933; yet sport, travel, and fashion remained his favorite subjects.[39] Wolff never joined the Nazi Party but in 1930 became a member of Rosenberg's Fighting League. His contribution to Heinrich Hauser's homage to the Opel company, *Im Kraftfeld von Rüsselsheim* (1940, In the forcefield of Rüsselsheim), illustrates his overall approach: the use of photography in displays of industrial might and national greatness and the full compatibility of the cult of the machine with the heroism of the worker. Recent years have seen a reappraisal of Wolff's contribution to modern photography, with some calling his oeuvre a visual primer of Germany during the first half of the twentieth century.

Meanwhile, the name of Erna Lendvai-Dircksen (1883–1962) remains closely identified with her ambitious multivolume project *Deutsche Volksgesicht* (1932– 1944, The face of the German Volk) and the problematic role of photography in the advancement of ethnonationalism. In her words, photography was "a powerful language of communication that conveys a point of view [Anschauung]. Point of view is everything."[40] Lendvai-Dircksen started out as an accomplished portraitist with her own photo studio in Weimar Berlin and developed a special sensibility for her (female) subjects that invites comparisons to other women photographers such as French Florence Henri and Hungarian Lucia Moholy. After 1933, she devoted herself almost exclusively to her magnum opus, a photographic compendium of Germanic peoples according to geographic regions (e.g., Mecklenburg, Pomerania, Lower Saxony) and a nostalgic overview of traditional folk culture and rural life. Less known is Lendvai-Dircksen's romance with industry and technology that produced a decidedly masculinist version of the new Germany. In fact, it would be difficult to distinguish her book on the Nazis' most ambitious public works project, titled *Reichsautobahn: Mensch und Werk* (1937, Man and work), from Lewis Hine's New Deal–era homage to *Men at Work* (1932) without taking into account the con-

---

39 For instance, photographs by Wolff can be found in two photobooks edited by Friedrich Heiss: *Deutschland zwischen Nacht und Tag* (1934) and *Der große Auftrag: Vier Jahre deutsche Werkarbeit 1933–1936* (1937).
40 Erna Lendvai-Dircksen, in *Meister der Kamera erzählen*, ed. Wilhelm Schöppe (Halle-Saale: Wilhelm Knapp, 1935), 35.

textual factors that made Lendvai-Dircksen as well as Wolff effective propagandists for the German war machinery.

The contribution of these photographers to the discourse of workerdom can be examined through the constitutive tension between class and race and their reconciliation in the idea of community. For both, the empowerment of the German worker was predicated on the alliance between German industry and the Nazi state and the implementation of the leadership principle in work community and folk community. It would be easy to use gender to explain the differences between Wolff and Lendvai-Dircksen, with the first ultimately exonerated as a modern technocrat and the second denounced as a *völkisch* ideologue. The postwar career of Wolff as an early chronicler of the Economic Miracle and Lendvai-Dircksen's quick fall into oblivion have encouraged such tendencies in the scholarship. Accordingly, Wolff is claimed for a transnational history of interwar photography that includes many European exiles and émigrés, and Lendvai-Dircksen, like Riefenstahl, dismissed as that rare woman in a male-dominated profession who aligns herself with the Nazi regime in order to realize her artistic ambitions. Their books' covers, with *Work!* announcing its modernist credentials through sans serif fonts and with *Work Shapes the Face* communicating its *völkisch* leanings through an archaizing Gothic script, certainly support such readings. For Wolff, the relationship between man and machine is indeed key to his staging of industrial modernity, with the machine often placed in the center of the composition, whereas Lendvai-Dircksen is interested only in men's faces as an expression of their attitudes toward work. Yet it is Wolff who, in the book's preface, proudly declares his faith in National Socialism and who includes an excerpt from a 1937 Führer Reichstag speech. By contrast, Lendvai-Dircksen adds maudlin poems by Emil Maier-Dorn to present her book as a reflection on the difference between profession and calling (*Beruf* vs. *Berufung*). In the end, both photobooks must be read as part of the same ideological project, namely the creation of a collective face of the working people out of the many faces of individual workers. What that ambitious project looked like in a collaborative effort can be seen in the Strength through Joy-publication *Das Gesicht des deutschen Arbeiters* (1938, The face of the German worker) to which Wolff and Lendvai-Dircksen contributed.[41]

Work!, the Wolff book published in conjunction with the "Give Me Four Years' Time" traveling exhibition, consists of two hundred black-and-white images printed in high-quality photogravure, with descriptive captions in German, English,

---

[41] Gerhart Nesch, ed., *Das Gesicht des deutschen Arbeiters: Sonderheft der NS-Gemeinschaft "Kraft durch Freude" zum Tag der deutschen Arbeit 1938* (Berlin: Verlag der Deutschen Arbeitsfront, 1938). The book includes thirteen images by Lendvai-Dircksen and six by Wolff.

Fig. 6.7: Wolff, *Arbeit!*, 50.

and French. The plain beige cover and the title scribbled in cursive evoke the hands-on, can-do attitude that presumably could be found in factories all across Germany: from the Zeppelin shipyard in Friedrichshafen, the Junghans watch manufacturer in Schramberg, the MAN machine factory in Augsburg, the Gute Hoffnungshütte complex in Oberhausen to the automobile manufacturer Opel in Rüsselsheim and the electrical company Siemens-Schuckert in Berlin (see figure 6.7). The book opens and closes with Wolff's personal reflections on the importance of *Werkfotografie*, with the neologism referring both to the process and the site of industrial production. For him, the essence of work photography lay in its experiential and communicative nature. Against the cool detachment of his Weimar precursors, he insisted on the cognitive effects of authentic experience: "What I saw with my eyes, I (incontrovertibly) have seen. But what I understood through the eyes of others, I have *experienced.*"[42] He describes speaking with the workers in the factories, watching them handle tools and materials, and gaining a deeper understanding of their contribution to "the miracle of the rebirth of the German worker and the German people."[43] In capturing this dialogic quality, the work photographer must "record the expression of full commitment to work as reflected in the face of the workers" and, in turn, reassure the working man that "the [photographic] *image* can reconquer his place in the heart of our peo-

---

42 Wolff, "Wunder!," in *Arbeit!,* 21.
43 Wolff, "Wunder!," 22.

ple."⁴⁴ A clearer argument for the identity of populist, *völkisch*, and National Socialist positions in the photographic registers of Nazi Sachlichkeit would be difficult to find.

Wolff's contribution to the discourse of workerdom can be further clarified through his use of descriptive captions and the sequential logic inherent in the book format. Setting the mood, the symbolically charged image of a weaving loom on the first pages prompts the (rhetorical) question: "Faced with such machine giants, who does not at once think of the thousands of white- and blue collar workers [Arbeiter der Stirn und der Faust] who had to invent and build these 'fanatics of work'?"⁴⁵ These imagined thousands are ever present behind the individual workers quietly honing their skills in the optical, mechanical, or chemical industries and the small groups working together in coal mines and steel mills. The book starts out with craftspeople (e.g., weavers, potters, shoemakers, locksmiths), devotes the main section to skilled industrial workers (e.g., milling cutters, lens polishers, spool winders), and concludes with an homage to the heroic world of steel and coal (e.g., smelters, colliers). Most images showcase specific technical procedures, processes, and operations. For instance, the section on automobiles contains captions such as "forging a back axle," "drilling a cylinder bloc," "mounting a crankshaft," and, finally, "testing the motor." Many images come with predictable sayings on the importance of strength and the mastery of tools. Faces in close-up allow Wolff to register the sense of intense concentration or the feeling of deep satisfaction but it is working hands that time and again connect his images to a transnational and transhistorical iconography of work:

> Could there be a more pictorial representation of "work" than those two pairs of hands? Here the oil- and polish smeared hand of a needle maker who scratches surgical needles – hard, strong, and with a grip like a bench vise. There the hand of a metal worker who is assembling a gearbox – touching, sensing, almost tender hands that "know" how to handle the living organism of the machine.⁴⁶

Formally, Wolff draws on conventions in the representation of labor and industry developed in the late nineteenth century. Surrounded by fire and steam, steelworkers receive the most dramatic treatments. Captured as dark silhouettes, they become Promethean figures in an eternal struggle with the elements and offer heroic

---

44 Wolff, "Werkphotographie, eine Gegenwartsaufgabe!," in *Arbeit!*, 26. A very practical definition of work photography is offered by Renger-Patzsch in a pamphlet from the mid-1930s titled *Neues fotografieren: Vier plaudern aus der Schule über Heimat- Werk- Zeit- Familien-Foto* (Stuttgart: J. Hauff, n.d.), 8–10.
45 Wolff, *Arbeit!*, 36.
46 Wolff, *Arbeit!*, 76–77.

reenactments of the human will. Coal miners and construction workers are shown in small groups that attest to the importance of teamwork. Some machines resemble monumental sculptures that dwarf those manning their controls; others invite associations with experiences of synergy and flow. Extreme close-ups are reserved for highly skilled workers and their specialized tools: reading glasses and magnifying lenses, measuring cups and flasks, and tiny pipettes and tweezers. Perhaps a self-referential moment, one image depicts an optical worker testing a lens (see figure 6.8). The difference to Lendvai-Dircksen's treatment of a worker's hand at the lever is very revealing.

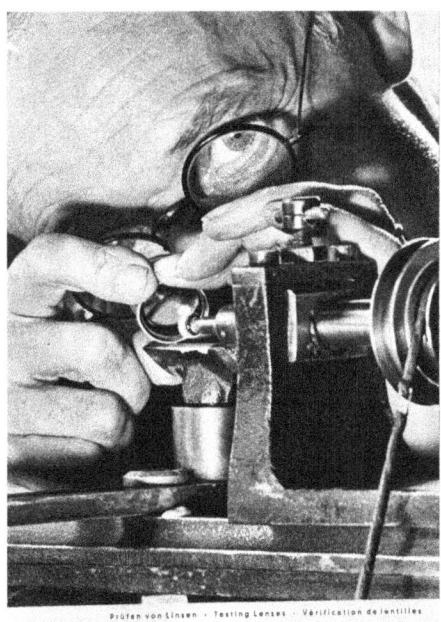
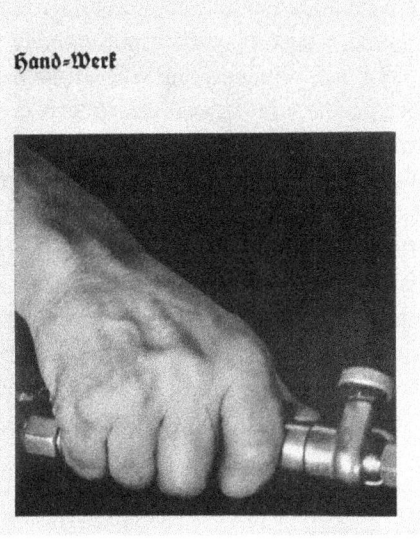

Fig. 6.8: Wolff, *Arbeit!*, 77.

Fig. 6.9: Erna Lendvai-Dircksen, *Arbeit formt das Gesicht. Aus dem Archiv der Henschelwerke*, words by Emil Maier-Dorn (Magdeburg: Wohlfeld, 1938), n.p.

Wolff presents his iconography of *Work!* within a National Socialist worldview, whereas Lendvai-Dircksen develops her argument in *Work Forms the Face* from a corporate perspective in the war economy (see figure 6.9). She combines the classificatory principles of visual ethnography with the formal conventions of portrait photography and, in the process, creates a conventionally anthropocentric but ultimately race-based physiognomy of work. Commissioned by the Henschel Werke in Kassel, her book features ninety-five portraits of blue- and white-collar workers, with about half shown at their workplaces. Originally a manufacturer of transportation equipment, Henschel after 1933 began to specialize in heavy tanks and airplane engines. During the war, the company grew to an enormous industrial complex with mass housing for more than thirty thousand workers and camps for about six thousand forced laborers. The original assignment taken on by Lendvai-Dircksen was to create a document of Henschel's commitment to the nobility of work (*Adel der Arbeit*).[47] In showing "how work forms the face, and how the nobility and blessing of work are reflected in the face,"[48] she not only draws on physiognomic categories to visualize racialized and gendered conceptions of workerdom. In her selection and presentation of these images, she also reaffirms an essential aspect of workerdom, namely its moral claims on values such as competence, achievement, and commitment to the greater good.

As the title suggests, *Work Shapes the Face* is based on three propositions: that work, whether physical or intellectual, leaves traces in the face, that these traces can be preserved and deciphered, and that they are irreducible to conventional notions of social type and professional habitus. Lendvai-Dircksen's assertions that photography "has become a powerful language of communication that conveys its view without mediation. And point of view [Anschauung] is everything"[49] speak precisely to the desired convergence of image, vision, and worldview in the making of the work community and, by extension, folk community. Yet unlike the folk community, whose ontological status is made visible through the transformation of multitudes into the fascist mass ornament, the work community becomes

---

[47] Attributed to Hitler, the phrase and related slogans could be found on lapel pins, calendars, art works, banners, and murals. The importance of the phrase is recognized in the titles of Peter Schirmbeck's *Adel der Arbeit: Arbeiter in der Kunst der NS-Zeit* (quoted in chapter 5) and Wolfgang Eggerstorfer's *Schönheit und Adel der Arbeit: Arbeitsliteratur im Dritten Reich* (quoted in chapter 3).
[48] W. H., "Geleitwort," in Erna Lendvai-Dircksen, *Arbeit formt das Gesicht*, Aus dem Archiv der Henschelwerke, text by Emil Maier-Dorn (Magdeburg: Wohlfeld, 1938), n.p. For an example of the ideological functions of the new face of work, see Oskar Krüger, "Das neue Gesicht der deutschen Arbeit," in *Arbeitertum* 4.2 (1934): 15–16.
[49] Erna Lendvai-Dircksen, in *Meister der Kamera erzählen*, ed. Wilhelm Schöppe (Halle-Saale: Wilhelm Knapp, 1935), 35. On the photographer, see Ulrich Hägele, "Erna Lendvai-Dircksen und die Ikonografie der völkischen Fotografie," in *Menschbild und Volksgesicht: Positionen zur Porträtfotografie im Dritten Reich, Berliner Blätter; Ethnografische und ethnologische Beiträge 36 Sonderheft*, ed. Katharina Berger, Falk Blask, Thomas Friedrich et al. (Münster: LIT, 2005), 78–98. On the discourse of physiognomy in her work, see Claudia Schmölders, "Das Gesicht von 'Blut und Boden': Erna Lendvai Dircksens Kunstgeografie," in Diehl, *Körper im Nationalsozialismus*, 51–78 and Andrés Mario Zervigón, "The Timeless Imprint of Erna Lendvai-Dircken's 'Face of the German Race,'" in *Photography in the Third Reich*, 98–128 and Franziska Schmidt, "Volksgesicht als Menschengesicht: Die Fotobücher von Erna Lendvai-Dircksen," both in *Autopsie*, 2:574–591.

accessible only through partial reenactments of the relationship between man and machine. With the shift from crafts to industries, the process-based nature of work gradually disappears from view while the machine becomes too large to be captured within the picture frame. Wolff evokes the machine's immense powers through the typical hand movements performed by one skilled worker within the larger process of production; his approach is metonymic, as it were. Drawing on metaphoric functions, Lendvai-Dircksen focuses on the worker's face (or hand) as the expression of a productive life – which also means, a life in service to the community. Filled with what she calls her "great love for the monumentality and eternity of the face of the folk,"[50] she references two ideological narratives, recognition of the goals shared by the workers of the fist and forehead and promotion of the corporatist principles that make the factory community an extension of the Nazi state.

Notwithstanding Lendvai-Dircksen's focus on the folk, questions of class clearly informed her selection and presentation of photographs. Examined individually, they reveal very little about the ideological work they perform within the photobook format. About half of the images depict blue-collar workers identified as such by their jackets and overalls. Many are shot in three-quarter view, with dramatic side-lighting emphasizing the men's sincerity and determination. Meanwhile, the soft-lit portraits of upper-level administrators recall the official headshots typical of corporate settings – were it not for the Nazi Party pins on their lapels. The numerous images of hands filing, sanding, drilling, hammering, and sauntering evoke the ethos of *Handwerk* (literally: hand work) in the tradition of Albrecht Dürer. Once again, the similarities with Lerski's series on the hands of kibbutz workers function as a necessary reminder of the indeterminacy of the photographic image and its embeddedness in very different discourses of work, identity, and nationhood.

Lendvai-Dircksen's consistent choice of narrow framing, balanced composition, and neutral background indicates that her images, too, must be read as part of a unified whole – that is, as part of the discourse of workerdom. The book starts out with a section on apprentices, showing handsome (and mostly blond) youngsters at their workbenches or in consultation with their masters.

---

50 Erna Lendvai-Dircksen, *Das deutsche Volksgesicht* (Berlin: Kulturelle Verlagsgesellschaft, 1932), 6. The project grew into five-volume work featuring the peoples of Schleswig-Holstein, Mecklenburg/Pomerania, Tyrol/Vorarlberg, Lower Saxony, and Hesse. On physiognomic thought in photobooks of the 1920s and 1930s, see Wolfgang Brückle, "Kein Portrait mehr? Physiognomik in der deutschen Bildnisphotographie um 1930," in *Gesichter der Weimarer Republik: Eine physiognomische Kulturgeschichte*, ed. Claudia Schmölders and Sander L. Gilman (Cologne: DuMont, 2000), 131–155.

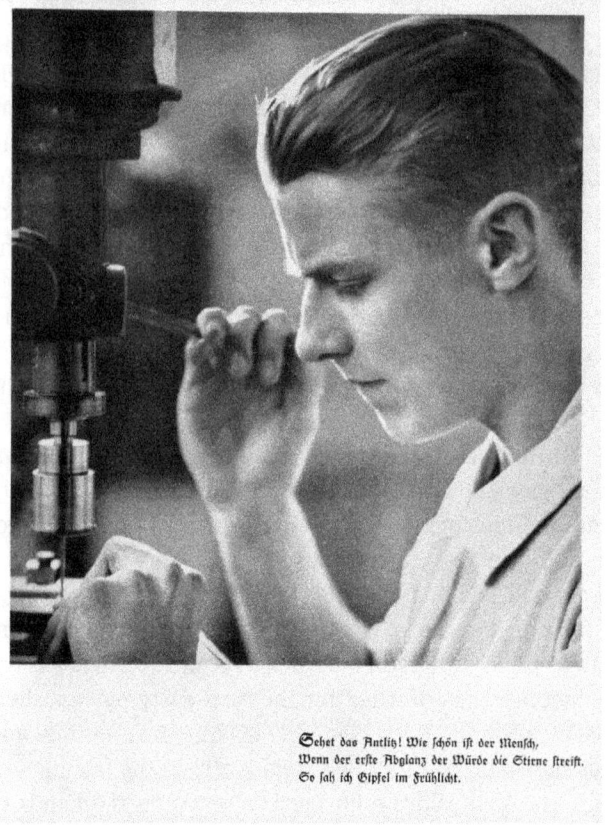

Fig. 6.10: Lendvai-Dircksen, *Arbeit formt das Gesicht*, n.p.

The commentary "Look at that face! How beautiful is man when the first flicker of dignity touches his forehead" describes the process of interpellation into workerdom as one of becoming German in the racial sense (see figure 6.10). The next section introduces the factory's corporate leaders, head engineers, and old master craftsmen, with their somber expressions a testament to the weight of responsibility. Specialized metal workers dominate the last section on "Montage." Recognizable by their *Blaumännner* overalls, they at last also introduce the product and purpose behind their shared efforts – namely the Henschel aircraft engines built for warfare. All of the portraits acknowledge the constitutive tension between typicality and individuality, with the images of young apprentices and old craftsmen recognizing the contribution of different generations to the making of the work community, and with the attention to individual characteristics gesturing toward a fantasy of diversity that is immediately disproven by the exclusion of women.

As in other treatments of workerdom, the equation of work with masculinity becomes the essentializing mechanism that sustains the equivalencies between race and class. Like Riefenstahl, Lendvai-Dircksen shows an appreciation for masculine beauty that highlights angular faces and lean muscles and celebrates self-control and restraint as quintessentially male characteristics. How much modernity and masculinity are treated as synonymous in *Work Shapes the Face* is indirectly confirmed by the equation of femininity with the lost culture of the folk in her magnum opus.

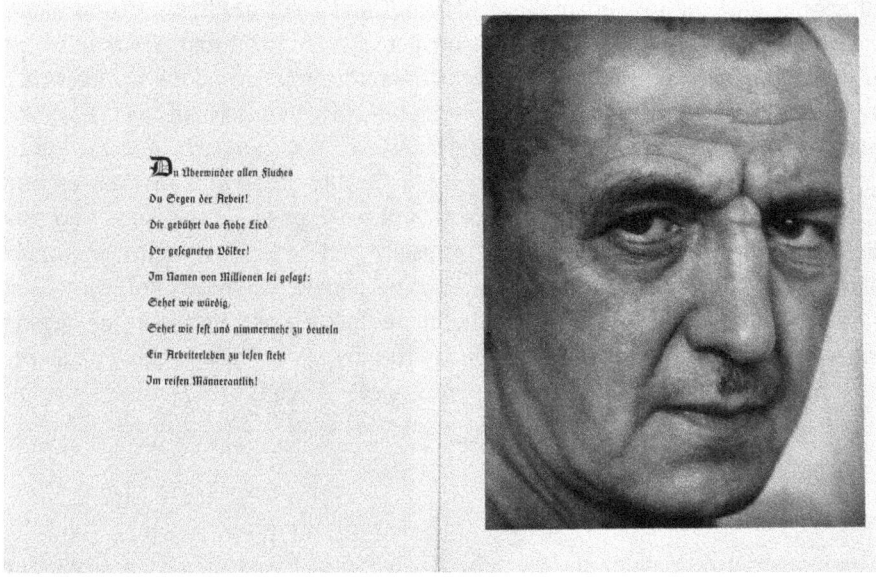

Fig. 6.11: Lendvai-Dircksen, *Arbeit formt das Gesicht*, n.p.

The poems by Emil Maier-Dorn provide additional ideological scaffolding for Lendvai-Dircksen's choices. A committed Nazi, Maier-Dorn starts out by defining the conditions for joy in work: "The calling of all those with the right worldview lies in the balance between what one can and what one must. [...] Everyone may be blessed to work where he feels joy. But he also has the duty to endure where the dark sides of life prevail."[51] His comments presuppose a process of physiognomic inscription by which the cool, hard metal, the raw material, leaves an indelible imprint on the workers' faces: "The iron itself / Is an ironclad teacher: / Sincerity, precision, / Mastery, sobriety, and seriousness, / These traits can be found

---

51 Emil Maier-Dorn, "Beruf und Berufung," in *Arbeit formt das Gesicht*, n.p.

everywhere."[52] To prevent possible misreadings, Maier-Dorn ends his musings with a verb from the vocabulary of antisemitism that, in an ironic reversal, only underscores the unreadability of these faces: "In the name of millions it be said: / see how dignified? See how easy it is to read a worker's life in a mature man's face / and not to have to resort to quibbling [deuteln]!"[53] (see figure 6.11).

Both *Work!* and *Work Forms the Face* take advantage of implicit and explicit claims about the readability of faces that informed Weimar social photography and gained heightened relevance in combination with racial theory. A telling remark by Nazi-era critic Friedrich Sieburg on the ideal-typical face of the worker illustrates how the images provided by Wolff and Lendvai-Dircksen were meant to be understood: "It is a serious, concentrated, almost sculptured face that is completely immersed in the work and does not want to look beyond the workbench. It is a pious face absorbed in the task. It is the only face that Germany has. All others are sketches or caricatures. It is *the* German face."[54] A short article in the appropriately named journal *Schönheit der Arbeit* (Beauty of labor) elaborates on how the aesthetic choices – in this case, by two photographers – contribute to a thus defined project of workerdom. Its conclusion: "An artist who wants to capture this beauty of work cannot fall back on false pathos; he should not inject false heroism into a world that is already heroic in and of itself. Heroic in the appearance of an austerity that in fact is innate to true heroism."[55] There could be no better characterization of the photographic project of Wolff and Lendvai-Dircksen.

IV

The industrial film added the element of rhythm to the visualization of workerdom. It drew on the avant-garde films of the 1920s, especially their formal explorations of movement in conjunction with montage. Whether in experimental films or city symphonies, rhythm allowed filmmakers to conjure the tempo, vitality, and energy of modern life and evoke the spirit of modernity through its audiovisual attractions. In the industrial films made after 1933, rhythm came to stand for the inevitability of modernization – even if its appearance was limited to short

---

52 Maier-Dorn, "Beruf und Berufung," n.p.
53 Maier-Dorn, *Arbeit formt das Gesicht*, n.p. A similar tone can be found in his contribution to Lendvai-Dircksen's Reichsautobahn book: "Those who flee real work and noble battle have abandoned their God. / Go ahead, reach eternity through work—and learn to hate the chatterers." *Reichsautobahn: Mensch und Werk* (Bayreuth: Gauverlag, 1937), n.p.
54 Friedrich Sieburg, *Es werde Deutschland* (Frankfurt am Main: Societät, 1933), 97.
55 Anon., *Schönheit der Arbeit*, 1 May 1936, 1.

montage sequences in otherwise conventional works. As a formal principle, rhythm promised liberation from social determinations and submission to an abstract principle or structural law. But as a bodily sensation, rhythm also served as a reminder of the physical nature of manual work, especially fieldwork, a connection recognized early on by ethnographic studies of work songs and explored further in the time-motion studies carried out by Frederick Taylor and other proponents of scientific management.[56]

Like industrial photography, the industrial film reconciled competing tendencies and contradictory elements: belief in the importance of technical progress and industrial growth, on the one hand, and fear of domination by the machine and its destructive impact on the old traditions of work, on the other; affirmation of the German worker as master over the machine, on the one hand, and implementation of disciplinary regimes through hard and soft power, on the other.[57] The industrial film has always been a hybrid genre combining documentary, narrative, and experimental elements and serving informative, instructional, and propagandistic purposes. Shown as part of propaganda campaigns and cultural events, the films produced during the Nazi years were usually intended for general audiences, in contrast to the instructional films made for training purposes.[58] Corporate perspectives predominated, despite occasional demands for more work films (*Arbeitsfilme*) that favored the perspective of the workers.[59] Various attempts at developing a National Socialist theory of documentary could not resolve the tension between the genre's presumably objective recording of physical reality, its heroic view of industry and technology, and its romantic fantasy of folk and community.[60] Instead, the official demands for visually and emotionally appealing treatments fur-

---

56 For an ethnographic perspective on the relationship between work and rhythm, see Karl Bücher, *Arbeit und Rhythmus*, 2nd enl. ed. (Leipzig: B. G. Teubner, 1899).
57 On this point, see Peter Zimmermann and Kay Hoffmann, eds., *Geschichte des dokumentarischen Films in Deutschland, Vol. 3: 'Drittes Reich' 1933–1945* (Stuttgart: Philipp Reclam jun, 2005), esp. the sections on "Neusachlicher Technikkult" and "Mobilisierung der 'Werkgemeinschaft'" (231–256). For more general points, see Vincenz Hediger and Patrick Vonderau, eds., *Films that Work: Industrial Film and the Productivity of Media* (Amsterdam: Amsterdam University Press, 2009), esp. "Record, Rhetoric, Rationalization: Industrial Organization and Film" by the editors (35–50).
58 This distinction is based on Thomas Elsaesser, "Propagating Modernity: German Documentaries from the 1930s: Information, Instruction, and Indoctrination," *The Oxford Handbook of Propaganda Studies*, ed. Jonathan Auerbach and Russ Castronovo (Oxford: Oxford University Press, 2013), 237–260.
59 For example, "Der Wunsch eines deutschen Arbeiters: Der Arbeitsfilm," *Völkischer Beobachter, Norddeutsche Ausgabe*, 9 September 1937.
60 See Hans-Jürgen Brandt, *NS-Filmtheorie und dokumentarische Praxis: Hippler, Nodan Junghans* (Tübingen: Niemeyer, 1987).

ther blurred the distinction between the shorter industrial film and longer cultural film, with the former regularly shown at Leistungsschauen and the latter an integral part of the typical movie program of newsreel and feature film. Last but not least, there was growing pressure on documentary filmmakers, especially by the Propaganda Ministry, to support the war effort through forms of identification typically found in classical narrative.

The thematic choices of the industrial film after 1933 tend to reflect the economic and political interests of its commissioning organizations. The German Labor Front advertised the new culture of work with titles such as *Arbeiter heute* (1935, Workers today), *Kameraden der Arbeit* (1938, Comrades of labor), and *Sieg der Arbeit* (1940, Victory of labor). The team around Svend Noldan produced *Schönheit der Arbeit* (1934, Beauty of labor) and *Deutsche Arbeitsstätten* (1940, German workplaces) as homages to the technocratic mindset shared by technical elites and party functionaries in the vein of Todt, Speer, and others.[61] Repeatedly, Ruttmann used his skills at associative montage in filmic apotheoses of German steel. His UFA production *Metall des Himmels* (1935, Metal from the sky) includes a veritable compendium of set pieces from the technological imagination: machine parts (cogwheels, pistons, levers), metal pieces (steel sheets, tubes, bars), and industrial processes (cutting, bending, hammering). The bombastic musical score and bellicose voice-over commentary leave no doubt about the film's propagandistic intent. The same can be said about its planetary narrative that starts with the birth of meteors and ends with German aviation, or the mythological framing that establishes a direct link between Siegfried's sword Nothung and modern steel constructions, or the cut from children's toys to warplanes that makes warfare part of everyday life. The closing words "German folk, German work, German steel" in *Metal from the Sky* could also be applied to *Mannesmann* (1937), which was commissioned by the large steel pipe manufacturer, and of wartime propaganda films such as *Deutsche Waffenschmieden* (1940, German armories) and *Deutsche Panzer* (1940, German tanks).

Famous for his apotheosis of Weimar culture in *Berlin, die Sinfonie der Großstadt* (1927, Berlin, the symphony of a big city), Ruttmann (1887–1941) was the most prolific director of industrial films during the Weimar and Nazi years and the most accomplished documentary filmmaker associated with New Objectivity. *Acciaio*

---

[61] Martin Loiperdinger, "Neue Sachlichkeit und Nationalsozialismus: Zur Ambivalenz von Walter Ruttmanns Filmen für das 'Dritte Reich,'" *Perspektiven des Dokumentarfilms*, ed. Manfred Hattendorf, *Diskurs Film* 7, (1995): 43–56. Also see Heinz-B. Heller, "'Stählerne Romantik' und Avantgarde: Beobachtungen und Anmerkungen zu Ruttmanns Industriefilmen," in *Triumph der Bilder: Kultur– und Dokumentarfilm vor 1945 im internationalen Vergleich*, ed. Peter Zimmermann and Kay Hoffmann (Constance: UVK, 2003), 105–118.

Fig. 6.12: *Acciaio/Arbeit macht glücklich* (Walter Ruttmann, 1933), Deutsches Filminstitut & Filmmuseum, Frankfurt am Main/Plakatarchiv/Nachlass Erich Meerwald.

(Steel), an Italian production shot at the Terni Steelworks in Umbria and originally released in Germany under the title *Arbeit macht glücklich* (Work makes you happy), represents his contribution to a fascist modernism that was part and parcel of the European project of "Work and Joy" and its eponymous publication *Arbeit und Freude* (see figure 6.12). The film's significance for this chapter, however, lies in its failure to interpellate the worker into a fascist narrative of industrial modernity – that is, a narrative with a psychological template for "happiness" through work. Reviewers acknowledged the director's artistic ambition but criticized the lack of integration between scenes of work in the steel mill, everyday life in the village, and a barely developed love story involving two steelworkers (Mario and Pietro) and a young woman (Gina). The original plan had been to create a storyline, based on a story by Luigi Pirandello, that identified the conditions detrimental to joy in work and, by extension, productivity. In *Steel*, that impediment is romantic love – specifically, the disruptive effect of women and sexuality on workplace safety. After a barely averted accident, one worker remarks: "See what happens when you think about girls?" As if proving the point, the romantic rivalry between two good friends takes a tragic turn when one of them dies in a fatal accident in the foundry. Initially, the community blames the other, but the forgiveness of the dead man's father allows the accused in the end to rejoin the work community – and imagine a future together with his beloved Gina.

Steel's artistic shortcomings point to the difficulties of defending the emotional world of workerdom against the eruptions and disruptions of individual desire. Promising that "work makes you happy," *Steel* communicates this message primarily through formal means: the close-ups of machine parts and men's faces, the interplay of light and shadow inside the forge, the montage of human bodies and geometrical forms, the vacillation between rapid editing and contemplative long shots, and, above all, the almost symbiotic relationship between man, steel, and fire. For the steelworkers, work provides order and structure and creates a sense of achievement and belonging. Through the daily rhythms marked by the factory siren and the collective ritual of punching in and out, a relationship is established between self and world that can be measured in the products of men's labor. Working with steel allows them to acquire a protective armor against the exigencies of everyday life, including romantic love. Michael Cowan is right to point to the biopolitical ambitions behind the form-giving power attributed to abstraction – in this case, Ruttmann's extensive use of montage.[62] Unfortunately, in *Steel*, the strategies for controlling populations fail on the visual and narrative level. Work is not confirmed as the main source of happiness – other human beings are.[63]

---

[62] Michael Cowan, *Walter Ruttmann and the Cinema of Multiplicity: Avant-garde—Advertising—Modernity* (Amsterdam: Amsterdam University Press, 2014), especially chapter 4 on "'Überall Stahl': Forming the New Nation in Ruttmann's Steel and Armament Films (1934–1940)," 133–172.
[63] The same conclusion could be reached about *Das Stahltier* (1935, The steel animal) directed by Willi Zielke as a commission by the Deutsche Reichsbahn on the occasion of the centennial of the German railroad. Concerned with the problem of joy in work, the film shows how a *Werkstudent* (trainee) overcomes his initial difficulties relating to the track workers during required job training at a rail yard by drawing on the powers of storytelling; in the process, he finds a renewed sense of purpose. His joy in work is conveyed through several montage sequences in which he describes

Fig. 6.13: *Hände am Werk* (Walter Frentz, 1935), Bundesarchiv PLAK 105/14321.

The ability to combine narrative and nonnarrative elements through the power of music makes Walter Frentz's *Hände am Werk: Ein Lied von deutscher Arbeit* (1935, Hands at work: a song of German work) a much more successful filmic treatment of workerdom (see figure 6.13). Shot in what looks like the Ruhr region, the Upper

---

the beauty of the steam engine, its energy as a living being, and its shiny beauty as a work of metal. Rejected by the Reichsbahn as an incoherent mix of montage sequences, documentary scenes, historical flashbacks, and narrative fragments, *The Steel Animal* was released in a shortened version only after the war. Working in a very different tradition than Ruttmann, Zielke repeatedly used his skills as a cinematographer to attack social inequities and promote class reconciliation. *Arbeitslos: Ein Schicksal von Millionen* (1933) addresses the problem of mass unemployment through a mixture of staged scenes involving men from the unemployment exchange, realistic episodes of working-class life, and montage sequences that aim at a Brechtian alienation effect. Commissioned by the Nazi Party, a longer version titled *Die Wahrheit: Ein Film von dem Leidensweg des deutschen Arbeiters* (1932–1934) draws on very different aesthetic registers by using idealized worker figures and the rousing effects of choral speaking to answer the question "Why?" (i.e., working-class suffering) with an emphatic endorsement of Hitler and the Nazi Party.

Middle Rhine Valley, and the area around Lake Constance, *Hands at Work* takes the didactic tone of the cultural film and infuses it with artistic ambition, national(ist) pride, and *Heimat* sentiment. The inclusion of a Hitler speech during the 1934 May Day celebration on Berlin's Tempelhofer Feld confirms their combined propagandistic functions. (That sequence was cut from existing copies, reducing the original 54' to 48' in length.) Produced by the Propaganda Ministry, the film is an homage to the German worker and, by extension, the folk community. It is best described as a symphonic poem held together by what critics at the time hailed as the organic unity of image, music, and voice. The familiar trope of hands at work traces the spectacle of modern industry back to the traditional crafts but also connects the country's vineyards, fields, and forests to the remarkable advances in highway construction. That socialist communitarianism and rural utopianism were not unique to National Socialism has been shown by Ofer Ashkenazi, who identifies very similar tendencies in cultural films made in the name of leftwing Zionism.[64]

In modeling this communal ethos, *Hands at Work* took a collaborative approach to filmmaking. The project was conceived by Walter Frentz (1907–2004), who worked as a cinematographer for Riefenstahl on *Triumph of the Will* and *Olympia* and who, because of his extensive involvement with Ufa newsreels and wartime propaganda, has been called "the eye of the Third Reich."[65] The rousing musical score by Walter Gronostay, a Schönberg student, was recorded after the completion of the editing process, and the Thingspiel-like commentary by Otto Heinz Jahn was post-synchronized to fit with the four distinct symphonic parts. Not surprisingly, an observer on the studio lot during sound recording commented favorably on the film's community effect (*Gemeinschaftswirkung*).[66] After the premiere, reviewers offered plenty of praise. "Captivating impressions not just of the strength and joy in work but also of the good spirit found among all those in National Socialist Germany who have been integrated into the culture of work and, as a result, found an active, happy life," concluded the *Kinematograph*.[67]

---

64 For a comparative perspective, see Ofer Ashkenazi, "The Bifurcating Heritage of Weimar Culture in Helmar Lerski and Walter Frentz's *Kulturfilms*," *German Studies Review* 40.1 (2017): 527–548.
65 On Frentz, see Karl Stamm, "Avantgarde und Propaganda: Der Film 'Hände am Werk,'" in *Das Auge des Dritten Reiches: Hitlers Kameramann und Fotograf Walter Frentz*, ed. Hans Georg Hiller von Gaertringen (Munich: Deutscher Kunstverlag, 2006), 50–61. Also see Boris von Brauchitsch, ed., *Der Schatten des Führers: Der Fotograf Walter Frentz zwischen Avantgarde und Obersalzberg* (Berlin: Braus, 2017).
66 Curt Belling, review of *Hände am Werk*, *Kinematograph* 38, 22 February 1935.
67 Anon., "*Hände am Werk*, Welturaufführung in Saarbrücken," *Kinematograph* 45, 5 March 1935.

The first act of *Hands at Work*, which is set among the steel mills and coal mines of the Ruhr region, starts out as an homage to the machine but soon settles on its main goal, the introduction of the worker – specifically, his hands – as the main protagonist in the new culture of work. To quote the voice-over (3:15'): "No machine is so enormous that it can hide the man standing being it. [...] But what kind of men are these?" To answer this question, Frentz chooses the format of a typical day in a nation at work. Close-ups of hands setting wheels, belts, and pumps into motion are followed by images of miners hammering, drilling, and shoveling underground, with the montage effect reminiscent of the opening sequence of Ruttmann's *Berlin* film. Brought together through the formal principles of repetition and variation, these individual shots give rise to a collective "we" unbounded by geography or industry. After a short lunch break, the workday continues and, with it, the film's homage to the worker as the true master of the machine (16:00'): "It is not the machines that create the work. [...] Only the hands control the work, with one push of the finger, with one grip of the hand, with their constant movements. Our hands at work."

The second act is devoted to those cultivating soil and forest and practicing the old crafts. The unexpected look back to an idealized country life serves two purposes, to establish continuity between tradition and modernity and create the sense of social coherence needed to face the challenges of the present. Under the heading "We Created," the third act showcases the achievements of German industry through a series of images of bridges and towers, locomotives and airplanes – but this time without the presence of hands. The final act "We Are Creating" turns to the Reich's ambitious public works projects, including housing estates, and ends with scenes from the German Alpine Road construction. At last, the commentator summarizes the film's underlying message (25:05): "Work for everyone and to every work its rightful place, a country large enough for living, a folk united in work." Extending the ethos of workerdom to a future that includes expansionist ambitions, the closing declaration "We Will Create" moves the scene from the clearing of land to the conquest of space made possible through a Zeppelin built in Friedrichshafen.

To conclude, industrial photography and film during the Third Reich played a key role in defining the visible and invisible aspects of work, class, and race and in demarcating the boundaries beyond which representations had to be prevented, forbidden, or closely controlled. The implicit realism of the photographic (or filmic) image – the promise to offer privileged access to physical reality – implicated the new visual media more extensively in the regime's strategies of exclusion than traditional art forms such as painting and sculpture. For that reason, it makes sense to end this chapter by acknowledging the discrepancy between the official iconography of work and the photographs and films that showed actual working condi-

Fig. 6.14: Woman worker with aerial bomb, Maschinenfabrik Meer, Mönchengladbach, February 1941, Ruth Hallersleben/Fotoarchiv Ruhrmuseum.

tions. Intended for official use only, these other images of "German" labor give credence to Rolf Sachsse's description of "photography as a medium that teaches how to look away."[68] Accordingly, the idealized work community portrayed in *Work Forms the Face* cannot be discussed without at least a reference to the forced laborers at Henschel, whose conditions of abjection had nothing in common with the proscribed feelings of joy and pride. Few visual records exist of what has been described as extermination through labor, but the obsession with joy in work cannot be fully understood without some recognition of these structuring absences. Similarly, the marginalization or, in the case of Lendvai-Dircksen, exclusion of women workers must be acknowledged, however briefly, by evoking the very different perspective offered by Ruth Hallersleben, a contemporary of Lendvai-Dircksen who took countless photographs of women workers in the coal and

---

[68] Rolf Sachsse, *Die Erziehung zum Wegsehen: Fotografie im NS-Staat* (Dresden: Philo Fine Arts, 2003), 14.

steel industries of the Ruhr region.[69] The conditions under which her portraits of average-looking, middle-aged women wearing aprons and kerchiefs found no place in the male iconography of industrial labor must be considered as important to the male discourse of workerdom as the dynamics of absence and presence that link the official performances of joy in work to the conditions of abjection in the labor camps (see figure 6.14). How these divisions between visibility and invisibility, and between inclusion and exclusion, extended to the entire sphere of life will be examined in the final chapter on Beauty of Labor and the aestheticization of work. As one Nazi-era scholar phrased it: "The German folk conquers joy, the joy of creating and working, the joy in all things beautiful and noble. In so doing, it conquers for itself eternal life."[70] In the context of workerdom, this "joy in all things beautiful and noble" requires closer consideration, especially as regards its significance for a better understanding of the Nazi culture of work, its populist appeals to the folk and the people and its coordinated techniques of aestheticization and emotionalization.

---

69 Ursula Peters, ed., *Ruth Hallensleben: Frauenarbeit in der Industrie: Fotografien aus den Jahren 1938–1967* (Berlin: Dirk Nishen, 1985) and Georg Herpertz and Jörg Boeström, *Ruth Hallensleben—Industrie und Arbeit* (Essen: Ruhrlandmuseum, 1990)
70 Köllinger, "Die Arbeitsfreude," 62.

Chapter 7
The German Worker and the Beauty of Labor

> Beauty of Labor, Socialism of Action
> Motto of "Beauty of Labor"

Beauty as a socialist practice – that is the bold promise made by the Amt "Schönheit der Arbeit" ("Beauty of Labor" Office) founded in 1933, headed by Albert Speer, and located within the German Labor Front.[1] The book title in the epigraph succinctly summarizes the biopolitical project that the previous two chapters have mapped through the interrelated themes of "pride in work" and "joy in work." Beauty may seem an unexpected ingredient in the transition from class-based definitions of "worker" to the abstract category of "work" as the new locus of collective identifications. Yet given the inordinate attention to the arts during the Third Reich, it should come as no surprise that beauty, the very subject of aesthetics after all, played a key role in transforming the work community into a model of the folk community.[2] Traditionally, beauty has been seen as inseparable from goodness and truth, examined through objective and subjective criteria, linked to phenomena of nature as well as culture, sometimes described as a source of pleasure and desire, and at other times defined as the sensory appearance of an idea. In its various initiatives, Beauty of Labor drew heavily on the formative and transformative qualities of the beautiful to imagine the new culture of work as a utopia of unalienated labor and blissful communitarianism. In line with the office's socialist rhetoric, this aestheticizing perspective was presented both as an alternative to the ugliness of profit and capital and a facilitator in the convergence of work and leisure in the terms of biopolitics.

The implicit assumptions about beauty and its associations with pleasure and discipline made it very appealing to the proponents of workerdom – namely as a standard for workers' attitudes and behaviors and a measure of their active participation in (the performance of) work community. As a solution to problems in the workplace, beauty stood for ergonomic principles and sanitary facilities, worker housing and continuing education, and company health programs and sports teams. Yet as a conduit to feelings and sensations, beauty also offered a

---

[1] Anatol von Hübbenet, ed., *Schönheit der Arbeit, Sozialismus der Tat* (Berlin: DAF, 1936). Inside the booklet the slogan becomes "'Schönheit der Arbeit' ist Nationalsozialismus der Tat" (n.p.)

[2] For a recent study that examines the connection between work community and folk community, see Frank Becker and Daniel Schmidt, eds., *Industrielle Arbeitswelt und Nationalsozialismus: Der Betrieb als Laboratorium der "Volksgemeinschaft" 1920–1960* (Essen: Klartext, 2020).

model for the liberation of the German worker from the injustices of class oppression and his initiation into a new world committed to the values of cooperation and commitment. Describing this new society created through work as beauty and beauty as work, DAF functionary Herbert Steinwarz called Beauty of Labor "an innate law, a moral obligation. It is a National Socialist term through and through because a part of revolutionary consciousness lives in and through it."[3] Once beauty was established as an integral part of "German work" and "German character," its other qualities would become obvious as well: connecting the people to the arts, achieving harmony between nature and technology, modeling the unity of work and life, and so forth.

Previous chapters on workers' sculpture as well as industrial painting, photography, and film have shown how expressions of pride and joy redefined the meaning of the worker in the Nazi dictatorship. It is then only logical that the final chapter consider the unique role of beauty in shifting the site of identifications to the abstract category of work and, by extension, creating an opening for corporatist ideas about labor, industry, and the state. As will be shown, beauty functioned as an important conduit in the ongoing adaptation of the dream of work community to the goals of the racial state. The themes of joy and pride still acknowledged the worker as an individual or collective actor, with proletarian influences a continuing source of anxieties about residual class-based attachments. As a quality inherent in a person, place, or practice, beauty shifted the site of identification from workers as laboring bodies to work as a quantifiable product and process. The ultimate goal? Not simply an increase in productivity, but an emotional realignment that replaced proletarian rage, despair, and resentment with German joy, pride, and, as their aesthetic equivalent, beauty. The complete absorption of the work community into the folk community, however, was predicated on the exclusion of anything or anyone marked as Other, including the proletarian elements that had required continuous strategies of appropriation during the early years of the regime. After all, to create a "Europe without proletarians," to cite an article published in 1944, involved neutralizing the meaning of "worker" in the context of class society while utilizing its emotional energies for the project of total mobilization.[4] The representatives of Beauty of Labor were confident that their ambi-

---

3 Herbert Steinwarz, *Wesen, Aufgaben und Ziele des Amtes "Schönheit der Arbeit"* (Berlin: DAF, 1937), 5.
4 Werner Kahl, "Europa ohne Proletarier," *Das neue Europa: Mitteilungen über das englisch-amerikanische Geschichtsbild* 4.7/8 (1944): 5–8. Written by Werner Scheunemann, a similar piece with the same title appeared on the cover of *Arbeitertum* 13.9 (1944): 1–2. On the European perspective, also see Benjamin G. Martin, *The Nazi-Fascist New Order for European Culture* (Cambridge, MA: Harvard University Press, 2016).

tious goals would be realized: "The 'prole' is dead," they declared, "the term has been erased from the consciousness of the German people and will never again be brought back to life."[5]

If the nineteenth century was haunted by the problem of labor, the early twentieth century had to make sense of an ever-closer connection between production and consumption and, by extension, between work and leisure. The forces of globalization, then called Americanization, weakened the bonds between capitalism and the nation-state. Meanwhile, the Soviet Union offered a compelling alternative by aligning the project of industrialization with the social utopia of communism. Fascist movements throughout Europe responded to these challenges by paying closer attention to the reproduction of labor power, whether in the context of family policies, women's organizations, or leisure activities. Using consumption and entertainment as alternative sites of group identification, they took advantage of the rise of modern mass society and the greater mobility between social classes in modern democracies. Through the structures created by Beauty of Labor and Strength through Joy, workerdom, too, began to extend deep into the private sphere, beginning with close attention to anything from recreational activities and voluntary associations to individual tastes, attitudes, and beliefs. If folk community can be described as a project of social engineering, Nazi biopolitics aimed at complete control of the population through emotions, perceptions, and experiences. As Robert Ley explained, "in Germany, nothing is a private matter anymore" – whether industrialist, worker, bourgeois, peasant, or civil servant, all were now "soldiers of Adolf Hitler."[6]

The focus on the aestheticization of work and, closely related, the dissolution of the boundaries between public and private life are inseparable from the project of the historical avant-garde and what Peter Bürger calls the sublation of art into life.[7] Scholars identify its radical program with the various artistic movements that, under the influence of World War I and the October Revolution, proclaimed the identity of artistic and political revolutions. On the radical Left, the politicization of the avant-garde found privileged expression in proletarian culture, from the Proletkult movement in the Soviet Union to international proletarian-revolutionary literature and the doctrine of socialist realism.[8] Against this long tradition

---

5 Anatol von Hübbenet, ed., *Schönheit der Arbeit, Sozialismus der Tat* (Berlin: DAF, 1936), n.p.
6 Robert Ley, *Soldaten der Arbeit* (Munich: Franz Eher, 1938), 71.
7 Peter Bürger, *Theory of the Avant-Garde*, trans. Michael Shaw, foreword Jochen Schulte-Sasse (Minneapolis: University of Minnesota Press, 1984).
8 *The Proletarian Dream* examines the connection between artistic and political revolution in chapters on Franz Seiwert of the Cologne Progressive and John Heartfield's photomontages for AIZ. It also expands the meaning of radicalism to include proletarian children's literature and

of reading the avant-garde project as a leftist – that is, a radically democratic – project, Boris Groys has argued for its logical culmination in the total art of Stalinism. It would be tempting to apply his argument about art in a totalitarian society to Nazi Germany, as well, and to its own transformation of modernism into "the will to power as art."[9] A comparison of the culture of work in Stalinist Russia and Nazi Germany would show that aestheticization was indeed inseparable from the kind of emotionalization that produced happiness Soviet style and German joy in work. Yet can Groys's conclusion that "the Stalin era satisfied the fundamental avant-garde demand that art cease representing life and begin transforming it by means of a total aesthetic-political project"[10] also be applied to the Third Reich, where distinctions between high art and functional design remained a powerful reminder of the continuing existence of class hierarchies and distinctions? An answer can be found in the prevalence especially in architecture and design of what has been called *gemäßigte Moderne* (moderate modernism), which offered a compromise between modernity and tradition, art and industry, and drew heavily on the project of life reform to achieve these larger goals under the existing conditions of capitalist modernity.

The historical avant-garde was a driving force behind the dissemination of the aesthetic into all spheres of modern life. Yet equally important were the reform movements of the turn of the century that, from architecture and furniture to clothing and sports, sought to reconcile technology and industry with existing culture and society. Sometimes ignored because of their modest ambitions and conciliatory tones, these movements accommodated countercultural, communitarian, conservative, and *völkisch* tendencies. In architecture, folk traditions and regional styles inspired modern interpretations in the context of Weimar-era *Neues Bauen* (New Building); in design, the Deutscher Werkbund proposed to reconcile the perspectives of art and industry. Nostalgia for the world of crafts and guilds and visions of romantic agrarianism found expression in what *völkisch* activists promoted as new models of communitarianism. All proved entirely compatible with

---

pedagogy as well as proletarian sexuality, conceptualized by Wilhelm Reich in the context of Sex-pol.
9 The reference is to David Roberts, "The Will to Power as Art," in *The Total Work of Art in European Modernism* (Ithaca, NY: Cornell University Press, 2011): 232–254. On the power of beauty in fascist mobilizations, also see Franz Dröge and Michael Müller, *Die Macht der Schönheit: Avantgarde und Faschismus oder die Geburt der Massenkultur* (Hamburg: Europäische Verlagsanstalt, 1995).
10 Boris Groys, *The Total Art of Stalinism: Avant-Garde, Aesthetic Dictatorship, and Beyond*, trans. Charles Rougle (Princeton: Princeton University Press, 1992), 36. For a Nietzschean version of the Stalinism argument, see Bernice Glatzer Rosenthal, *New World, New Myth: From Nietzsche to Stalinism* (University Park: Penn State University Press, 2002).

technocratic rationality as well as racial theory, complicating any neat distinctions between progressive and reactionary modernism and limiting the heuristic value (beyond questions of periodization) of related categories such as Nazi Sachlichkeit.[11]

Could Robert Paxton's definition of fascism as "regressive ideas, progressive techniques" also be applied to the program of Beauty of Labor?[12] One way of answering or rephrasing the question involves looking at the main protagonists and initiatives that connect the conservative Deutscher Werkbund, founded in 1907, to Beauty of Labor and that inform their various proposals for bringing affordable design to the masses and making beauty an integral part of everyday life. The overdetermined function of the qualifier "German" in aligning this version of life reform with modernization is well researched; the contribution of former *Bauhäusler* to the Nazi culture of work has only recently been recognized. Yet whether as a vitalist reaffirmation of life or a radical spatial intervention, the (re)making of society through architectural forms, materials, objects, and practices always involved the terms – class, mass, folk, and the people – used to deal with a society in transition (or crisis) and find solutions in the languages of labor and industry.

Last but not least, Beauty of Labor is inseparable from the profound changes in the reorganization of work and leisure first undertaken by the mass organizations of Fascist Italy. The historical avant-garde explored the possibilities of fun and play in Dada performances and modern dance experiments. An Americanized culture industry turned the pursuit of happiness into the kind of marketable goods modeled by the Hollywood dream factory and translated into the experiential registers of what Siegfried Kracauer called the cult of diversion. Yet the ascendancy of white-collar society and its leisure culture did not simply bring more individual freedom and a democratization of taste but also gave rise to a homogeneous mass audience and the techniques of subjectivization captured by Kracauer in the evocative image of the mass ornament.[13] While Americanism continued to provide the magic formula for the ascendancy of the modern culture industry, including its Nazi version, the Italian leisure organization Opera Nazionale Dopolavoro (ONP)

---

11 The scholarship on fascist, reactionary or Nazi modernism is extensive. For three contributions by historians, see Jeffrey Herff, *Reactionary Modernism: Technology, Culture, and Politics in Weimar and the Third Reich* (New York: Cambridge University Press, 1984); Peter Fritzsche, "Nazi Modern," *Modernism/Modernity* 3.1 (1996): 1–22; and Paul Betts, "The New Fascination with Fascism: The Case of Nazi Modernism," *Journal of Contemporary History* 37.4 (2002): 541–558.
12 See Robert O. Paxton, *The Anatomy of Fascism* (New York: Vintage, 2004), 1–23.
13 See Siegfried Kracauer, *The Mass Ornament: Weimar Essays*, intr. and trans. Thomas Y. Levin (Cambridge, MA: Harvard University Press, 2005). The collection includes his influential essays on "The Cult of Diversion" and "The Mass Ornament."

became the main source of inspiration for Beauty of Labor's vision of a culture of work that extended from factory architecture and workplace design to cultural events and leisure activities to the invisible world of feelings, sensibilities, and mentalities.

A comparison to socialist realism clarifies once more in what ways Beauty of Labor moved beyond conventional beautification projects to utilize the transformative potential of beauty as a tool of coercion and consent. In the same way that socialist realism in the words of Evgheny Dobrenko functioned as *"an institution for the production of socialism,"*[14] the Nazi culture of work created the settings and practices through which workerdom could be realized. The result was not only a reversal of the relationship between representation and reality. The aestheticization of work also established the frameworks of interpretation in which the equality of manual and mental work or the union of worker and soldier seemed real and true despite evidence to the contrary. To quote Dobrenko once more, *"the more socialism realized itself, the more life was de-realized. The mechanism for realizing socialism and simultaneously de-realizing life was what we call Socialist Realism."*[15] Something similar can be said about Beauty of Labor and National Socialism.

With aestheticization and emotionalization treated as corresponding strategies of interpellation, this chapter introduces the utopian project of Beauty of Labor through a perspective on workerdom that at first seems far removed from any beautification programs: Ernst Jünger's 1932 essay on *Der Arbeiter: Herrschaft und Form* (The worker: domination and form). Presenting the worker as a new type, Jünger's controversial argument establishes a baseline of dystopian thinking against which the biopolitical vision of the work-state associated with Beauty of Labor comes into clearer view. The self-representation of Beauty of Labor in select DAF publications will then be used to identify the aestheticizing strategies involved in the comprehensive reconceptualization of work and leisure in the name of workerdom. Based on these findings, the conclusion revisits Walter Benjamin's influential aestheticization-of-politics argument and its resonance in prevailing definitions of Nazi culture to draw attention to the genealogies of a modern culture of work that continues to haunt authoritarian and democratic societies to this day.

---

14 Evgeny Dobrenko, *Political Economy of Socialist Realism*, trans. Jesse M. Savage (New Haven: Yale University Press, 2007), xii. Emphasis in original.
15 Dobrenko, *Political Economy*, 19. Emphasis in original.

I

In *The Worker*, Ernst Jünger (1895–1998) envisions the future of a work-state in which all class distinctions have disappeared and standardization and massification become naturalized. Just like Winnig's *From Proletariat to Workerdom*, Jünger's controversial work projects the profound transformations of modern class society and capitalist modernity onto the overdetermined figure of the worker. An advertisement by the Hanseatische Verlagsanstalt describes Jünger's book as a "Generalstabswerk [work of the general staff] of workerdom" and Winnig's book as "the Song of Songs of German workerdom," with the military and religious metaphors identifying their respective takes on the problem and its solution.[16] Like Winnig, Jünger saw the worker as a future type equally removed from the bourgeois and the proletarian. But where the former turned to the preindustrial past as a model for the coming work community, the later used the worker-type in order to make sense of the total mobilization of technology in the name of the coming work-state.[17]

Jünger's relevance to this discussion lies in his close attention to the role of new technologies of vision in imagining a postbourgeois subject for the new culture of work. Conceived as a companion piece to *The Worker*, Jünger's *Die veränderte Welt* (1932, The transformed world), features two images that perfectly capture his pronouncements on the worker as a new type. Titled "fantastic impressions from an industrial boiler," one image depicts two workers in full protective gear. The other shows a futuristic-looking steelworker pouring iron ore. "Not a medieval alchemist but a modern worker in an asbestos suit," reads the caption (see figure 7.1).[18] Both images corroborate Jünger's conclusion that, in the experience of modernity, "technology is our uniform."[19] The consequences for man (and) machine become observable and interpretable in the form of accidents, breakdowns,

---

16 Rudolf Craemer, *Der Kampf um die Volksordnung: Von der preussischen Sozialpolitik zum deutschen Sozialismus* (Hamburg: Hanseatische Verlagsanstalt, 1933), 303.
17 For a contemporary study that includes chapters on Winnig and Jünger, see Hannah Vogt, *Der Arbeiter: Wesen und Probleme bei Friedrich Naumann, August Winnig, Ernst Jünger* (Grone-Göttingen: August Schöne, 1945). For a philosophical dissertation that focuses on Jünger's contribution, see Erich Brock, *Das Weltbild Ernst Jüngers: Darstellung und Deutung* (Zurich: M. Niehans, 1945).
18 Edmund Schultz, ed., *Die veränderte Welt: Eine Bilderfibel unserer Zeit*, with texts by Ernst Jünger (Breslau: Wilhelm Gottlieb Korn, 1933), 49. For an English translation, see Brigitte Werneburg and Christopher Phillips, "Ernst Jünger and the Transformed World," *October* 62 (1992): 42–64. On Jünger's photobooks, see Isabel Capeloa Gil, "The Visuality of Catastrophe in Ernst Jünger's *Der gefährliche Augenblick* and *Die veränderte Welt*," *KulturPoetik* 10.1 (2010): 62–84.
19 Ernst Jünger, *On Pain*, trans. and intr. David F. Durst, preface by Russell A. Berman (New York: Telos, 2008), 31.

failures, and catastrophes. Subtitled "a picture book of our times," *The Transformed World* uses the photo camera, "an expression of our particularly cruel way of seeing,"[20] to strip away the delusions of bourgeois liberalism, its desire for security, harmony, and comfort, and to uncover the new regimes of perception, sensation, and surveillance. The photographic apparatus not only models the detachment necessary for accepting the ubiquity of violence in modern life but also trains appreciation for what Jünger calls the technological mask. The affinity between the camera eye and social typology, in turn, provides the tools for analyzing the making of a postclass and postindividual world, a world conceived, constituted, and controlled by and through technology. In the words of Jünger: "Total mobilization is far less consummated than it consummates itself; in war and peace, it expresses the secret and inexorable claim to which our life in the age of masses and machines subjects us. It thus turns out that each individual life becomes, ever more unambiguously, the life of a worker."[21]

Jünger first wrote about the power of photography and the problem of visibility in his introductions to *Das Antlitz des Weltkrieges: Fronterlebnisse deutscher Soldaten* (1930, The face of the World War: accounts from the front by German soldiers) and *Ein Bilderwerk zur Geschichte der deutschen Nachkriegszeit: Das Gesicht der Demokratie* (1931, A picture book on the history of the German postwar period: the face of democracy). Both works document how traumatic war experiences and fundamental social changes are inscribed into the faces of modern men and, if deciphered properly, bring forth the steely face of modernity. Technology surrounds men on the modern battlefield and in the city streets, accounts for the ubiquity of danger and violence in everyday life, and contributes to the experience of shock and the acceptance of pain – all tropes first explored by Jünger in his autobiographical account of trench warfare in the enormously successful *In Stahlgewittern* (1920, Storm of steel) and the accompanying philosophical 1922 essay "Der Kampf als inneres Erlebnis" (1922, The inner experience of battle). The projection of the war experience onto the modern world and the closely related embrace of violence as a legitimate political means henceforth dictated (if not haunted) Jünger's reflections on the failure of the bourgeoisie, the disappearance of the proletariat, and the emergence of an entirely new kind of society embodied by the worker as a type. One year after the Nazi rise to power, he posed the question: "What role does pain play in the new race we have called the worker that is now making its

---

20 Jünger, *On Pain*, 40.
21 Ernst Jünger, "Die totale Mobilmachung," in Ernst Jünger, ed., *Krieg und Krieger* (Berlin: Junker & Dünnhaupt,1930), 15–16. Available in English translation in Richard Wolin, *The Heidegger Controversy: A Critical Reader* (Cambridge, MA: MIT Press, 1992), 119–139.

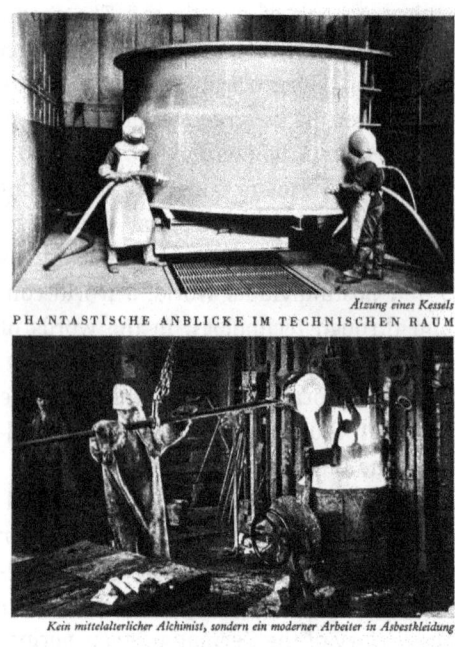

Fig. 7.1: Edmund Schultz, ed., *Die veränderte Welt: Eine Bilderfibel unserer Zeit*, with texts by Ernst Jünger (Breslau: Wilhelm Gottlieb Korn, 1933), 49.

appearance on the world historical stage"?[22] His answer? Pain functions as a shorthand, physiological as well as psychological, for the acceptance of violence as an integral part of modernity and a conduit to the new culture of work that, in its aesthetic ambitions, rejects both the moralism and utopianism of socialist narratives stuck in the nineteenth century. Scholar Karl-Heinz Bohrer has located a thus defined aesthetics of terror within a longer tradition of pessimistic romanticism.[23]

The Worker was published in 1932 as the number of unemployed reached six million, as KPD and NSDAP promised radical solutions in the name of workers, and as the democratic practices and liberal presumptions of the Weimar Republic

---

22 Jünger, *On Pain*, 2. Similar points are made in "On Danger (1931)," trans. Donald Reneau, *New German Critique* 59 (1993): 27–32. An English translation of *In Stahlgewittern* was published by Penguin in 2004 as *Storm of Steel*.
23 Karl-Heinz Bohrer, *Die Ästhetik des Schreckens: Die pessimistische Romantik und Ernst Jüngers Frühwerk* (Munich: Hanser, 1987), esp. 413–422.

came under enormous pressure from all sides.[24] None of these developments are acknowledged in the essay, but they provide the historical backdrop against which Jünger set out to examine the conditions of work in modern societies and project their long-term effects onto a future in a state of total mobilization. Notwithstanding his elitist contempt for the Nazis as plebeians, his intellectual formation is inseparable from broader trends in rightwing thought. The scholarship on *The Worker* cites the conservative revolution (via Carl Schmitt), National Bolshevism (via Otto Strasser), cultural pessimism (via Oswald Spengler), and Prussian socialism (via Ernst von Salomon) and, repeatedly nihilism (via Friedrich Nietzsche) as important influences. Jünger shared their hatred of liberal democracy and its ethos of tolerance and openness and welcomed the demise of bourgeois individualism and, with it, of nineteenth-century class society. Terms such as soldierly nationalism and steely romanticism, the latter a phrase often used by Goebbels, have been used to describe his exultation of the war experience, his antihumanist conception of technology, and his aristocratic cult of masculinity. Jünger's debt to the historical avant-garde, especially futurism, and his place within European modernism have been recognized in comparative studies on reactionary modernism, fascist modernism, or, as the Nazi equivalent of socialist realism, heroic realism.[25] His contribution to the worker question has been much more difficult to categorize, given his almost religious belief in organizations as a spiritual and aesthetic phenomenon. His use of the essay form with its mixture of philosophical speculations and quotidian observations may have added to these difficulties and taken away from some of the more provocative insights.

The critical reception of *The Worker* at the time was decidedly mixed, with neologisms such as *Werkstattlandschaft* (industrial landscape), *Planlandschaft* (planned environment), or *Arbeitsdemokratie* (worker democracy) inviting vastly different interpretations. In an early review in *Völkischer Beobachter*, Thilo von Trotha followed the official party line and rejected the book because of its author's insuf-

---

24 The phrase was coined by Kurt Hiller in "Linke Leute von rechts," *Die Weltbühne* 28.2 (1932): 153–158.
25 For accounts that focus on his political biography, see Hans-Peter Schwarz, *Der konservative Anarchist: Politik und Zeitkritik Ernst Jüngers* (Freiburg: Rombach, 1962) and Otto Ernst Schüddekopf, *Linke Leute von Rechts: Die nationalrevolutionären Minderheiten und der Kommunismus in der Weimarer Republik* (Stuttgart: Kohlhammer, 1980). On the larger intellectual formation, see Robert Heynen, *Degeneration and Revolution: Radical Culture Politics and the Body in Weimar Germany* (New York: Haymarket, 2015), 107–134. On the connection between war experience and new modes of perception, see Marcus Paul Bullock, *The Violent Eye: Ernst Jünger's Visions and Revisions on the European Right* (Detroit: Wayne State University Press, 1992).

ficient attention to racial questions.²⁶ Having just signed the writers' proclamation of loyalty to Hitler, Gottfried Benn recognized a kindred spirit when he related *The Worker* to "the new concept of the state that dissolved the by now unproductive Marxist opposition of employer and employee into a higher community that, following Jünger, may be called 'worker' or National Socialism."²⁷ Meanwhile, in *Widerstand*, Ernst Niekisch succumbed to wishful thinking when he described *The Worker* as "a philosophy of German Bolshevism, which is free of all Marxism."²⁸ As Jan Robert Weber has shown, a surprising number of commentators after 1933 continued to treat Jünger as a National Bolshevik and assume that the work-state and related terms referred to the Soviet Union.²⁹ Seeing in Jünger an important interlocutor, Martin Heidegger focused on the philosophical questions raised by what he calls a Nietzschean "metaphysics of the properly understood, that is, imperial communism cleansed of all 'bourgeois' notions."³⁰ Discussions continue to this day on whether *The Worker* is to be read as a protofascist text or a diagnosis of fascism, whether it is a prophetic essay on the technological age or a perpetuation of the war experience, whether it belongs to the arsenal of the conservative revolution or the genealogy of posthumanist thought, and whether it is a devastating indictment of bourgeois individualism and democratic liberalism or an all-too familiar male flirtation with nihilism and authoritarianism.³¹

---

26 Thilo von Trotha, "Das endlose dialektische Gespräch," *Völkischer Beobachter*, 22 October 1932, Beiblatt.
27 Gottfried Benn, "Der neue Staat und die Intellektuellen," *Gesammelte Werke in vier Bänden*, ed. Dieter Wellershoff (Wiesbaden: Limes, 1968), 4:1006.
28 Ernst Niekisch, quoted by Jost Hermand, "Explosions in the Swamp: Jünger's *The Worker* (1932)," in *The Technological Imagination: Theories and Fictions*, ed. Teresa de Lauretis, Andreas Huyssen, and Kathleen Woodward (Madison: University of Wisconsin Press, 1980), 123–131.
29 See Jan Robert Weber, "'Der Arbeiter' und seine nationalbolschewistische Implikation: Ein Beitrag zur Rezeptionsgeschichte," in *Totalität als Faszination: Systematisierung des Heterogenen im Werk Ernst Jüngers*, ed. Andrea Benedetti and Lutz Hagestedt (Berlin: De Gruyter, 2018), 435–464.
30 Martin Heidegger, *Zu Ernst Jünger*, in *Heidegger Gesamtausgabe IV Abteilung: Hinweise und Aufzeichnungen*, Band 90, ed. Peter Trawny (Frankfurt am Main: Klostermann, 2004), 40.
31 The scholarship on *The Worker* is extensive. For a summary of its critical reception, see Marianne Wünsch, "Ernst Jüngers *Der Arbeiter*: Grundpositionen und Probleme," in *Ernst Jünger: Politik—Mythos—Kunst*, ed. Lutz Hagestedt (Berlin: De Gruyter, 2004), 459–476. On Jünger's definition of work, see Laurence Paul Hemming, "Work as Total Reason for Being: Heidegger and Jünger's *Der Arbeiter*," *Journal for Cultural Research* 13.3 (2008): 231–251. As part of larger discourses on gender, see Todd Samuel Presner, "The End of Sex and the Last Man: On the Weimar Utopia of Ernst Jünger's 'Worker,'" *Qui parle* 13.1 (2001): 103–136. In relation to the concept of individuality, see David Pan, "The Sovereignty of the Individual in Ernst Jünger's *The Worker*," *Telos* 144 (2008): 66–74. On the work's contribution to the aestheticization of politics argument, see David Roberts,

In the most basic sense, *The Worker* sets out "to make the form of the worker visible, namely as an effective force that has already intervened powerfully in history and that masterfully determines the forms of a changed world."[32] Understanding the broader implications means separating the worker as a new type from the working class as defined by Marxist theories and Social Democratic politics. Workers, Jünger explains, are neither an estate nor a class defined by, and against, the bourgeoisie. Released from the antagonism of class struggle, they stand for a society beyond classes. Both workers and capitalists are products of the nineteenth century – as are the main ideologies, socialism and nationalism, born of the history of class struggles. In order to understand the radically new quality of the worker, it is necessary "to distinguish between the worker as a nascent power on which the fate of the country rests and the garbs in which the bourgeoisie disguised this power" (14). Jünger's rejection of socialism and nationalism as ill-equipped to support these developments and his simultaneous insistence that "the rise of the worker is synonymous with a new rise for Germany" (14) bring out the contradictions that place *The Worker* inside and outside Nazi ideology. They also prefigure the extensions of the political into all spheres of life, later to be called biopolitics, that in 1932 still lacked an adequate terminology.

Empowered by technology, the form (*Gestalt*) of the worker in Jünger stands for a new society and a new state created through, and sustained by, total mobilization. His expanded definition of work has profound implications for every aspect of public and private life. In the age of the worker, he explains,

> there can be nothing not understood as work. Work is the rhythm of the fist, of thoughts, of the heart; it is life by day and night, science, love, art, faith, religion, war; it is the oscillation of the atom and the forces that move stars and solar systems [...] To be a worker, the repre-

---

The Total Work of Art in European Modernism (Ithaca, NY: Cornell University Press, 2011). On the worker and the notion of totality, also see Sandro Gorgone, "Ernst Jünger und die metaphysische Kategorie der Totalität," in *Totalität als Faszination: Systematisierung des Heterogenen im Werk Ernst Jüngers*, ed. Andrea Benedetti and Lutz Hagestedt (Berlin: De Gruyter, 2017), 153–162. For a very different reading that emphasizes the ontology of the worker, see Vincent Blok, *Ernst Jünger's Philosophy of Technology: Heidegger and the Poetics of the Anthropocene* (London: Routledge, 2017). For a recent discussion indebted to New Modernism studies, see Carl Gelderlos, *Organic Modernism: The New Human in Weimar Culture* (Evanston, IL: Northwestern University Press, 2020), 147–174.

32 Ernst Jünger, *The Worker: Domination and Form*, ed. Laurence Paul Hemming, trans. Bogdan Costeda (Evanston, IL: Northwestern University Press, 2017), xxxi. All subsequent quotations will appear in the text in parentheses. The work first appeared in 1932 in the rightwing Hanseatische Verlagsanstalt. Later reflections on the work appear in Ernst Jünger, *Maxima—Minima: Adnoten zum "Arbeiter"* (Stuttgart: Klett-Cotta, 1983).

sentative of a great form entering history, means to take part in a new humanity destined for domination (40).

The momentous shift from the individual work-character, where work is related to moral values and social obligations, to the total work-character, where work is performed collectively and anonymously, makes work the ultimate purpose and measure of life or, rather, existence: rationalized, standardized, and collectivized. This process, he explains, is part of "the emergence of a will to race-formation – to produce a certain type whose endowment is more standardized and more aligned to the tasks of an order determined by the total-work-character" (66). Specifically, "the mobilization of the world through the form of the worker" (100) relies on technology as both facilitator and accelerator in the emergence of new types of work-states. The cult of work as a heroic act makes workers and soldiers part of the same imperial project; the perpetuation of "battle as inner experience" defines this man-machine interface in decidedly militaristic and mechanistic terms.

At first glance, *The Worker* reads like an organizational blueprint for the German Labor Front. The descriptions of workers and soldiers serving at the front called "Germany" resemble DAF wartime propaganda; the appeals to workers to treat machines as bodily extensions sound as if taken from DAF tracts and treatises. At times, Jünger's predictions on the management of labor relations in the totalitarian state show an almost uncanny foresight, with his detailed comments on everything from mass-produced furniture to uniform work clothes anticipating concrete proposals by Beauty of Labor and Strength through Joy. At other moments in the essay, his almost compulsive references to discipline, determination, and above all *Haltung* (bearing) reproduce the vanquished world of Prussianism and fail to conceive of the joy and pride that, too, would become an integral part of Nazi biopolitics.

In fact, the reorganization of work and leisure undertaken by the German Labor Front was much more transformative than Jünger's conception of the work-state as an extension of war; his vision of the future proved just as obsolete as, in his opinion, the demands of the workers' movement. In that sense, Jünger's work-state seems frozen in time – not by the mask of technology but by that of masculinity. Projecting then-current developments into a dystopian future haunted by the past, he is blind to the growing significance of the Nazi culture industry and its claims on leisure time. Not only is his future state conceived, populated, and run by and for men; women, children, and families are entirely absent from its immaculate conception. Modeled on the military, the technocratic imagination in *The Worker* remains untouched by the consumer culture that, associated with white-collar society, contributed to the erosion of traditional gender roles and class divisions. Rather than submitting to the terror of functionality and efficiency, Beauty of Labor promised joyful consent to domination – a very different model of hegemony indeed. In the end, the total mobilization achieved by Beauty of Labor proved much more all-encompassing given its full coordination of the emotionalization and aestheticization of work. The typical worker of the Third Reich portrayed by Wilhelm Lotz, editor of the *Schönheit der Arbeit* journal, not only had nothing in common with the stereotypical proletarian of the past – with his haggard face, empty eyes, ragged clothes, hungry children, and suffering wife – their world also bore no resemblance to the worker-state as conjured by Jünger:

> In the industrial plant today, the worker listens to the most valuable music. Art exhibitions come to him in the factory; he dines with quality tableware in artistically and tastefully furnished rooms. He exercises on the company's athletic grounds; he reads books from the company library, listens to lectures on professional and general topics. [...] All of that has an influence on the approach to personal life, his domesticity, his customs and manners. Here something really important is being realized, namely the formation of a new way of life for the German worker.[33]

II

According to the Nazi Party Organization Book, the Deutsche Arbeitsfront (DAF, German Labor Front) was "the organization of all working Germans of the forehead and the fist."[34] In 1931, the year of its founding, DAF declared "the deproletarianization of the German working class" its foremost goal.[35] This is how DAF leader Robert Ley summed up their mission: "From proletarian to master – that is our socialism."[36] Elsewhere he clarified what was required of every German: "To be a socialist means practicing community on a daily basis."[37] In his explanations of how the Nazis took possession of the socialist narrative, the DAF leader returned

---

33 Wilhelm Lotz, *Schönheit der Arbeit in Deutschland* (Berlin: Deutscher Verlag, 1940), 62.
34 Reichsorganisationsleiter der NSDAP, ed., *Organisationsbuch der NSDAP*, 5th ed. (Munich: Franz Eher, 1938), 185. For overviews, see Arbeitswissenschaftliches Institut der DAF, *Die Deutsche Arbeitsfront: Wesen—Ziele—Wege* (Berlin: Verlag der Arbeitsfront, 1943) and Gerhard Starcke, *Die Deutsche Arbeitsfront: Eine Darstellung über Zweck, Leistungen, und Ziele* (Berlin: Verlag für Sozialpolitik, 1940). For Nazi-era dissertations on DAF and KdF, see Paul Bruns, "Wesen und Bedeutung der Deutschen Arbeitsfront: Ein Beitrag zu ihrer Würdigung als Wegbereiterin einer neuen Sozialordnung" (PhD diss., University of Leipzig, 1937) and Hans Krapfenbauer, "Die sozialpolitische Bedeutung der NS-Gemeinschaft 'Kraft durch Freude'" (PhD diss., University of Nuremberg, 1937).
35 Anon., *Arbeitertum*, 1 September 1931.
36 Robert Ley, *Vom Proleten zum Herrn* (Berlin: Verlag Deutsche Arbeitsfront, 1940), 11.
37 Robert Ley, "Glied der Gemeinschaft," in *Arbeit und Waffe: Worte an Arbeiter und Soldaten*, ed. Herwarth von Renesse (Leipzig: Nordland, 1940), 67.

time and again to the Weimar years: "1. The worker was robbed of all will to self-assertion through being degraded to a proletarian. 2. In accordance with Jewish-Marxist thought, the worker became the declared enemy of the soldier, and everything military was ignored, dismissed, and ridiculed."[38] Fulfilling its "organizational dream,"[39] the German Labor Front set out to restore the worker's innate sense of joy and pride and make worker and soldier part of the larger struggle for national and racial self-determination. Politically, this required what Ley as late as 1940 called the "destruction of capitalism, eradication of the plutocracy, and establishment of the conditions under which a socialist Germany could be built."[40]

The appropriation of proletarian identifications by the discourse of workerdom involved two steps: the absorption of the language of anticapitalism into that of antisemitism, and the substitution of race for class as the formative element in the imagination of folk community. The Nazis' instrumentalization of anticapitalist rhetoric, in turn, pivoted on the distinction between productive industrial capital and parasitic financial capital familiar from antisemitic slogans such as *schaffendes, nicht raffendes Kapital* (productive rather than money-grabbing capital). After the Nazi takeover of power, paeans to the workers of the forehead and the fist united against an external enemy channeled such pseudosocialist slogans increasingly through antisemitic propaganda. With "folk" and "work" treated as coterminous, the communitarian vision of *Arbeitsgemeinschaft* (community of work) would become one with the economic goals of *Leistungsgemeinschaft* (community of achievement). Reproducing the Nazi leadership principle in the relationship between corporate leader and workforce, a thus defined work community reconciled two incompatible aspects of workerdom, namely hierarchy with its structures of domination and submission and community with its emphasis on unity and harmony.

Scholars agree on many points related to the reorganization of labor and the redefinition of work after 1933: the central role of RAD and DAF in neutralizing the politically organized working class, the role of biopolitical ideas in establishing the racial state, and the calculated appropriation of socialist rhetoric, ritual, and symbolism by the Nazi Party. The year "1933" meant the banning of all labor unions and political parties and the dismantling of the entire structure of laws, rules, and practices that, after decades of labor struggles, brought the workers hard-won rights and protections. During the last years of the Weimar Republic, the National-

---

38 Robert Ley, "Der wehrhafte Arbeiter," *Arbeitertum* 11.16 (1942): 3.
39 This is the title of a chapter in Ronald Smelser, *Robert Ley: Hitler's Labor Front Leader* (Oxford: Berg, 1988), 149–179.
40 Robert Ley, *Unser Sozialismus—der Haß der Welt* (Berlin: Verlag der Deutschen Arbeitsfront, c. 1940), 24.

sozialistische Betriebszellenorganisation (NSBO, National Socialist Factory Cell Organization) infiltrated factories and became associated with the socialist wing of the Nazi Party.[41] Until its dissolution in 1935, the NSBO still acknowledged workers' grievances about poor working conditions and continued to advocate for higher wages. Meanwhile, the German Labor Service built on government solutions to mass unemployment that, in 1931, included the Freiwillige Arbeitsdienst (FAD, Voluntary Labor Service). Starting in 1935, the compulsory paramilitary Reichsarbeitsdienst (RAD, Reich Labor Service) provided cheap labor for large-scale public works projects such as the Reichsautobahn.[42] In the words of Helmut Stellrecht, a party functionary responsible for the indoctrination of German youth, the Reich Labor Service represented "a revival of the socialist idea" based on the participation of all social groups in the folk community.[43] As a RAD manual admonished its young readers: "Work! For work is a blessing and not a curse. Life is work and struggle. And therein lies its meaning."[44] Meanwhile, the DAF-based Arbeitswissenschaftliche Institut (Work Science Institute) absorbed DINTA (Deutsches Institut für technische Arbeitsschulung), an industry-run managerial training institute that used quantitative research to provide "scientific" evidence for the importance of joy and pride in work.[45] What that meant can be in seen in typical titles such as *Das Ringen um die Arbeitsidee* (1938, The struggle for the idea of work), where DINTA founder Karl Arnhold called for a more soldierly habitus among the workers, here called *Mannschaft* (squad or team).[46]

At the height of its power, the German Labor Front operated as what Rüdiger Hachmann describes as an economic empire within the Reich, complete with its own financial institutions, publishing houses, insurance companies, and construc-

---

[41] For two case studies that focus on Nazi infiltration of the labor unions, see Volker Kratzenberg, *Arbeiter auf dem Weg zu Hitler: Die nationalsozialistische Betriebszellen-Organisation. Ihre Entstehung, ihre Programmatik, ihr Scheitern 1927–1934* (Frankfurt am Main: Peter Lang, 1987) and Gunther Mai, "National Socialist Factory Cell Organisation and the German Labour Front: National Socialist Labour Policy and Organisations," in *The Rise of National Socialism and the Working Classes in Weimar Germany*, ed. Conan Fischer (Providence: Berghahn, 1996), 117–136.

[42] On the similarities between the Reich Labor Service and the Civilian Conservation Corps (CCC), see Kiran Klaus Patel, *Soldiers of Labor: Labor Service in Nazi Germany and New Deal America, 1933–1945*, trans. Thomas Dunlap (New York: Cambridge University Press, 2008).

[43] Helmut Stellrecht, *Arbeitsdienst und Nationalsozialismus* (Berlin: Ernst Siegfried Mittler, 1934), 42.

[44] Wilhelm Decker, *Der deutsche Weg: Ein Leitfaden zur staatspolitischen Erziehung der deutschen Jugend im Arbeitsdienst* (Leipzig: Koehler & Amelang, 1933), 119.

[45] On the Arbeitswissenschaftliche Institut, see Karl Heinz Roth, *Intelligenz und Sozialpolitik: Eine methodisch-historische Studie am Beispiel des Arbeitswissenschaftlichen Instituts der Deutschen Arbeitsfront* (Munich: K. G. Saur, 1993).

[46] See Karl Arnhold, *Das Ringen um die Arbeitsidee* (Berlin: DAF, 1938).

tion firms.⁴⁷ The original goal may have been the demolition of labor unions and the mandatory membership of workers in one organization that would henceforth manage all interactions between employers and employees. This relationship soon extended beyond the workplace to include cultural events, educational initiatives, and the kind of recreational activities provided by the NS-Gemeinschaft "Kraft durch Freude" (Strength through Joy). Offerings ranged from factory sports leagues and handicraft circles for women to the mass-organized vacations that brought DAF members to the Norwegian fjords on brand-new KdF cruise ships or housed them in enormous complexes such as the Baltic beach resort town of Prora.⁴⁸ More than anything, these initiatives captured the sense of excitement during the first years of the regime and, in later years, helped to distract participants from the unfulfilled promises of higher wages and shorter workdays. Of greatest relevance for this discussion, Strength through Joy was part of a fundamental rearticulation of the relationship between work and leisure in which aestheticization served key functions: through the extensive marketing and branding campaigns for Strength through Joy initiatives, through the design of its signature products and programs, and through the biopolitical principles implied by its programmatic name.

With the greedy and corrupt Ley at its helm, the German Labor Front thrived on a polycratic system of leadership held together by feuding functionaries with overlapping responsibilities. This culture of disorganization (or centralized decentralization) contributed to ongoing rivalries with the Nazi Party and disagreements with powerful corporate leaders. To use Max Weber's term, DAF functioned like a charismatic bureaucracy; it was heavily dependent on media representations in order to solidify its power base among the workers and realize its political ambitions beyond the workplace. Beauty of Labor developed ambitious plans for modernizing factories and workplaces in line with new productivity and efficiency standards. The *NS-Musterbetrieb* (model factory) became a favorite showcase for the importance of *Menschenführung* (organizational leadership) in increasing *Leis-*

---

47 The term is taken from Rüdiger Hachtmann, *Das Wirtschaftsimperium der Deutschen Arbeitsfront 1933–1945* (Göttingen: Wallstein, 2012), which is the most extensive study on the subject. On the Reich Ministry of Labor, including its complicated relationship to DAF, see Alexander Nützenadel, ed., *Bureaucracy, Work and Violence: The Reich Ministry of Labour in Nazi Germany*, trans. Alex Skinner (New York: Berghahn, 2020). For a historical survey, also see David Meskill, *Organizing the German Workforce: Labor Administration from Bismarck to the Economic Miracle* (New York: Berghahn, 2010).

48 On the KdF organization, see Shelley Baranowski, *Strength through Joy: Consumerism and Mass Tourism in the Third Reich* (Cambridge: Cambridge University Press, 2004). The growing attention to consumer culture can be seen in Pamela E. Swett, Corey Ross, and Fabrice d'Almeida, eds., *Pleasure and Power in Nazi Germany* (London: Palgrave Macmillan, 2011) and Julia Timpe, *Nazi-Organized Recreation and Entertainment in the Third Reich* (London: Palgrave Macmillan, 2017).

tungswille (the will to achieve) as well as *Schaffensfreude* (the joy to create).[49] Some scholars have pointed out that Beauty of Labor had no real power aside from inspecting existing factories, rewarding exemplary facilities, and shaming noncooperative owners by calling them *Schädlinge am Volkskörper*, parasites on the body of the folk. The limited interest among factory owners to receive the distinction "model factory" should not take away from the official rhetoric that beautification was essential to efficiency and productivity, including the production of consent. On the contrary, the dissonance between fantasy and reality only added to the significance of symbolic politics within the new culture of work.

The diverse collective imaginaries associated with workerdom gave a history to the biopolitical project that, through the means of aestheticization, aligned public and private life with the goals of the Nazi state. Beauty, in this context, provided the sensory pleasures and affective bonds that allowed German workers "to experience 'communal work' on the level of the corporation and 'national work' on the level of the entire state."[50] Up until the war, DAF promoted the rewards of workerdom across the entire range of media and exhibition practices. Aestheticization and emotionalization functioned as corresponding strategies in their narratives of communalization. The appeal to beauty as a prefiguration of happiness proved an essential part of the intended emotional effects. Numerous publications written for workers or concerned with workers established the larger context in which beauty was to be understood as a relational category – that is, an initiation into the feelings of unity and harmony soon to be experienced in reality. The official DAF organ *Arbeitertum* (discussed in chapter 6) and similar publications saw work as the necessary link between individual and community and emphasized its ability to inspire new forms of sociability and rituals of belonging. Published annually, the *Kalender der deutschen Arbeit* (Calendar of German work) issued by DAF offered a mixture of historical anecdotes, propaganda slogans, and folksy wisdom. Modeled on the *Arbeiter-Kalender* (Workers' calendar) popular since the beginning of the workers' movement, the National Socialist version adapted the existing iconographies of working-class masculinity and preindustrial folk culture to new propagandistic functions. These changes can be traced through calendar covers that first announced the union of workers of the forehead and the fist (1934), then appealed to the union of workers and peasants (1939), and, during the war, celebrated the union of workers and soldiers (1940, 1941, 1942, 1943). Other mass-cultural rep-

---

49 See Theo Hupfauer, "Der Nationalsozialistische Musterbetrieb," *Schönheit der Arbeit* 2.2 (1937): 50–51.
50 Manfred Seifert, *Kulturarbeit im Reichsarbeitsdienst: Theorie und Praxis nationalsozialistischer Kulturpflege im Kontext historisch-politischer, organisatorischer und ideologischer Einflüsse* (Münster: Waxmann, 1996), 8.

resentations relied on consumerist choices and lifestyle brands to promote the ideal of the German worker. Even the Dresden-based Greiling cigarette brand added a series of photographs titled *Adel der Arbeit* (1934, Nobility of work) to its catalog of cigarette picture albums.

Meanwhile, work- and industry-themed exhibitions showcased the regime's achievements through a combination of informative displays, artworks, public lectures, and festive events. Many exhibitions combined the heroic style of neoclassicism with the functionalist aesthetic of the Bauhaus. Herbert Bayer, who had contributed to the visual presentation of the 1931 Exhibition of the Building Workers Union and the 1933 Camera Exhibition in Berlin, ended up designing the displays, posters, and exhibition catalogue for the influential 1934 *Deutsches Volk – deutsche Arbeit* (German folk – German work) Exhibition in Berlin. During the 1930s, modern exhibition design, from the treatment of space and place to the use of photography, typography, and graphic design, emerged as an artistic medium in its own right and proved ideally suited for totalitarian regimes advertising their accomplishments in the technocratic idioms of industrial modernity.[51] Organized around the theme of work and community and its ever-expanding meanings, later *Leistungsschauen* included the 1937 *Schaffendes Volk* (Working folk) in Düsseldorf, the 1938 *Gesundes Leben, frohes Schaffen* (Healthy life, happy work) in Berlin, and the 1939 exhibition *Kraft durch Freude* (Strength through joy) in Hamburg.[52] The biopolitical concepts – folk, life, health, joy, and strength – referenced in the exhibitions' titles established a clear connection between work and race whose significance for the emotional health of the people was further clarified in a catalogue for the 1937 *Schönheit der Arbeit* exhibition. To once again quote Ley: "The productive German is called upon to enjoy his work; he should practice his profession and approach his daily tasks with a sense of joy. It is not enough for

---

51 On Nazi exhibition culture, see Michael Tymkiw, *Nazi Exhibition Design and Modernism* (Minneapolis: University of Minnesota Press, 2018) and, for a comparative study, Vanessa Rocco, *Photofascism: Photography, Film, and Exhibition Culture in 1930s Germany and Italy* (London: Bloomsbury, 2020), especially chapters 1 and 3.

52 On Italian Fascism, see Victoria de Grazia, *The Culture of Consent: Mass Organization of Leisure in Fascist Italy* (Cambridge: Cambridge University Press, 1981); Simonetta Falasca-Zamponi, *Fascist Spectacle: The Aesthetics of Power in Mussolini's Italy* (Berkeley: University of California Press, 1997); and Ruth Ben-Ghiat, *Fascist Modernities: Italy, 1922–1945* (Berkeley: University of California Press, 2010). For a comparative study, see Daniela Liebscher, *Freude und Arbeit: Zur internationalen Freizeit- und Sozialpolitik des faschistischen Italien und des NS-Regimes* (Cologne: SH-Verlag, 2009). On the Italian connection in a European context, see Benjamin G. Martin, *The Nazi-Fascist New Order for European Culture* (Cambridge, MA: Harvard University Press, 2016).

us to have brave people, they also have to be happy and joyous."[53] Beauty of Labor even put together guidelines for art exhibitions in factories, convinced that learning how to appreciate art would allow workers to overcome the detrimental effects of Marxist workers' education and open up to the spiritual reward of a folk-based workerdom. Whether exhibiting art in factories or bringing workers to museums, DAF functionaries saw painting and sculpture as useful tools in highlighting the artistic dimensions of work and showing the existence of beauty in everyday life.[54] Similar ideas stood behind the information campaigns that educated Germans about the benefits of a safe, quiet, well-lit, and clean workplace: the 1935 *Lärmbekämpfungswoche* (noise abatement week), the 1935 "Gutes Licht, gute Arbeit" (good light, good work) campaign, and the 1937 traveling exhibition "Saubere Menschen im sauberen Betrieb (Clean people in clean factories).

The influence of industrial and organizational psychology is most apparent in the International Central Bureau "Work and Joy" founded at the 1936 World Congress for Leisure Time and Recreation in Hamburg. Treating work as part of a whole new way of life, German presenters lectured on topics such as "World Views and Recreational Activities," "Joy in Work through Beautiful and Attractive Work Places," and "The Influence of Work on Art and Culture," topics that once again confirm the organizers' ambition to make the culture of work a model for public and private life.[55] Published in several languages, the Bureau's journal *Freude und Arbeit* (1936–1943, Joy and work) distributed its colorful images and stories of happy, healthy workers all across Europe. The focus on Italy and the Balkan countries must be seen as part of broader geopolitical ambitions, including initial competition with the International Labor Office in Geneva. These collaborations across borders indicate the degree to which ideologies of work and leisure were part of the Reich's preparation for war, with Central Europe suddenly placed in an awkward position between Fascist Italy and Nazi Germany.

---

53 Robert Ley, preface, *Führer durch die Ausstellung Schönheit der Arbeit und Die Arbeit in der Kunst München, 16 October 1937 – 6 Nov. 1937* (Munich: Deutsche Arbeitsfront, 1937), 4.
54 For an example of such initiatives, see the publication by the KdF Amt Feierabend, *Der Arbeiter und die bildende Kunst: System und Aufgabe der Kunstausstellungen* (Berlin: Kraft durch Freude, 1938) or the songbook *Werkleute singen: Lieder der NS-Gemeinschaft Kraft durch Freude* (Kassel: Bärenreiter, 1936).
55 See *Bericht über den Weltkongress für Freizeit und Erholung, Hamburg, vom 23. bis 30. Juli 1936* (Hamburg: Hanseatische Verlagsanstalt, 1937). Also see the extensive bibliography on the topic presented in *Freude und Arbeit: Bibliographische Materialien zum 3. Weltkongress "Arbeit und Freude," Rom 1938* (Berlin: Zentralbüro "Arbeit und Freude," 1938).

III

As part of the German Labor Front, Beauty of Labor set out to improve working conditions through good form and design and, in so doing, create joyous workers. Yet even its most practical solutions included the kind of ideological work involved in glossing over the contradictions at the heart of the new culture of work. For on the one hand, DAF reorganized and redefined working bodies in accordance with Fordist models, *völkisch* ideas, racist theories, and corporatist (and corporate) principles. Its initiatives perpetuated the confidence in technological solutions and methods of rationalization that fueled the intense German interest in Fordism since the Weimar years. The constitutive tension between scientific management and good design, public health and social hygiene, and techniques of self-improvement and technologies of surveillance made all of these initiatives an integral part of Nazi biopolitics. On the other hand, the ubiquitous expressions of institutional optimism, including the belief that everything could be managed and controlled, and the actual limits of DAF's power, whether in dealings with factory owners, local officials, or groups of workers, point to the compensatory function of the obsession with beauty, the performative nature of the evocation of joy, and the hidden anxieties about the unresolved social question.

Beauty of Labor promoted a wide range of initiatives in support of this new culture of work: through the building of meeting rooms, communal libraries, and sports facilities for factory workers; the use of decorative elements (mosaics, frescos, wall inscriptions) in designing common areas; and the establishment of best practices in the design of group showers, locker rooms, and so forth. Aimed at professionals, a book series published between 1936 and 1941 included volumes on workplace furniture and design, good lighting and proper ventilation, canteen kitchens and dining halls, as well as factory staircases, hallways, and access roads.[56] Combining modernist and regionalist elements, DAF furniture and tableware adopted the standards of affordable functionality established by the Werkbund. The Rosenthal tableware used in many factory canteens is a good example of the desired balance between comfort, modesty, and restraint associated with that tradition. Needless to say, the cult of work community also inspired a fair amount of kitsch, from bronze desk sculptures featuring workers inside the signa-

---

[56] Titles in the Fachschriftenreihe des Reichsamtes "Schönheit der Arbeit" include *Speiseräume und Küchen in gewerblichen Betrieben* (1938), *Das Kameradschaftshaus im Betrieb* (1939), *Das Möbelbuch* (1942), and *Der Umkleide-, Wasch- und Baderaum in gewerblichen Betrieben* (1942).

ture DAF cogwheel or the ubiquitous "Work Dignifies!" motto carved on pins, plaques, medals, and decorative daggers.[57]

Multidisciplinary perspectives can be very helpful when it comes to the contested status of modernism and modernity and what both contributed to the imaginaries of class and folk as mediated by Beauty of Labor. Diverging definitions and assessments often reflect disciplinary differences between social and cultural historians and literary and visual arts scholars. For historians, the modernizing ambitions of the Nazi regime remain closely tied to the nation-state and the crisis moments that fueled its violent eruptions during the first half of the twentieth century. For others, fascist modernism can only be examined within a European framework, both as regards the transnational project of the historical avant-garde and the connections among rightwing intellectuals in Germany, Italy, and France. The scholarship on Beauty of Labor reflects the difficulties of conceptualizing a technocratic aesthetic in relation to biopolitics – that is, the extension of work into the spheres of life. In one of the earliest studies, Anson Rabinbach calls the fascist aesthetics of production "an attempt to legitimize political rule through aesthetic symbolization."[58] Along similar lines, Peter Labanyi argues that Beauty of Labor offered more than "an aesthetic façade *within* the workplace" and concludes that "'beauty' was not simply an attempt to put a 'human' face on capitalist rationality, it was simultaneously – and primarily – *in the servic*e of this rationality."[59] In the first monograph on Beauty of Labor, Chup Friemert describes its program as a coordinated strategy for achieving social consent through new imaginaries organized around the idea of work. Developed and tested within the sphere of production, its conception of the aesthetic was no longer limited to individual convictions and experiences. To paraphrase Wolfgang Fritz Haug from that book's preface, the aesthetics of production was neither a quality inherent in the

---

[57] On the Nazi anti-kitsch campaign and the underlying official anxieties, see Natalia Skradol, "Fascism and Kitsch: The Nazi Campaign against Kitsch," *German Studies Review* 34.3 (2011): 595–612.

[58] Anson G. Rabinbach, "The Aesthetics of Production in the Third Reich," *Journal of Contemporary History* 11.4 (1976): 43, in (revised form in) *The Eclipse of the Utopias of Labor* (New York: Fordham University Press, 2018), 125–152. For a transnational perspective, also see Charles Maier, "Between Taylorism and Technocracy: European Ideologies and the Vision of Industrial Productivity in the 1920s," *Journal of Contemporary History* 5.2 (1970): 27–61. For comparative perspectives on industrial modernity during the interwar years, see Stefan J. Link, *Forging Global Fordism: Nazi Germany, Soviet Russia, and the Contest over the Industrial Order* (Princeton: Princeton University Press, 2020), especially chapter 4 on Nazi Fordism (131–171).

[59] Peter Labanyi, "Images of Fascism: Visualization and Aestheticization in the Third Reich," in *The Burden of German History 1919–45*, ed. Michael Laffan (London: Methuen, 1988), 168.

material object nor an expression of subjective taste.⁶⁰ For that reason, it must be treated as a subject-object relationship grounded in the social and economic contradictions of its times. Accordingly, the main function of the fascist aesthetics of production was to constitute the work community as a model of the folk community and establish the *Werk* (in the double sense of work and factory) as a central locus of collective identifications. Aestheticization and emotionalization in this context served two additional functions, to keep alive the socialist utopia of nonalienated labor and to affirm the modernist belief in social change through good design.

In its various publications, Beauty of Labor followed a modernist narrative in which form indeed follows function, namely as an agent of social change – but also of racial awakening. Many of the proposals for improved air circulation and lighting schemes rehearse standard arguments by Wilhelmine and Weimar-era reformers, as do the more ambitious plans for workers' education and workers' sport. In fact, the monthly *Schönheit der Arbeit* (1936–1939) was edited by Lotz, formerly the editor of the Werkbund's *Die Form: Zeitschrift für gestaltende Arbeit* (1922–1935) and read by professionals trained in the organic modern styles favored by Peter Behrens, Wilhelm Wagenfeld, and Herbert Bayer. Their influences are on full display in the special (last) issue of *Die Form* 10.7 (1935) that emulates the minimalist style and reformist zeal familiar from many Weimar-era publications. At the same time, the fixation on workers' happiness suggests a fundamental realignment of priorities evident in the before-and-after comparisons that promise to turn "miserable, unhealthy places of drudgery into places of happy work" and to make "work the joyous meaning of life."⁶¹ What that process looked like in practice can be seen in the many illustrations showcasing the failures of the Weimar system. As one caption reads: "Loveless, neglected, run-down – that's how hundreds of thousands of factories still look today. The balance sheet of a company without the mission 'joy in work' is indeed negative."⁶²

---

60 Wolfgang Fritz Haug, Introduction, Chup Friemert, *Produktionsästhetik im Faschismus: Das Amt "Schönheit der Arbeit" von 1933 bis 1939* (Munich: Damnitz, 1980), 6–10. On some of the conceptual and disciplinary issues, see John Heskett, "Art and Design in Nazi Germany," *History Workshop* 6 (Autumn 1978): 139–153. On the role of government policies in the history of modern German design by the same author, see "The Role of Government Policy on German Design," in *A John Heskett Reader: Design, History, Economics*, ed. Clive Dilnot (London: Bloomsbury Academic, 2016), 140–174.
61 Karl Kretschmer, preface, *Die Form* 10.7 (1935): 161 and 163. Other journals published special issues in conjunction with *Schönheit der Arbeit*, including *Baugilde* (May 1937) and *Westermanns Monatshefte* (February 1937).
62 *Die Form* 10.7 (1935): 172.

In *Schönheit der Arbeit*, the habitual calls for cleanliness and orderliness as the foundation of joy in work and the detailed proposals for improvements in workplace design culminated in the aestheticization of work through the emotional rewards of communitarianism. In a typical journal issue, panoramas of empty factory halls and offices and closeups of new prototypes for canteen flatware and tableware alternate with scenes of happy workers at rest and play, performers in the self-representation of Beauty of Labor and extras in the making of Nazi biopolitics. The overall impression of Nazi Germany is that of a worker's paradise and industrial arcadia. At last, it seems, the technocratic mentality from the Weimar years has been mellowed by a "warmer" communitarianism, complete with cute stories and funny cartoons about a new generation of workers eager to fit in and take part. The habitus of sobriety, still present in the journal's section on examples of outstanding design, is now overlain by a joyous commitment to service for, if not submission to, the common good. In the first issue of *Schönheit der Arbeit*, Ley announced this reorientation when he gushed about factories "where a community of men, with hearts and hands, work together in the service of German life."[63] Rejecting false pathos and artificial heroism, the pompous DAF leader described the "heroic clothed in the robe of austerity, the mark of true heroism"[64] as the only appropriate aesthetic register for the ambitious social project pursued by Beauty of Labor. The repeated references to "life" in advertisements for the journal confirm the strong influence of *Lebensphilosophie*, a German version of vitalism, on its highly eclectic mixture of functionalist, technocratic, biologistic, and corporatist elements.[65]

Three points are noteworthy in the self-representation of Beauty of Labor on the pages of *Schönheit der Arbeit:* an affinity for small and medium-size factories that are family owned, highly specialized, and located in the countryside; close attention to female workers (e. g., company childcare, women's clubs) that may be a function of the conventional equation of women with beauty; and a seemingly endless fascination with leisure and recreation: workers resting in rattan chairs, playing tennis on clay courts, tending to company gardens, dining in factory canteens, and so forth. In order to make these images readable, the editors frequently added narrative elements that tied these moments of joy and pride to gendered identifications. Highlighting the process of initiation into workerdom, the photo story of one young woman's first workday at an industrial laundry – called "a fateful moment" – ends with a sense of gratification that "in a few minutes, Hilde will be-

---

63 Robert Ley, Introduction, *Schönheit der Arbeit* 1 (1936): 1.
64 Robert Ley, Introduction, 1.
65 Advertisement for *Schönheit der Arbeit*, in *Taschenbuch "Schönheit der Arbeit,"* 277.

come a member of the workforce [Gefolgschaftsmitglied]."⁶⁶ In a recurring section called "After the Work Day," short stories by Erich Grisar model the right and wrong ways to be a German worker, for instance by rewarding proper work habits with a happy love story.⁶⁷ Combining photos and drawings, "How Paul Was Converted" offers a lesson on proper behavior as a grumpy middle-aged worker, used to grabbing a quick bite at his workstation, finally recognizes that it is better to join his coworkers at the canteen table.⁶⁸ Last but not least, a cartoon by Emmerich Huber titled "The Hostile Brothers" instructs readers how to create their own happy workplace: by identifying the cause of one worker's discontent, informing their supervisor, talking with colleagues, and (in this case) deciding to clean up the workshop themselves. The lesson learned by this particular disgruntled worker? "He once again felt happy and free / and experienced time and again: that work happens more easily / when workers do it surrounded by beauty."⁶⁹

Das Taschenbuch Schönheit der Arbeit (1938, The beauty of labor handbook) edited by Anatol von Hübbenet popularized many of these ideas for a broader readership, including those without any connection to labor or industry. At the outset, the KdF functionary made clear that beautification involved creating "a comradely connection to the folk and respect for the working man," in short: a set of feelings related to work.⁷⁰ For the individual worker this meant "that he must give his best for the community."⁷¹ Contributing a preface in his role as General Building Inspector for the Reich Capital, Speer called on factory owners to eliminate all residues of the "heavy and ugly atmosphere poisoned by class struggle and mutual mistrust" and admonished workers to develop the proper attitude toward work. After all, "The goal is to create a beautiful and dignified work environment so they can perform their daily assignments with joy and pride."⁷²

The preoccupation with beauty as an aesthetic experience invariably highlights its ideological function in defining the work community through and against its various others. This normative, if not punitive aspect of beauty can be recon-

---

66 Artur Fenners, "Der erste Arbeitstag," *Schönheit der Arbeit* 2.1 (1937): 12 and 22.
67 For example, Erich Grisar, "Das große Los," *Schönheit der Arbeit* 2.4 (1937): 104 and passim. In fact, Schönheit der Arbeit functionary Bruno Malitz wrote a novel about the beautification of a factory, *Arbeiter, Geschichte einer Werktreue* (Berlin: Wilhelm Limpert, 1942).
68 "Wie Paule bekehrt wurde," *Schönheit der Arbeit* 2.11 (1937): 451.
69 "Die feindlichen Brüder," *Schönheit der Arbeit* 2.1 (1937): 44–45. Text by Hans Gartmann, drawings by Emmerich Huber.
70 Anatol von Hübbenet, ed., *Das Taschenbuch Schönheit der Arbeit* (Berlin: Amt "Schönheit der Arbeit" Verlag der DAF, 1938), 22. The booklet includes photos by Paul Wolff.
71 Anatol von Hübbenet, "Schönheit der Arbeit, ein Triumph des Gemeinschaftswillens," in *Kalender der deutschen Arbeit 1937* (Berlin: DAF, 1936), 142.
72 Albert Speer, Geleitwort, *Taschenbuch Schönheit der Arbeit*, 8 and 17.

structed through the *Taschenbuch*'s sequential presentation of a typical workday within the photobook format. From the factory gate with its simple signage, the reader arrives inside the production halls, marvels at clean and neat workplaces, notices functional furniture and good lighting, recognizes quality tools and protective gear, and takes note of the many (but not too many) office-appropriate potted plants. The biopolitical ambitions of Beauty of Labor come into closer view through the intense focus on practices related to the working body. The demand for clean workers in clean factories finds telling expression on countless pages devoted to changing rooms, shower stalls, and bathrooms. The close attention to physical and mental health is captured in beautiful images of first aid stations, worker canteens, fitness rooms, green spaces, and outdoor sports facilities. Related social initiatives and intentions are on full display in the *Kameradschaftsräume and -häuser* (literally: comradeship rooms and houses) built exclusively for political meetings, rallies, and ceremonies and adorned with mosaics, frescos, and wall slogans about the joys of work. One image of women workers all clad in white, taking a break in the company park, comes with the simple caption: "Work and Joy" (see figures 7.2 and 7.3).

Fig. 7.2: Anatol von Hübbenet, ed., *Das Taschenbuch Schönheit der Arbeit* (Berlin: Verlag der DAF, 1938), 79.

Fig. 7.3: *Das Taschenbuch "Schönheit der Arbeit,"* 124.

The redesign of workshops according to ergonomic and hygienic criteria, the insistence on proper lighting and air circulation, the renovation of changing rooms and washrooms, the addition of public greens and sports facilities, and the selection of quality wall paints and appropriate decorative elements all served to strengthen the equation of work with beauty and of beauty, by extension, with joy. To quote one poster: "Beautiful places of work equal great joy in work." As the examples below illustrate, the absence of joy stood for the all-too-familiar markers of otherness in Nazi ideology: filth, clutter, darkness, and disease – traits associated with the unruly proletarian and the greedy Jewish capitalist. In the model factory, deproletarianization could only be achieved through a thorough clean-up campaign. Using the comparative perspective of "before and after," a series of posters in the modern *Sachplakat* (object poster) style developed originally by Ludwig Hohlwein depicted the proposed improvements with clear didactic purpose (see figures 7.4 and 7.5). Promising "Joy in Work through Friendly Work Places" and "Joy in Work through Beautiful Canteens," each poster is divided into an upper and lower part, with a worker's hand pulling down a colorful canvas representing the new culture of work. Thus, a bright workplace with quality tools above is juxtaposed to a grey mess of tools and materials below; a nicely set lunch table with flowers above is compared to workers hastily devouring their home-made lunch at the workplace.[73]

The emphasis on industrial hygiene can be traced back to turn-of-the-century reform movements that treated public health as an important part of social reform. However, the fixation on cleanliness here and elsewhere also reveals how antisemitism suffused the self-presentation of Beauty of Labor. The almost compulsive evocation of dirty factories and unkempt workers sheds light on the deep fears and resentments directed against both the proletarian and the capitalist and gives terrifying new meaning to the term "industrial hygiene." Filth and clutter functioned not only as tropes signifying capitalist greed, comparable to the "dirty, ugly Jew" in antisemitic propaganda; they also helped to legitimize solutions where cleanliness served as a shorthand for racial health. To quote Ley once more, the Marxists "are partly to blame for the German worker's feeling of inferiority. Since all he heard was 'dirty' factory, we should not be surprised that he saw himself as a dirty worker."[74] For DAF functionaries, the first step toward a solution was obvious: "Whoever wants to eliminate the class struggle, would first have to remove the stain of dirtiness from the work and, hence, the workers."[75] Tellingly,

---

73 Reprinted in a special issue of Die *Form* 10.7 (1935): 191.
74 Robert Ley, "Die Gründung der NS Gemeinschaft 'Kraft durch Freude,'" in *Durchbruch der sozialen Ehre*, 42.
75 Quoted by Friemert, 191. First published in *Blätter für soziale Praxis* 46.19 (1937): 252.

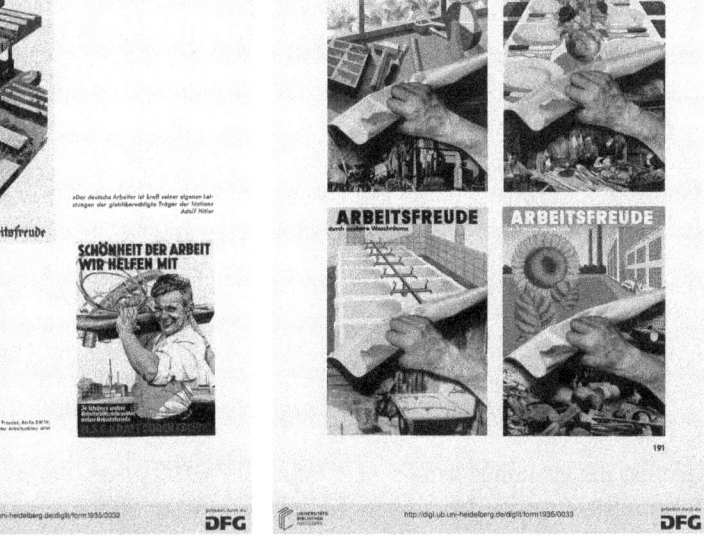

Fig. 7.4: "So und nicht so" and "Schönheit der Arbeit. Wir helfen mit," posters reprinted in *Die Form* 10.7 (1935): 190.

Fig. 7.5: "Arbeitsfreude" posters, reprinted in *Die Form* 10.7 (1935): 191.

the campaigns against dirt not only identified those to be excluded from the folk community, they also established rules and regulations for those to be included. This new order left little room for individual choice; to quote yet another Nazi official: "We have replaced class struggle with the spirit of working camaraderie. [...] Everyone must join the unified front of production. Everyone must recognize that they are all dependent on each other. The folk comes first, and then the individual. Only when we think along these lines can the true folk community be created."[76]

The aestheticization of work in Nazi Germany marks the endpoint of a long development that started with the workers' movement of the nineteenth century and profoundly influenced the reform movements of the turn of the century. Today Beauty of Labor may be most remembered for its architecture and design initiatives, but it played an even more important role in establishing the very conditions of Nazi biopolitics. Measured by the sheer quantity of publications about beauty and work, it is all the more surprising that the aestheticization of politics remains the main category through which the fascist aesthetic has been theorized.

---

76 *Rheinische Landeszeitung* quoted in Friemert, 129.

In closing, it may therefore make sense to summarize the various functions of the aestheticization of work through Walter Benjamin's famous definition of fascism as the aestheticization of politics. The phrase's original appearance in the epilogue to "The Work of Art in the Age of Mechanical Reproducibility" from the mid-1930s provides a first indication of how much the politics of emotion in fascism was tied to new mass media and mass cultural practices and in what ways it has since been equated with an expanded meaning of the political as spectacle, performance, and fantasy. Often forgotten, the key passage in Benjamin begins with an explanation for the broad support for the Nazi movement among the working class:

> Fascism attempts to organize the newly proletarianized masses while leaving intact the property relations which they seek to eliminate. It seeks its salvation in granting expression to the masses – but on no account granting them rights. The masses have a *right* to changed property relations; fascism seeks to give them *expression* in keeping these relations unchanged. *The logical outcome of fascism is an aestheticizing of political life.*[77]

Against the economic determinism of orthodox Marxism, Benjamin insists on the legitimacy of the workers' desire for self-expression. At the same time, he connects the strategy of aestheticization to the perpetuation of the conditions of production under capitalism, with the result that, for him, the politicization of art under communism offers the only valid strategy of resistance available at the time.

On the one hand, the Marxist analysis of class blinds Benjamin to the populist elements shared by socialist and fascist movements, starting with the people's need for strong identifications and powerful emotions. From his use of proletarianization in describing the experience of downward mobility during the economic depression to his overestimation of communist sympathies among the politicized workers, his analysis reproduces the constellation of utopian anticapitalism, Bolshevist vanguardism, and economic determinism that sustained the Weimar Left's romance with the Soviet Union. On the other hand, his description of fascism as an expressive modality opens up a radically new perspective on politics in the age of modern mass media and new social movements. "Aestheticization" under these conditions refers, first of all, to the insertion of aesthetic practices into the power structures, processes, and relations normally placed outside the arts in the traditional sense and far removed from the institutions of high culture. More specifically, the term draws attention to the collective identifications organized through aesthetic forms, styles, and experiences. The latter point in fact provides

---

[77] Walter Benjamin, "The Work of Art in the Age of Its Technological Reproducibility: Second Version," in *The Work of Art in the Age of Its Technological Reproducibility and Other Writings on Media*, ed. Michael W. Jennings, Brigid Doherty, and Thomas Y. Levin (Cambridge, MA: Harvard University Press, 2008), 42.

the departure for Benjamin's influential reading of the avant-garde project as the sublation of art into life and its historical connection – in ways reminiscent of Jünger – to war as the formative experiential model of modernity. This is made clear in his polemical conclusion that humankind's "self-alienation has reached the point where it can experience its own annihilation as extreme pleasure. *Such is the aestheticizing of politics, as practiced by fascism. Communism replies by politicizing art.*"[78]

The political alternatives identified with the fascist aestheticizing of politics and the communist politicizing of art may have made sense in the context of the prewar years, with Nazi power at its height and Benjamin laying out strategies of resistance from his Parisian exile. But the romance with (a narrowly defined) politically engaged art has also blinded subsequent generations of scholars to the fluid boundaries between the aestheticization of politics and the politicization of art and made them beholden to interpretative categories that, whether framed in terms of left vs. right, subversive vs. affirmative, or inclusive vs. exclusive, downplay the complexities of aesthetic experiences and political commitments. At the same time, the historically specific nature of the antifascist formation remains ill-suited to account for the changing currency of aestheticization in the age of the culture industry and the society of the spectacle. As a result, critical readings of Benjamin tend to place his argument within genealogies of contemporary thought that, whether in the language of ideology critique or poststructuralism, link the diagnosis of aestheticization to questions about (post)modernity, culture, and democracy.[79] For reasons that require a more detailed cultural-historical account, to be attempted in the third volume, questions of labor (until recently) have generated little interest in German studies and the figure of the worker has (almost) disappeared from the social imagination. Perhaps Benjamin's historical confrontation between the aestheticization of politics and the politicization of art has outlived its critical usefulness in postclass societies that establish their

---

78 Benjamin, "The Work of Art," 41. Emphasis in original.
79 Critical responses to the aestheticization of politics argument can be found (in chronological order) in Russell Berman, *Modern Culture and Critical Theory: Art, Politics, and the Legacy of the Frankfurt School* (Madison: University of Wisconsin Press, 1989), esp. 27–41; Lutz Koepnick, "Fascist Aesthetics Revisited," *Modernism/Modernity* 6.1 (1999): 51–73; Carsten Strathausen, "Nazi Aesthetics," *Culture, Theory and Critique* 42.1 (1999): 5–19. For a special emphasis on modernist genealogies, see Brett Wheeler, "Modernist Reenchantments I: From Liberalism to Aestheticized Politics" and "Modernist Reenchantments II: From Aestheticized Politics to the Art Work," *German Quarterly* 74.3 (2001): 223–236 and 75.2 (2002): 113–126, respectively. From the German perspective, compare Karlheinz Barck, "Konjunktionen von Ästhetik und Politik oder Politik des Ästhetischen," in *Ästhetik des Politischen, Politik des Ästhetischen*, ed. Karlheinz Barck and Richard Faber (Würzburg: Königshausen & Neumann, 1999), 97–120.

structures of inequality and strategies of exclusion along very different fault lines. In light of growing concerns about the condition of precarity, rising inequality, and the future of work, it may be high time to rediscover a very different fascist legacy with an equally complicated political history and theoretical legacy known as the aestheticization of work.

Afterword

Research on *The Nazi Worker* began with questions about the survival of proletarian identifications after 1933 – survival both in the form of class-based stories and images and in the context of new social imaginaries. The return to the archives yielded surprising results: first, the class struggles of the Weimar years remained an important reference point during the first years of the Nazi regime; second, enormous political will and creative energy were spent on establishing workerdom as the Nazi version of the working class; and third, the new culture of work played a key role in linking the work community to the folk community and changing the meaning of work and worker in the process.

As in *The Proletarian Dream*, understanding the textual productivity surrounding the figure of the worker required a return to the archives, to unknown, forgotten, and neglected texts. It meant treating discourse as a social practice and recognizing the power of social imaginaries. In this volume, it also meant expanding the definition of culture to include corporate branding and work psychology, distinguishing official cultural policies from actual artistic practices, and avoiding reductionist readings that treat everything as a reflection of Nazi ideology. With these caveats in mind, the discourse of workerdom has been reconstructed through a two-pronged approach: attention to the strategies of appropriation and adaptation through which class-based identifications were replaced by race-based ones, and awareness of the forms of emotionalization and aestheticization through which oppositional practices were turned into hegemonic ones.

As the seven chapters have shown, the textual productivity inspired by the figure of the worker and the heightened relevance attributed to the culture of work represent clear evidence of the continued relevance of questions of class and labor after 1933. More specifically, the countless images and stories attest to the surprising adaptability of class and folk as social imaginaries, their association with socialist, nationalist, and populist positions, and their very different functions in workers' poetry and prose fiction, industrial painting and photography, as well as in the Thingspiel movement and Beauty of Labor initiative. Neither a reflection of social reality nor a mere function of Nazi ideology, these imaginaries in turn are inseparable from the longer histories of industrialization, capitalism, and class society and the related genealogies of socialist, nationalist, and populist notions of community, folk, and the people. To acknowledge this complicated interplay of regional, national, and international perspectives, the selection of materials and the organization of chapters have highlighted the historically specific ways in which literature, criticism, theater, painting, sculpture, photography, and film contributed to three overlapping discourses: the uniquely German discourse of workerdom, including its connection to ethnonationalism, antisemitism, and communitarianism; the transnational culture of industrial modernity, including its affinities with the machine aesthetic and technocratic rationality; and the emotionalization and aestheticization of work, including the similarities with contemporaneous developments in Fascist Italy and the Soviet Union.

The main function of workerdom in the Third Reich was to replace class-based with race-based definitions of community and change the meaning of nation, folk, and people in the process. But this strategy of appropriation and instrumentalization was not without its complications and contradictions. On the one hand, the discourse of workerdom became part of a dynamic of coercion and consent, a process of interpellation through which workers could be integrated into the new culture of work, including its corporate interests and corporatist ideas. On the other hand, the proletarian remained a destabilizing force, whether in the form of specific feelings, beliefs, or attachments or through the retelling and restaging of past struggles and different futures. Here, the emphasis on feelings such as pride and joy in work has proven crucial for reconstructing the interrelated strategies of emotionalization and aestheticization that aligned the culture of work with the interests of the Nazi state and laid the foundations for Nazi biopolitics.

If the study of German working-class culture is to involve more than antiquarian interest or leftist nostalgia, it must develop the larger questions about work and class across the ideological divides and violent ruptures of modern German history and consider the unique configurations of nationalism, socialism, and populism that made the worker such a central figure – as a social and political type, an artistic and literary subject, and a figure of identification and projection. Untangling all of these elements means moving beyond the rigid left-right distinctions that have blinded scholars to the fluidity of class-based identifications and imaginaries and allowed them to underestimate the emotions mobilized by social and political movements. It means focusing not on questions of identity but on processes of identification; it means reading work-related images and stories with a clear view toward their affective intensities and performative effects; and it means paying close attention to work as part of working-class culture and the changing configurations of nationalism and socialism. Last but not least, tracing these cultures of work across the 1933 and 1945 divides means extending the historically specific meanings of work and worker from the divisions of the Cold War to very different yet uncannily familiar contemporary phenomena personified by the migrant, related to service work, and identified with the conditions of precarious life.

With very contemporary investments but a deep commitment to the historical archives, the multivolume project of *The Proletarian Dream* recognizes the radical otherness of the worker as "the last great emblem of social mobilization,"[1] with "last" marking our own distance from social movements in which the working class embodied dreams of revolution and self-liberation. On the one hand, making productive use of this estrangement from the past requires closer attention to the iconographies of work and class that accompanied the master narratives of modern capitalism and industrial modernity in democracies as well as dictatorships. On the other, taking seriously the identifications mobilized by socialist, nationalist, and populist appeals to the people involves treating workerdom as an integral part of the culture of class and work in modern German history. Especially in the name of a forward-looking history of the Left and what has taken its place in contemporary social movements and identity politics, it is important to acknowledge the historical connection of socialism to modern democracy. At the same time, in the interest of a cultural history of work, class, and nation not constrained by the master narratives of socialism, it is imperative to recognize the historical affinities with nationalism and populism, including their nondemocratic versions, and make the insights gained from the study of working-class culture available to the problems of postclass and post-work societies.

---

1 Christoph Schmidt, *Vom Messias zum Prolet: Arbeiter in der Kunst* (Stuttgart: Franz Steiner, 2010), 11.

Select Bibliography

The following includes important English and German-language monographs on the topics addressed in individual chapters:

Annuß, Evelyn, *Volksschule des Theaters Nationalsozialistische Massenspiele* (Munich: Wilhelm Fink, 2019).
Bajor, Frank and Michael Wildt, eds., *Volksgemeinschaft: Neue Forschungen zur Gesellschaft des Nationalsozialismus* (Frankfurt am Main: Fischer, 2009).
Barbian, Jan-Pieter, *Literaturpolitik im NS-Staat: Von der "Gleichschaltung" bis zum Ruin* (Frankfurt am Main: Fischer, 2010).
Barron, Stephanie, ed., *"Degenerate Art": The Fate of the Avant-Garde in Nazi Germany* (New York: Harry N. Abrams, 1991).
Berswordt-Wallrabe, Silke von, Jörg-Uwe Neumann, and Agnes Tieze, eds., *"Artige Kunst": Kunst und Politik im Nationalsozialismus* (Bielefeld: Kerber, 2017).
Birdsall, Carolyn, *Nazi Soundscapes: Sound, Technology, and Urban Space in Germany, 1933–1945* (Amsterdam: Amsterdam University Press, 2012).
Böhnigk, Volker and Joachim Stamp, eds., *Die Moderne im Nationalsozialismus* (Bonn: University Press, 2006).
Bons, Joachim, *Nationalsozialismus und Arbeiterfrage: Zu den Motiven, Inhalten und Wirkungsgründen der nationalsozialistischen Arbeiterpolitik vor 1933* (Pfaffenweiler: Centaurus, 1995).
Brenner, Hildegard, *Die Kunstpolitik des Nationalsozialismus* (Reinbek: Rowohlt, 1983).
Bussmann, Georg, ed., *Kunst im 3. Reich: Dokumente der Unterwerfung* (Frankfurt am Main: Zweitausendeins, 1980).
Campbell, Joan, *Joy in Work, German Work: The National Debate* (Princeton: Princeton University Press, 1989).
Carsten, Francis Ludwig, *The German Workers and the Nazis* (Aldershot: Scholar Press, 1995).
Cuomo, Glen R., ed., *National Socialist Cultural Policy* (New York: St. Martin's Press, 1995).
Denkler, Horst and Karl Prümm, eds., *Die deutsche Literatur im Dritten Reich: Themen Traditionen Wirkungen* (Stuttgart: Reclam, 1976).
Drewniak, Boguslaw, *Das Theater im NS-Staat: Szenarium deutscher Zeitgeschichte 1933–1945* (Düsseldorf: Droste, 1983).
Eggerstorfer, Wolfgang, *Schönheit und Adel der Arbeit: Arbeiterliteratur im Dritten Reich* (Frankfurt am Main: Peter Lang, 1988).
Eichberg, Henning, Michael Dultz, Glen Gadberry, and Günther Rühle, eds., *Massenspiele: NS-Thingspiel, Arbeiterweihespiel und olympisches Zeremoniell* (Stuttgart: Friedrich Frommann-Holzboog, 1977).
Fischer, Conan, ed., *The Rise of National Socialism and the Working Classes in Weimar Germany* (Providence: Berghahn, 1996).
Fleckner, Uwe, ed., *Angriff auf die Avantgarde: Kunst und Kunstpolitik im Nationalsozialismus* (Berlin: Akademie, 2007).
Föllmer, Moritz, *Culture in the Third Reich* (Oxford: Oxford University Press, 2020).
Frecot, Janos et al., eds., *Zwischen Widerstand und Anpassung: Kunst in Deutschland 1933–1945* (Berlin: Akademie der Künste, 1978).

Friemert, Chup, *Produktionsästhetik im Faschismus: Das Amt "Schönheit der Arbeit" von 1933 bis 1939* (Munich: Damnitz, 1980).
Gadberry, Glen W., ed., *Theatre in the Third Reich, the Prewar Years: Essays on Theater in Nazi Germany* (Westport, CT: Greenwood Press, 1995).
Gilman, Sander L., ed., *NS-Literaturtheorie: Eine Dokumentation*, preface Cornelius Schnauber (Frankfurt am Main: Athenäum, 1971).
Graeb-Könneker, Sebastian, *Autochtone Modernität: Eine Untersuchung der vom Nationalsozialismus geförderten Literatur* (Opladen: Westdeutscher Verlag, 1996).
Herf, Jeffrey, *Reactionary Modernism: Technology, Culture and Politics in Weimar and the Third Reich* (Cambridge: Cambridge University Press, 1984).
Heuel, Eberhard, *Der umworbene Stand: Die ideologische Integration der Arbeiter im Nationalsozialismus* (Frankfurt am Main: Campus, 1989).
Hinz, Berthold, *Die Malerei im deutschen Faschismus: Kunst und Konterrevolution* (Munich: Carl Hanser, 1974).
Kater, Michael H., *Culture in Nazi Germany* (New Haven: Yale University Press, 2019).
Keele, Max H., *Nazis and Workers: National Socialist Appeals to German Labor, 1919–1933* (Chapel Hill: University of North Carolina Press, 1972).
Ketelsen, Uwe-Karsten, *Literatur und Drittes Reich* (Vierow bei Greifswald: SH-Verlag, 1992).
Ketelsen, Uwe-Karsten, *Völkisch-nationale und nationalsozialistische Literatur in Deutschland 1890–1945* (Stuttgart: Metzler, 1976).
Loewy, Ernst, *Literatur unterm Hakenkreuz: Das Dritte Reich und seine Dichtung* (Frankfurt am Main: Fischer, 1983).
London, John, ed., *Theatre under the Nazis* (Manchester: Manchester University Press, 2000).
Maertz, Gregory, *Nostalgia for the Future: Modernism and Heterogeneity in the Visual Arts of Nazi Germany* (Stuttgart: ibidem, 2019).
Mason, Timothy W., *Nazism, Fascism, and the Working Class: Essays by Tim Mason*, ed. Jane Caplan (Cambridge: Cambridge University Press, 1995).
Mason, Timothy W., *Social Policy in the Third Reich: The Working Class and the "National Community"* (Oxford: Oxford University Press, 1997).
Menger, Michaela, *Der literarische Kampf um den Arbeiter: Populäre Schemata und politische Agitation im Roman der späten Weimarer Republik* (Berlin: De Gruyter, 2016).
Michaud, Eric, *The Cult of Art in Nazi Germany*, trans. Janet Lloyd (Stanford: Stanford University Press, 2004).
Paul, Gerhard, *Aufstand der Bilder: NS-Propaganda vor 1933* (Berlin: Dietz, 1992).
Peters, Olaf, *Neue Sachlichkeit und Nationalsozialismus: Affirmation und Kritik 1931–1947* (Berlin: Dietrich Reimer, 1998).
Petropoulos, Jonathan, *Art as Politics in the Third Reich* (Chapel Hill: University of North Carolina Press, 1996).
Potter, Pamela M., *Art of Suppression: Confronting the Nazi Past in Histories of the Visual and Performing Arts* (Berkeley: University of California Press, 2016).
Rabinbach, Anson, *The Human Motor: Energy, Fatigue, and the Origins of Modernity* (Berkeley: University of California Press, 1992).
Rabinbach, Anson and Sander L. Gilman, eds. *The Third Reich Sourcebook* (Berkeley: University of California Press, 2013).
Reichel, Peter, *Der schöne Schein des Dritten Reiches: Faszination und Gewalt des Faschismus* (Munich, 1991).

Rocco, Vanessa, *Photofascism: Photography, Film, and Exhibition Culture in 1930s Germany and Italy* (London: Bloomsbury, 2020).
Schäfer, Hans Dieter, *Das gespaltene Bewußtsein: Deutsche Kultur und Lebenswirklichkeit 1933–1945* (Munich: Hanser, 1981).
Schirmbeck, Peter, *Adel der Arbeit: Der Arbeiter in der Kunst der NS-Zeit* (Marburg: Jonas, 1984).
Schneider, Michael, *Unterm Hakenkreuz: Arbeiter und Arbeiterbewegung 1933 bis 1939* (Bonn: Dietz, 1999).
Schnell, Ralf and Martin Rector, eds., *Kunst und Kultur im deutschen Faschismus* (Stuttgart: Metzler, 1978).
Schütz, Erhard, *Mediendiktatur Nationalsozialismus* (Heidelberg: Winter, 2019).
Steber, Martina and Bernhard Gotto, eds., *Visions of Community in Nazi Germany: Social Engineering and Private Lives* (Oxford: Oxford University Press, 2014).
Steinweis, Alan E., *Art, Ideology, and Economics: The Reich Chambers of Music, Theater, and the Visual Arts* (Chapel Hill: University of North Carolina Press, 1996).
Stommer, Rainer, *Die inszenierte Volksgemeinschaft: Die "Thing-Bewegung" im Dritten Reich* (Marburg: Jonas, 1985).
Strobl, Gerwin, *The Swastika and the Stage: German Theater and Society, 1933–1945* (Cambridge: Cambridge University Press, 2007).
Taylor, Brandon and Winfried van der Will, eds., *The Nazification of Art: Art, Design, Music, Architecture, and Film in the Third Reich* (Winchester, 1990).
Tymkiw, Michael, *Nazi Exhibition Design and Modernism* (Minneapolis: University of Minnesota Press, 2018).
Van Dyke, James A., *Franz Radziwill and the Contradictions of German Art History, 1919–1945* (Ann Arbor: University of Michigan Press, 2010).
Van linthout, Ine, *Das Buch in der nationalsozialistischen Propagandapolitik* (Berlin: De Gruyter, 2012).
Vondung, Klaus, *Völkisch-nationale und nationalsozialistische Literaturtheorie* (Munich: List, 1973).
Webster van Tonder, Christopher, *Photography in the Third Reich: Art, Physiognomy and Propaganda* (London: Bloomsbury, 2020).
Wildt, Michael and Marc Buggeln, eds., *Arbeit im Nationalsozialismus* (Munich: Oldenbourg, 2014).
Wulf, Joseph, *Theater und Film im Dritten Reich: Eine Dokumentation* (Gütersloh: Sigbert Mohn, 1964).
Würmann, Carsten and Ansgar Warner, eds., *Im Pausenraum des "Dritten Reiches": Zur Populärkultur im nationalsozialistischen Deutschland* (Berne: Peter Lang, 2008).
Zimmermann, Peter and Kay Hoffmann, eds., *Geschichte des dokumentarischen Films in Deutschland, vol. 3: "Drittes Reich" 1933–1945* (Stuttgart: Philipp Reclam jun., 2005).

Index of Names

Abbott, Berenice   167
Abel, Theodore   49, 52, 54, 59, 71
Adler, Alfred   160
Alexander, Gertrud   90
Annuß, Evelyn   105, 120
Arnhold, Carl   205
Arnold, Heinz Ludwig   76
Arntz, Gerd   128, 143
Arvidsson, Stefan   32
Ashkenazi, Ofer   186

Bade, Wilfrid   63
Bakhtin, Michael   51
Ballhause, Walter   164
Baluschek, Hans   143 fn41, 150
Bangert, Otto   39
Bartels, Adolf   86
Bartetzko, Dieter   104
Barthel, Max   16, 68, 80 – 81, 89 – 90, 113
Bayer, Herbert   132, 208, 212
Becher, Johannes R.   90
Behrens, Peter   212
Benjamin, Walter   102, 125, 195, 218 – 219
Benn, Gottfried   200
Beyer, Paul   109
Biallas, Hans   42, 168
Biermann, Karl Eduard   150
Bloch, Ernst   10, 37, 76, 94 – 95
Block, Max Paul   165
Böhme, Herbert   114
Bohrer, Karl-Heinz   198
Bourke-White, Margaret   167
Braumüller, Wolf   106 – 108, 115, 120
Braune, Rudolf   90
Brecht, Bertolt   92, 103
Bredow, Gustav Adolf   134
Breker, Arno   126, 132, 134, 141
Briefs, Götz   161 – 162
Bröger, Karl   80 – 81., 86, 89., 169
Brüssow, Hans   80
Bücher, Karl   161
Buchhorn, Josef   107
Bürger, Peter   192

Campbell, Joan   159
Carossa, Hans   32
Clark, Katerina   66
Claudius, Hermann   81
Courbet, Gustave   142

Damus, Martin   133
Debabov, Dmitri   167
Debord, Guy   102
Diederichs, Peter   80\
Diers, Marie   61
Diesel, Eugen   165 – 166
Dobrenko, Evgheny   195
Drexler, Anton   43 – 45
Dwinger, Edwin Erich   32

Eggerstorfer, Wolfgang   94
Eichberg, Henning   104, 108
Eichelberger, Kurt   131
Eisenlohr, Michael Friedrich   89
Eiserlo, Hans   81
Engelke, Gerrit   80 – 81
Euringer, Richard   17, 23, 100, 103, 115 – 118
Ewers, Hanns Heinz   52, 54, 64

Feder, Gottfried   43 – 45
Fischer, Eugen Kurt   120
Fischer-Lichte, Erika   105, 109
Freiligrath, Friedrich   87
Friemert, Chup   211 – 12
Frohme, Karl   87

Gallas, Helga   93
Gent, Paul   88
Gerlach, Kurt   162
Gerwin, Franz   124, 144
Gessner, Richard   144
Giese, Fritz   161
Glaser, Waldemar   54 – 55
Goebbels, Joseph   24, 27, 45, 53, 56 – 58, 110 – 111, 137, 162, 199
Goes, Gustav   115
Göring, Hermann   124, 144, 162

Gothe, Richard 156
Gotto, Bernard 7
Graf, Oskar Maria 80
Gramsci, Antonio 30
Griebel, Otto 129
Griese, Friedrich 162
Grimm, Hans 32
Grisar, Erich 92, 214
Gronostay, Walter 186
Gropius, Walter 103
Grossberg, Carl 130, 132, 143
Grosz, George 25 n11, 128
Grotewohl, Otto 136
Groys, Boris 193
Günther, Hans 64

Hachmann, Rüdiger 205
Hadamovsky, Eugen 56–57
Haid, Walter 39
Hallersleben, Ruth 188
Härtle, Heinrich 156
Hartmann, Bernd (Wiedenbrück) 134
Haug, Wolfgang Fritz 211–212
Hauser, Heinrich 167, 171
Heartfield, John 25, 128, 164 n23, 192 n8
Heidegger, Martin 200
Heine, Heinrich 87
Heiß, Friedrich 165
Heller, Leonid 65–66 182
Henri, Florence 171
Herder, Johann Gottfried 43
Herkner, Heinrich 160
Hermann, Gustav 162
Herwegh, Georg 87
Heynicke, Kurt 100, 110, 113, 115–116, 118–119, 122–123
Hine, Lewis 167, 171
Hinz, Berthold 27, 147 f.
Hitler, Adolf xiii, 1124–27, 31, 37, 42–43, 49, 52., 58–59, 62–64, 66–68, 71–72, 81, 108, 110, 123–125, 131, 136, 162, 176 fn47, 18., 192, 200
Höger, Fritz 115
Hohlwein, Ludwig 216
Hoppé, Emil Otto 149, 165
Horneffer, Ernst 161

Hübbenet, Anatol von 214–215
Huber, Emmerich 214

Iffland, Frank 134
Imdahl, Max 142

Jahn, Otto Heinz 186
Janensch, Gerhard Adolf 134
Jelken, Ernst 53, 86
Johst, Hanns 107
Jung, Patrick xv, 148–149
Jünger, Ernst 18, 33, 133,195–203, 219
Jünger, Friedrich Georg 33,

Kammerer, Ernst 138–140
Kampf, Arthur 29, 31, 39, 57, 65, 80, 86, 114 f., 143, 161, 165, 196 f.
Karrasch, Alfred 56
Kauffmann, Fritz Alexander 145, 148
Ketelsen, Uwe-K. 78, 92, 101, 120
Kindermann, Heinz 80, 107
Kläber, Kurt 80
Klemperer, Victor 5, 22
Koelle, Fritz 17, 124–125, 127–129, 131, 133, 135–142, 152
Kollwitz, Käthe 24, 25 fn.11., 80, 128, 135, 142
Korsch, Karl 160
Kracauer, Siegfried 194
Kraeplin, Emil 161
Kreis, Wilhelm 115
Krenzler, Guenter 161

Laban, Rudolf 104, 113
Labanyi, Peter 211
Laclau, Ernesto 9, 23–24, 79
Langenbucher, Hellmuth 76, 112
Lassalle, Ferdinand 87
Laubinger, Otto 120–121
Lauer, Erich 114
Lefort, Claude 21
Lehmann, Hans-Thies 102
Leibl, Wilhelm 142
Lendvai-Dircksen, Erna 18, 153, 157, 163, 165, 168–172, 175–180, 188
Lepp, Adolf 87
Lersch, Heinrich 16, 78, 80–86, 89, 93
Lerski, Helmar 170, 177

Index of Names

Lethen, Helmut   93
Ley, Robert   28, 45, 137, 153, 156, 192, 203–204, 206, 208, 213, 216
Liebermann, Max   143
Loeb, Minna   86
Lohmann, Heinz   55, 58
Lorch, Willi   61
Lotz, Wilhelm 203, 212
Luckhardt, Hans and Wassili Luckhardt   115
Lüdtke, Alf   72

Magilow, Daniel   164
Maier-Dorn, Emil   172, 179–180
Maillol, Aristide   139
Man, Hendrik de   104, 161
Marszolek, Inge   111
Marx, Karl   13, 28, 37, 58, 136
Mason, Timothy   71–72
Meinecke, Friedrich   7
Meinholz, Anton   166
Mellon, Arthur   74
Menger, Michaela   65
Menz, Egon   105
Menzel, Adolph   143
Mercker, Erich   xv, 17, 124–125, 127–131, 133, 145–146, 148–153
Meunier, Constantin   139, 143
Millet, Jean-François   142
Moeller van den Bruck, Arthur   28, 33
Moholy, Lucia 171
Molenaar, Herbert   114
Möller, Eberhard Wolfgang   97–98, 101, 106, 114, 118, 120
Moraller, Franz   112
Moshamer, Ludwig   115
Most, Johann   88
Muckow, Reinhold   168
Mühle, Hans   16, 81
Müller, Traugott   104, 117, 122
Müller-Schnick, Erich   114–115.
Munter, Hans   42

Nadler, Josef   35, 68, 82
Nagel, Otto   25 fn11, 129
Naumann, Friedrich   37
Nelissen-Haken, Bruno   112
Niedecken-Gebhard, Hanns   104

Niekisch, Ernst   32, 38, 200
Nierentz, Hans-Jürgen   114
Niessen, Carl   97
Nietzsche, Friedrich   40, 199
Niven, Bill   109
Noldan, Svend   182

Paul, Gerhard   27
Petzold, Kurt   80–81
Picco-Rückert, Ria   144, 146
Pinder, Wilhelm   142
Piscator, Erwin   103–104
Potter, Pamela   11
Propf, Robert   134
Protzen, Carl Theodor   144

Querner, Curt   129

Rabinbach, Anson   133, 158, 211
Reich, Lilly   132
Reich, Wilhelm   193 fn8
Reichel, Peter   12
Reineke-Altenau, Karl   145
Reinhardt, Max   103
Reisse, Hermann   55
Renger-Patzsch, Alfred   166–167, 171
Retzlaff, Erich   170
Riefenstahl, Leni   97, 100, 104, 120–121, 126, 172, 179, 186
Riehl, Wilhelm Heinrich   159
Rittich, Werner   148
Rodchenko, Alexander   167
Rodin, Auguste   139
Rohe, Mies van der   132
Rosenberg, Alfred   53, 106, 110–113, 137, 156, 171
Rühle, Jürgen   93
Rülcker, Christoph   93–95
Ruttmann, Walter   18, 153, 157, 182–185, 187

Sachsse, Rolf   188
Salomon, Ernst von   199
Sander, August   164, 169–170
Schäfer, Hans Dieter   12,
Schaller, Fritz   115
Scheler, Max   7
Schemm, Hans   59

Schenzinger, Karl Aloys   54, 58, 63–64, 66
Schinkel, Friedrich   33
Schirach, Baldur von   66
Schirmbeck, Peter   141
Schlösser, Reinhard   109
Schmitt, Carl   27, 32, 46, 199
Schneider, Michael   72
Scholter, Hans   134
Schönlank, Bruno   80
Schramm, Wilhelm von   109
Schröder, Alfred C.   62–63
Schulz, Hans Hermann   86
Schumann, Gerhard   114
Schütz, Erhard   123
Schweitzer, Hans (i.e., Mjölnir)   24–26
Shaikhet, Arkady   167
Sheeler, Charles   167
Skoronel, Vera   113
Sombart, Werner   7, 33
Speer, Albert   104, 111, 126, 182, 190, 214
Spengler, Oswald   33, 37, 199
Spranger, Eduard   161
Stapel, Wilhelm   74–75,77
Starcke, Gerhard   56
Steber, Martina   7
Steinhoff, Hans   67
Steinwarz, Herbert   191
Stellrecht, Helmut   205
Stetler, Pepper   164
Stollmann, Rainer   93
Strasser, Gregor   28–29 38, 46, 56, 111
Strasser, Otto   56, 199, 111, 199
Strobl, Gerwin   102
Suleiman, Susan Rubin   51

Theweleit, Klaus   3 fn 2
Thorak, Josef   134, 141

Tillich, Paul   33, 45–46
Tinnefeld, Eleonore   86
Todt, Fritz   124, 130, 146, 167, 182
Tonder, Christopher Webster van   157
Tönnies, Ferdinand   7
Tritschler, Alfred   170
Trotha, Thilo von   199
Trümpy, Berthe   113
Trunz, Erich   107

Van linthout, Ine   66
Viera, Josef   55, 64
Vogt, Hannah   35, 196

Wagenfeld, Wilhelm   212
Walser, Martin   82
Wangenheim, Gustav von   113
Weber, Jan Robert   200
Weber, Max   115, 159, 206
Weerth, Georg   87
Weitling, Wilhelm   37
Wernicke, Lotte   113
Wessel, Horst   52, 55, 60, 62–64, 67–68., 136
Wichert, Ernst   132
Wigman, Mary   104
Williams, Raymond   10, 76
Winkler, Otto   134
Winnig, August   15, 22–24, 28, 30–44, 46–47., 135, 162, 196
Wolff, Paul   18, 149, 153, 155–157, 163, 165., 168–175, 177, 180
Wundt, Wilhelm   161

Zielke, Willy   153, 184–186n 63
Zille, Heinrich   164

www.ingramcontent.com/pod-product-compliance
Lightning Source LLC
Chambersburg PA
CBHW050522170426
43201CB00013B/2050